FRENCH COURT DANCE AND DANCE MUSIC
A Guide to Primary Source Writings 1643-1789

III-75 Louis César de la Baume le Blanc, duc de LA VALLIÈRE, *Ballets, opéra, et autres ouvrages lyriques* . . . (Paris: C. J. Baptiste Bauche, 1760). Minuet danced at the full-dress ball given by the king, February 24, 1745, in the riding school of the Grande Écurie, Versailles, with full orchestra. [New York Public Library at Lincoln Center, Astor, Lenox, and Tilden Foundations, Music Division, Mus. Res. MFCB (France); inserted between pp. 204 and 205.]

FRENCH COURT DANCE AND DANCE MUSIC
A Guide to Primary Source Writings
1643-1789

by
Judith L. Schwartz
and
Christena L. Schlundt

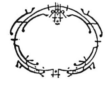

DANCE AND MUSIC SERIES No. 1

PENDRAGON PRESS
STUYVESANT, NY

Musicological Series by Pendragon Press

Aesthetics in Music
Annotated Reference Tools in Music
Festschrift Series
French Opera in the 17th and 18th Centuries
Giovanni Battista Pergolesi:The Complete Works/Opere Complete
The Historical Harpsichord
The Juilliard Performance Guides
Monographs in Musicology
Musical Life in 19th-Century France
RILM Retrospectives
The Sociology of Music
Thematic Catalogues

Library of Congress Cataloging-in-Publication Data

Schwartz, Judith L. (Judith Leah), 1943-
    French court dance and dance music.
    (Dance and Music No. 1)
    Includes index.
    1. Dancing--France-- History--17th century--Bibliography.
2. Dancing--France--History--18th century--Bibliography.
3. Dance music--France--17th century--History and criticism--
Bibliography. 4. Dance music--France--18th century--History
and criticism--Bibliography. I. Schlundt, Christena L.II. Title.
III. Series.
Z7514.D2S3 1987 [GV1649] 016.7923'0944 87-14888
ISBN 0-918728-72-X (lib. bdg.)

CONTENTS

LIST OF ILLUSTRATIONS

PREFACE

This project originated in 1973 when, upon discovering our common
interest, we joined forces to offer an interdisciplinary course in French
court dance to students of music and dance at the University of California at Riverside. In gathering material for teaching and study, we
found a dearth of organized information about sources and resources
both for dance history in general and for French court dance specifically. With the intent of assisting others in similar circumstances, we
later undertook to expand for publication the meager checklists prepared for our students. Since that time, a bloom of scholarship in the
field of French Baroque music and dance has produced many worth-
while studies and a flurry of reprints. Listing and classification of the
rapidly proliferating secondary literature must await some future effort. For the present, we restrict ourselves to primary sources in the
form of published writings and hope that in the future dance bibliography will receive the professional attention it deserves.

Many hands and minds contributed to this project. We owe special
acknowledgment to Meredith Ellis Little for permitting access to her
inventory of the choreographic sources; to Wendy Hilton and Shirley
Wynne for helpful criticism; and to George R. Hill for generous coun-
sel on bibliographic matters. Thanks are due the library staffs of the
Bibliothèque National, Bibliothèque de l'Opéra, and Bibliothèque de
l'Arsenal, Paris; the Library of Congress, Washington; the New York
Public Library; the Newberry Library, Chicago; the Harvard University Library; the Stanford University music library; the university libraries at campuses of the University of California at Berkeley, Irvine,
Los Angeles, and Riverside; Northwestern University; New York University; and the University of Chicago. In addition we wish to thank

the many student assistants, too numerous to name here, who over the years did much laborious checking and compiling.

Judith L. Schwartz
Associate Professor of Music
History and Literature,
Northwestern University, School
of Music

Christena L. Schlundt
Professor of Dance, Program in
Dance, University of California
at Riverside

Summer, 1986

INTRODUCTION

Growing interest in classic French music and theatrical entertainment has brought with it awareness of the prominent role of dance in French culture of the 17th and 18th centuries. Primary sources from which social and theatrical dances of the period may be reconstructed have inspired much ethusiasm on the part of performers and students of the French classic period. Such enthusiasm easily turns to frustration, however, at the lack of bibliographic control in the field of dance history. The present effort does not pretend to do more than begin the process of listing and describing sources useful to the reconstruction of classic French dance of court and theater, as well as its music.

The subject of this work is social and theatrical dance of the French royal court from the reign of Louis XIV through the French revolution. Dance was the one domain in which France achieved artistic sovereignty over the rest of Europe. Performers of all nations acknowledged French dance expertise, training under French dancers, composing charming dance airs in the French manner, and gracing court entertainments in imitation of the balls and ballets of Versailles. A record of their accomplishments comes down to us in fragmentary fashion through a variety of documents of the period, both technical and critical, representing creators, observers, and teachers of an art that quickly became the lingua franca of social entertainment.

Purpose. The aim of this work is to facilitate reconstruction of French court dancing of the 17th and 18th centuries in its contemporary setting. As part of the dance in its context, we understand not only the technique and ethos of movement, but the nature of sounds accompanying such movement and the space containing it. When dance is thus understood in a broad sense as multimedia entertainment coordinating movement with musical and visual design, then music and theater (or spatial setting) become important components of the reconstruction process.

xiii

Reconstructing movement for the dance involves knowledge of technique and performance. In addition to instruction manuals and choreographic treatises, however, such knowledge can be acquired from sources devoted to related subjects, such as aesthetics and criticism, choreography, chronicle (descriptions of performances), pedagogy, notation, classification of dance types and of forms of entertainment, or social graces. Movement in the dance is thus understood to involve not merely form and mechanical gesture, but spirit, expression, or character as well.

Reconstructing music to accompany dancing involves knowledge not only of dance-music composition, but of contemporary performances as well. Of considerable importance to authentic style are distinctions between dance types and the details of musical structure and expression for each. The first task is thus to seek information on form, character, and composition of dance pieces. Of no lesser importance, however, are details of contemporary performance relevant to dance music, including appropriate accompaniment, articulation, dynamics, expression, instrumentation, embellishment, deviation from notated rhythm, tempo, temperament, conventions in singing and playing individual instruments, and conventions regarding accompaniment and improvisation. These aspects of the resultant sound are not merely superficial additions, but essential components of the style, elements that evoke time, place, and function quite as readily as do meter, form, or texture. We thus consider relevant to the reconstruction of dance music any aspect of musical performance, composition, aesthetics and criticism, and classification of genres that contributes to a distinction between French and other regional styles (e.g. Italian, German, Spanish) or between Baroque or Classic and other period styles. The search for such information leads to investigation of broad topics that, though pertinent to French Baroque or Classic music in general, are also applicable to French court dance music in particular.

Reconstructing the visual and spatial context of the dance requires knowledge of both the physical and the functional settings in which the dance was performed. Construction of theaters and ballrooms, design of stage sets and ballroom decoration, afford ideas of physical setting. Information about various genres of theatrical or social entertainment as well as specific productions (including details of dramatic scenario and continuity, decoration, costume, allegorical device, masks, properties, and machines) reveals the role of dance within larger forms.

Technical and administrative aspects of theatrical production provide clues not only to the visual and spatial setting, but also to the social milieu within which dance became such an important cultural medium in 17th and 18th-century Europe.

Scope and organization. The sources of information here described consist of printed matter issued during the reigns of Louis XIV, XV, and XVI, representing the period 1643-1789. The work focuses upon writings that bear directly or indirectly upon French court dance and its music, its practitioners in France, and its imitators abroad. It does not include important non-verbal primary sources for dance and music: the choreographies in Feuillet notation and the musical scores (except when these appear in conjunction with a verbal contribution). The choreography sources will be described and indexed in Meredith Ellis Little's forthcoming thematic catalogue. This Guide is intended to be used as a companion to Little's catalogue. While most of the publications cited here are French, many with foreign imprints attest to the assimilation of French court dance in Britain, the German-speaking lands, the Iberian peninsula, Italy, and the Netherlands.

Three separate listings each arrange individual titles alphabetically by author. The first of the three annotated lists presents 17th and 18th-century writings devoted to French court dance and dancing (in both its social and theatrical context), compiled by Christena L. Schlundt. The second list treats selected writings about music and other subjects that bear upon dance music in the French style, both its creation and its performance, compiled by Judith L. Schwartz. The third list offers a selection of tangentially related writings that establish the physical, social, or cultural setting and the aesthetic background to French court dance and its music, compiled jointly. A foreword to each section describes the extent and classification of material both included and excluded from the ensuing annotated list. It also refers to modern secondary literature of importance to the subject, providing a list of reference works used in compiling the annotations. The short-title list that follows the three parts of the Guide combines titles from all three lists in chronological order of first publication.

The index serves as a guide to subjects, names, and publication titles mentioned in the annotations as well as in the main bibliographic entries for individual items. Index entries for technical details, such as Dance Performance—Steps, or Musical Performance—Rhythm: *notes inégales,* are designed to make the index a starting point for dance and music research.

The bibliographic entry. Each entry provides the author's full name and dates as verified in recent reference works, especially in *The new Grove dictionary of music and musicians* (London 1980). The title for the first known edition appears in full, reproducing the orthography and wording of the original when possible. First edition titles not seen by the compilers were taken from RISM B-VI (or other sources) and are therefore subject to editorial change or error passed on by that source. In all instances diacritical marks have been altered to conform to modern usage.

Subsequent editions to 1800 are cited in chronological order, represented by either a short reference ("2nd ed.") or by a short or complete title, if significantly different from previous titles. For each edition cited, the city, publisher, and date of publication are indicated, normally followed by the number of pages. If the publication history is sufficiently long, it will be replaced by a reference to a secondary source that provides the information. Reference to a modern facsimile reprint follows the specific edition represented in the facsimile. Further citations indicate modern editions in the original language and modern translations. Only publication in book form is considered, even though many titles are now available in microform.

Although the compilers attempted to examine personally each edition of a given work, they did not always succeed. An asterisk (*) therefore marks the edition(s) seen, to which the commentary most directly applies. The remaining editions may possibly differ in content or organization, and information about them may be subject to errors passed along by secondary sources. The annotations comment variously on the orientation, scope, and contents of the works, as well as their relevance to the subject at hand. They may also compare a work with others of its type, indicating borrowing and plagiarism.

ABBREVIATIONS

b.	=	born
c.	=	century
ca.	=	circa
ch.	=	chapter
d.	=	died
ed.	=	edition, edited
f.	=	folios; following page
facs.	=	facsimile
ff.	=	following pages
fig.	=	figure(s)
fl.	=	flourished
MGG	=	*Die Musik in Geschichte und Gegenwart*
MMMLF	=	Monuments of Music and Music Literature in Facsimile
p.	=	page; total number of pages
par.	=	paragraph
pp.	=	inclusive pages
pl.	=	plate(s)
pseud.	=	pseudonym
q.v.	=	quod vide (which see)
RISM	=	*Répertoire international des sources musicales*
s.d.	=	sine die (without date)
s.l.	=	sine loco (without place of publication)
transl.	=	translation, translated
v.	=	volume(s)

PART I

WRITINGS ON DANCE AND DANCE NOTATION

FOREWORD

The writings discussed in the following section pertain either to dance—its nature, structure, and function—or to dance performance: positions, steps *(pas)*, arm movements *(ports de bras)*, use of space, rhythm, tempo, and relationship to accompanying music *(cadence)*. They include information about one or both contexts of French dance—dance of the theater and dance of the ballroom—as it flourished during the period 1643-1789.

Annotations for individual entries provide first a summary of the contents of the writings. Then detail specific to dance and dance practice is described.

Classification of Material. The 17th and 18th centuries saw the publication of numerous books devoted entirely to dance and its performance. The dance historian who relied solely on these, however, would miss the greater amount of dance information found in writings that include dance as one of several fine arts. As the premise justifying this combined bibliography assumes, much information on dance is available in musical writings. Thus the works described in the three sections of this Guide include in addition to dance publications many books that make important statements about dance even though their relevance may not be apparent in the titles. In contrast to Parts II and III, which offer merely a personal selection of relevant literature, Part I attempts a comprehensive listing of dance literature for the period. As a general orientation to the scope of these writings on dance, the following classification accounts for works listed in this section.

I. Literature of Dance
   A. DICTIONARIES AND ENCYCLOPEDIAS OF DANCE
      Anon. *Encyclopédie méthodique,* Compan

B. HISTORY OF DANCE
   1. *General*: Bonnet, Cahusac, Gallini *Treatise*, Ménéstrier *Des Ballets*, Weaver *Essay*
   2. *Period or Country*: Moreau, Rojo de Flores, Uriot
C. AESTHETICS OF DANCE
   Angiolini *Dissertation*, Angiolini *Lettere*, Borsa, Jenyns, Laus de Boissy, Lecointe, Noverre *Due lettere*, Noverre *Lettres*

II. Dance Instruction and Study
   A. GENERAL
      Bonin, Borin, Minguet, Pasch, Pauli, Saint Hubert, Taubert, Weaver *Anatomical*
   B. TEACHING AND INSTRUCTION MANUALS (How to teach)
      Bacquoy-Guédon, Lauze, Sol
   C. PERFORMANCE MANUALS (How to perform; "L'art de bien danser")
      Behr *L'art*, Behr *Wohlgegründete*, Boném, Chavanne, Dubois, Dufort, Esquivel, Ferriol, Gallini *Critical*, Guillaume, Kattfuss, Lambranzi, Lang, Lange, Lepitre, Magri, Rameau *Le Maître*, Tomlinson *Art*
   D. NOTATION MANUALS (How to write and read; "L'art d'écrire et de lire")
      Clément, Feldtenstein, Feuillet *Chorégraphie*, Feuillet *Neuvième recüeil*, Feuillet *Première receüil*, Feuillet *Recüeil de contredanses*, Feuillet *Recüeil de danses* (Pécour 1704), Gaudrau, Guillemin, Magny, Malpied *Élémens*, Malpied *Traité*, Pemberton *Essay*, Rameau *Abbrégé*, Tomlinson *Six dances*
   E. DANCES
      Feuillet *Le passepied*, Ménéstrier *L'Autel de Lyon*, Pemberton *The pastorall*, Theobold *Perseus and Andromeda*, Thurmond *Harlequin Doctor Faustus*, Weaver *Judgment of Paris*, Weaver *Loves*, Weaver *Orpheus*

Exclusion of Material.
1. As stated in the Introduction, this Guide does not include the nonverbal primary sources for dance, the dances recorded in *chorégraphie*. Exceptions contain verbal material of historical interest.

2. This Guide does not include comprehensive information about the contredanse, primarily because Jean Michel Guilcher has listed the sources in his definitive study of the contredanse from its origins during the reign of Louis XIV through the second half of the 19th century (*La contredanse et les renouvellements de la danse française,* Paris: Mouton, 1969). The publications of the early (for our period) English authority John Playford bear directly upon this kind of dancing. His work on the English country dance, *The English dancing master* (London: Thomas Harper, 1651 and many subsequent editions), is therefore not included here.

3. This Guide does not include works on dance that were reprinted during this period but first published at an earlier time. Examples are the 1529 *Antonius arena provincialis* and the 1596 *Orchestra* by Sir John Davies.

4. This Guide does not include manuscript materials no matter how historically vital to the period. An example would be the 13 volumes preserved at Turin that contain details of entertainments given at the court of Savoy between 1640 and 1680, some of which were seen in France.

5. This Guide does not include several seemingly relevant works that upon examination proved to have no information bearing directly upon music or dance. The most conspicuous of these are Pierre Jean Baptiste Nougaret's *Anecdotes des beaux-arts* (Paris: J. F. Bastien, 1776-1780), which despite mention of music and literature in the title deals mainly with painting, sculpture, and architecture; and the same author's *La mort de l'opéra comique,* a satire.

Secondary Literature and Reference Works.

No attempt has been made to cite secondary sources pertinent to each individual item in the Guide. For compiling bibliographic information and historical-critical summaries of items in the Guide, the following proved useful.

CHRISTOUT, Marie Françoise. *Le ballet de cour de Louis XIV.* Paris: A. & J. Picard, 1967.

_____. *Le merveilleux et le "théâtre du silence."* Paris: Mouton, 1965.

De HOOP, Loes and Freek PLIESTER. *Handlist of the dance collection* [of Daniel François Scheurleer]. The Hague: Gemeente Museum, 1982.

DERRA DE MORODA, Friderica. *The dance library: a catalogue.* München: Robert Wölfle, 1982.

_____. "Die Tanzliteratur des achtzehnten Jahrhunderts," in *Sammeln und Bewahren: Beiträge zur Kunst, Literatur und Buchgeschichte,* pp. 150-57. München: Wölfle, 1973.

Enciclopedia dello spettacolo. Ed. by Silvio d'Amico and Francesco Savio. Rome: 1954-1968.

FLETCHER, Ifan Kyrle. *Biographical descriptions of forty rare books relating to the art of dancing in the collection of P. J. S. Richardson, O.B.E.* London: The Dancing Times, 1954. 20p.

FORRESTER, F. S. *Ballet in England: a bibliography and survey.* London: The Library Association, 1968. (ca. 1700-1966)

GUILCHER, Jean Michel. *Le contredanse et les renouvellements de la danse française.* Paris: Mouton, 1969.

HILTON, Wendy. *Dance of court and theater: the French noble style 1690-1725.* Princeton, N.J.: Princeton Book Co., 1981.

KUNZLE, Régine. "In search of l'Académie Royale de Danse." *York dance review,* v. 7 (1978), pp. 3-13.

LESLIE, Serge. *Bibliography of the dance collection of Doris Niles and Serge Leslie.* London: Beaumont, 1966-1974.

MICHEL, Arthur. "The ballet d'action before Noverre." *Dance index,* v. 6 no. 3 (1947), pp. 1-73.

The new Grove dictionary of music and musicians. Ed. by Stanley Sadie. London: Macmillan, 1980.

PETERMANN, Kurt. *Tanzbibliographie.* Leipzig: VEB Bibliographisches Institut, 1966.

PRUNIÈRES, Henry. *Le ballet de cour en France.* Paris: Henri Laurens, 1914.

REBMAN, Elisabeth Huttig. "Chorégraphie: an annotated bibliography of eighteenth century printed instruction books." M.A. thesis, Stanford University, 1981.

RILM abstracts (Répertoire international de littérature musicale). New York: RILM abstracts, 1967- .

RISM B-VI (Répertoire international des sources musicales, series B, v. VI): *Écrits imprimés concernant la musique.* Ed. by François Lesure. München-Duisberg: G. Henle, 1971.

SULZER, Johann Georg. *Allgemeine Theorie der schönen Künste.* Leipzig: Wiedman, 1794.

SWIFT, Mary Grace. "The three ballets of the young sun." *Dance chronicle,* v. 3 no. 4 (1978-1980), pp. 361-72.

WINTER, Marian Hannah. *Pre-romantic ballet.* London: Pitman, 1974.

WITHERELL, Anne L. *Louis Pécour's 1700 Recüeil de dances.* Ann Arbor, MI: UMI Research Press, 1983.

In addition, catalogues were consulted for the following libraries: New York Public Library at Lincoln Center, Astor, Lenox, and Tilden Foundations, Dance Collection and Music Collection; Paris, Bibliothèque de l'Arsenal (August Rondel Collection).

ANNOTATED LIST OF WRITINGS

1 ANGIOLINI, Gasparo (1731-1803)

Dissertation sur les ballets pantomimes des anciens, pour servir de programme au ballet pantomime tragique de Semiramis, composé par Mr. Angiolini maître des ballets du théâtre près de la cour à Vienne, & représenté pour la première fois sur ce théâtre le 31 janvier 1765. À l'occasion des fêtes pour le mariage de sa majesté le roi des Romains.

Vienne: Jean Thomas de Trattner, 1765.

*Ed. with Italian commentary by Walter Toscanini, Milan: Achille Bertarelli, 1956. viii+55p.

A lucid defense of dance as a medium for tragedy, this short essay shows how 18th-c. ballet masters who wished to use dance for the expression of action sought support in the writings of Lucian and Horace, who described so vividly the power of their contemporary dance pantomimists in ancient Rome. Determined that dance be more than a display of technique, Angiolini argues in favor of dances that move the spectators to terror and compassion similar to that experienced by the ancients. He also discusses the various classes of expressive dance then current: *danse grotesque, danse comique, danse de demi-caractère,* and the most sublime, *danse pantomime-tragique.*

2 ANGIOLINI, Gasparo (1731-1803)

Lettere di Gasparo Angiolini a monsieur Noverre sopra i balli pantomimi.

*Milano: Giovanni Batista Bianchi, 1773; 112p.

These two letters bear upon the debate between the French choreographer J. G. Noverre (q.v.) and the Italian Angiolini concerning the origin of the *ballet d'action.* Angiolini here as elsewhere claims precedence for

9

his teacher F. A. Hilverding, who was actively producing this kind of ballet in Viennese theaters as early as 1740 through 1758, before going to Russia. Although Noverre, during his time in Vienna, benefited from the dancers trained by Hilverding, he never acknowledged his predecessor in his own famous *Lettres* (q.v.). For Noverre's lofty answer to Angiolini, see his *Due lettere scritte a diversi sogetti.*

3 ANONYMOUS

Encyclopédie méthodique. Arts académiques, équitation, escrime, danse, et art de nager.
*Paris: Panckoucke; Liège: Plomteux, 1786; 445p. (V. 69 of the *Encyclopédie méthodique;* illustrative plates are in v. 190. The complex publishing history of this work will not be dealt with here.)

The section on dance (pp. 312-424) consists of alphabetically arranged articles on dance steps and other topics relevant to dancing. Many of them derive literally from Diderot's *Encyclopédie* (q.v.); the article Chorégraphie (pp. 383-95) reproduces verbatim the *Encyclopédie* article by L. J. Goussier, with his two plates as well. Much of the additional material—such as the entries for Bal (pp. 312-16), Ballet (pp. 317-73), and Bras (pp. 374-83), or the untitled section on dance in general under Courante (pp. 397-416)—derives from P. Rameau's *Le maître à danser* (q.v.), L. de Cahusac's *Dance ancienne et moderne* (q.v.), and J. G. Noverre's *Lettres* (q.v.). Only a few dance types are treated: Bocane (p. 374), Bourrée (p. 374), Contredanse (p. 395), Courante (p. 397), Menuet (pp. 418-19), Passepied (p. 420), and Rigaudon (p. 423). In addition, dance terms singled out for definition are Balancé (pp. 316-17), Battement (pp. 373-74), Cabriole, Cadence, Chassé (p. 383), Contretemps (pp. 395-96), Coupé (p. 396), Coupé de mouvement (pp. 396-97), Entrechat (pp. 416-17), Fleuret (p. 417), Gaillarde (pas de, p. 417), Gargouillade (pp. 417-18), Glissé, Jetté, Marcher (p. 418), Mouvement, Ouverture des jambes (p. 419), Pas (pp. 419-20), Pirouette (p. 420), Position (pp. 420-21), Révérence (pp. 421-23), Saillie (pp. 423-24), Saut, Sissone, and Tombé (p. 424). Spanish equivalents for French dance terms may be found in a Spanish translation of the volume as *Encyclopedia metódica, artes académicos* (Madrid: Imprenta de Sancha, 1791).

4 BACQUOY-GUÉDON, Alexis (fl. 1780)

Méthode pour exercer l'oreille à la mesure dans l'art de la danse.
Amsterdam, Paris: Valade, ca. 1784; 56+20p.
*Facs. reprint, Genève: Minkoff, 1972.

This dancing master's guide to eurhythmics provides a course of instruction designed to teach pupils with no ear for rhythm how to hear rhythm, meter, and phrasing and how to mark time appropriately for the minuet and contredanse. The author describes a series of physical gestures (pp. 14-19), made to music in the accompanying second part, that permit the pupil to develop a sense of the dance rhythm. He also describes in some detail the minuet (pp. 9-19, which he favors for its gravity and grace over the all too popular contredanse) and contredanse (pp. 20-24), emphasizing character and structure. Remarks on the importance of 4-bar phrasing culminate in suggestions for coordinating the preliminary honors with the music in certain minuets with atypical phrasing. The 20 pages of music provide tunes to accompany the series of exercises, primarily minuets and contredanses. The first 6 contredanses resemble gavottes in musical structure; later ones exemplify French (6/8), English (2), and German (2/4) types, as well as a march and rigaudon to which the author's principles may be applied. A diagram of the floorplan of the minuet closes the book (Part 2, pp. 19-20).

The author continues his discussion of the ballroom minuet in a contemporary supplement now in the Scheurleer collection, his *Considérations sur la danse du menuet* (*2nd ed., Paris: Valade, ca. 1784; 9p.). He praises the exceptional beauty and majesty of the danced minuet, the cultivation of which develops in young persons the noble countenance, the well-bred assurance that enhances esteem. He then proposes modifications in dancing the ordinary minuet that would eliminate what he considers to be two faults: the dance phrase lengths not coinciding with the musical phrase lengths, and the irregular number of dance phrases, varying according to the taste of the dancer. He shows how exact counting can correct each fault and, in addition, shorten the performance duration of an individual minuet to about three minutes. This enables more dancers to have the pleasure of dancing, eliminating the boredom that inspires the demand for contredanses and threatens the abandonment of so noble and interesting a dance as the minuet.

5 BEHR, Samuel Rudolph (1670-1716)

L'art de bien danser, oder: die Kunst wohl zu Tantzen, worinnen

11

gewiesen wird I. La méthode d'informer dans la belle-danse. II. La méthode d'informer dans la danse-haute. III. La méthode d'informer dans la comique & grotesque. Nemlichen: I. Die Art und Weise zu informiren im doucen- und niedrigen Tantzen. II. Die Art und Weise zu informiren im hohen theatralischen Tantzen. III. Und dann im lustigen und verstellten Tantzen. Worbey mit anzutreffen: 1. Viele Inventiones unterschiedener curiösen Entrées und Balets. 2. Ein Bericht von dem Tantzen der Alten, und noch heut zu Tage von dem Tantzen unterschiedener fremder Nationen. 3. Etliche Anmerckungen von dem Tantzen gar unvernünfftiger Creaturen. 4. Ein Anhang zur Tantz-Kunst gehörigen Reguln. 5. Von denen Nahmen und Ursprunge unterschiedenen Täntze. Und 6. Die Summarien dieses gantzen Buchs. Welches alles auf das allerfleissigste so wohl aus eigner Invention, als auch aus unterschiedener gelehrten Leute Schrifften (und in specie derer, die von der Tantz-Kunst vieles geschrieben haben) zusammen getragen, und nebst einer ausführlichen Vorrede, welche von allen Exercitiis handelt, der galanten Welt ediret worden. Leipzig: Martin Fulde, 1713; (8)+135p.

> *Facs. reprint, Leipzig: Zentralantiquariat der DDR; München: Heimeran, 1977 (Documenta choreologica, 2); (8)+135+lix p. German commentary and index by Kurt Petermann.

According to Petermann in his commentary to the 1977 reprint, the author of this concise treatise on French dancing may have been the first to describe French dancing in a German language publication. (See also Behr's *Wohlgegründete Tantz-Kunst.* Petermann, pp. xvii-xviii, mentions titles of three other works by Behr, virtually unknown: (1) *Anleitung zu einer wohlgegründeten Tantz-Kunst, so er aus vielfältiger Praxis in sehr vielen merckwürdigen Opern, Bällen, Balletts etc. angemercket, welcher auch etliche Bogen von des Autoris Composition untersch. Courantes, Menuets, Passepieds, Bourées, Sarabandes, Entrées, Gigues, Chaconnes, Gavots etc. zum divertissement angehenckt. Mit Titelkupfern.* Leipzig: Christoph Heydler, 1703. (2) *Anderer Theil Tantz-Kunst, oder ausgesiebte Grillen, sowohl über sein herausgegebenes Tantz-Buch selbst.* . . . Leipzig: Christoph Heydler, 1703. (3) *Curieuser Tantz-Informator, welcher durch angenehme Discurse, Beschreibung artiger Qualitäten mancher tantzenden Personen in seiner Information sich darstellt.* Leipzig: Christoph Heydler, 1703.)

L'art de bien danser is in 8 parts. Part 1 (pp. 17-38) discusses the low or ballroom dances, with the *révérences,* steps, arm and leg coordination, carriage, and *cadence* fundamental to the Minuet, Passepied, and Courante. Part 2 (pp. 38-53) treats high or theatrical dance—the formation of steps, the composition of entrées and ballets, their melodies, their expression, instruction for the dancer, decoration (machines, stages, costumes, personnel), and the activities of the dancing master. Part 3 (pp. 53- 56) similarly deals with comic and grotesque dances, those for commedia dell'arte figures. Part 4 (pp. 57- 96) describes characteristics of specific dances; Behr gives details for selected entrées from ballets such as *Le ballet des furies.* Part 5 (pp. 96-109) presents a conventional history of dance among the ancients and in foreign countries, e.g. China. Part 6 (pp. 109-11) continues with dances of national origin, such as the Tarantella. Of greatest interest is the list of 32 principles of good dancing in Part 7 (pp. 111-17). Part 8 (pp. 118-24) gives the names and origins of various dance types, e.g. Sarabande.

6 BEHR, Samuel Rudoph (1670-1716)

Wohlgegründete Tantz-Kunst. So er auff Begehren seiner Herren Scholaren und vielen andern Lieb-Habern der edlen Tantz-Kunst, zum drittenmahl, vermehrter, verbessert, und anitzo aber mit unterschiedenen Kupffern und Figuren heraus gegeben.
*Leipzig: Joh. Heinichens Wittwe, 1709; [viii]+81p.

This historical, philosophical, and practical treatise on the dance traces its presence in civilization from Greek antiquity to the present, with special emphasis on the role of dancing masters, who must know mathematics, musical instruments, and the composition of music as well as understand poetry (pp. 1-28). The proper performance of dance gestures (such as the "Porte de Brah" [sic]) is illustrated by drawings of a male dancer in short coat, wrist ruffles, tight hose and plumed hat. Heeled shoes adorn completely turned-out legs, attached to which are numbers keyed to descriptive passages in the text. Figure 2 can be described as first position elevated to the tips of the toes.

Essential requirements for the dancing master include a natural carriage, a repertory of steps with clarity of movement connecting them, and a feeling for cadence and rhythm, as well as knowledge of deportment, bows, and etiquette appropriate to the dance (pp. 38-46). After generally characterizing a good entrée (pp. 47-51), Behr examines the components of a ballet (pp. 52- 60): its opening ("Ouverture"), plot or action, figures and steps, scenic decorations, costumes and machines, and closing ("das Grand Ballet"). Short discussions of familiar dances

I-6 Samuel Rudolph BEHR, *Wohlgegründete Tantz-Kunst* (Leipzig: Joh. Heinichens Wittwe, 1709), frontispiece. Domestic dancing lessons with the teacher playing violin and pupils reading dance notation. [Haags, Gemeente Museum, Dance collection, Scheurleer Handlist No. 54]

I-6 Samuel Rudolph BEHR, *Wohlgegründete Tantz-Kunst* (Leipzig: Joh. Heinichents Wittwe, 1709), pp. 32-35. Four individual dancing figures, numbered to illustrate the text. [Haags, Gemeente Museum, Dance collection, Scheurleer Handlist No. 54]

and their national origins follow: Sarabande, Chaconne, Folie d'Espagne, Canary, Castainettes, Pavane, Galliard, Gigue, Pergamasces,
Branle, Gavotte, Courante, Menuet, and Rigaudon (pp. 60-67).

Brief advice on music and instruments appears on pp. 67-73: a grand
ballet needs a triumphant melody, using oboe and violin. The final section contains names of 61 dance steps or gestures (Battement, Assemblé,
eine halbe Piroüete, Pas de Baladin), supposedly accompanied by illustrations in which male and female figures are identified by the letters
M[ann] and F[rau]. (The copy in the Daniel François Scheurleer collection in the Gemeente Museum, the Hague, apparently contains no such
illustrations.)

7 BONÉM, Natal Jacome

*Tratado dos principaes fundamentos da dança obra muito útil,
não sõmente para esta mocidade, que quer aprender a dançar
bem, mas ainda para as pessõas honestas, e polidas, aś quaes
ensina as regras para bem andar, saudar e fazer todas as cortezias, que convémem [sic] as assembleas adonde o úzo do mundo a
todos chama.*
*Coimbra: Irmaos Ginhoens, 1767; 138p.

This tract, similar to dancing manuals in other languages, devotes a
chapter to each of the fundamentals of French dance: carriage of the
body (ch. 1), walking (ch.2), assuming the 5 positions (ch. 3), bowing
in general (ch. 4) and in particular (ch. 5), how a woman walks and
presents herself (ch.6), different kinds of bows (ch. 7), entering a room
(ch. 8), behaving during a ball (ch. 9), bowing before beginning the
dance (ch. 10). The final portion of the book discusses the steps of the
minuet (ch. 11), the movement of the arms in the minuet (ch. 12), style
in general (ch. 13), and arm movements in general (ch. 14). The work
represents a very few on this subject in Portuguese.

8 BONIN, Louis

*Die neuste Art zur galanten und theatralischen Tantz-Kunst.
Worinnen gründliche Nachricht anzutreffen wie dieses höchst-
nützliche Exercitium sowol vor Alters als anjetzt beschaffen; auch
wie man zur richtigen Erlernung desselbigen und zu manirlichen
Auffführungen sowol unter seines gleichen als unter fürnehmen
Personen gelangen kan. Deme bygefüget was für Requisita zu*

I-8 Louis BONIN, *Die neuste Art zur galanten und theatralischen Tantz-Kunst* (Frankfurt, Leipzig: Joh. Christoff Lochner, 1711), frontispiece. Dancing lesson with teacher, violinist, pupils. [New York Public Library at Lincoln Center, Astor, Lenox, and Tilden Foundations, Dance Collection, [*MGRK]]

einen rechtschaffenen Tantz-Meister gehören damit er einen guten Scholaren machen sich selbsten aber bey Hofe in Assembléen, Bällen, Redouten und Masqueraden etc. desgleichen in Opern und Comoedien auf dem Theatro will sehen lassen. Der heutigen galanten Welt zum Nutzen und Ergötzen an das Liecht gestellet von Louis Bonin, fürstl. Sachsen-Eisenachischen privilegirten Tantz-Meister auf der welt-berühmten Universität Jena. Samt einer Vorrede von Meletaon.
*Frankfurt, Leipzig: Joh. Christoff Lochner, 1711; 270p.

Bonin was a Frenchman, a pupil of P. Beauchamps who had gone to the University of Jena as dancing master. By means of his position and this instructional text in German, he helped bring French court dance to Germany. His first chapter (pp. 1-5) seeks the origins of dance in antiquity, the second (pp. 6-11) defends its spirituality. The next chapters give an overview of dance as entertainment (pp. 11-13), in the military (pp. 14-16), and in the theater (pp. 16-21). He discusses the prevalent attitudes about dance, its misuse, its usefulness (pp. 21-55), and its types (pp. 56-60). The next chapters specifically concern the character of the upright dancing master (his learning, his dress, pp. 70-110), the ballroom and ballroom etiquette (how to enter, exit, bow, pp. 110-38), and details of the Courante (pp. 138-42), Minuet (pp. 142-57), and other dances (pp. 157-60). Treating separately the dance of the theater from that of the ballroom, Bonin discusses the dance and music for entrées in opera, operettas, comedies, and pastorals, including grotesque and comic dances (pp. 160-221), and for private assemblies and balls (pp. 42-46, 221-70). There is a particularly interesting set of guidelines for judging dances and dancing masters. The book documents the presence in Germany of French-born dancing masters, who worked beside French-trained German masters to cultivate French court dancing in German theaters and private residences.

9 BONNET, Jacques (1664-1724)

Histoire générale de la danse, sacrée et profane, ses progrès et ses révolutions, depuis son origine jusqu'à présent. Avec un supplément de l'histoire de la musique, et le paralèle de la peinture et de la poésie.
*Paris: d'Houry fils, 1723; xl+269p.
   Facs. reprint, Genève: Minkoff, 1969.
   *Facs. reprint, Genève: Slatkine, 1969.

Facs. reprint, Bologna: Arnaldo Forni, 1972.
Paris: d'Houry fils, 1724; xl+269p.

In the first 4 chapters (pp. 1-69), the dance of ancient Egypt, Greece, and Rome and the sacred dance of the Hebrews and early Christian church are discussed as precursors of ballets (enumerated pp. 83-89) produced at European courts, 1450-1723. In his historical survey, the author selects for description *Le grand balet du roy* of 1664 (pp. 94-107) and *Le balet de la nuit* of 1657 (pp. 109-110) from France and *Le balet du tabac,* ca. 1675 (pp. 107-9) in Lisbon. *Bals de cérémonie,* says the author, take their rules and precepts from the ancients and were at their height under Charles IX, Henri III, and Henry IV; he describes the best of them (pp. 112-45). *Bals masqués* (pp. 146-60) and the performances of *danseurs de corde* and *voltigeurs* (pp. 161-82) are similarly treated. This history, put together by Bonnet from the manuscripts of Pierre Bourdelot, is important not only in itself, but because it was quoted as authoritative by later historians such as Louis de Cahusac (q.v.). The appended material on music history (pp. 183-211) supplements his earlier *Histoire de la musique et de ses effets* (q.v.). A comparison between poetry and painting (pp. 213-69) closes the book. An "Ode de la danse" of 1714 appears in full (pp. 138-45).

10 BORIN

L'art de la danse.
*Paris: Jean Baptiste Christophe Ballard, 1746; viii+26p.

The author acknowledges Pierre Rameau's *Le maître à danser* (1725, q.v.), but he believes its merits should not prevent other treatises from being of use to the public. His, he declares, is a methodical summary of his own reflections on the grace and perfection of the steps. He finds nothing to complain about in the dancers of the day; in fact, he finds their manner so affecting that it succeeds in moving audiences much as the ancient pantomimists' did. The importance of pleasing action in civil life provides another reason for learning to dance, he argues, since dancing contains the first principles of the art of pleasing by actions. Briefly and succinctly, the usual technical details are presented: how to walk, bow, perform the steps, carry the arms, follow rhythm, and compose dances. The presentation is succinct, the tone as gracious, light, and positive as the dancing described. There are no illustrations.

11 BORSA, Matteo
Saggio filosofico sui balli pantomimi seri dell'opera.
Lettra prima, 30 febbrajo 1782, v. 5, pp. 137-51.
Lettra terza, 1 febbrajo 1783, v. 6, pp. 153-69.
*Ed. by Carlo Amoretti and Francesco Soave in *Opuscoli scelti
sulle scienze e sulle arti.* 22 v. Milano: Guiseppe Marelli, 1778-
1803.

These two letters, selected from philosophical essays written in 1782
and 1783, document the ascendency of the *ballet d'action,* here called
serious pantomime ballet, at the end of the 18th c. In the first letter,
Borsa laments the passing of the greatness characterizing Renaissance
spectacles that preceded opera, which he discusses in other letters. But
upon what is the success of an opera based? "Tutto e ballo . . ." (v. 1,
p. 38). It is the dancing that prompts criticism, discussion, and meta-
physical speculation. Borsa then proceeds to the same, in letter 1 on
ballet and mime (discussed separately) and letter 2 on the combination of
the two into the present unified dance spectacle. Starting with the Greek
philosophers and the Roman historians, Borsa traces the unification of
dance and pantomime through the writings of C. F. Ménéstrier (q.v.), J.
B. Du Bos (q.v.), and others, ending with J. G. Noverre (q.v.) and G.
Angiolini (q.v.).

12 CAHUSAC, Louis de (1706-1759)
La danse ancienne et moderne ou traité historique de la danse.
3v.
*La Haye: Jean Neaulme, 1754; xxxiv+168p., 180+xxxiip.,
168+xxivp.
  Facs. reprint, Genève: Slatkine, 1971.
German transl. of v. 1 in *Sammlung vermischter Schriften zur
Beförderung der schönen Wissenschaften und der freyen Künste.*
5 v. Berlin: Friedrich Nicolai, 1759-1762.

This treatise on the history and aesthetic of dance aimed to further not so
much the technique as the poetic essence of dance as an art. As the
introduction clearly states (p. 17), dance is the art of gesture and, like
other arts, must have expressive meaning. Thus Cahusac transfers Bat-
teaux's (q.v.) philosophy of art imitating nature directly to the art of
dance. He provides a detailed history of the dance, whole sections of
which were reprinted in the Diderot-d'Alembert *Encyclopédie* (q.v.)

and in the works of other writers who sought to disparage contemporary dance. V. 1 treats dance among the ancients; v. 2 continues the subject (pp. 1-126), then brings the story up to the 17th c., with descriptions of French court entertainments (pp. 126-80). V. 3 continues the history, emphasizing the author's opinion, especially in the last part, that narrative-expressive dancing *(ballet d'action)* is superior to all other kinds. The dancer Marie Sallé and ballet-master Jean Baptiste de Hesse are cited as having the power to express all human passions. The treatise closes with rules for making dances, rules derived from ancient Greek rhetoric: exposition, development, and denouement. Modern grand ballet, insisted Cahusac—that of pattern and technique, devoid of rhetorical or expressive content—was nothing more than a masked ball. His rationale for expressive dance was later taken up by J. G. Noverre (q.v.) as his own.

13 CHAVANNE, J. M. de

Principes du menuet et des révérences, nécessaires à la jeunesse de savoir, pour se présenter dans le grand monde.
*Luxembourg: les héritiers d'André Chevalier, 1767; 55p.

In this highly derivative instruction manual (for parents who wish to reinforce the dancing master's tutelage at home), Chavanne aimed to make accessible the methods of Feuillet and Pécour, as well as those of his own teacher Fonville, to young people inexperienced in social graces. Without acknowledgement, the book draws heavily upon the first 25 chapters of Pierre Rameau's *Le maître à danser* in overall organization and content; many chapters are indeed abridgements or close paraphrases of Rameau's text. Unlike Rameau, Chavanne provided no pictorial illustrations, probably since the book was intended to supplement rather than replace the dancing master's instructions.

Ch. 1-15 (pp. 9-31) deal with carriage and walking (pp. 9-11), positions (pp. 11-15), and a variety of bows for different situations (pp. 15-27), with a separate section on bows for young ladies (pp. 28-31), rearranging, contracting, or augmenting Rameau's material. The remainder of the book deals with the minuet, beginning with Rameau's chapters on fundamental movements of hip, knee, and instep (ch. 16, pp. 31-33) and on *demi-coupés* (ch. 17, pp. 33-35). General observations on dancing the minuet (ch. 18-21, pp. 35-39) precede description of minuet steps (ch. 22- 25, pp. 41-47). Ch. 26-28 (pp. 47-49) briefly tell how to dance the ordinary minuet, with comments on the use of arms and presentation of hands (pp. 47-49). Ch. 29 (pp. 50-52) discusses proper etiquette at balls. The final chapter (pp. 53-55) surveys dances currently in vogue, including the minuet (as "the most noble of all the dances"), French and English contredanses, the German Allemande, and the Polonoise.

14 CLÉMENT

Principes de corégraphie ou l'art d'écrire et de lire la danse par caractères démonstratifs accompagné d'un passe-pied et d'une allemande à quatre à la Dauphine, approuvé par M^{rs}. de l'Académie Royale de Musique et de Danse.
*Paris: Denis, 1771; 36+(17)p.

Clément claims no originality. He wishes only to facilitate learning of the dance notation called *chorégraphie* (published by R. A. Feuillet, *Chorégraphie,* 1700, q.v.) so that dances can be read as easily as a musician reads a piece of music. To accomplish this he explains terms, orientation within the ballroom, the signs for positions and steps, floor patterns, the relationship of steps to the musical measure, carriage of the arms, and composite steps *(pas composées).* Appended are two of his dances for practice: *Passepied à la dauphine* (2 couples, pl. 1-8) and *Allemande à la dauphine* (2 couples, pl. 1-8).

15 COMPAN, Charles (b. ca. 1740)

Dictionnaire de danse, contenant l'histoire, les règles et les principes de cet art, avec des réflexions critiques, et des anecdotes curieuses concernant la danse ancienne et moderne; le tout tiré des meilleurs auteurs qui ont écrit sur cet art.
*Paris: Cailleau, 1787; xvi+395p.
    *Facs. reprint, New York: Broude Bros., 1974 (MMMLF, 84).
    Facs. reprint, Genève: Minkoff, 1980.
    2nd ed., Paris: Servière, 1802; xvi+395p.

The most authoritative 18th-c. dance dictionary derives its information from Greek and Roman writers on dance of the ancients, Thoinot Arbeau on Renaissance dancing, and, for contemporary dance, Cahusac (q.v.), Noverre (q.v.), and Bonnet (q.v.). In his preface, Compan describes the 3 principal aspects of dance as the "mechanical" (having to do with notation, or *chorégraphie)*, the "poetical" (aesthetic or theoretical aspect), and the historical. In addition, articles deal with steps and other elements of technique (Coupé, p. 106; Glissade, 165; Jetté, 187-88; Pirrouette, 298-99; Tombé, 374-77) and dance types (Allemande, pp. 8-9; Bocane, 34; Bourrée, 35-6; Branle, 37-40; Canarie, 41-42; Chaconne, 47-48; Contredanse, 101; Forlane, 157-58; Gaillarde, 162; Gavotte, 163; Gigue, 164-65; Kalenda, 193-94; Loure, 196-97; Menuet, 231-39; Musette, 247-48; Pavane, 294-95; Rigaudon, 322-23; Sarabande, 346-47; Tordion, 377), as well as with general topics (Bal, pp. 12-25; Ballet, 27-32; Danse, 111-29; Théâtre, 367-72). A long article on *Chorégraphie* compares it favorably to another system of dance notation by M. Favier.

16 DUBOIS

Principes d'allemandes.
*Paris: author [1780 or 1790]; 25p.+12 engravings.

For each figure of the allemande, a brief description accompanies a clear engraving by Madame Annereau. These illustrations and their commentary provide information on costume, style, and especially on the use of the arms.

17 DUFORT, Giambatista (fl. 1728)

Trattato del ballo nobile . . . [Trattato del minuetto]. Indirizzato all'eccellenza delle signore dame, e de'signori cavaliere napoletani.
*Napoli: Felice Mosca, 1728; 12+160p.
*Facs. reprint, England: Gregg International, 1972.

By publishing this manual for the use of his pupils in Naples, the French trained dancing master Dufort helped disseminate French dance abroad by providing Italian equivalents for French dance terms (listed pp. 27-28). Using the dance notation known as *chorégraphie,* as well as verbal description, he discusses the five positions and problems of coordinating movement with music. He then briefly explains *chorégraphie* in order to use it further in describing steps (pp. 29-100). Information on the use of arms, the performance of bows, tracing the floor pattern, and the cultivation of style close this section (pp. 93-116). The treatise on the minuet (pp. 117-49) is similarly organized. A final section treats briefly the contredanse (pp. 150- 55) and bows other than in dancing (pp. 156-60).

I-16 DUBOIS, *Principes d'allemande* (Paris: auteur, 1780 or 1790), Figures 2 and 3. Hand-holding positions for the allemande. [New York Public

Library at Lincoln Center, Astor, Lenox, and Tilden Foundations, Dance
Collection, [*MGO p.v. 23. Res.]]

25

18 ESQUIVEL NAVARRO, Juan de (17th c.)

Discursos sobre el arte del dancado y sus excelencias y primer origen, reprobando las acciones deshonestas.
*Seville: Juan Gomez de Blas, 1642; [29+103p., irregularly numbered].
Facs. reprint, Madrid: Hauser y Menet, 1947.

Discursos is one of only 3 extant dance manuals published in Spanish during the period 1643-1789. It is included here to represent the kind of dance that prevailed at the Spanish court, where continual French influence eventually brought French dance to Spain during this period. The result is seen in the 1745 *Reglas utiles* by Ferriol y Boxeraus (q.v.) and the 1758 *Arte de danzar* by Minguet e Yrol (q.v.). Like French dancing manuals, this book deals with the virtues of dancing, its origins and first practitioners (ch. 1), the requirements for a dancing master—his manner, discipline and body proportions—(ch. 3), dancing style to be taught in dancing schools (ch. 4 and 5), and a description of teachers then in vogue (ch. 6 and 7). But quite non-French are some of the passionate and fiery movements asked for in ch. 2 on performance. The author does deal, however, with pure technique, treating performance on both feet, to the side, while turning, one foot circling in the air, cabrioles, bows, carriage of the body, and floor plans. Even the etiquette of proper gift-giving to the master is discussed (ch. 7).

19 FELDTENSTEIN, C. J.

Erweiterung der Kunst nach der Chorographie ᵀsic] zu tanzen, Tänze zu erfinden und aufzusetzen; wie auch Anweisung zu verschiedenen National-Tänzen; als zu Englischen, Deutschen, Schwäbischen, Pohlnischen, Hannak-Masur-Kosak- und Hungarischen; mit Kupfern; nebst einer Unzahl Englischer Tänze.
*Braunschweig: 1772; [viii]+109p.
Zweyter Theil. Nebst vier und zwanzig Englischen Tänzen, und sechs Cottillons (Quadrillen) sammt Figuren.
Braunschweig: 1775; 35p.
Braunschweig: 1776; 35p.

This manual documents the late 18th-c. use of *chorégraphie* among German dancing masters. This dance notation, first published in 1700 in France by R. A. Feuillet *(Chorégraphie,* q.v.), was intermittently used, adapted, attacked, and ignored by dancing masters. Here it figures as

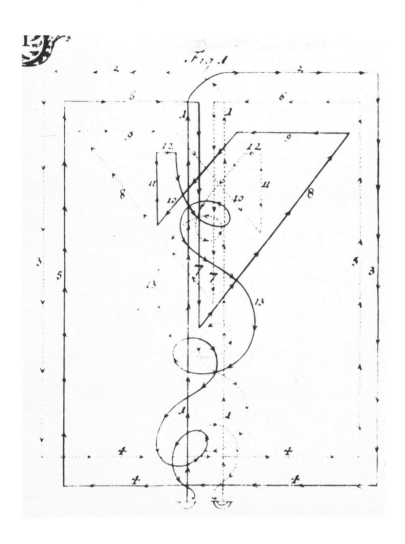

I-19 C. J. FELDTENSTEIN, *Erweiterung der Kunst nach der Chorographie zu tanzen* (Braunschweig: 1772), Tabula 1, Figure 1. Dance notation showing the track for an entire dance in a single diagram. [Haags, Gemeente Museum, Dance Collection, Scheurleer Handlist No. 66]

part of an overview of dance as a "science." All the elements of the system are presented: orientation within the ballroom, floor plans, body position on the track (pp. 49-56), symbols (pp. 57-64), and the *révérence* (pp. 68-72). The only specific court dance type treated is the minuet (pp. 73-83), after which the many national dances listed in the title are described. Of special interest are the clearly drawn "tabula," large pull-out illustrations: I—floor plans, II— *chorégraphie* symbols, III— minuet floor plans, IV— contredanse floor plans, V-VIII—music and floor patterns for contredanses. The second volume consists of 24 English dances and 6 cotillons diagrammed in 10 "tabula," only the first of which has a musical score linked by phrase numbers to the floor pattern. The overwhelming number of contredanses testifies to the prevalence of that type over the summarily treated minuet. The author earlier published a work entitled *Die Kunst, nach der Chorégraphie zu tanzen und Tänze zu schreiben, nebst einer Abhandlung über die äusserliche Wohlanständigkeit im Tanzen* (Braunschweig: Schröder, 1767; 55p.).

20 FERRIOL Y BOXERAUS, Bartholomé

Reglas utiles para los aficionados a danzar. Provechoso divertimiento de los que gustan tocar instrumentos; y advertencias polyticas a todo genero de personas. Illustradas con laminas, y aumentados varios assumptos...unico, en España, de la chorographia, Amable, contradanzas, etc.
*Copoa [i.e. Malaga]: Joseph Testore, 1745; 16+298p.

One of apparently 3 extant dance manuals published in Spanish during this period (including Juan de Esquivel Navarro's *Discursos sobre el arte del dancado,* 1642, q.v., on Spanish dancing and Pablo Minguet e Yrol's *Arte de danzar,* 1758, q.v.), this treatise documents the widespread influence of French court dance. Divided into 4 "tratados," it first discusses the origin, usefulness, advantages, and difficulties of dance; how to choose a teacher, how to judge good dancing, how to be up-to-date; and ball ceremonies and courtesies. Before describing the 5 positions, the author inserts a useful table (pp. 68-69) of French terms, their pronunciation, and their Spanish equivalents. He acknowledges Pierre Beauchamps, "el primer author de esta danza," and other French masters. Bowing and manipulation of the hat are illustrated with drawings similar to those in Pierre Rameau's *Le maître à danser* (q.v.). This first part closes with a long chapter on all the various steps of French dance, beginning with 5 types of minuet step. Tratado 2 gives corresponding information about the use of the arms. Tratado 3 deals at

28

length with the minuet (with drawings and floor patterns), the *passapié* (with floor patterns), and *chorégraphie* (with charts and accompanying verbal explanations), closing with the dance *Amable,* with verbal description (pp. 232-35) and chorégraphie diagrams with notated music (pp. 236-41). Tratado 4 is devoted to the etiquette and performance of *contradanzas.* An appended table provides equivalents in Castillian Spanish for terms in Italian, English, and Catalan. It is followed by several *contradanzas* both verbally described and notated in *chorégraphie* with music.

21 FEUILLET, Raoul Auger (ca. 1659-1710)
Chorégraphie ou l'art de décrire la dance par caractères, figures et signes démonstratifs, avec lesquels on apprend facilement de soymême toutes sortes de dances. Ouvrage très-utile aux maîtres à dancer et à toutes les personnes qui s'appliquent à la dance.
*Paris: auteur, Michel Brunet, 1700; 106p.
    *Facs. reprint, New York: Broude Bros., 1968 (MMMLF, 130).
    Facs. reprint, Hildesheim: Georg Olms, 1974.
*2nd ed., augmented with 4 tables of supplementary steps. Paris: auteur, Michel Brunet, 1701.
    Facs. reprint, Bologna: Arnaldo Forni, 1969.
Paris: 1709.
Paris: Dezais, 1713; 95p. (With preface by Dezais.)
English paraphrase by Paul Siris as *The art of dancing, demonstrated by characters and figures whereby one may learn easily and of one's self all sorts of dances, being a work very useful to all such as practice dancing, especially masters. Done from the French of Monsieur Feuillet, with many alterations in the characters, and an addition of the English Rigaudon, and French Bretagne, by P. Siris.*
*London: author, 1706; 52p.
English transl. by John Weaver as *Orchesography or the art of dancing, by characters and demonstrative figures. Wherein the whole art is explain'd; with compleat tables of all steps us'd in dancing, and rules for the motions of the arms, etc. Whereby any person (who understands dancing) may of himself learn all manner of dances. Being an exact and just translation from the French of Monsieur Feuillet.*

29

*London: H. Meere for the author,1706; 59p.

*Facs. reprint, England: Gregg International, 1970.

Facs. reprint, New York: Dance Horizons, 1971.

*Facs. reprint in Richard Ralph, *The life and works of John Weaver* (New York: Dance Horizons, 1985), pp. 173-285.

*2nd ed. *To this edition is added the Rigadoon, the Louvre, & the Brittagne, in characters, with the contents, or index . . .* London: John Walsh, 1722; 120p.

Feuillet's *Chorégraphie* is the first publication of the dance notation system variously credited to Pierre Beauchamps, Louis Pécour, and Feuillet. (For an account of the problem of authorship for the system, see "Choregraphy: the dance notation of the 18th century," by Friderica Derra de Moroda, *The book collector, v.* 16/4 [winter 1967], pp. 450-76. On Beauchamps, see Régine Kunzle, "Pierre Beauchamp: the illustrious unknown choreographer," *Dance scope,* v. 8/2 [spring-summer 1974], pp. 32-42; v. 9/1 [fall-winter 1974-75], pp. 31-45.) This method of recording dance performance consists of signs for individual positions (pp. 1-8) and steps or *pas* (pp. 9-32, 43-46), including some for the arms (pp. 96-102), placed upon a track representing the floor pattern (pp. 33-42). Bar lines and step liaisons rhythmically coordinate the dance movements with the accompanying music (pp. 87-96, 103-6). A series of tables illustrates the steps in chorégraphie (pp. 47-86), including the Tems de courante, Pas de gaillarde, Demi-coupés, Coupés, Pas de bourrée ou fleurets, Jettées, Contretemps, Chassées, Pas de sissonne, Pirouettes, Cabrioles, Demi-cabrioles, Entre-chats, and Demi-entre-chats. Feuillet's text serves as a manual for a notation system that was used in varying degree throughout the 18th c., and thus as a key to the many dances recorded in this notation. It appeared in many translations and paraphrases.

Weaver's translation (dedicated to the English dancing master Isaac) slightly condenses and rearranges the text; it omits information on castanets and adds a table of abbreviations. In the 2nd ed., Weaver provides a table of contents and adds the following dances in Feuillet's notation: *The rigadoone* (composed by Isaac; couple, pp. 101-6), *The loure* (couple, pp. 107-12), and *The Bretagne* (couple, pp. 113-20). Siris' paraphrase of Feuillet's text offers another interpretation of Feuillet's intentions. In his preface, Siris provides information about Pierre Beauchamps, whom he credits with the invention of the notation first published by Feuillet. Other treatment of Feuillet's text includes versions in German by Taubert (q.v.), Italian by Dufort (q.v.) and Spanish by Ferriol y Boxeraus (q.v.) and Minguet e Yrol (q.v.).

Two collections of dances notated in *chorégraphie* (announced in the preface to *Chorégraphie*) are appended to the treatise in most publications of it. The first, *Recüeil de dances, composées par M. Feuillet, maître de dance* (*Paris: Feuillet & Brunet, 1700, 84p.; *facs. reprint, New York: Broude Bros., 1968; facs. reprint, England: Gregg International, 1970; facs. reprint, New York: Dance Horizons, 1970; *2nd ed., Paris: Feuillet & Brunet, 1701; Paris: 1709, 1713), contains the "most beautiful" *entrées de ballet,* representing both solo and ensemble ballet entries for male and female dancers: *Le rigaudon de la paix* (couple, pp. 1-7), *Gigue à deux* (couple, pp. 8-11), *Entrée à deux* (couple, pp. 12-16), *Autre entrée à deux* (couple, pp. 17-20), *Sarabande pour femme* (woman, pp. 21-24), *Sarabande pour homme* (man, pp. 25-28), *Sarabande espagnole pour homme* (man, pp. 29-32), *Folie d'Espagne pour femme* (woman, pp. 33-38), *Canarie à deux* (couple, pp. 39-40), *Gigue pour homme* (man, pp. 41-44), *Entrée pour homme* (man, pp. 45-48), *Autre entrée pour homme* (man, pp. 49-52), *Entrée grave pour homme* (man, pp. 53-59), *Entrée d'Apolon* (man, pp. 60-66), *Balet de neuf danseurs* (5 men, 4 women, pp. 67-83). The second, *Recüeil de dances composées par M. Pécour, pensionnaire des menus plaisirs du roy, & compositeur des ballets de l'Académie royal de musique de Paris. Et mises sur le papier par M. Feuillet, maître de dance* (*Paris: Feuillet & Brunet, 1700; 72p.; *facs. reprint, New York: Broude Bros., 1968; facs. reprint, England: Gregg International, 1970; facs. reprint, New York: Dance Horizons, 1970; 2nd ed., Paris: Feuillet & Brunet, 1701; Paris: 1709, 1713), contains the "most beautiful" ballroom dances composed by Louis Pécour: *La bourée d'Achille* (couple, pp. 1-11), *La mariée* (couple, pp. 12-21), *Le passepied* (couple, pp. 22-31), *La contredance* (couple, 32-36), *Le rigaudon des vaisseaux* (couple, pp. 37-42), *La Bourgogne* (couple, pp. 43-53), *La Savoye* (couple, pp. 54-61), *La forlana* (couple, pp. 62-67), *La Conty* (couple, pp. 68-72). An analysis of the dances in the second collection appears in Anne Witherell's dissertation, *Louis Pécour's 1700 Recueil de dances* (Ann Arbor, MI: UMI Research Press, 1983).

22 FEUILLET, Raoul Auger (ca. 1659-1710)

IX Recüeil de danses pour l'année 1711. Recüeillies et mises au jour par Mr. Feuillet, m^e. de danse.
*Paris: Dezais, [1709 or 1710]; 23p.

Little is known of Feuillet, the publisher of the dance notation manual *Chorégraphie* (q.v.). In the preface to this collection of dances for the

1711 ball season (part of an annual series), his student Dezais announces Feuillet's death at age 50, acknowledges his predecessor's pioneering work, and promises to carry on with the annual publication of new dances in chorégraphie. Those in this collection are *La nouvelle forlanne* by Pécour (couple, pp. 1-8), *Le passepied à quatre* by Feuillet (2 men, 2 women, pp. 9-16), and *La Médicis* by Feuillet (couple, pp. 17-23).

23 FEUILLET, Raoul Auger (ca. 1659-1710)

Le passepied nouveau. Dance de la composition de Monsieur Pécour, pensionaire des Menus Plaisirs du Roj et compositeur des ballets de l'Académie royalle de musique de Paris. Et mise au jour par Mr. Feuillet m^e. de danse.
*Paris: 1700; 10p.

A note in the preface states that upon receiving dance airs from dancing masters in the provinces or in foreign courts, Feuillet would send back stylistically appropriate dance compositions recorded in chorégraphie notation. This passepied in notation is for a couple.

24 FEUILLET, Raoul Auger (ca. 1659-1710)

Pr Receüil [sic] de danses de bal pour l'année 1703 de la composition de M. Pécour et mis au jour par M. Feüillet, m^e. de danse, auteur de la chorégraphie.
*Paris: Feuillet, 1702; 3+27p.

After the successful publication of a dance notation system *(Chorégraphie,* q.v.) and 2 collections in this notation of dances by himself (1700) and by Louis Pécour (1700), Feuillet began to publish ballroom dances in an annual series. Each November a collection of new dances appeared for the coming season, at least as late as 1724. (The series continued in the hands of his pupil Dezais after Feuillet's death.) In his advice to readers, Feuillet here urges them to learn chorégraphie. It is easier than one might imagine, he writes; anyone can learn it in very little time, as others in France and in foreign countries have shown. The two dances, both for one couple, are *Les contrefaiseurs contre-dance* (couple, pp. 1-11) and *La paysanne* (couple, pp. 12-27).

25 FEUILLET, Raoul Auger (ca. 1659-1710)
Recüeil de contredances, mises en chorégraphie, d'une manière si aisée, que toutes personnes peuvent facilement les apprendre, sans le secours d'aucun maître et même sans avoir eu aucune connaissance de la chorégraphie.
*Paris: Feuillet, 1706; [xxxii]+192p.
  Facs. reprint, New York: Broude Bros., 1968 (MMMLF, 135).
English transl. by John Essex as *For the furthur* [sic] *improvement of dancing, a treatis of chorography or ye art of dancing country dances after a new character, in which the figures, steps, & manner of performing are describ'd, & ye rules demonstrated in an easie method adapted to the meanest capacity. Translated from the French of Monsr. Feuillet, and improv'd w[i]th many additions, all fairly engrav'd on copper plates, and a new collection of country dances describ'd in ye same character by John Essex dancing master.*
London: I. Walsh & P. Randall, J. Hare, 1710; 88p.
  *Facs. reprint, England: Gregg International, 1970.
  Facs. reprint, New York: Dance Horizons, 1970.

This contains a simplified explanation of some elements of chorégraphie, here adapted for the notation of contredanses. The opening section entitled "Éléments ou principes de chorégraphie" (pp. [i-xxxii]; pp. 1-24 in Essex's transl.) describes the symbols for the track, feet, hands, and arms; the steps; and the relation of floor patterns to musical notation. The subsequent section of notated contredanses provides music and floor patterns for 32 dances, each for 4 couples. The translation by John Essex substitutes other dances, while retaining two from Feuillet's original collection *(La pantomime, La Gasconne).*

26 FEUILLET, Raoul Auger (ca. 1659-1710)
Recüeil de dances contenant un très grand nombres des meillieures entrées de ballet de Mr. Pécour, tant pour homme que pour femmes, dont la plus grande partie ont été dancées à l'Opéra. Recüeillies et mises au jour par Mr. Feüillet, m^e. de dance.
*Paris: Feuillet, 1704; [x]+228+16p.
  Facs. reprint, Bologna: Arnaldo Forni, 1969.
  *Facs. reprint, England: Gregg International, 1972.

*English transl. by John Weaver of the prefatory *Traité de la cadence* as *A small treatise of time and cadence in dancing, reduc'd to an easy and exact method. Shewing how steps, and their movements, agree with the notes, and the division of notes, in each measure.* London: Meere, 1706; 8+[5]p.

Facs. reprint, England: Gregg International, 1971.

Facs. reprint, New York: Dance Horizons, 1971.

Facs. reprint, New York: Broude Bros., 1968. (MMMLF, 128)

Facs. reprint in Richard Ralph, *The life and works of John Weaver* (New York: Dance Horizons, 1985), pp. 359-72.

This collection of theatrical dances contains two types of relevant historical information. First, the prefatory "Traité de la cadence" amplifies with additional examples Feuillet's earlier instuctions (in *Chorégraphie*, q.v.) on how to coordinate the dance steps and the music. Second, 25 of the 35 duet and solo dances here notated in *chorégraphie* provide the names of the dancers and the opera or ballet associated with the first performance. (Such information, leading to appropriate libretti, musical scores, and costume illustration, assists greatly in the reconstruction of a dance in its original context.) The dances here notated are: *Sarabande* (woman, p. 1-4); *Entrée . . . Ballet du Carnaval de Venise* (Mlle Victoire, pp. 5-9); *Chacone de Phaeton* (woman, p. 10-19); *Passacaille . . . Opéra de Scilla* (Mlle Subligny, pp. 20-35); *Entrée espagnolle . . . Ballet de l'Europe galante* (Mlle Subligny, pp. 36-40); *Gigue* (Mlle Subligny in England, pp. 41-47); *Menuet . . . Ballet des Fragments de Mr de Lully* (Mr du Moulin, Mlle Victoire, pp. 48-50); *Entrée [Forlane] . . . Ballet des Fragments de Mr de Lully* (Mlles Victoire and Dangeville, pp. 51-56); *Entrée [Menuet rondeau] . . . Opéra d'Omphalle* (Mr Balon, Mlle Subligny, p. 57-63); *Entrée . . . Opéra de Thézée* (Mr Balon, Mlle Subligny, pp. 64-67); *Entrée . . . Ballet des Fragments de Mr de Lully* (Mr Balon, Mlle Subligny, pp. 68-73); *Entrée espagnolle . . . Ballet de l'Europe galante* (Mr Balon, Mlle Subligny, pp. 74-78); *Passacaille . . . l'Opéra de Persée* (Mr Balon, Mlle Subligny, pp. 79-90); *2 Entrées . . . Opéra de Persée* (Mr Balon, Mlle Subligny, pp. 91-108); *Entrée . . . Opéra d'Hésionne* (Mr Dumirail, Mlle Victoire, pp. 109-116); *autre Entrée . . . Opéra d'Hésionne* (Mr Balon, Mlle Subligny, pp. 117-121); *Entrée . . . Opéra d'Aretuse* (Mr Balon, Mlle Subligny, pp. 122-26); *Sarabande . . . Opéra de Tancrède* (Mr Blondy, Mlle Victoire, pp. 127-31); *Contre-dance . . . Opéra de Tancrède* (Mr Dumirail, Mlle Victoire, pp. 132-38); *2 Entrées pour un berger et une bergère . . . Opéra d'Ullisse* (Mr Dumoulin l'aîné, Mlle Danjeville, pp. 139-47); *Entrée . . . Opéra de Cadmus* (Mr l'Evêque,

Mr Danjeville l'aîné, pp. 148-53); *Sarabande . . . Opéra Alside* (Mr Pissetot, Mr Chevrier, pp. 154-57); *Canary . . . Opéra de Didon* (Mr Pissetot, Mr Chevrier, pp. 158-63); *Entrée . . . Ballet de l'Europe galante* (Mr Pissetot, Mr Chevrier, pp. 164-68); *Loure . . . Opéra de Scilla* (Mr Blondy, Mr Philbois, pp. 169-75); *Chaconne* (man, pp. 176-84); *Chaconne de Phaeton* (man, pp. 185-94); *Entrée d'Appolon* (man, pp. 195-201), *l'Aimable Vainqueur* (man, pp. 202-9); *Sarabande* (man, pp. 210-15); *Entrée* (man, pp. 216-20); *Folies d'Espagne* (man, pp. 221-24); and *Sarabande* (man, pp. 225-28). Music for each of the dances appears in a 16-page appendix.

27 GALLINI, Giovanni Andrea Battista (1728-1805)

Critical observations on the art of dancing; to which is added a collection of cotillons or French dances.
*London: author, [1770?]; 184+10+[101]p.
London: author, 1772; 184+10+[101]p.

The first two chapters (pp. 1-118) contain a history of dance, which (as in Gallini's 1762 *Treatise,* q.v.) is largely indebted to Cahusac's *La danse ancienne et moderne* (q.v.), without acknowledgment. Ch. 3 "On the air and port of the person" (pp. 119-52) summarizes the positive traits a student acquires from learning how to dance: a head erect without stiffness, a body upright without affectation, a gait firm and assured without heaviness, a bearing light and airy without indecency. A poem in celebration of Mr. Marcell, Gallini's master, is appended. A "Description of several steps and movements practiced in the art of dancing" (pp. 159-84) describes the ballroom, provides a glossary, explains floor patterns, illustrates the true and false positions, comments on a few steps, and denigrates the use of *chorégraphie,* or dance notation. The cotillons or French dances may have had a separate title page as *A new collection of forty-four cotillons. With figures properly adapted; also the music for six select dances, two of which may be used as cotillons* (London: author, n.d.). This part begins with "General rules" (pp. 3-10), includes an index, then provides the music in 46 numbered plates, each with a separate page of description. There are 4 additional musical numbers for dancing.

28 GALLINI, Giovanni Andrea Battista (1728-1805)
A treatise on the art of dancing.
London: author, 1762; xvi+292p.
London: author, 1765; xvi+292p.
*London: author and R. Dodsley, 1772; xvi+292p.
  *Facs. reprint, New York: Broude Bros., 1967 (MMMLF, 48).
London: author and R. Dodsley, 1775; xvi+292p.

To a great deal of historical material derived from Cahusac's *La danse ancienne et moderne* (q.v.), Gallini adds quotations (pp. 140-43) from the educational writings of John Locke. A survey of dancing by country in Europe (pp. 181-94), Asia (pp. 195-208), Africa (pp. 209-16), and America (pp. 217-25) is followed by more quotations from Cahusac on pantomime (pp. 227-62), as well as the latter's rules for making dances (pp. 262-72). The book closes with the description of two comic dances (pp. 273-92).

29 GAUDRAU
Novueau [sic] *recüeil de dances de bal et celle de ballet contenant un très grand nombres des meillieures entrées de ballet de la composition de Mr. Pécour tant pour hommes que pour femmes qui ont été dancées à l'Opéra. Ouvrage très util aux maîtres et à toutes les personnes qui s'apliquent à la dance. Recüeillies et mises au jour par Mr. Gaudrau M^e. de dance et de l'Accadémie Royalle de Musique à Paris.*
*Paris: Gaudrau, [ca. 1712-1715]; 4p.+108pl.

The dedication and preface to this collection of notated dances give important information about the identity of the author of the notation system *chorégraphie*. Gaudrau states plainly that Pierre Beauchamps invented the art of notation and R. A. Feuillet then profited from its publication *(Chorégraphie,* q.v.). By this time, Gaudrau explains, Louis Pécour has succeeded Beauchamps in the composition of ballets and has asked Gaudrau to put together this collection. It begins with 9 ballroom dances: *La royalle* (couple, pp. 1-5); *Le cherubain* (couple, pp. 6-7); *La bourée de Mlle Charolois* (couple, pp. 8-11), *La badine* (couple, pp. 12-15); *La contredance* (couple, pp. 16-18), *La gaillarde* (couple, pp. 19-22); *La Bourbon* (couple, pp. 23-25); *Menuet à quatre* (2 couples, pp. 26-33); *Rigaudon à quatre* (2 couples, pp. 34-41). It continues with threatrical dances. Of 30 dances, 23 name the original dancers and work in which the dance was performed (in a manner similar to the Feuillet *Recüeil* of 1704, q.v.). The dances are: *Entrée . . . Thézée* (Mr Balon, Mlle Subligny, pp. 1-4); *Entrée . . . Méleâgre* (Mr Dumoulin, Mlle Guiot, pp. 5-10); *Entrée . . . Philomelle* (Mr Dumoulin, Mlle Guiot, pp. 11-14); *Gigue . . . Philomelle* (Mr Dumoulin, Mlle Guiot, pp. 15-16); *Entrée d'un pastre et d'une pastourelle . . . Feste venitienne* (Mr Dumoulin, Mlle Guiot, pp. 17-19); *2me Entrée des Festes venitienne* (Mr Dumoulin, Mlle Guiot, pp. 20-22); *Entrée pour un berger et une bergère . . . Opéra de Sémelée* (Mr Dumoulin, Mlle Guiot, pp. 23-26); *Entrée d'un pastre et d'une pastourelle . . . Opéra de Sémelée* (Mr Dumoulin, Mlle Guiot, pp. 27-32); *Sarabande . . . Opéra d'Yssée* (Mr Dumoulin l'aîné, Mlle Chaillous, pp. 33-35); *Entrée . . . Opéra d'Hézionne* (Mr Dumoulin l'aîné, Mlle Chaillou, pp. 36-38); *Entrée . . . Opéra d'Hézionne* (Mr Dumoulin l'aîné, Mlle Chaillon [sic], pp. 39-42); *Canarye . . . Triomphe de l'Amour* (Mlle Provost, Mlle Guiot, pp. 43-45); *La Paysanne* (couple, pp. 46-50); *Entrée . . . Opéra d'Yssée* (Mlle Provost, Mlle Guiot, pp. 51-56); *La Muszette . . . Opéra de Callirhoé* (Mlle Provost, Mlle Guiot, pp. 57-60); *Entrée de deux Bacchante . . . Philomelle* (Mlle Provost, Mlle Guiot, pp. 61-63); *Entrée de deux femme . . . Feste venitienne* (Mlle Provost, Mlle Guiot, pp. 64-66); *Entrée seul pour une femme* (Mlle Guiot, pp. 67-68); *Gigue pour une femme seul* (pp. 69-72); *Entrée pour une femme seul* (Mlle Guiot, pp. 73-74); *Gigue pour une femme . . . Opéra de Tancrède* (Mlle Guiot, pp. 75-76); *Entrée pour une femme . . . Opéra d'Athis* (Mlle Guiot, pp. 77-78); *Passacaille pour une femme . . . Opéra d'Armide* (Mlle Subligny en Angleterre, pp. 79-86); *Loure de deux homme . . . Galaté* (Mr Blondy, Mr Marcel, pp. 87-90); *Entrée de deux homme . . . Opéra de Persé* (Mr Marcel, Mr Gaudrau, pp. 91-94); *Entrée de deux homme . . . Feste venitienne* (Mr Blondy, Mr Marcel, pp. 95-98); *Entrée de Cithe . . . Amours déguisez* (Mr Blondy, Mr Marcel, pp. 99-101); *Entrée seul pour un homme . . . Thézé* (Mr Klin, pp. 102-3); *Entrée seul pour un homme* (pp. 104-6); *Entrée seul pour un homme* (pp. 107-8). The airs for these dances were published separately.

30 GUILLAUME, [Simon]

Caractères de la danse allemande figurés en taille douce telle quelle s'exécute au Wauxhall de cette ville. Avec l'explication des pas et enchaînemens où se trouve un recueil de contredances et menuets les plus nouveaux; et des notes historiques sur l'origine et l'utilité de la danse. Dedié au beau sexe par Guillaume, maître de dance.

*Paris: author, [1769?]; 31p.+12pl.

Almanach dansant, ou positions et attitudes de l'allemande, avec un discours préliminaire sur l'origine et l'utilité de la danse, dedié au beau sexe . . . pour l'année 1770.
*Paris: author, 1770; 31p.+12pl.
Almanach . . . pour l'année 1771. Paris: author, [1771].

Acknowledging his debt to Bonnet *(Histoire générale de la danse,* q.v.), the author gives a summary history, then tries to persuade all to an interest in dance. If the reader wishes to be grave, the menuet is good for those who are not agile. Has one a need to exercise the legs? There are fast and difficult dances in which the body must be speedy. Does one wish to exercise and excite all parts of the body? One can dance the allemande. It takes its name from Germany, but it is performed very differently in Paris, and the author wishes to record this difference. Some say the dance is too simple, too well known, he admits, but simplicity is essential to it. Then follows an explanation of the *pas de l'allemande* and details on how to pass from one person to the next. The 12 beautiful plates each have an explanatory paragraph, but the graphic and unstilted poses teach without need of words—a beautiful book. For information on the *Recueil de contredances et menuets les plus nouveaux* mentioned in the title (which has a separate title page and is dated 1716 in the copy seen), see J. M. Guilcher, *La contredanse* (Paris: Mouton, 1969).

31 GUILLEMIN

Chorégraphie, ou l'art de décrire la danse.
*Paris: l'auteur, Petit, 1784; 35p.

The author of this manual published late in the century laments the neglect of *chorégraphie,* the dance notation introduced by Feuillet in 1700 *(Chorégraphie,* q.v.), and the substitution of "une *chorégraphie* bâtarde." His manual is, however, a summary treatment of the system: a short glossary of basic terms, the usual description of the ballroom, the body orientation, the floor pattern, and symbols of the most basic steps. The only dance discussed is the minuet (step of 2 movements), including a survey of its manner of performance rather than its technique. Brief *chorégraphie* charts (pp. 17-21) and advice to students (p. 35) flank the *chorégraphie* with music for four dances: a partial *Menuet de la cour* by Gardelle (couple, pp. 21-22), a *Menuet dauphin* by Marcelle (couple, pp. 23-28), *La chasse de Lagarde* by Gardelle (couple, pp. 29-30), and *Les tricotets* (male, pp. 31-34).

32 JENYNS, Soame (1704-1787)
The art of dancing, a poem in three cantos.
London: J. Roberts, 1729; 55p.
Facs. reprint, London: Dance Books; Princeton, NJ: Princeton Book Company, 1978. Ed. by Anne Cottis.
*In *Poems,* London: R. Dodsley, 1752; pp. 3-29.
1770 or 1771.
Ed. by Charles Nelson Cole in *Works of . . . ,* 2nd ed., 4 v. V. 1, pp. 1-30. London: T. Codell, 1793.
  Facs. reprint, England: Gregg International, 1970.
Poems by . . . containing the art of dancing, and other pieces, with the author's life. In *The literary miscellany,* XX. London: G. Nicholson, 1804; 25p.

This poem limns the female as a dancing muse, beautiful in repose but devastating in the motions of the dance. In describing her dances, Jenyns characterizes the minuet as a maze, the louvre as slow, with a majestic pace, and the jigg as sprightly. A long section gives advice on dress proper for dancing—skirt not too heavy, hoop not too large, colors not unmatching, garter not insecure, heel not too high, fan not awkwardly handled. He distinguishes between the levels of ability required for stage and ballroom dancing, but at no level does he tolerate slipshod performance. If a person cannot master the court dances from France, it is best to remain with the less demanding country dances. Even there, one must keep true time, catch the beat before beginning, keep eyes off the ground, but not stare about. France is the leader in dance, having produced not only the forms of the dance (Rigadoon, Louvre, Borée, Courant ["unpractis'd long," p. 17], the immortal Minuet, the smooth Bretagne), but a dance notation *(chorégraphie)* that enables one to write down every step for posterity. Another section describes the rise of country dance from a jovial pastime to an artistic entity, still however somewhat boisterous when performed at balls. Thus in charming verse, Jenyns offers a view of ballroom etiquette and dance in 1729.

33 KATTFUSS, Johann Heinrich

Chorégraphie, oder vollständige und leicht fassliche Anweisung zu den verschiedenen Arten der heut zu Tage beliebtesten gesellschaftlichen Tänze für Tanzliebhaber, Vortänzer und Tanzmeister. Erster Theil.
*Leipzig: Heinrich Graff, 1800; xiv+[xv]+208+[12]p.

The recent availability on microcards of the Daniel François Scheurleer collection, in The Hague's Gemeente Museum, has revealed the existence of this book on *chorégraphie,* dated a full century after the first appearance of the dance notation system in 1700 in the publications of Raoul Feuillet (q.v.). As the title indicates, this book is for dance lovers, dancing demonstrators, and dancing masters. After an introduction in which Kattfuss acknowledges his debt to his predecessors Thoinot Arbeau *(Orchésographie,* 1589) and Feuillet, the author opens his book with a section on rhythm (pp. 7-15) and irrhythm (pp. 16-19). An explanation of *chorégraphie* signs and their meanings (pp. 20-26) is illustrated in fold-out diagrams, showing the *chorégraphie* signs in their usual boxes. The signs are not exact duplicates, but rather adaptations of the Feuillet symbols. The sign remains similar (with the circular mark at the bottom, the usual line bisected by the "rise" or "spring" marks), but at the top a shoe-shape (similar to an Arthur Murray shoe-diagram) is attached. This shoe-shape is used in many ways—to denote the five positions, to tract pirouettes, and to make tracks on the "Z" figure of the minuet, for example. The number of each box is keyed to the verbal explanations. Practical instruction in the carriage of the body as well as in dancing occupies pp. 27-64, with frequent reference to positions notated on the fold-out charts. Bows *(Complimenten)* in general, those for women, the *pas de Menuet,* the minuet itself, presentation of the hand, the divisions of the minuet, its *pas coulée, pas balancé,* and *pas battu,* lead into a final discussion of the complete minuet (pp. 65-93). More advice is offered the scholar on the value of learning the minuet, and overall rules for dancing follow (pp. 94-106). After this major portion of the book devoted to the minuet as "dem schönsten und schwersten Tanze" (p. 93) follows a section on other kinds of dances, which are merely cited in brief as those one should know: Saraband, Passepied, Passacaille, Musette, Loure, Folie d'Espagne, Gavotte, Gigue, and Rigaudon. A middle section reflects the era, being devoted to the Contredance (pp. 109-44), the Waltz or Ländler (pp. 149-54), a patterned dance called the Conversation (pp. 155-63), and information on balls (pp. 163-79), at which such dances as the Schöttische or Eccossaise, the Allemande, Quadrille, and the Polonaise might be performed (pp. 181-

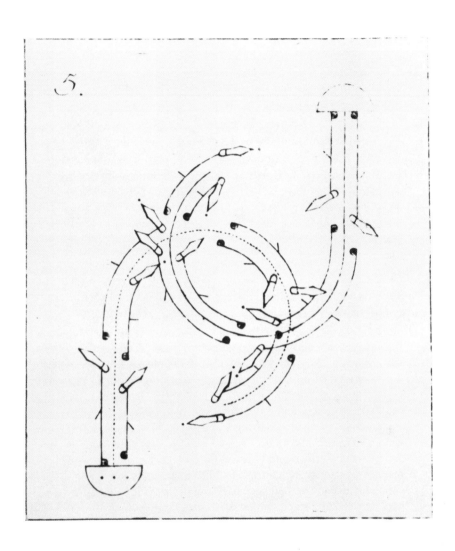

I-33 Johann Heinrich KATTFUSS, *Chorégraphie, odor vollständige und leicht fassliche Anweisung* (Leipzig: Heinrich Graff, 1800). Dance notation for presenting right hands in the minuet. [Haags, Gemeente Museum, Dance Collection, Scheurleer Handlist No. 70]

41

92). Rules for health close the book (pp. 193-204), followed by pages of a quadrille and some dance cards. Throughout, fold-out plates with Feuillet notation illustrate the text.

34 LAMBRANZI, Gregorio (fl. early 18th c.)
Neue und curieuse theatralische Tantz-Schul. Deliciae theatrales.
Nürnberg: Johann Jacob Wolrab, 1716; 50f.+51f.

> Facs. reprint, Leipzig: Peters, 1975; 50+51+xviip. With German commentary by Kurt Petermann and English transl. by Michael Talbot.

English transl. by F. Derra de Moroda, ed. with a preface by Cyril W. Beaumont as *New and curious school of theatrical dancing.* *London: Imperial Society of Teachers of Dancing, 1928; 27p.+50pl.+6p.+51pl.

*Reprinted, Brooklyn, N.Y.: Dance Horizons, 1966.

*Facs. publication of the original manuscript (Munich, Bayerische Staatsbibliothek), with commentary by F. Derra de Moroda. Brooklyn, N.Y.: Dance Horizons, 1972; [xvi]p.+86pl.+key to comparison of plates.

Beside the noble court dance, popular theatrical dance flourished during the 17th and most of the 18th centuries. Lambranzi's work is an extraordinary source of information about the dance pantomime practiced by popular *commedia dell'arte* performers on the stages of the fair theaters, the Théâtre Italien, and the Opéra Comique. The 101 plates, prepared from Lambranzi's own drawings and beautifully engraved by Johann Georg Puschner, show costumed dancers on the stage. Each bears instructions in German and Italian for use by dancing masters wishing to recreate or parody the dances. The life-like illustrations provide detail concerning costume (height of heel, use of masks, genre of dress), production (backdrops and wing pieces, stages), steps (including those for court dances: Sarabande, Folie d'Espagna, Bourrée, Rigaudon, Menuet; and dances with military, commercial, or sports themes), stage business (humor, continuity—by means of a series of plates), and music (by means of the musical notation at the top of each plate). When read in combination with Magri's *Trattato teorico-prattico de ballo* (q.v.), a lively picture of dance in the popular theater emerges. See also the scenarios in Le Sage's *Le théâtre de la foire.*

35 LANG, Franciscus (1654-1725)

Dissertatio de actione scenica, cum figuris eandem explicantibus, et observationibus quibusdam de arte comica. Auctore P. Francisco Lang Societatis Jesu. Accesserunt imagines symbolicae pro exhibitione & vestitu theatrali. Superiorum permissu, sumptibus Joan, Andreae de la Haye, Bibliopolae Academici Ingolstadii.
Monachii: Typis Mariae Magdalenae Riedlin, Vidux, 1727; 154p.

*Facs. reprint and German transl. by Alexander Rudin as *Abhandlung über die Schauspielkunst mit erläuternden Abbildungen und einigen Bemerkungen über die dramatische Kunst von P. Franz Lang aus der Gesellschaft Jesu. Beigefügt sind symbolische Bilder für die theatralische Aufführung und Bekleidung. Mit Erlaubnis der Oberen. In Verlegung Johann Andreae de la Haye, Akademischen Buchhändlers zu Ingolstadt.* Bern, München: A. Francke, 1975; 383p. (pp. 1-154, 155-383).

Lang was one of the French Jesuits who, like his predecessor C. F. Ménéstrier (q.v.) during the era of the *ballet de cour,* was a leader in his order's use of dance and drama for furthering the fundamental tenets of Catholicism. The *Dissertatio* is essentially an instruction manual for the expressive use of the body. Students trained in these techniques were then to participate effectively—with conviction and emotion—as actors and dancers in operas, pastoral plays, Alexandrine tragedies, court pageants, and ballets. The first 2 chapters define and defend the skills taught (pp. 11-17), the next 5 give specific instruction on the use of the parts of the body (17-45), and 2 delineate the body's overall effect (45-56). The next chapters (pp. 56-71) discuss elements of production: use of declamation, relationship to the playwright, interplay of acting and dialogue. The book closes with 4 chapters (pp. 71-106) on the drama in general, on comedy and tragedy, on the unity of time and place, and on the contribution of the stage scene. Of special interest is the section (pp. 107-54) entitled "Imagines symbolicae" with suggestions (gestures to use, objects to carry, costumes to wear) for personifying abstract symbols (amor, fortitudo, matrimonium) as well as mythological characters (Mars, Volcanus) on the stage. Rudin's German translation includes an essay on Lang's life and work (pp. 313-32), bibliographies of Lang's works, his references, and works on Lang (pp. 333-39), notes explaining textual problems (pp. 340-44), notes on the text (pp. 345-75), and an index and table of contents.

36 LANGE, Carl Christoph

Anfangsgründe zur Tanzkunst, in welchen denenjenigen, die sich in der Aufführung von dem gemeinen Mann zu unterscheiden, und bey der galanten Welt beliebt zu machen gedenken, eine gefälligmachende Art gezeiget wird.
*Erlangen: Johann Carl Tetzschner, 1751; [10]+90p.
2nd ed., Erlangen: Johann Dietrich Michael Kammerer, 1765; 80p.

This dancing master's manual provides specific information on good health, decorous dress (proper colors, appropriately seasonal, with all cleanliness), and unaffected mein (pp. 8-22); body placement (allignment, the 5 positions; pp. 23-31) and the walk or march (pp. 32-38); and bows and courtesies (decorum, manipulation of the hat, the approach, details for the gentleman and for the lady; pp. 39-90). The author's attitude, mirroring one expressed in Pierre Rameau's *Le maître à danser* (q.v.), is best exemplified in his restatement of the proverb: "den Vogel kennt man an den Federn."

37 LAUS DE BOISSY, Louis de

Lettre critique sur notre danse théâtrale addressée à l'auteur du Spectateur français, par un homme de mauvaise humeur.
Paris: Louis Jorry fils, Lesclapart, 1771; 27p.
*Published as part of a collection of the author's works *(L'art d'aimer,* etc.). Londres: J. F. Bastien, 1772; 27p.

This critical reply originated on September 20, 1771. The author had gone, as he did once a year, to the Académie Royale de Musique to see the dancers Gaetano Vestris and Dlle. Anne Heinel. They might have danced, he argues, but they did not—since they did not meet his definition of true theatrical dance: "l'art de rendre les diverses impressions de l'âme par les mouvemens variés des différentes parties du corps. . . . Les pas ne sont que le méchanisme de la danse . . . ; la pantomime en est l'âme et la vie. La danse . . . doit être une imitation des actions et des passions humaines: donc elle ne sera rien sans la pantomime. La danse, unié à la pantomime est un art; la danse, séparée de la pantomime, n'est plus qu'un métier" (p. 6). Since true theatrical dances must be the imitation of something else, the senior Vestris was not a dancer, because he was always himself, not the person he should be representing. To support his argument, Laus de Boissy harks back to the ancients, then calls for the ingenious J. G. Noverre (q.v.) to come produce his admirable ballets in Paris. Then he gives examples of expressionless dancing—especially in *Les pas de furies*—similar to those that fill Noverre's *Lettres* (q.v.). The author appends a postscript in which he quotes Diderot, who, Laus de Boissy triumphantly points out, confirms this same position in his *Le fils-naturel* (1757).

38 LAUZE, F. de

Apologies de la danse et la parfaicte méthode de l'enseignement tant aux cavaliers qu'aux dames.
[s.l.]: 1623; 69p.
  Facs. reprint, Genève: Minkoff, 1977.
  *Facs. reprint with English transl. and commentary by Joan Wildeblood. Introduction, pp. 1-33; text and translation, pp. 34-153; music transcribed by Eduardo M. Torner, pp. 154-160; simplified instructions, pp. 162-217; bibliography and index, pp. 218-221. London: Frederick Muller, 1952.

This instruction manual devotes itself to the practice of dance in the early 17th c., while offering a glimpse of contemporary dance aesthetic. It derives support from evidence in the writings of classical antiquity and in ecclesiastical tracts encouraging the use of *danses mesurées* with certain motets. In addition to deportment, treated separately for gentlemen and ladies, and some steps (e.g. Capriole), specific dance types are discussed, notably the Courante (pp. 88-100; 146-48 in the 1952 ed.), Bransles (pp. 100-13; 134-46), and Gaillarde (pp. 114-22; 148-52). Turn-out is already recommended for certain steps. The 1952 edition interleaves Wildeblood's translation with the facsimile original text; Torner's music is selected from Marin Mersenne's *Harmonie universelle* (q.v.). The notes make comparisons with contemporary documents on deportment and dancing.

39 LECOINTE, Jean

Apologie de la danse: son antiquité, sa noblesse, et ses avantages. Avec une dissertation sur le menuet.
Paris: 1752.
*English transl. as *An apology for dancing: shewing its antiquity, excellence and advantages.*
London: Kippax, 1752; xvi+59p. (Pages numbered 17-75.)

Writing in his preface that "I pretend to be nothing but a simple lover of dancing, who writes for his own pleasure, and without any other view than that of amusement" (p. xiv; his constitution was too weak to perform), the author begins with history, but his mind wanders to thoughts on love, with ramblings on dance's origins, examples of its partisans, samples of its virtues, and advice for its selection. In the "Dissertation upon the Minuet" (pp. 57-75), Le Cointe claims to present "the true idea of the taste and graces requisite in the elegant execution of it" (p. 57). A story about a dancing master of elegant bearing being mistaken for a nobleman is his only illustration. The author's enthusiasm borders on parody, evident in his excitement about the minuet: "All other dances are as much inferior to this, as the languid light of the stars is to the bright refulgency of the sun" (pp. 67-68). But alas, the dissertation comes to a close, and only a footnote on the last page describing a *contretems* provides any technical information.

40 LEPITRE, Jean Charles Louis

L'art de la danse oder allgemein fassliches vollständiges Taschenlehrbuch zur leichten und angenehmen Erlernung der eleganten und höheren Tanzkunst nach einer ganz neuen Methode von Jean Charles Louis Le Pitre vermehrt mit einer ausführlichen Abhandlung von der Nothwendigkeit, den Nützen und Werth der Tanzkunst, so wie auch mit den nothwendigen Gesundheitsregeln und einer schönen Anweisung sur la bonne conversation et l'air noble auf Bällen und beim Tanzen für Herren und Damen aller gebildeten Stände, vorzüglich aber für Lehrer der Tanzkunst, Familien auf dem Lande, Erzieher und jede Bildungsanstalt von T. F. Campe, und einer Vorrede von D. B.
*Paris, St. Petersburg, Wien, Berlin: [s.d.]; xxiv+xxiii+206p.

After a philosophical introduction and a "detailed treatise on dance and the art of dance," Lepitre describes briefly the 5 positions, the bow, and

the minuet (pp. 24-45). Although he emphasizes that without a knowledge of the minuet, other dances can not be performed with proper style,
most of the book concentrates on the English dance, its steps (pp. 46-
99), floor patterns (pp. 99-110), a minuet (quadrille) for 4 and 6 (pp.
110-25), turns and hops (pp. 126-37), and assorted dances (quadrilles;
pp. 138-58). Aesthetic commentary (art dance is an imitation of nature)
and advice on achieving a noble bearing are then followed by a closing
summary (pp. 159-206).

41 MAGNY, Claude Marc (1676-1727)

*Principes de chorégraphie, suivis d'un traité de la cadence, qui
apprendra les tems et les valeurs de chaque pas de la danse,
détaillés par caractères, figures et signes démonstratifs.*
*Paris: Duchesne et de la Chevardière, 1765; [vii]+244p.
Facs. reprint, Genève: Minkoff, 1984.

Apparently not ever in general use, even during the years immediately
following Feuillet's publication in 1700 of the notational system (*Chorégraphie,* q.v.), dance notation had in the second half of the 18th c. not a
few detractors (such as Noverre, q.v.), but also advocates such as
Magny. Magny's *Principes* was one of five extant French manuals on
dance writing to appear after 1750, with two by Malpied (*Élémens de
chorégraphie,* 1762; *Traité sur l'art de la danse,* ca. 1770, q.v.), Guil-
lemin's *Chorégraphie* (1784, q.v.), and Clément's *Principes de corégraphie* [sic] (1771, q.v.). (For two in German, see Kattfuss and Feldtenstein.) In his preface, Magny claims to have developed, extended,
put in order, proved, and augmented Feuillet's principles, but his book
shows little change from the master's manual of 1700. He explains the
principles of the system (pp. 1-50), then provides a series of tables with
the steps in *chorégraphie:* the Tems de courante, Pas de gaillarde (pp.
51-53), Demi-coupés (pp. 54-60), Coupés (pp. 61-71), Pas de bourrée
(pp. 74-83), Jettés (pp. 84-88), Contretems (pp. 89-98), Chassés (pp.
99-100), Sissonnes (pp. 101-2), Pirouettes (pp. 103-6), Cabrioles (pp.
107-9), Entrechats (pp. 110-12), and several Pas détachés (pp. 111-13).
Added is a section on cadence (pp. 119-38), with signs for the *pas de
menuet* used to illustrate coordination with the music. Further information on the menuet is found at the end of the book (pp. 240-44). Magny
appends dances in *chorégraphie* with music, including two by Marcel:
Menuet de la reine (couple, pp. 139-44) and *Menuet Dauphin* (couple,
pp. 145-57); three by Pécourt: *L'allemande* (couple, pp. 165-73), *La
mariée* (couple, pp. 175-82), and *Aimable vainqueur* (couple, pp. 183-

88); and one by Magny himself: *Menuet d'Exaudet* (pp. 157-64 [music in Gaston Vuillier's *A history of dancing* (New York: Appelton, 1898), p. 148]). Then follows a section on the contredanse and the use of *chorégraphie* in recording it (pp. 209-10), including examples: *Le quadrille* (2 couples, pp. 189-99), *Le ballet champestre* (2 couples, pp. 200-8), *La croix de Lorraine* (2 couples, pp. 211-23), *Le ballet valois* (2 couples, pp. 224-32), *L'interrompu* (4 couples, pp. 233-36), and *Les petits bosquets* (4 couples, pp. 237-39). The three dances by Pécour date from the turn of the 18th c., while the others represent a later taste.

42 MAGRI, Gennaro (fl. 1779)

Trattato teorico-prattico di ballo.
*Napoli: Vincenzo Orsino, 1779; 143+101+[36]p.

"Gennaro Magri's *Trattato teorico-prattico di ballo* is the most invaluable 18th-century treatise on ballet technique." Marian Hannah Winter makes this observation in *The pre-romantic ballet* (London: Pitman, 1974, p. 152), because Magri treats in painstaking detail all genres of dance, not just the noble. Frankly acrobatic movements abound, many of which appear in the illustrations of Lambranzi's *Neue und curieuse theatralische Tantz-Schul* (1716, q.v.).

In two parts, the treatise opens with general statements on the dance— its utility and discipline, the qualities of the *ballerino,* the presence and movements of the body (pp. 13-22). "Della cadenza" asserts that performers must be able to discern perfectly the two meters, binary and ternary, to which all music is basically reduced. The interaction between dance and its accompanying music is emphasized. Magri insists upon the importance of the dancer knowing music, while at the same time the musician must be alert to the practicalities of dance and provide music suited to the specific theater (pp. 22-26). The five positions of the feet (including the false) and how to perform them in the air, with force and with style, lead into a discussion of steps *(passi),* which forms the principal portion of Part 1. Beginning with the *passo naturale,* innumerable kinds are described: the walk, Piegare (Plié), Rilevare (Rélevé), Degage, Battimento, the Tordichamp (pp. 30-140). Sections are devoted to the Coupè and the Mezzo coupè, with similar treatment of the Gettato (Jetté), Tombè, Eschapè, Sissonne, Chassè, Contratempo, and Fuetè ("un passo assai brillante," p. 43). Here are found descriptions of Pistoletta a terra, Tortiglie, Passobilanciato, Gagliarde, Sarabonda, Balonnè, Deviluppe, Glissade, Passo unito (Assemblé), Balottè (not to be confused with the Balonnè), Ambuette, Fleuret, Brise, and Rigaudon. Link-ing steps like the Flinc, combined steps like the Pas trusè and the Passo di ciaccono are treated. The Flinc can finish a Capriol, of which there are 23 kinds (pp. 118-40).

Of the serious *passi*, the *courante* with both three and four movements, the *pas de bourée* with nine variations (simple, open, crossed, in the air, etc.), are all treated in Part 1 (pp. 55-68), preceding a full discussion of the minuet in Part 2 (pp. 14-34), including its origin, bows, *passi* and *tempi* (*quattrotre* and *tripola* with multiples) and figures. The use of the arms is discussed, including how to offer the hands; all three kinds of *ballerini* can use the arms in the four positions of *basse, a mezz'aria, alte,* and *sforzate* (the French *les grands bras*). Closing this section is advice to the performer on how to do the minuet well despite its difficulty, to the teacher to help the beginner, and to the male to accompany the *Dama*. The rest of Part 2 (pp. 34-100), plus five tables of symbols and 26 pull-out diagrams (one of which is musical notation), is devoted to *contradanze*.

43 MALPIED

Élémens de chorégraphie contenant la description de plusieurs pas et les mouvemens en usage dans l'art de la danse suivant les principes de M. Feuillet, rédigés, augmentés et suivis d'une nouvelle contredanse par M. Malpied.
*Paris: Malpied, Guersan, 1762; 37p.

Malpied adapts the dance notation of Feuillet *(Chorégraphie,* q.v.) to contredanses. The whole system, simplified clearly and laconically, as he says, is explained and illustrated in the first 18 pages. The contredanse as a type is described verbally (pp. 19-22), and the contredanse *La Française,* with airs closely coordinated to dance figures, is presented in the adapted notation (pp. 23-35). Of greatest interest are *chorégraphie* signs to denote the movement of arms, hands, and even fingers.

44 MALPIED

Traité sur l'art de la danse.
Paris: Bouin, [ca. 1785]; 122p.
Seconde édition augmentée d'une grande quantité de pas tant anciens que modernes avec leurs explications à chacun.
Paris: Bouin, [s.d.]; 166p.
*Facs. reprint, England: Gregg International, 1972.

De la Division des Tems de l'Air
avec les Tems des Bras.

Il faut d'abord avoir les deux bras un peu ouverts
en dehors à côté de soi

Pour marquer le 1.ᵉ Tems ou est le Signe frappé
il faut laisser tomber les mains en dedans sur les
poches de l'habit.

Pour marquer le 2.ᵉ Tems il faut ouvrir les bras en.
les arrondissans du poignet et du coude imperceptiblem'

Pour indiquer le 3.ᵉ Tems, il faut ouvrir les deux bras
et les mains en dehors en les écartant un peu du corps.

Pour marquer le 4.ᵉ Tems, Il faut laisser tomber les
mains, en arriere sur les poches de l'habit ou est le
Signe frappé, ce qui fait le 4.ᵉ Tems, et la Seconde
mesure, pour marquer le 5.ᵉ Tems il faut rouvrir les
bras à côté de soi,

Pour le 6.ᵉ Tems, il faut rétourner les mains et les
bras un peut en dedans sans les approcher de soi

On remarquera qu'il faut deux Mesures à trois
tems pour un pas de Menuet, voici la vraie mani-
-ere de battre la Mesure avec les Bras dans le Me-
-nuet pour trouver tous les tems des Bras qui ont
rapport au Tems de l'Air

Voyez L'Exemple dans la Page cy après.

I-44 MALPIED, *Traité sur l'art de la danse* (Paris: Bouin, ca. 1785),
pp. 90-91. Text and notation coordinating arm motions with the music.
[Haags, Gemeente Museum, Dance Collection, Scheurleer Handlist
No. 69]

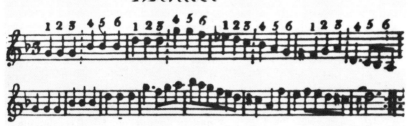

Menuet

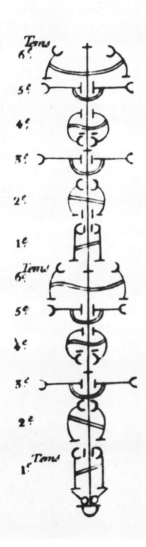

Late 18th-c. advocates of *chorégraphie,* the dance notation published by Feuillet *(Chorégraphie,* q.v.), had at their disposal Malpied's presentation with its minor revision of the system. Malpied's is one of the last comprehensive *chorégraphie* manuals of the period. The opening section follows the custom of similar books by discussing the plan of the room or theater, the position of the dancers' bodies, and the floor pattern. Next comes the signs for the five positions (the false ones have been dropped) and the steps on the floor pattern, with several examples (Pas assemblé, Pas battu). A middle section (pp. 60-104) contains the tables of signs for the Pas de gaillarde (p. 60), Tems de courantes (pp. 60-61), Demi-coupés (pp. 62-66), Coupés (pp. 67-77), Pas de bourée ou fleurets (pp. 78-86), Jettés (pp. 87-89), Contre-tems (pp. 90-96), Chassés (pp. 97-98), Pas de sissonne (p. 99), Pirouettes (pp. 100-1), Cabrioles (pp. 102-3), and Entrechats (p. 104). The section on cadence (pp. 105-24) explains how musical meter and rhythm are expressed in the dance notation. Malpied's most important contribution to our knowledge of 18th-c. dance is in the section "Da la manière de présenter les mains" (pp. 125-37), in which he gives the most specific information we have on the five arm positions, here written down in *chorégraphie,* with numbered examples clearly showing sequence. A final section (pp. 138-47) offers a "Dissertation sur les pas du menuet," in which numerals in the notation of the minuet steps show when the metric beats of the music fall. It is followed by a detailed minuet in *chorégraphie* (13 figures and a final bow). Here, too, Malpied pays unusual attention to the arms, the hands, and even the fingers.

45 MÉNÉSTRIER, Claude François (1631-1705)

L'Autel de Lyon, consacré à Louis Auguste, et placé dans le temple de la gloire. Ballet dédié à sa majesté en son entrée à Lyon.
*Lyon: Jean Molin, 1658; [vii]+60p.
Portion entitled "Remarques pour la conduite des ballets" reprinted in M. F. Christout, *Le ballet de cour de Louis XIV, 1643-1672* (Paris: A. & J. Picard, 1967), pp. 221-26.

This *livret* (libretto) to a ballet in three parts provides the text of the recitatives and verbal description of the danced entrées (Part I, 6 entrées; Part II, 10 entrées; Part III, 8 entrées and a grand ballet). In his "remarks on the conduct of ballets" (pp. 50-56), the author offers his aesthetic rationale (derived from writings of Lucian and Aristotle) for the production of ballet. Ballet encompasses all the arts, he observes; its subject need not be realistic, since stage machines allow depiction of supernatural and extraordinary actions. Variety and diversity are recommended, but the most important ingredient is a clever and agreeable subject. Out of this subject grow the characters, melodies, apparatus, structure, and recitation. An appendix provides information on heraldic devices and emblems.

46 MÉNÉSTRIER, Claude François (1631-1705)
Des ballets anciens et modernes selon les règles du théâtre.
Paris: René Guignard, 1682; 54+323p.
*Facs. reprint, Genève: Minkoff, 1972.
Paris: Robert Pépié, 1684.
Paris: Robert Pépié, 1685.
Paris: Robert Pépié, 1686.

In this, the first printed history of ballet, Ménéstrier used historical and contemporary documents to provide extensive information on 17th-c. dance. He spoke with authority, because he himself was a peripatetic master of ceremonies known throughout Europe for his triumphs, pageants, fêtes, horse ballets, and wedding and funeral ceremonies. Although he described the use of pantomime both among the ancients and his contemporaries, Ménéstrier in his reporting concentrated less on movement per se than on other aspects of production. He treats here all elements of public spectacle and ceremony, including choice of subject, poetry, characterization, dance steps, costume (describing elaborate devices and specific symbolic reference), sets and mechanical stage accessories, music (of specific instrumentation and appropriate mood), and even the use of rope dancers, acrobats, children, and animals. His extensive description of specific productions offers unique first-hand information about the 17th-c. *ballet à entrées.*

47 MINGUET E YROL, Pablo (fl. 1733-1775)
Arte de danzar à la francesa, adornado con quarenta y tantas laminas, que enseñan el modo de hacer todos los passos de las danzas de corte, con todas sus reglas, y de conducir los brazos en cada passo; y por chorographia demuestran como se deben escribir, y delinear otras; obra muy conveniente, no solamente à la juventad, que quieren aprendar el bien danzar, sino aûn à las personas civiles, y honestas, à quien les enseña las reglas para

53

bien andar saludar, y hacer las cortesias, que convienen en qualesquier suerte de personas.
*Madrid: author, 1758; 40+60p.
Madrid: author, 1768; 64p.
Quadernillo curioso de veinte contradanzas nuevas, escritas de todas quantas maneras se han inventado hasta aora; tienen la musica muy alegra, y con su baxo.
*Madrid: author, [1758]; 18p.
Breve tratado de los passos del danzar à la española, que oy se estilan en las sequidillas, fandango, y otros tañidos.
*2nd impression, Madrid: author, 1764; 18p.

Bound together in Paris, Bibliothèque de l'Arsenal (Ro 9939), these treatises witness the spread of French dance into Spain. *Arte de danzar* offers condensed versions of P. Rameau's *Le maître à danser* (q.v.) and R. A. Feuillet's *Chorégraphie* (q.v.), with superior illustrations and Spanish terminology. Part 2 contains 18 *contradanzas* written in *chorégraphie*, with music and verbal explanation: *La estrella, La idea buena, La invencion bella, La greca marrucca, Los petimetres, Los muchachos, Los prefumidos, Sequidillas y fandango, Los bailarines, La macarena, La disereta, La pastoril, La diligenta, La malagueña, La catalana, El suple seguidillas, La alemana y la de teatro.* Six *danzas* or *minuetes* follow: *El minuete régular, El minué de Alcides, El passepiéd comun, El passepié de España, La guastala, e minué de entrequatro.* Other *danzas* are *La bretaña, El rigodon, Las folias, El amable vencedor, El charman vainqueur, La boréa y cortesana.* In *Quadernillo curioso,* the author explains the signs he uses, describes the differences between *contradanzas* and *seguidillas,* and stresses the style of performing. *Breve tratado* contains a list and explanation of steps, the general rules, and a summary of differences among Italian, French, and English dances. For discussion of this rare item, see Friderica Derra de Moroda, "A Spanish book of 1758: another 18th-century book discovery," *Dancing times* (July 1931), pp. 336-38. For titles of other writings on dance by this author, see *The new Grove dictionary,* v. 12, p. 334.

48 MOREAU DE ST.-MÉRY, Médéric Louis Elie (1750-1819)

Danse. Article extrait d'un ouvrage de M. L. E. Moreau de St-Méry. Ayant pour titre: Répertoire des notions coloniales. Par ordre alphabétique.
Philadelphie: l'auteur, 1796; 62p.
*English transl. with introduction by Lily and Baird Hastings as

*Dance: an article drawn from the work by M. L. E. Moreau de
St.-Méry entitled: Repertory of colonial information, compiled
alphabetically (1796).*
Brooklyn, N.Y.: Dance Horizons, 1975; 3+73p.

Although this book primarily describes dance of the Creoles in North
American colonies, evidence of the spread of French court dancing to
the western hemisphere surfaces in several references to French dancing
practiced by colonial proprietors of sugar and indigo plantations. Remarks emphasizing proper dress and strict etiquette intermingle with
those mentioning Allemandes, the Anglaise, and the Minuet, said to be
having difficulty holding their own against the popular Contredanse.
The list of dancers at the Paris Opéra—Guimard, Vestris, Miller,
Gardel—indicates that Moreau was thoroughly familiar with dance in
France. For a detailed analysis of this work, believed to be the earliest
book on dance printed in the United States, see Lillian Moore, "Moreau
de Saint-Méry and 'Danse,' " *Dance index,* v. 10/1 (October 1946),
pp. 229-60. Moore makes clear how this small book was used by Carlo
Blasis for his *Code of Terpsichore* (1828). For related information on
dance in the culture described by Moreau de St.-Méry, see his *Description topographique, physique, civile, politique et historique de la partie
française de l'Isle Saint-Dominque,* 2 v. (Philadelphia, 1797-1798),
abridged, transl., and ed. by Ivor D. Spencer as *A civilization that per-
ished: the last years of white colonial rule in Haiti* (Lanham, MD: University Press of America, 1985).

49 NOVERRE, Jean Georges (1727-1810)
*Due lettere scritte a diversi sogetti: 1 Lettere a madame XXX
sopra i balli di Apelle e Campaspe e de Adele dati da Mons.
Noverre nel teatro di Milano 1774 [pp. 3-14] 2 Risposta alla me-
desima diretta a madame [pp. 15-37].*
*Napoli: 1774; 37p.

These two letters bear upon the debate between Noverre and G. Angiolini over the origins of the *ballet d'action.* The first discusses the
division of the spectators at Milan either for Noverre or for Angiolini;
the second follows up with additional arguments. For the attack that
prompted this reply by Noverre, see Angiolini's *Lettere.* Additional literature on the debate is cited in *The new Grove dictionary,* v. 13, pp.
441-44.

50 NOVERRE, Jean Georges (1727-1810)
Lettres sur la danse et sur les ballets.
Lyon: Aimé Delaroche, 1760; [vi]+484p.
*Stuttgardt: Aimé Delaroche, 1760; [vi]+484p.
Facs. reprint, New York: Broude Bros., 1967 (MMMLF, 47).
Louisbourg: 1766. Condensed as v. 1 of *Théorie et pratique de la danse simple et composée; de l'art des ballets; de la musique; du costume et des décorations.* V. 2 is entitled *Programmes de grands ballets historiques, héroïques, poëtiques, nationnaux, allégoriques et moraux de la composition de M. Noverre.* V. 3-6 contain the scores for *Musique des ballets composée d'après les programmes de Mr. Noverre,* including *Médée et Jason* by Jean Joseph Rodolphe (v. 3, p. 2), *La mort d'Hercule* by Johann Florian Deller (v. 3, p. 89), *Psyché et l'amour* by Rodolphe (v. 3, p. 175); *Les jalousies du serail* by Granier (v. 4, p. 3), *Orphée et Euridice* by Deller (v. 4, p. 77), *Hypermnestre* by Rodolphe (v. 4, p. 147); *Alceste* by Deller (v. 5, p. 3), *Renaud et Armide* by Rodolphe (v. 5, p. 112), *Les fêtes Hyménée* by Deller (v. 5, p. 154); *Enée et Lavine* by Deller (v. 6, p. 3), *Alexandre* by Deller (v. 6, p. 109), *L'enlèvement de Proserpine* by Renaud (v. 6, p. 87). V. 7-8 contain drawings by René-Louis Boquet: *Desseins des habits de costume pour le ballet,* with costume sketches for *Médée et Jason* (v. 7, p. 3), *La mort d'Hercule* (v. 7, p. 17), *Psyché* (v. 7, p. 37), *Jalousies du Serail* (v. 7, p. 54), *Orphée et Eurydice* (v. 7, p. 70), *Hypermnestre* (v. 8, p. 2), *Alceste* (v. 8, p. 19), *Renaud et Armide* (v. 8, p. 39), *Pyrrhus et Polixène* (v. 8, p. 62), *Les fêtes Hyménée* (v. 8, p. 74), *Enée et Didon* (v. 8, p. 98). V. 9 contains sketches by Boquet, entitled *Habits du costume pour différents caractères de danse, d'opéra, de comédie, tragédie et de bal,* for *Enée et Lavinie* (p. 2), *Alexandre* (p. 21), *l'Enlèvement de Proserpine* (p. 37), *Idée de la Henriade* (p. 63), *Don Quichotte* (p. 77), *Ballet hongrois* (p. 91). V. 10 contains sketches by Boquet, entitled *Habits de costume pour l'exécution des ballets,* including *Habits serieux pour des pas de deux et entrées seuls* (p. 1) and *Habits comique et demi-caractère pour des pas de deux et entrées seuls* (p. 52). V. 11 contains Boquet's sketches *Pour différents caractères de danse, tragédie, opéra, comédie et de bal* (p. 11), with information about price, fabrics, and construction of costumes.

Vienna: Johann Thomas von Trattner, 1767; 444p.

Amsterdam: 1787.

2nd ed., London, Paris: veuve Duchesne, 1783; 363p. (Noverre's new introduction expresses his happiness at the changes his letters have stimulated in the intervening 20 years.)

St. Petersbourg: Jean Charles Schnoor, 1803; v. 1, [vii]+240+[ii]p.; v. 2, [v]+240+[ii]p. Appears as v. 1 and 2 of *Lettres sur la danse, sur les ballets et les arts.* V. 3, entitled *Observations sur la construction d'une salle de l'Opéra de Paris et programmes de ballets* (1804; iii+224+iip.), contains scenarios for Noverre's *Les Horaces et les Curiaces, Euthyme et Eucharis, Médée, Les graces, Renaud et Armide, Adèle de Ponthieu, Psyché et l'amour, Enée et Didon, Hymenée et Cryséis, La mort d'Hercule, Les amours de Vénus, Apelles et Campaspe, La rosière de Salency, Pyrrhus et Polixène,* and *La descente d'Orphée aux enfers.* V. 4 (1804; iii+256+iip.), similarly titled, contains *La mort d'Agamemnon, Le jugement de Paris, Les danaïdes, L'epouse persanné, Alceste, Alexandre, Belton et Eliza,* and *Iphigénie en Tauride.*

*Paris: Léopold Collin; La Haye: Immerzeel, 1807; v. 1, xvi+468p.; v. 2, 520p. Appears as *Lettres sur les arts imitateurs en général et sur la danse en particulier.* V. 2 contains synopses for Noverre's *La mort d'Agamemnon* (pp. 344-68), *Les graces* (pp. 369-94), *Les danaïdes* (pp. 394-410), *Le jugement de Paris* (pp. 411-24), *Adèle de Ponthieu* (pp. 425-38), *Psyché et l'amour* (pp. 439-56), *Enée et Didon* (pp. 457-72), *Belton et Eliza* (pp. 473-84), *Alceste* (pp. 485-98), *Ballet d'Alexandre* (pp. 499-502), and *Apelles et Campaspe* (pp. 503-517).

Reprinted as *Noverre: Lettres sur la danse et sur les ballets in édition de luxe,* with a biography by André Levinson. Paris: Ducharte, Van Buggenhoudt, 1927. Paris: Éditions de la Tourelle, [1927]; iv+242p., 25pl.

*Edited by Fernand Divoire as *Lettres sur la danse et les arts imitateurs.* Paris: Editions Lieutier, 1952; 357p. With a biography (pp. 333-42), list of ballets by Noverre (pp. 344-46), detailed scenario of Noverre's *ballet tragique, Jason et Medée* (pp. 348-53), and bibliographical material.

German transl. by Johann Joachim C. Bode and Gotthold Ephraim Lessing as *Briefe über die Tanzkunst und über die Bal-*

lette. Hamburg, Bremen: Johann Heinrich Cramer, 1769; 358p.
Italian transl. by Domenico Rossi as *Lettere sopra la danza e sopra gli balli.* Napoli: 1778.
English transl. as v. 1 and 2 of *The works of Monsieur Noverre.*
London: G. Robinson [et al.], [1783]; v. 1, lxviii+232p.; v. 2, 258p. V. 3, xii+330p., contains scenarios of ballets: *The Danaïdes* (p. 1), *Rinaldo & Armida* (p. 29), *Adela of Ponthieu* (p. 53), *The Graces* (p. 93), *The Horatii and Curiatii* (p. 145), *Agamemnon Revenged* (p. 183), *Apelles and Campaspe* (p. 263), *The Amours of Venus* (p. 285), *Alceste* (p. 301).

Facs. reprint, New York: AMS Press, 1978.
Russian transl. as *Pisma o tantse i baletakh.* Leningrad: Akademia, 1927; 319p., 8pl.
*English transl. with commentary by Cyril W. Beaumont as *Letters on dancing and ballets.* London: C. W. Beaumont, 1930; viii+169p., 12pl. (Transl. of 1803 ed.)

   *2nd. ed. with revised introduction. London: C. W. Beaumont, 1951; xiii+169p., 12pl. *Facs. reprint, Brooklyn, N.Y.: Dance Horizons, 1966; 169p.

   Excerpt (letters 2 and 4) in Selma Jeanne Cohen, *Dance as a theatre art* (New York: Dodd, Mead & Co., 1975), pp. 57-64.
Spanish transl. by Pablo Palant as *Cartas sobre la danza.* Buenos Aires: Anaquel, [1945]; 181p.
Spanish transl. by Susana Uriburu as *Cartas sobre la danza y sobre los ballets,* with Levinson's 1927 biography. Buenos Aires: Centurion, [1946]; 272p.
Russian transl. by A. G. Movshensona as *Pis'ma o tantse i baletakh.* Leningrad: Iskusstvo, 1965; 374p.

More than the earlier efforts of Angiolini and others to establish dramatic pantomime ballet, this famous book on dancing and the theater fostered awareness of the dramatic function of theatrical dance. Noverre saw the *ballet d'action* as a work unifying ballet and pantomime. He believed that both music and movement should be subservient to dramatic expression. Many of his demands for reform of the ballet paralleled those of the composer Gluck, for whose operas Noverre choreographed ballets. In the 1952 critical edition of this classic text for both theater and dance history, Fernand Divoire has traced a total of 35 letters by Noverre and shown that no previous edition, including the first, contained all of them. They are: Letter 1 (pp. 11-16), "Renaissance de l'art de la danse;'' 2 (pp. 17-22), 3 (pp. 23-29), 4 (pp. 30-36), ''Des spectacles des anciens et surtout de la pantomime;'' 5 (pp. 37-42), ''Division de la danse'' [danse mécanique ou d'exécution, danse pantomime ou en action]; 6 (pp. 43-47), 7 (pp. 48-55), ''Qualités nécessaires au maîtres de ballets;'' 8 (pp. 56-66), 9 (pp. 67-72), ''Des connaissances d'anatomie nécessaires au maître de ballets;'' 10 (pp. 73-84), ''Études du maître de ballets;'' 11 (pp. 85-87), ''Choix des sujets;'' 12 (pp. 88-92), 13 (pp. 93-98), ''De la composition des ballets,'' and ''Règles à suivre;'' 14 (pp. 99-104), 15 (pp. 105-110), ''De la disposition des parties principales et des parties accessoires;'' 16 (pp. 111-17), ''Défauts de nos premiers ballets;'' 17 (pp. 118-39), ''Des ballets d'Opéra;'' 18 (pp. 140-63), ''De l'expression de la figure. Inconvenient des masques;'' 19 (pp. 164-69), ''De la composition des corps de ballets;'' 20 (pp. 170-78), ''Des coryphées;'' 21 (pp. 179-86), ''Des costumes;'' 22 (pp. 187-97), ''De l'accord du geste avec la pensée et les mouvements de l'âme;'' 23 (pp. 198-206), 24 (pp. 207-22), ''De la conformation du danseur;'' 25 (pp. 223-234), ''De la chorégraphie;'' 26 (pp. 235-48), 27 (pp. 249-65), ''Sur les ballets de l'auteur;'' 28 (pp. 266-86), ''Résumé général sur les ballets;'' 29 (pp. 287-91), ''Sur les sujets de la danse en 1740;'' 30 (pp. 292-96), 31 (pp. 297-302), ''Sur les principaux sujets de la danse de l'Opéra depuis 1740;'' 32 (pp. 303-7), ''Sur les maîtres de ballets de l'Opéra;'' 33 (pp. 308-14), ''De quelques autres compositeurs de ballets;'' 34 (pp. 315-25), 35 (pp. 326-30), ''Des danseurs actuels de l'Opéra.''

51 PASCH, Johann

Beschreibung wahrer Tanz-Kunst. Nebst einigen Anmerckungen über Herrn J.C.L.P.P. zu G. Bedencken gegen das Tantzen und zwar, wo es als eine Kunst erkennet wird. Worinnen er zu behaupten vermeynet dass das Tantzen wo es am besten ist nicht natürlich, nicht vernünfftig, nicht nützlich, sondern verdammlich und unzulässig sey, mit angeführtem Text des Herrn Gegners.
*Franckfurt: Wolffgang Michahelles & Johann Adolph, 1707; 36+475+6p.

Facs. reprint, Leipzig: Zentralantiquariat der DDR, 1975 (Documenta choreologica, 16).

In the first sections of the book (pp. 1-63), Pasch turns to philosophy and history to prove the true worth of dance as an art. After this preparation, he then states the requirements of a good dancing master (pp. 64-

76: *l'esprit sage, l'esprit savant, bel esprit, l'esprit de negotiation).*
Practical aspects are taken up in the next section on composition (pp. 77-
81, with a reference to Beauchamps' "erfindenen Characteren," i.e.
chorégraphie) and on execution (pp. 82-85). The dancing master of true
art dance should be a scholar and have knowledge of music and mime,
as well as all the tricks needed for good theatrical presentations (pp. 86-
90). An interesting Appendix A lists how true art dance is misused by
pedants; a second list shows how it is recognized by those who respect
its inherent virtues (pp. 110-35). The last part (pp. 138-475) contains
Herr Gegner's reflections against dance, interspersed with Pasch's annotations refuting that writer page by page.

52 PAULI, Carl (fl. 1756-1777)

*Élémens de la danse par Charles Pauli, maître à danser à
l'Université de Leipsic. Très humblement dédiés à tous ceux de
quelque sang et qualité qu'ils soient qui lui sont l'honneur de se
servir de son instruction et qui fréquentent ses leçons pour la
danse.*
*Leipzig: Ulr. Chret. Saalbach, 1756; 96p.

This book documents how French court dance, its literature, and its
history were disseminated abroad in the mid-18th c. The body of the
work consists of quotations from the most important dance histories and
aesthetics treatises, strung together as a textbook for Pauli's students
(presumably at the University of Leipzig, where he was dancing master). A bibliography on p. 11 cites works by Lucian, Ménéstrier's *Des
ballets* (q.v.), Bonnet's *Histoire générale* (q.v.), Du Bos' *Réflexions
critique* (q.v.), and Cahusac's *Dance ancienne* (q.v.). In addition, the
author later refers to Batteux's *Les beaux-arts* (q.v.) and Feuillet's
Chorégraphie (q.v.). On p. 78, Pauli reproduces the introduction to the
Lettres Patent establishing the Académie Royale de Dance (q.v.) and
part of the *Discours académique* that marked the event. In his preface,
Pauli asks if it be considered strange that he offer this book in French in
the heart of Germany. He counters that he would not know how to do
otherwise, for in the land of dance, the language used is French. The
French have originated the dance of the time, cultivated and polished it,
invented its dance notation, *chorégraphie,* and enriched the art with
terms significant and proper. Anyone learning to dance must adopt the
French terms, pronounce them distinctly, and write them correctly or be
ridiculed.

53 PEMBERTON, E[benezer (1671-1717)]

An essay for the further improvement of dancing; being a collection of figure dances, of several numbers, compos'd by the most eminent masters; describ'd in characters after the newest manner of Monsieur Feuillet, by E. Pemberton. To which is added, three single dances, viz. a chacone by Mr. Isaac, a passacaille by Mr. l'Abbé, and a Jig by Mr. Pécour, master of the Opera at Paris. London: J. Walsh, J. Hare, author, 1711; [5]p.+[54]pl.

*Facs. reprint, England: Gregg International, 1970; [72p.].

Facs. reprint, New York: Dance Horizons, 1970.

Pemberton cites the advantages of the dance notation made available to the dancing public by Feuillet *(Chorégraphie,* q.v.) and his English translators. With this collection of dances in *chorégraphie,* he answers requests from dancing masters "remote from London" who urged him to publish for their benefit. In the future, observes Pemberton, it will be as ridiculous to teach dancing without *chorégraphie* as music without notes. Most of the dances offered here use the simplified notational system adapted by Feuillet for his contredanse collection of 1706 (q.v.). The music and floor patterns are fully indicated, but for the steps only minimal detail appears, with the expectation that the dancing master use steps appropriate to the level of his pupils. The dances in this simplified notation offer further evidence concerning the makeup of provincial dance classes, in that they are all to be performed by groups of ladies, ranging from 3 to 12 in number: *An ecchoe* [borée] by Groscort (3 women, pl. 1-6), *Minuet* by Holt (4 women, pl. [7-10]), *Minuet* by Caverley (5 women, pl. [11-14]), *Minuet* by Shirley (6 women, pl. [15-18]), *[Minuet]* by Prince (8 women, pl. [19-22]), *[Jigg]* by Couch (9 women, pl. [23-25]), *[Jigg]* by Hickford (10 women, pl. [26-27]), *Minuet* by Priest (12 women, pl. [28-31]). The three additional dances are each for a presumably accomplished female soloist, with the steps fully indicated in *chorégraphie: Chacone* [minuet] by Isaac (female, pl. [34-45]), *Passacaille* by Abbée (female, pl. [46-53]), *Jigg* by Pécour (female, pl. [54-58]).

54 PEMBERTON, E[benezer (1671-1717)]

The pastorall. Mr. Isaac's new dance, made for her majestys [sic]
birthday 1713. The tune by Mr. Paisible. Engraven in characters
and figures for ye use of masters. Writ by Mr. Pemberton.
*London: J. Walsh, J. Hare, [1713]; 10p.

After the translation into English of Feuillet's dance notation manual
(Chorégraphie, q.v.), English dancing masters such as Pemberton began to publish dances in *chorégraphie.* Like other dances Pemberton
published, this one has a preface by the author advocating general use of
dance notation. Refuting claims that the system was too difficult to
learn, Pemberton argues that dancing masters should consider notation
to be as much a part of instruction in dance as in music. Answering
complaints that *chorégraphie* does not record the specific manner of
performance, Pemberton observes that the same could be said about
music or even common literary printing; yet no one for this reason suggests abandoning musical notation or printing.

55 RAMEAU, Pierre (fl. early 18th c.)

Abbrégé de la nouvelle méthode dans l'art d'écrire ou de traçer
toutes sortes de danses de ville . . . Ouvrage très utile pour toutes
personnes qui ont sçu ou qui apprennent à danser, puisque par le
secour de ce livre, on peut se remettre facilement dans toutes les
danses que l'on a appris.
*Paris: auteur, 1725; 112p.+83pl.
   *Facs. reprint, England: Gregg International, 1972.

A supplement to Rameau's verbal description of dance steps in *Le ma-*
ître à danser of the same year, the *Abbrégé* in Part 1 explains a somewhat more precise version of *chorégraphie* (the dance notation method
first published in 1700 by Feuillet, q.v.), with plates comparing Feuillet's and Rameau's notation. Part 2 contains "12 of Pécour's most beautiful dances," each for one couple, recorded in Rameau's refined notation: *La bourée d'Achille* (pl. 1-9), *La mariée de rollant* (pl. 10-17), *Le*
passepied (pl. 18-25), *La bourgogne* (pl. 26-33), *La forlanne* (pl. 34-
38), *Aimable vainqueur* (pl. 39-44), *Menuet d'Alcide* (pl. 45-50), *La*
bachante (pl. 51-57), *L'allemande* (pl. 58-64), *La Bretagne* (pl. 65-71),
La nouvelle forlanne (pl. 72-75), and *La royalle* (pl. 76-83). Regarding
variants in this collection among different copies, see Serge Leslie, *A*

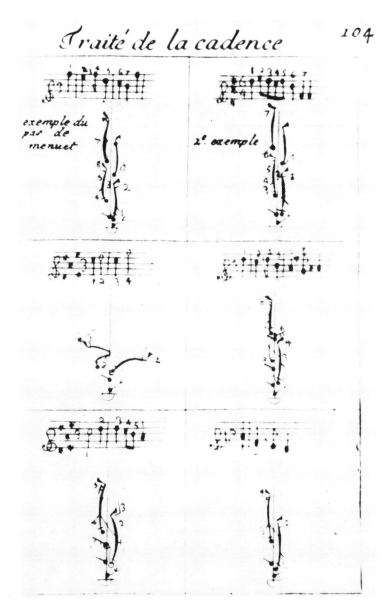

I-55 Pierre RAMEAU, *Abbrégé de la nouvelle méthode dans l'art d'écrire ou de traçer toutes sortes de danses de ville* (Paris: auteur, 1725), p. 104. Notation coordinating music and dance steps for the minuet. [Haags, Gemeente Museum, Dance Collection, Scheurleer Handlist No. 58]

bibliography, v. 2, pp. 436-37 and v. 3, p. 213. (The dances were all published previously in Feuillet's original notation.)

56 RAMEAU, Pierre (fl. early 18th c.)

Le maître à danser, qui enseigne la manière de faire tous les différens pas de la danse dans toute la régularité de l'art, et de conduire les bras à chaque pas. Enrichi de figures en taille douce servant de démonstration pour tous les différens mouvemens qu'il convient de faire dans cet exercice. Ouvrage très-utile nonseulement à la jeunesse qui veut apprendre à bien danser, mais encore aux personnes hônnetes et polies, et qui leur donnent des règles pour bien marcher, saluer et faire les révérences convenables dans toutes sortes de compagnies.

*Paris: Jean Villette, 1725; xxiv+272p.

*Facs. reprint, New York: Broude Bros., 1967 (MMMLF, 45).

2nd ed., Paris: Villette, 1734.

3rd ed., Paris: Rollin fils, 1748.

English transl. by John Essex as *The dancing-master: or the art of dancing explained. Wherein the manner of performing all steps in ball dancing is made easy by a new and familiar method. In two parts. The first, treating of the proper positions and different attitudes for men and women, from which all the steps are to be taken and performed; adorned with instructive figures; with a description of the menuet figure, shewing the beautiful turns and graceful motions of the body in that dance. The second, of the use and graceful motion of the arms with the legs in taking the proper movements and forming the contrasts, with figures for the better explanation. The whole containing sixty figures drawn from the life, and curiously engraved on copper plates.*

London: J. Essex and J. Brotherton, 1728; xxxii+160p.+57pl.

2nd ed., with new engravings by G. Bickham Jr. and additional approbation by Anthony l'Abbé, dancing master to the royal family. London: J. Essex and J. Brotherton, 1731.

*Portions, with engravings and musical notations, published by George Bickham, Jr. as *An easy introduction to dancing or the movements in the minuet fully explained.* London: Cooper, 1738; 5p.+7pl.

Portuguese transl., of portions of the 1725 ed., by Joseph Thomas Cabreira as *Arte de dançar à franceza, que ensina o modo de fazer todos os differentes passos de minuete, com todas as suas regras, e a cada hum dellos o modo de conduzir os brazos: obra muito conveniente, naò sŏ à mocidade, principalmente civil, que quer aprender a bem dançar; mas ainda a quem ensina as regras para bem andar, saudar, e fazer as cortezias, que convém a qualquer classe de pessŏas.*

*Lisboa: Francisco Luiz Ameno, 1760; 22p.

Madrid: Cabreira, 1768.

Facs. reprint in Jose Sasportes, *História de dança em Portugal.* Lisbon: Fundação Calouste Gulbenkian, 1970; pp. 387-416.

English transl. of the 1725 ed. by Cyril W. Beaumont, with Bickham's plates from the 2nd English ed., as *The dancing master.* London: Beaumont, 1931.

*Facs. reprint, New York: Dance Horizons, 1970.

Facs. reprint, England: Gregg International, 1972.

Spanish transl. of Beaumont's 1931 ed. by Susana Uriburu as *El maestro de danza, version castellana del texte inglés.* Buenos Aires: Centurion, 1946.

With this instruction manual, Rameau provided the classic textbook of social dancing for the early 18th century. His book contains a detailed description of the minuet considered fundamental to research on this dance.

Simple engravings effectively illustrate the positions, carriage, walking, moving from one position to another, bowing (including manipulation of the hat, walking and bowing for women, and proper etiquette at balls; pp. 1-66), in addition to specific steps and other elements of technique. Reference numbers on dancers' limbs and diagrams representing figure guides on the ballroom floor, or gesture guides in the air, precisely link the illustrations to the text. Clothing, wigs, and spatial relationships and patterns shown in the drawings (which are signed "P. Rameau invenit et fecit") provide additional detail.

Part 1 treats positions, steps, and the structure of specific dances, while Part 2 deals with the use of the arms in dancing. The 42 chapters of Part 1 begin with basic positions (ch. 1-8, pp. 1-21), fundamental movements of hip, knee, and instep that comprise the various *pas* or steps of the dance (ch. 19, pp. 67-70, with ch. 20, pp. 71-75, devoted to the *demi-coupé),* as well as bows and etiquette (ch. 9-18, pp. 22-66). Ch. 21-25 (pp. 76-109) describe steps and other performance details of the minuet, including movements of the arms. Ch. 26-27 deal with the courante and its steps, ch. 28-42 with additional steps: Pas de bourrées or Fleurets, various Coupés, Pas de gaillarde, Pirouettes, Balancés, Pas de sissonne, Pas de rigaudon, Jettés, Contretems de gavotte (forward, to the side), various Chassés, Sallies, Ouvertures de jambes, and various Battemens.

The 16 chapters of Part 2 begin with general treatment of positions, elevations, and movements of the arms, in combination with wrists, neck, and shoulders (ch. 1-5, pp. 191-209). General coordination of arms and feet occupies ch. 6, while ch. 7-16 (pp. 210-71) describe how to coordinate arm motions with specific dance steps treated in Part 1. Rameau's instructions for dancing the ordinary minuet are discussed in detail in Wendy Hilton's *Dance of court and theater: the French noble style 1690-1725* (Princeton, NJ: Princeton Book Company, 1981).

57 ROJO DE FLORES, Felipe
Tratado de recreaciòn instructiva sobre la danza.
*Madrid: en la Impreta Real, 1793; 127p.

This rare Spanish dance treatise is devoted largely to the nature (pp. 1-8) and history (pp. 9ff.) of dance generally, with sections devoted to different regions and nations, especially Spain (pp. 85-118, 120). Treatment of "English dance" is brief, including mention of the Jiga, Saltar[ella], Zarabande, and Allemandos. The section on French dance consists of quotations from Brossard (q.v.).

58 SAINT-HUBERT, de (fl. 1625)
La manière de composer et faire réussir les ballets.
Paris: F. Targa, 1641.
*English transl. by Andrée Bergens as "How to compose a successful ballet," with introduction by Marie Françoise Christout, in *Dance perspectives,* 20 (1964), pp. 4-25 (introduction), 26-35 (text), 36-37 (notes).
English transl. by Andrée Bergens in *Dance as a theatre art,* ed. by Selma Jeanne Cohen (New York: Dodd, Mead, & Co., 1975), pp. 31-37 (slightly abridged).

Clear and concrete, this brief treatise tells much about the structure and aesthetic of the *ballet à entrées* during the reign of Louis XIII. Considering dance entertainments as one of three principal forms of noble exercise, Saint-Hubert distinguishes between expressive types *(sérieux, grotesque)* and levels of complexity (a great or royal ballet with 30 entrées, a fine ballet with at least 20, and a small ballet with 10 to 12). A good ballet depends upon a good subject, to which all melodies, steps, etc. must be subservient. The dancing should be suited to the characters represented, without interfering with the identifying properties carried by the dancers. It should be tailored to suit the performers' varying abilities and rehearsed, not improvised. Costumes, scenery and machines should similarly relate to the subject. Of special interest is the author's insistence that the final form of a given ballet production be the result of one person's authority in selection, so as to avoid excesses that mar the harmony of the whole.

59 SOL, C.

Méthode très facile et fort nécessaire pour montrer à la jeunesse de l'un et l'autre sexe la manière de bien dancer. Suggérer aux maîtres d'une capacité médiocre, de bons principes, et faire connaître aux parens mêmes, si leurs enfans sont bien enseignez.
*Den Haag: auteur, 1725; 96p.

Sol writes that he does not pretend to be a complete master, but is publishing this book in order to help those who have worked only under inadequate dancing masters. He approaches his subject primarily as a teacher, dividing his pupils into three kinds: those with no talent, those with a little talent and much interest, and those with great talent and great interest. All should learn dancing, since even the untalented will learn confidence and develop grace. All dancing masters should learn the dance notation called *chorégraphie* (q.v.) in order to acquire easily the new dances from Paris or to remember precisely those already learned. Sol's manual is pedagogical in orientation. As in the preface, the sections dealing with dance technique emphasize presentation of the subject to pupils: Part 1 on bows and courtesies (pp. 21-27), the minuet (pp. 28-44), use of the arms and presenting the hands (pp. 44-55); Part 2 on the steps (pp. 55-90).

60 TAUBERT, Gottfried (b. ca. 1673; fl. 1717)

Rechtschaffener Tantzmeister, oder gründliche Erklärung der frantzösischen Tantz-Kunst, bestehend in drei Büchern, deren das erste historice des Tantzens Ursprung, Fortgang, Verbesserung, unterschiedlichen Gebrauch, Zulässigkeit, vielfältigen Nutzen, und andere Eigenschafften mehr, untersuchet; das andere methodice des so wol galanten als theatralischen frantzösischen Tantz-Exercitii Grund-Sätze ethice, theoretice und practice, das ist: was in dem prosaischen Theile zu der äusserlichen Sitten-Lehre und gefällig-machenden Aufführung: was in dem poëtischen Theile zu der theoretischen Wissenschafft und Betrachtung so wol der niedrigen Kammer- als hohen theatralischen Tänze: und was in Praxi so wol zu der regelmässigen Composition, und geschicklichen Execution, als gründlichen Information dieser beyden Haupt-Theile gehöret, deutlich zeiget; anbey wird, nebst einer ausführlichen Apologie für die wahre Tantz-Kunst, der Haupt-Schlüssel zu der Chorégraphie, oder Kunst alle Tänze durch Characteres, Figuren, und allerhand Zeichen zu beschreiben, als welches ingeniöse Werck vormals durch Msr. Feüillet, Tantzmeister in Paris, ediret, anizo aber, nebst den Kupfferstichen, von dem Autore aus dem frantzösischen in das teutsche, und in diesen Format gebracht worden, zu finden seyn; und das dritte discursive derer Maitres, Scholaires, Assemblées, Balls, Hochzeit-Täntze, und anderer Tantz-Compagnien Requisita, wie sie nemlich beschaffen seyn sollen, und unterweilen beschaffen sind, zulänglich erörtert. Endlich ist ein vollständiges Register aller eingebrachten Sachen beygefüget worden.
Leipzig: Friedrich Lanckischens Erben, 1717; 8+1176+54p.

*Facs. reprint, with commentary by Kurt Petermann, München: Heimeran; Leipzig: Zentralantiquariat der DDR, 1976 (Documenta Choreologica, 22); 661+662+52+xxxii p.
English transl. by Angelika Gerbes of excerpts on the minuet in Selma Jeanne Cohen, *Dance as a theatre art* (New York: Dodd, Mead & Co., 1975), pp. 42-51.

The most extensive treatise on French court dance ever produced, Taubert's opus falls into three parts: dance history; current dance practices (especially for varieties of the courante, minuet, and bourrée); dance pedagogy and dance usage at balls and festivals, etc. After an introduction, Book 1, on dance in general, devotes 12 chapters (pp. 45-82) to its origins and antiquity, defending the holy position it held among the ancients. Ch. 13-33 (pp. 82-288) briefly describe contemporary processions, balls, and carnivals, with a lengthy defense of such dancing when properly done by respectable persons (with special advice for ladies). Book 2 concentrates on French dance practice, with the first 6 ch. (pp. 289-382) devoted to dance as a true art, defending it as Christian and God-pleasing. Ch. 7-11 (pp. 382-430) begin the discussion of proper performance—presentation, dress, carriage and walking—while ch. 12-16 (pp. 430-87) are devoted entirely to the *révérences*. Ch. 17-24 (pp. 488-568) discuss specific steps (both *pas simples* and *pas composés)*, following the musical cadence (i.e. coordinating steps and music), floor patterns, and developing *bon air* (proper bearing, especially in the *porte de bras)*. Ch. 25-29 (pp. 568-614) present the Courante (with 6 dances in *chorégraphie* without music). Following the same ·order as Feuillet's *Chorégraphie* (q.v.), ch. 36-43 (pp. 675-735) present the French *pas composés*. Ch. 44-45 (pp. 736-916) are exclusively devoted to a section of the 1701 edition of *Chorégraphie:* pages 747-97 contain Feuillet's characters, examples coordinating musical measures and dance steps, and entire examples in *chorégraphie,* all in boxes numbered 1 to 836. Pages 799-902 provide a German translation of Feuillet's text pertinent to the previous numbered illustrations. Three dances in *chorégraphie* with music then follow: *Folie d'Espagne pour femme* (woman, pp. 903-7; in Feuillet's 1700 *Recüeil*, pp. 35-38), *Sarabande pour un homme* (man, pp. 908-11; in Feuillet's 1704 *Recüeil*, pp. 225-28), *Gigue à deux* (couple, pp. 912-15; in Feuillet's 1700 *Recüeil*, pp. 8-11). Specifically entitled "On theatrical dancing," the last section of Book 2 devotes ch. 46-47 (pp. 917- 40) to *ballet sérieux* and *ballet comique,* while ch. 48-51 (pp. 941-72) deal with all aspects of composing *entrées* and *ballets*. Book 3 has three parts, dealing with dancing masters (ch. 1-6, pp. 973-1040), their pupils (ch. 7-9, pp. 1041-99), and *assemblées,* balls, and other festivals (ch. 10-12, pp. 1100-76). Taubert also provides a 51-page index. Study and evaluation of this encyclopedic work has only just begun. For differing opinions on its value to present scholarship, see Petermann's essay in the 1976 facsimile reprint; Angelika Renate Gerbes' dissertation, *Gottfried Taubert on social and theatrical dance of the early eighteenth century* (Ohio State University, 1972; see Appendix B for excerpts in English translation), and Marian Winter's *Pre-romantic ballet* (London: Pitman, 1974), pp. 45-47.

61 [THEOBALD, Lewis (1688-1744)]

Perseus and Andromeda as it is performed at the Theatre Royal in Lincoln's Inn-Fields.
*London: Tho. Wood, 1730; 17p.

This pantomime devised by Theobald for "Lun" (John Rich) clearly shows the double plots characteristic of this type of theater: alternating masque and harlequinade, with no relationship between the two. This was one of the most successful of Lun's performances, using ingenious stage tricks as Harlequin. Music by Johann Ernst Galliard survives.

62 THURMOND, John (fl. 1720s)

Harlequin Doctor Faustus, with masque of the deities.
*London: W. Chetwood, 1724; 24p.

This description of one of the two most frequently performed pantomimes of the period in England is unusually detailed in itself and can be augmented with contemporary accounts. The first part, in which the devil and related supernatural characters use tricks and devices to frighten in dumb show, was followed by the second, in which spectacular heavenly deities reassured with singing and dancing. It is an example of pantomime in which *commedia dell'arte* characters carried the action of the piece alone until the masque at the end, when trained dancers such as Hester Santlow performed as Diana and Mr. Thurmond himself performed a pyrrhic dance as Mars. Part of the music by Henry Carey survives. (The British Library has three additional entertainments by Thurmond: the above combined with *Apollo and Daphne, or Harlequin's metamorphoses* and *Harlequin's triumph,* London 1727; *Harlequin sheppard, a night scene in grotesque characters,* London 1724; and *The miser, or Wagner and Abericock,* London 1727).

63 TOMLINSON, Kellom (fl. early 18th c.)

The art of dancing explained by reading and figures; whereby the manner of performing the steps is made easy by a new and familiar method: being the original work first design'd in the year 1724, and now published by Kellom Tomlinson, dancing-master.
London: author, 1735; xxiii+159+35p.
*Facs. reprint, England: Gregg International, 1970.

*Facs. reprint, New York: Dance Horizons, 1970.
2nd ed., London: author, 1744; 160p.

In the continuing debate on the value of dance notation, Tomlinson takes
the position that *chorégraphie* is indeed very useful (he includes two
very minutely detailed plates explaining *chorégraphie),* but only to
dancing masters. This book, with its verbal description of the steps and
its figures illustrating the positions and floor patterns, is nevertheless
usable by all. While Tomlinson's subject matter bears resemblance to P.
Rameau's *Le maître à danser* (1725, q.v.), published in England in a
translation in 1728, the preface pointedly claims no relationship and
expresses indignation that Rameau's English translator John Essex published before he (Tomlinson) could finance the publication of his own
treatise written in 1724, a year prior to Rameau's. The work seems to be
Tomlinson's own. Book 1 covers material similar to Rameau's, but with
different order and emphasis. Book 2 devotes 12 chapters to the Minuet
(pp. 103-41), one to timing (pp. 141-52), and one to arms (pp. 152-56),
with a closing chapter on Country Dancing (pp. 156-59). The author
continually refers to the illustrations in the 35 plates at the end. These
charming illustrations are more sophisticated, though less relaxed look-
ing, than those in Rameau's treatise. *Chorégraphie* appearing with the
dancing figures in the illustrations is coordinated to music in staves at
the top of the plate. A complete minuet choreography appears in *chorégraphie* in the final plate. There is a frontispiece engraving of the author.
I. K. Fletcher *(Bibliographical descriptions)* points out that the frontispiece was probably inserted, since it bears two dates, "R.d.V. Bleek
Pinxit 1716" and "F. Morellon la Cave Sculpsit 1754," the latter date
being 10 years after the publication of the second edition.

64 TOMLINSON, Kellom (fl. early 18th c.)

*Six dances compos'd by Mr. Kellom Tomlinson. Being a collec-
tion of all the yearly dances, publish'd by him from the year 1715
to the present year, viz. I. The passepied. Round O. II. The shepherdess. III. The submission. IV. The Prince Eugene. V. The address. VI. The gavot. The submission writ, as it was perform'd at
the Theatre in little Lincoln's-Inn-Fields, by Monsieur and Mademoiselle Salle, the two French children.*
[London: author, 1720; 45p.]
   *Facs. reprint, England: Gregg International, 1970.
   *Facs. reprint, New York: Dance Horizons, 1970.

Tomlinson dedicates his collection of 6 dances to the ladies, to help his pupils retain their lessons. As in his later *Art of dancing* (q.v.), he urges them to learn *chorégraphie,* the art of notating dances in written characters, "which art is now become equal, and of the same use, with notes, etc. in musick." Skill in learning dances "by book," he urges, enhances quickness and accuracy in learning and recall. The 6 dances recorded in *chorégraphie* appear here in the reverse order of their dates of original publication: *Gavot* (1720, tune by Tomlinson; couple, pl.[1-4]), *The address* (1719, tune by Babell; couple, pl.[6-11]), *Prince Eugene* (1718, tune by Loeillet; couple, pl.[13-20]), *The submission* (1717, tune by Loeillet; couple, pl.[22-28]), *The shepherdess* (1716, tune by Loeillet; couple, pl.[30-34]), *Passepied round O* (1715, tune by Loeillet; couple, pl.[36-40]).

65 URIOT, Joseph

Description des fêtes données pendant quatorze jours à l'occasion du jour de naissance de son Altesse Serenissime Monseigneur le Duc Regnant de Wurtemberge et Teck.&&& le onze fevrier M DCC LXIII.
*Stoutgard: Christophe Fredric Cotta, 1763; 176p.

While lamenting the impossibility of describing such rich festivities, Uriot proceeds to give details day by day of one of the many festivals at Stuttgart when J. G. Noverre was choreographer there. Ballets treated are *Medée et Jason* (pp. 39-45), *Orphée e Eurydice* (pp. 45-51), *Triumphe de Neptune* (pp. 51-54), *Psyché* (pp. 59-63), *Mort d'Hercule* (pp. 63-70), and *Ballet d'Armide* (pp. 139-47). Uriot describes them in their context as part of a whole series of entertainments that included a review of troups, a gala, an opera, a masked ball, Mass in the morning, and a French comedy at night, a *fête* at the palace at Louisbourg, fireworks, a tragedy, a hunt for game (listed) in the morning, and a concert at night, culminating in a Carrousel.

66 WEAVER, John (1673-1760)

Anatomical and mechanical lectures upon dancing wherein rules and institutions for that art are laid down and demonstrated, as they were read at the academy in Chancery Lane.

*London: J. Brotherton, W. Meadows (J. Graves, W. Chetwood), 1721; xii+156p.

*Facs. reprint in Richard Ralph, *The life and works of John Weaver* (New York: Dance Horizons, 1985), pp. 855-1031.

In what is probably the first book on the physical anatomy of dancing, Weaver applies to dance the information available to him on muscle and skeletal structure, and on their functions in movement. He believed that the technical proficiency acquired in dance training was the means by which the art imitated nature, in accordance with the leading aesthetic position of the 18th c. The book established critical standards in this art never before given such serious attention. See especially his "rules and institutions for dancing," which include advice on the significance for dance of music, rhetoric, and painting.

67 WEAVER, John (1673-1760)

An essay towards an history of dancing, in which the whole art and its various excellencies are in some measure explain'd. Containing the several sorts of dancing, antique and modern, serious, scenical, grotesque, etc. with the use of it as an exercise, qualification, diversion, etc.

*London: Jacob Tonson, 1712; 172p.

*Facs. reprint in Richard Ralph, *The life and works of John Weaver* (New York: Dance Horizons, 1985), pp. 389-672.

This essay presents dance as an art with a long and estimable history, especially among the ancients whom Weaver cites at length. From this background, Weaver develops an aesthetic based upon laws of nature, which for him meant imitation of nature through beautiful bodily movement—action, manners, passions. An early attempt to relate aesthetics specifically to dance, Weaver's book (and also his dances, q.v.) stands out in its advocacy of dance as a vehicle for dramatic expression.

68 WEAVER, John (1673-1760)

The judgment of Paris. A dramatic entertainment in dancing and singing, after the manner of the Greeks and Romans, as it is perform'd at the Theatre-Royal in Drury-Lane. The words by Mr. Congreve, set to musick by Mr. Seedo, compos'd by J. Weaver, dancing-master.

*London: J. Tonson, 1733; 12p.
*Facs. reprint in Richard Ralph, *The life and works of John Weaver* (New York: Dance Horizons, 1985), pp. 839-52.

This seems to be a setting of a 1701 libretto, with many songs by William Congreve. Little is known of the composer of the music, Mr. Seedo. The few movements for the pantomime Weaver required are for the specific emotions of admiration, love, respect, and desire; much use was made of machines for transporting the goddesses. This was the last choreography in which Weaver attempted to revive the ancient art of pantomime.

69 WEAVER, John (1673-1760)
The loves of Mars and Venus; a dramatick entertainment of dancing, attempted in imitation of the pantomimes of the ancient Greeks and Romans; as perform'd at the theatre in Drury-Lane.
*London: W. Mears, J. Browne, 1717; 28p.
  *Facs. reprint in Richard Ralph, *The life and works of John Weaver* (New York: Dance Horizons, 1985), pp. 735-62.
*Ed. and abridged, with introduction by P. J. S. Richardson as "An Early *ballet d'action,*" in *Dancing times,* series 2, no. 468 (Sept. 1949), pp. 697-700.
*Ed. by Peggy Van Praagh and Peter Brinson, in *The choreographic art* (London: Adam and Charles Black, 1963), pp. 279-83.
Ed. by Selma Jeanne Cohen, in *Dance as a theatre art* (New York: Dodd, Mead & Co., 1975), pp. 51-57.

This printed description of the action in a dramatic pantomime is one of about 20 English ones to survive from the first half of the 18th c. Intended as bait to lure customers, the circular was short, inexpensive, and soon thrown away. Weaver's preface makes elaborate claims for originality. His script gives complete descriptions of gesticulations and vivid synopses of acts (which have all been quoted extensively by dance writers since). Evidence, such as the inclusion of specific dances (a pyrrhic dance for followers of Mars, a passacaille for Venus), the exclusion of song texts, and the omission of grotesque characters, indicates that this was more nearly a ballet than a pantomime of the time. Also, excellent dancers such as the Frenchman Louis Dupré and Weaver himself were the performers. With clearly conceived dramatic action, *The loves* stands out amid the episodic works of this time as an early *ballet d'action,* a form associated with J. G. Noverre a half century later. Concerning music for Weaver's ballets, see George Dorris, "Music for the ballets of John Weaver," *Dance chronicle,* v. 3/1 (1979), pp. 46-60.

70 WEAVER, John (1673-1760)

Orpheus and Eurydice, a dramatick entertainment of dancing; attempted in imitation of the pantomimes, of the ancient Greeks and Romans, as perform'd at the Theatre Royal in Drury-Lane.
*London: W. Mears, J. Browne, W. Chettwood, 1718; 44p.
*Facs. reprint in Richard Ralph, *The life and works of John Weaver* (New York: Dance Horizons, 1985), pp. 765-812.

This is a two-part description of Weaver's second ballet, a tragedy taken from Horace, Ovid, and Virgil, the writings of whom are quoted as background for the ballet. The extent of Weaver's research into the origins of the fable is impressive, although he gives little specific information on his applications to movement. Effective dramatic foreshadowing and contrast are evident, however. Concerning music for Weaver's ballets, see George Dorris, "Music for the ballets of John Weaver," *Dance chronicle,* v. 3/1 (1979), pp. 46-60. For two other theatrical publications by Weaver, see Richard Ralph's collection of facsimiles.

PART II

WRITINGS PERTAINING TO DANCE MUSIC

FOREWORD

The writings in the following section pertain either to dance music—including composition, structure, character, and function of the various dance airs—or to performance practices applicable to dance music of the period 1643-1789, with reference to accompaniment, articulation, conducting, diction, dynamics, fingering, improvisation and variation, instrumentation, meter, ornamentation, pitch, rhythm, singing, tempo, temperament, voice culture, and playing instruments. With respect to performance, no attempt has been made to cite all sources relevant to these matters, nor even the most important sources. (For additional titles, consult Mary Vinquist and Neal Zaslaw, eds., *Performance practice: a bibliography* [New York: Norton, 1971] and supplements in *Current musicology,* numbers 12 and 15, as well as appropriate topical articles in *The new Grove dictionary*.) Rather, the performance information found in these sometimes obscure treatises and unexpected places serves to supplement that in better known sources of information. Annotations for individual entries provide either (1) a summary of passages devoted to dance music, (2) a list or description of passages devoted to specific performance practice topics, or (3) an overview of the contents.

Classification of material. While very few 17th and 18th-century authors devoted themselves to dance music per se, information can be gleaned from a wide variety of writings originally intended for other uses, the relevance of which may not be readily apparent. The works described in this section demonstrate what such literature may yield for the inquisitive performer of French dance music. The list does not pretend to be comprehensive; it represents rather a selection of available contemporary music literature, classifiable in the following manner:

I. Literature of Music
  A. PERIODICALS Christman, Hiller, Marpurg *Des critischen Musikus*, Reichardt
  B. DICTIONARIES AND LEXICONS Anon. *Kurzgefasstes*, Brossard, Busby, Grassineau, Hoyle, Koch, Meude-Monpas, J. J. Rousseau, Walther
  C. ENCYCLOPEDIAS OF MUSIC Blankenburg, Framéry, La Borde, Mersenne, Praetorius
  D. BIBLIOGRAPHIES Adlung
  E. HISTORY AND CRITICISM
     1. *General:* Burney *General*, Hawkins, Lacépède, Marpurg *Des critischen Musicus*
     2. *Period or country:* Blainville *Histoire*, Bollioud de Mermet, Bonnet, Burney *Present*, Cramer, Raguenet, Vogler

II. Musical Instruction and Study
  A. RUDIMENTS, PEDAGOGY, AND GENERAL Asaïs, Bordet, Brijon *L'Apollon*, Choquel, Dard, C. Denis *Nouvelle*, Dupont *Principes de musique*, Duval, Engramelle, Jones, Loulié, Lustig, Marcou, Marquet, Masson, Mattheson *Neu*, Mattheson *Vollkommene*, Metoyen, Montéclair *Nouvelle*, Montéclair *Petit*, Montéclair *Principes*, Tans'ur, Vagué
  B. COMPOSITION AND THEORY Albrechtsberger, Béthizy, Blainville *Ésprit*, d'Alembert, Daube, Drewis, Francoeur, Kirnberger *Recueil*, Koch, Kollmann, La Voye, Masson *Divers*, Masson *Nouveau*, Rameau *Traité*, Simpson
  C. ACCOMPANIMENT AND HARMONY Anon. *Rules*, Bordier, Gervais, Heinichen, Kellner, Langlé, Niedt, St.-Lambert *Nouveau*, Rameau *Code*, Rameau *Dissertation*, Rameau *Traité*
  D. TUNING AND TEMPERAMENT J. Denis
  E. INSTRUMENTAL TECHNIQUE
     1. *Bagpipe (Musette, Loure):* Borjon, Hotteterre *Méthode*
     2. *Brass and Percussion:* Altenburg, Anon. *Instruction*, Roeser
     3. *Harp:* Meyer
     4. *Hurdy-Gurdy:* Bouin, Corrette *Belle*, Dupuit
     5. *Keyboard:* Bach, Christman, Corrette *Maître*, Couperin,

80

5. *Keyboard:* Bach, Christman, Corrette *Maître,* Couperin, Delair, Despréaux, Heck, Kirnberger, Marpurg *Clavierstücke,* Prelleur, St.-Lambert *Principes,* Troufflaut, Türk

6. *Lute and Guitar:* Baron, Delair, Mace, Merchi *Guide,* Merchi *Traité*

7. *Mandolin:* P. Denis *Méthode,* Fouchetti, Leone

8. *String*

   a. *Violin:* Bailleux *Méthode raisonnée,* Bornet, Brijon *Réflexions,* Corrette *L'école,* Crome, Dupont *Principes du violon,* L'Abbé, Muffat, Prelleur, Tarade

   b. *Violoncello:* Corrette *Méthode théorique,* Cupis

   c. *Viol:* Danoville, Hely, Le Blanc, J. Rousseau *Traité*

   d. *Viole d'amour:* Milandre

9. *Woodwind:* Corrette *Méthode pour,* Francoeur, Freillon, Hotteterre *L'art,* Hotteterre *Principes,* Lorenzoni, Lusse, Mahaut, Mussard, Prelleur, Quantz, Roeser, Tromlitz

F. VOICE CULTURE AND SINGING Bacilly, Bailleux *Méthode . . . vocal,* Bérard, Blanchet, David, Corrette *Le parfait maître,* Durieu, Lacassagne, La Chapelle, L'Affilard, Lecuyer, Legat, Le Pileur, Millet, Morel, Prelleur, Raparlier, J. Rousseau *Méthod,* Villeneuve, Vion

G. GAMES Anon. *Anleitung,* Anon. *Ludus,* Hayn, Hoegi, Kirnberger, Lange, Stadler

Exclusion of material. Material deliberately excluded falls into the following categories (for complete citations, see RISM B-VI):

I. Literature of Music

   A. PERIODICALS that make no reference to French secular music (e.g. Cramer)

   B. DICTIONARIES in which definitions of dances and musical terms are too general to supply technical information (e.g. Wolf *Kurzgefasstes musikalisches Lexikon,* Anon. *Musikalisches Handwörterbuch)*

II. Musical Instruction and Study

   A. RUDIMENTARY OR GENERAL INSTRUCTION MAN-

UALS with too little to offer (e.g. Adgate, Buchholtz, Cajon, Montéclair *Leçons,* Moyreau, Roussel, Turner)

B. COMPOSITION AND COUNTERPOINT MANUALS oriented to polyphonic music (Baron, Kirnberger *Sing),* to German and Italian music only (Cousu, Demoz, Grétry, Kirnberger *Gedanke,* Nivers), or to late 18th-century cosmopolitan style (Gianotti, Lirou, Portmann, Riepel)

C. ACCOMPANIMENT AND THOROUGHBASS MANUALS not concerned with dance accompaniment, French bass figures, or figural accompaniment applicable to dance music (Ballière, Dandrieu, Daube, Frick, Grénerin, Hahn; Clément, Fleury, Keller, Lampe, Marpurg, Mattheson, Miller, Perrine, Rodolphe, Roussier)

D. SINGING OR KEYBOARD INSTRUCTION MANUALS directed only to performers of sacred music (Münster)

E. VOCAL AND INSTRUMENTAL INSTRUCTION MANUALS concerned only with German, English, or Italian music, or with the cosmopolitan music and performance technique of the late classic and early Romantic eras (Hiller, Kurzinger, Lasser, Mancini, Marpurg, Milchmeyer, Mylius, Petri, Playford, Printz; Bailleux, Cambini, Dreux, Durieu, Galeazzi, Ozi, L. Mozart, Raoul, Speer, Wiedeburg, Vander Hagen)

III. Music: Scores, including anthologies of ballet, keyboard, chamber, or social dance music; operas and ballets; etc. Exceptions contain a substantial preface, theoretical introduction, or other verbal contribution, such as the pedagogical essays in the Marpurg and Kirnberger *Recueils* of keyboard pieces. Collections of pieces *(leçons)* appended to treatises and tutors have been included when they contain pieces with French dance titles or musical character. While much information about musical performance and dancing may be gleaned from scores for operas, ballets, etc. (see especially the stage works of Lully and Rameau), their description better belongs in a separate study of scores.

Secondary literature and reference works. No attempt has been made to cite secondary sources pertinent to each individual item in the

Guide. Such literature is best sought in indexes of periodical and other literature (e.g. *RILM abstracts, Music index,* etc.), dissertation listings, and the bibliographies in reference works listed below.

For compiling bibliographic information and historical-critical summaries of items in the bibliography, the following secondary sources proved useful.

ADLUNG, Jacob. *Anleitung zu der musikalischen Gelahrtheit.* Erfurt: J. D. Jungnicol, 1758.

ALLEN, Warren Dwight. *Philosophies of music history.* New York: American Book Company, 1939; Dover, 1962.

ANTHONY, James R. *French baroque music from Beaujoyeulx to Rameau.* New York: W. W. Norton, 1974; rev. ed. 1981.

Baker's biographical dictionary of musicians. 6th ed. revised by Nicolas Slonimsky. New York: Schirmer Books, 1978.

BOYDEN, David D. *The history of violin playing from its origins to 1761.* London: Oxford University Press, 1965.

BROSSARD, Yolande de. *Musiciens de Paris, 1535-1792: actes d'état civil d'après le Fichier Laborde de la Bibliothèque Nationale.* Paris: A. et J. Picard, 1965.

CHARLES, Sydney Robinson. *A handbook of music and music literature in sets and series.* New York: The Free Press, 1972.

COHEN, Albert. "Early French dictionaries as musical sources," in *A musical offering: essays in honor of Martin Bernstein.* Ed. by E. Clinkscale and C. Brook. New York: Pendragon Press, 1977. (Pp. 97-112)

COOVER, James. *Music lexicography.* 3rd ed. Carlisle, PA: Carlisle Books, 1971.

Dictionnaire des lettres françaises: le dix-huitième siècle. Ed. by G. Grente, A. Pauphilet, L. Pichard, and R. Barroux. Paris: 1960.

EITNER, Robert. *Biographisch-bibliographisches Quellen-Lexikon der Musiker und Musikgelehrten der christlichen Zeitrechnung bis zur Mitte des 19. Jahrhunderts.* Leipzig: Breitkopf & Härtel, 1898-1904; New York: Musurgia, 1947.

The encyclopaedia britannica. 13th ed. London, New York: Encyclopaedia Britannica Company, 1926.

HARDING, Rosamond. *Origins of musical time and expression.* London: Oxford University Press, 1938.

HAWKINS, John. *A general history of the science and practice of music.* London: Payne and Son, 1776; J. Alfred Novello, 1853; New York: Dover, 1963.

HEYER, Anna Harriet. *Historical sets, collected editions, and monuments of music: a guide to their contents.* 3rd ed. Chicago: American Library Association, 1973.

ISHERWOOD, Robert M. *Music in the service of the king.* Ithaca, NY, London: Cornell University Press, 1973.

KASSLER, Jamie Croy. *The science of music in Britain, 1714-1830: a catalogue of writings, lectures, and inventions.* New York: Garland Publishing, 1979.

KRUMMEL, Don (ed.). *Bibliograhical inventory to the early music in the Newberry Library.* Boston: G. K. Hall, 1977.

MARCO, Guy A. *Information on music: a handbook of reference sources in European languages. I, Basic and universal sources.* Littleton, Co.: Libraries Unlimited, 1975.

Die Musik in Geschichte und Gegenwart. Ed. by Friedrich Blume. Kassel, Basel: Bärenreiter, 1949-1967.

National union catalog: pre-1956 imprints. London: Mansell, 1968- . (Washington, Library of Congress)

The new Grove dictionary of music and musicians. Ed. by Stanley Sadie. London: Macmillan, 1980.

New York Public Library. Dictionary catalog of the music collection. Boston: G. K. Hall, 1964-65; supplements, 1966-.

RATNER, Leonard G. *"Ars combinatoria:* chance and choice in eighteenth-century music," in *Studies in eighteenth-century music: a tribute to Karl Geiringer on his seventieth birthday.* Ed. by H. C. R. Landon and R. Chapman. New York: Oxford University Press, 1970. (Pp. 343-63)

REESE, Gustave. *Fourscore classics of music literature.* New York: Liberal Arts Press, 1957.

Riemann Musik Lexikon. 12th ed. Ed. by W. Gurlitt. Mainz: B. Schott's Söhne, 1959.

RILM abstracts (Répertoire international de littérature musicale). New York: RILM abstracts, 1967- .

RISM B-VI (Répertoire international des sources musicales. Series B, v. VI): *Ecrits imprimés concernant la musique.* Ed. by François Lesure. München-Duisburg: G. Henle, 1971.

SERAUKY, Walter. *Die musikalische Nachahmungsästhetik im Zeitraum von 1700 bis 1850.* Münster: 1929.

SCHNEIDER, Herbert. *Die französische Kompositionslehre in der ersten Hälfte des 17. Jahrhunderts.* Tutzing: Hans Schneider, 1972.

STRUNK, Oliver. *Source readings in music history from classical antiquity through the Romantic era.* New York: W. W. Norton, 1950.

WARNER, Thomas E. *An annotated bibliography of woodwind instruction books, 1600-1830.* Detroit: Information Coordinators, Inc., 1967. (Detroit Studies in Music Bibliography, 11)

WILLIAMS, David R. *A bibliography of the history of music theory.* 2nd ed. Fairport, NY: Rochester Music Publishers, 1971.

ANNOTATED LIST OF WRITINGS

1 ALBRECHTSBERGER, Johann Georg (1736-1809)

Gründliche Anweisung zur Composition mit deutlichen und ausführlichen Exempeln, zum Selbstunterrichte, erläutert; und mit einem Anhange: von der Beschaffenheit und Anwendung aller jetzt üblichen musikalischen Instrumente.

*Leipzig: Johann Gottlob Immanuel Breitkopf, 1790; 440p.

Ed. and enlarged by Ignaz Ritter von Seyfried as *J. G. Albrechtsberger sämtliche Schriften über Generalbass, Harmonie-Lehre und Tonsetzkunst zum Selbstunterrichte systematisch geordnet, mit zahlreichen aus dessen mündlichen Mittheilungen geschöpften Erläuterungs-Beyspielen und einer kurzen Anleitung zum Partitur-Spiel.*

Wien: A. Strauss, [1826]; 3 v.

Wien: T. Haslinger, [1837].

   Facs. reprint, Kassel: Bärenreiter, 1975.

French transl. by M. A. Choron as *Méthode élémentaire de composition.* Paris: Courcier, 1814.

English transl. of Seyfried's German ed. and of Choron's remarks from the French ed. by Arnold Merrick as *Methods of harmony, figured base, and composition, adapted for self-instruction.*

London: R. Cocks & Co., [1834].

London: R. Cocks & Co., [1844].

English transl. of Seyfried's ed. by J. F. Dugan, ed. by E. Woolf, as *Elementary work on the science of music; including thorough-bass, harmony, and composition.* Philadelphia: J. G. Osbourne, 1842.

English transl. of Seyfried's ed. by Sabina Novello as *Collected*

writings on thorough-bass, harmony, and composition, for self-instruction. (Music revised by Vincent Novello).
London: Novello, Ewer & Co., 1855.

In his only mention of dance music in this composition manual, Albrechtsberger declares that symmetrical phrasing ("Rhythmus," e.g. grouping in regular 2+2, 3+3, or 4+4 measure patterns) must be adhered to only in dance music ("National-Stücken," i.e. Menuet, Trio, Allemande, Sarabande, Gavotte, Courante, Rigadon, Gigue, Ballett, and "Liederchen"). He refers to writings of J. Riepel concerning "Rhythmus" and advises that such phrasing is not appropriate in longer pieces such as arias, symphonies, trios, and quartets.

2 ALTENBURG, Johann Ernst (1734-1801)
Versuch einer Anleitung zur heroisch-musikalischen Trompeter- und Pauker-Kunst, zu mehrerer Aufnahme derselben historisch, theoretisch und praktisch beschrieben und mit Exempeln erläutert.
Halle: Johann Christian Hendel, 1795; 144p.
  *Facs. reprint, Dresden: Richard Bertling, 1911.
  *Facs. reprint, New York: Broude Bros., 1966 (MMMLF, 36).
  Facs. reprint, Amsterdam: Antiqua, 1966.
  *English transl. by Edward H. Tarr as *Essay on an introduction to the heroic and musical trumpeters' and kettledrummers' art.*
Nashville, TN: The Brass Press, 1974.

Apparently written several decades before its publication date (i.e. before 1770), Altenburg's treatise remains the most comprehensive source of information about the trumpet and trumpet playing in the 18th c. and before. Part 1—historical and theoretical—treats the history of the instrument (emphasizing the socially exalted position of trumpeters in ancient times to justify their elevated status in the 17th and 18th c.), the organization of trumpeters' guilds in the Holy Roman Empire, the status and perquisites of trumpeters both in imperial and foreign service, and famous trumpeters past and present. Here we learn that the French employed German guild-trained trumpeters as well as non-guild musicians in its army. The discussion of contemporary instruments illuminates their materials and construction. Part 2 provides practical instruction. Ch. 8-11 cover embouchure, available pitches, mouthpieces, tuning bits, crooks, mutes, types of playing (military, ceremonial; high, low, clarino), and tonguing and huffing techniques in which the German trumpeters were said to excell. Altenburg describes five main types of military signals used in Germany and a sixth used in France, plus six additional ones, all bearing French names. Ch. 12 on composition for trumpet ensemble contains a Bourrée and Minuet for two trumpets, kettledrums, and string quartet. Ch. 13 on ornaments illustrates the Accent or Vorschlag, Nachschlag, Triller, Pralltriller, Mordent, Schleifer, and Bebung. Ch. 14-15 treat pedagogy in great detail, outlining the two-year apprenticeship training program. The final chapter on kettledrums treats briefly the history and modern construction of the instruments, their use (military, civil, divine) and proportionate numbers when played with trumpet choirs, and the various kinds of strokes. (Detailed engravings of an imperial kettledrummer and an imperial trumpeter of ca. 1700 added by Tarr in the English transl. amplify Altenburg's remarks on construction and attire.)

3 [ANONYMOUS]

Anleitung, so viel Walzer man will mit Würfeln zu componiren, ohne musikalisch zu seyn oder Composition zu wissen . . . Op. CXII.
*Berlin: Rellstab, [ca. 1790]; 8p.
Anleitung zum Componiren von Walzern so viele man will vermittlest zweier Würfel ohne etwas von der Musik oder Composition zu verstehen. Berlin: [Hummel], 1793. Attributed to W. A. Mozart.
**Anleitung, Walzer oder Schleifer mit zwei Würfeln zu componiren, so viele man will, ohne etwas von der Musik oder Composition zu verstehen . . . Par W. A. Mozart.* Bonn: N. Simrock, [ca. 1796]; 7p.
**Instruction pour composer autant de walzes que l'on veut par le moyen de deux dez sans avoir la moindre connoissance de la musique ou de la composition par W. A. Mozart.* Paris: Vogt, [ca. 1800]; 6p.

The waltz dice game most often attributed to W. A. Mozart was apparently first published by Rellstab in Berlin, attributed to C. P. E. Bach. It later appeared in several early 19th-c. (Worms: Johann Michael Gotz, [ca. 1800]; Hamburg: Kratsch; Paris: Vogt, [ca. 1800]; London: Wheatstone, 1806; Amsterdam: Henning) and even 20th-c. editions *(Musika-*

lisches Würfelspiel, Mainz: Schott, 1956; *Musik mit Würfeln,* Amsterdam: Heuwekemeijer, 1957; *Melody dicer,* Brighton, MA: Carousel, 1973). The text appears in German and French in the Rellstab edition; in German, French, English, and Italian in Simrock and Gotz; and in French only in Vogt. By rolling two dice and employing the two tables of numbers and one of musical measures, the player produces 16-measure C-major waltzes in keyboard score. The tables of numbers are the same as those found in minuet games attributed to Maximilian Stadler *(Table pour composer des menuets,* q.v.) and Joseph Haydn *(Gioco filharmonico).*

4 [ANONYMOUS] (before 1773?)
Instruction des tambours, et diverses batteries de l'ordonnance.
*Paris: gravée par Melle. Vendôme, [s.d.]; 4p.+4pl.

These instructions for the military drummer, with fife and drum signals for the infantry, establish absolute tempos for march music. Directions for marching indicate a duration of one second for each step ("pas"), or 60 steps per minute, except for *La charge,* which is twice as fast, or 120 per minute. Twelve signal calls coordinate the drum strokes with their respective fife or oboe melodies: *La généralle, L'assemblée, L'appel, Le drapeau, La marche, La charge, La retraite, La prière, La fascine ou bréloque, Le ban, L'ordre, L'enterrement.* The drumstroke notation shows left and right hand strokes, designating the name and showing the details of the stroke pattern (9 patterns are described and illustrated in the instructions), while indicating where in the measure each step begins. Each signal has a specific indication for tempo, e.g. two seconds per measure, one second per half-measure, etc. Signs for left and right foot coordinate the marcher's steps with the drum beats.

5 [ANONYMOUS] (Sometimes attributed to Johann Christoph and Johann David STÖSSEL)
Kurtzgefasstes musicalisches Lexicon, worinnen eine nützliche Anleitung und gründlicher Begriff von der Music enthalten, die Termini technici erkläret, die Instrumente erläutert und die vornehmsten Musici beschrieben sind, nebst einer historischen Beschreibung von der Music Nahmen, Eintheilung, Ursprung, Erfindung, Vermehrung und Verbesserung, biss sie zu itziger Vortrefflichkeit gelanget, auch wunderbaren Würckung und Ge-

90

brauch ingleichen ihren vornehmsten Cultoribus, so von der Welt Anfang bis auf unsere Zeit gelebet. Alles aus derer besten und berühmtesten Musicorum ihren Schrifften mit Fleiss zusammen gesucht, in alphabetische Ordnung gebracht und denen Liebhabern musicalischer Wissenschaften zu fernern Nachdencken wohlmeynend vorgestellet.
*Chemnitz: Johann Christoph und Johann David Stössel, 1737; 430p.
Chemnitz: Johann Christoph und Johann David Stössel, 1749; 431p.

Based on 17th and 18th-c. German musical treatises (Printz, Mattheson, et al.), the dictionary includes French, Italian, and Latin as well as German terms and names of composers and musicians. The historical introduction is drawn largely from W. C. Printz. Articles on dance types are more detailed and articulate than those in many other dictionaries, tending to relate the musical form to the dance itself. The article "Bourrée" describes musical structure and form of the dance, characterizing it as the third basic dance type after the minuet and courante. Included are the Allemanda, Ballet, Bourrée, Chaconne, Courante, Gavotte, Gigue, Menuët, Paduanna/Pavana, Passacaille, Passepieds, Rigaudon, Rondeau, Sarabande, and Suite.

6 [ANONYMOUS] (Sometimes attributed to Louis Balthasar de La CHEVARDIÈRE, fl. 1758-1785)
Ludus melothedicus ou le jeu de dez harmonique contenant plusieurs calculs par lesquels toute personne composera différents menuets avec l'accompagnement de basse en joüant avec deux dez même sans sçavoir la musique.
*Paris: de La Chevardière; Lyon: frères le Goux, [1758]; 15p.
Nouvelle édition, corrigée quant à la partie harmonique qui se trouve quelquefoix défectueuse dans la première édition donnée depuis peu à Paris. Liège: Benoît Andrez, [ca. 1759]; 15p.
Den Haag: Pierre Gosse, [s.d.].

This musical dice game, requiring one throw for each measure, produces pairs of 16-measure minuets in two parts (treble and bass), one in D major and one in A minor. For each throw, a numerical table coordinates the number on the dice with the number of the throw to indicate the proper selection from a chart of musical measures.

7 [ANONYMOUS]

Rules: or a short and compleat method for attaining to play a thoroughbass upon the harpsichord or organ. By an eminent master. Also an explanation of figur'd time, with the several moods & characters made use of in musick. To which is added, a dictionary, or explication of such Italian words, or terms, as are made use of in vocal, or instrumental musick.
*London: J. Walsh, [ca. 1730]; 42p.

The glossary section corresponds to *A short explication of such foreign words, as are made use of in musick books* (London: J. Brotherton, 1724). Both works have been attributed to J. C. Pepusch (see J. C. Kassler, *The science of music in Britain*). The French dance terms in this primarily Italian list are of interest chiefly as they indicate which dances were current among British amateurs in the early 18th c. Perfunctory definitions appear for Bourée, Forlana, Galliarda, Gavotta, Gigue, Loure, Minuet, Passepied, Rondeau, Sarabande, Tempo di Gavotta, Tempo di Minuetto, and Tempo di Sarabanda. The Gavotta receives the most extensive description commenting on length of structural sections in the tune. The Minuet is said to be so well known as to need no explanation.

8 AZAÏS, Hyacinthe (1741-ca. 1795)

Méthode de musique sur un nouveau plan à l'usage des élèves de l'école royale militaire. On a joint aux leçons un accompagnement de basse chiffrée; six trio qui peuvent être éxécutés par deux violons et une basse, quelques ariettes avec des accompagnements etc., un traité abrégé d'harmonie, et un dictionnaire de musique par M. Azaïs.
*Sorèse par Revel: auteur, [1776]; 173p.
Paris: Bignon, 1776.

While this elementary instruction manual offers no discussion of dance music per se, it uses dance melodies to illustrate various meters, modes, and rhythms, including 1 Contredanse en allemande, 1 Chaconne, 2 Gigues, 1 Loure, 1 March, 2 Menuets, 2 Rigaudons, 1 Sarabande, 1 Tambourin, and 2 Gavottes. The discussion of meter indicates for each meter which note values are to be played unequally. (The section on harmony derives chiefly from writings of P. J. Roussier, the dictionary from Rousseau's.)

9 BACH, Carl Philipp Emanuel (1714-1788)

Versuch über die wahre Art das Clavier zu spielen. Mit Exempeln und achtzehn Probestücken in sechs Sonaten erläutert . . . [Erster Theil.]
Berlin: Christian Friedrich Henning (In Verlegung des Auctoris), 1753; 135p.
2nd ed. Berlin: Georg Ludwig Winter (In Verlegung des Auctoris), 1759; 118p.
Leipzig: [Engelhardt Benjamin] Schwickert, 1780; 118p.
3rd ed., enlarged, with additional pieces. Leipzig: Schwickert, 1787; 103p.
Ed. by Walter Niemann from the 1759 ed. Leipzig: 1925.
*English transl. by William J. Mitchell as *Essay on the true art of playing keyboard instruments.* New York: W. W. Norton, 1949.
English transl. of ch. 2 in 0. Strunk, *Source readings in music history,* pp. 609-15.
French transl. of essential theoretical passages by Jean Pierre Muller in *Revue belge de musicologie* (1972-73), pp. 159-236.

While French contributions to C. P. E. Bach's keyboard practice are not clearly distinguished from other influences on this composer's mixed style, his essay is included here on account of its importance as one of the most important practical musical treatises of the 18th c. In clarity, scope, and detail it prevailed over all previous writings on keyboard playing and became a reference point for all later ones in the German language. Ch. 1 on fingering, which provides the basis (established by his father J. S. Bach) for modern keyboard fingering, agrees with Couperin's usage of the left thumb (though it goes further in turning under both thumbs in scale passages). Ch. 2 on embellishment emphasizes the melodic and harmonic functions of ornaments, specifying the exact musical context suited to each. Admiring the "precision" of French keyboard ornaments, Bach provides his own classification of short ornaments into 7 types (appoggiatura, trill, turn, mordent, compound appoggiatura, slide, snap, and fermata elaboration) and 24 subtypes, some standard and others admittedly "new." Ch. 3 on performance articulates an aesthetic most appropriate to expressive German music, specifically Bach's own. Bach consistently distinguishes between learned and galant styles, revealing his preference for the French-derived galant. Nevertheless, the attitude of unrestrained expressiveness and the unconventional formal processes he recommends depart considerably from French aesthetic and practice. This third chapter deals with

93

articulation, vibrato, portato, arpeggiation, rubato, and dynamic shading as means to his expressive ends. The first revised edition was the one of 1787; the intervening editions of 1759 and 1780 were minimally changed reissues. Mitchell's translation combines the original text of 1753 with the printed revisions of 1787, interpolating musical examples into the text. (A copy of the 1787 edition with Bach's hand written corrections and comments, as well as a 23-page manuscript appendix, known in the 1920s [see *MGG* I, 934], was announced for a facsimile publication apparently never realized.) The six sonatas intended to illustrate the essay originally appeared in a separate pamphlet and are not included in Mitchell's translation.

10 BACH, Carl Philipp Emanuel (1714-1788)

Versuch über die wahre Art das Clavier zu spielen. Zweyter Theil, in welchem die Lehre von dem Accompagnement und der freyen Fantasie abgehandelt wird.
Berlin: Georg Ludwig Winter (In Verlegung des Auctoris), 1762; 341p.
Leipzig: Schwickert, 1780; 341p.
2nd ed., Leipzig: Schwickert, 1797; 280p.
*English transl. by William J. Mitchell as *Essay on the true art of playing keyboard instruments.* New York: W. W. Norton, 1949.

The second part of Bach's famous keyboard instruction manual concentrates upon thoroughbass realization, accompaniment, and free improvisation. While Bach was familiar with Rameau's harmonic theory, his rejection of it in favor of his father's (J. S. Bach's) more practical, keyboard oriented intervallic instruction method brought him perhaps closer to pre-Rameau French thoroughbass teaching. Chords are grouped primarily according to bass notes, rather than roots; chords are identified by their function (or harmonic tendency) rather than merely by intervallic construction.

Chapters on accompaniment offer sound advice on various topics: unison textures, one-part accompaniment for the left hand, *points d'orgue;* appoggiaturas, syncopated notes, and dotted rhythms in the bass; volume control by means of fluctuating texture; cadenzas; figural accompaniment and other refinements; imitation; the need for bass figures; recognizing and dealing with passing tones (with specific remarks on Siciliana accompaniment, p. 414 in Mitchell's transl.); chords that anticipate their bass notes; recitative; changing notes; and bass themes.

While much of this commentary pertains more directly to German than to French style, Bach's perceptiveness on matters of concern to all accompaniment make this a universal handbook. The chapter on figural accompaniment (pp. 386ff. in Mitchell's transl.) provides later 18th-c. treatment of the subject discussed earlier by St. Lambert (q.v.), Heinichen (q.v.), and Mattheson (q.v.).

The justly famous chapter on improvisation and free fantasy, while bearing most directly on Bach's own fantasies, may serve as a guide to mid-18th-c. improvisation practice possibly applicable to preludes and dance introductions. Noteworthy are the strict limitations Bach imposes upon supposedly free form, which should follow a general ground plan and observe restrictions on the range and remoteness of modulation. Freedom applies more nearly to the manner of working out detail than to the plan as a whole. The first revised edition was the one of 1797; the intervening edition of 1780 was a virtually unchanged reissue of the original. Mitchell's translation combines the original text of 1762 with the printed revisions of 1797.

11 BACILLY, Bénigne de (ca. 1625-1690)

Remarques curieuses sur l'art de bien chanter, et particulièrement pour ce qui regarde le chant françois. Ouvrage fort utile à ceux qui aspirent à la méthode de chanter, surtout à bien prononcer les paroles avec toute la finesse et toute la force nécessaire; et à bien observer la quantité des syllabes, et ne point confondre les longues et les brefves, suivant les règles qui en sont établies dans ce traité.
Paris: auteur et Ballard, 1668; 428p.

2nd ed. entitled *Traité de la méthode ou art de bien chanter, par le moyen duquel on peut en peu de temps se perfectionner dans cet art, et qui comprend toutes les remarques curieuses que l'on y peut faire.* Paris: Guillaume de Luyne, 1671; 428p.

3rd ed. entitled *L'art de bien chanter de M. de Bacilly. Augmenté d'un discours qui sert de réponse à la critique de ce traité, et d'une plus ample instruction pour ceux qui aspirent à la perfection de cet art.* Paris: Guillaume de Luyne, 1679; 32+428p.

Facs. reprint, Genève: Minkoff, 1974.
4th ed., 1681.
*English transl. by Austin B. Caswell as *A commentary upon the art of proper singing*. Brooklyn, NY: Institute of Mediaeval Music, 1968.

One of the most important writings on French vocal performance in the latter 17th c., Bacilly's treatise offers extensive discussion of ornaments and improvised ornamentation, including divisions (variations) for *doubles*. Bacilly subordinates all elements of style and interpretation to the proper declamation of French texts, emphasizing the syllable length of words, rather than their meaning, as the determinant of ornament placement. The many musical examples he cites from *airs de cour* by Michel Lambert and others do not actually appear in musical form in the original editions; Caswell has sought them out from musical sources and inserted them into his translation.

Part 1, in 13 chapters, deals generally with the aesthetics, pedagogy, and performance of vocal music. Ch. 11 refers twice to dance music, first (p. 98) declaring that although Italian airs may be in some ways superior to French airs, even Italians agree that French dance airs, such as gavottes, sarabandes, and minuets, are quite as worthy as the grander (Italian) airs and as technically beneficial to the student. A second reference (pp. 105-8) informs us of the practice of altering the tempo in a dance type sung as an air, so as to make it more tender or expressive. Bacilly defends the skillful singer who slows the tempo of a gavotte or even disrupts its metric structure when adding appropriate ornaments to give the air more charm or refinement; his purpose is not to make the tune danceable. Other dance airs, such as the minuet or sarabande, may be slower in tempo than the corresponding dance but should not be metrically disrupted, as they lose their identity. Ch. 12 deals with vocal ornaments, including the Port de voix, Cadence, Double cadence, Demi-tremblement (Tremblement etouffé), Soûtien de la voix, Expression (Passioner), Animer, Accent (Aspiration, Plainte), and Diminution. Ch. 13 treats passages and diminutions suited to more extensive variation of the tune. Part 2 concerns French pronunciation as applied to declamation and singing. Bacilly shows the effect of diction on the vocal line and indicates how to ornament certain vowels. Part 3 applies quantitative rhythm to French poetry in the *air de cour,* providing rules for determining the length of syllables. According to Bacilly, the purpose of ornamentation is not display, but rhythmic accent; long syllables in the poetry are to be stressed with musical ornamentation. Long syllables receive a note of longer value than those for surrounding short syllables. Every long syllable approached melodically from above should be sung with some sort of *tremblement* or *cadence;* long syllables approached from below should be sung with one of the *ports de voix* described. (See Austin B. Caswell's article, ''Remarques curieuses sur l'art de bien chanter,'' *Journal of the American musicological society,* v. 20 [1967], pp. 116-20, and the introduction to his English transl.)

12 BAILLEUX, Antoine (ca. 1720-ca. 1798)

Méthode pour apprendre facilement la musique vocale et instru-mentale où tous les principes sont dévelopés avec beaucoup de clarté, et cent leçons dans le goût nouveau à une et à deux par-ties, ce qui enseigne en très peu de tems à solfier sur toutes les clefs, toutes les mesures et tous les tons. Ouvrage qui conduit jusqu'au dernier degré de perfection, tant pour la mesure que pour le goût du chant. Dédiée aux demoiselles pensionnaire de la Maison des Dames Réligieuses de la Croix.
*Paris: auteur, [1770]; 127p.

While there is no reference to dance music specifically, an excellent section on ornaments (pp. 103-117) and their use in French vocal music attempts to relate ornaments to musical character and to expression of words, emphasizing the importance of this relationship. Bailleux indi-cates various notations and terms for the same ornament with explicit examples of their use. Included are Liaison, Tremblement (appuyé, feint, double), Flaté, Tour de Gossier, Passage, Diminution, Trait, Son filé, Son enflé et diminué, Son glissé, Sanglot.

13 BAILLEUX, Antoine (ca. 1720-ca. 1798)

Méthode raisonnée pour apprendre à jouer du violon avec le doigté de cet instrument et les différents agréments dont il est susceptible, précédée des principes de musique, dédiée aux jeunes élèves.
Paris: auteur, [1798]; 46p.
  *Facs. reprint, Genève: Minkoff, 1972.

This elementary method devotes 13 pages to rudiments and 33 pages to music. On pages 9-13 appear fairly detailed descriptions of ornaments with multiple examples, including the Coulé, Port de voix, Chûte, Tremblement (appuyé, subit, feint, doublé), Pincé, Flatté, Balance-ment, Accent, Passage, Coulade, Trait, Son diminué, and Son glissé. Some compare one ornament to another (e.g. the Port de voix is the "renversement du coulé"), indicate appropriate dynamic inflection (e.g. the Coulé has wedge marks for crescendo and decrescendo), or draw parallels with the Italian counterpart (e.g. Balancement is equated with tremelo). The musical *leçons* include 14 minuets, as well as exer-cises in advanced bowing.

14 BARON, Ernst Gottlieb (1696-1760)

Historisch-theoretisch und practische Untersuchung des Instruments der Lauten, mit Fleiss aufgesetzt und allen rechtschaffenen Liebhabern zum Vergnügen herausgegeben.
*Nürnberg: Johann Friedrich Rüdiger, 1727; [30]+218+[4]p.
Facs. reprint, Amsterdam: Antiqua, 1965.
English transl. by Douglas Alton Smith as *Study of the lute.* Redondo Beach, CA: Instrumenta antiqua, 1976; ix+185p.

The last significant German baroque lutenist, Baron was influenced by French aesthetics, particularly the writings of Batteux and Rousseau. Part 2 of the treatise is devoted to technique and aesthetics of the instrument. In ch. 1, Baron defends the lute against the judgment of Mattheson. Ch. 2 describes the special beauties of the lute ("Von dem Genie zur Lauten"). Ch. 3 deals with fundamental technique: hand and body position, fingering, and tablature. Ch. 4 on ornaments treats only a few, mainly the Trillo and Mordant; he distinguishes between Mordant and Bebung, or moving the string back and forth. Ch. 5 on taste ("Von dem rechten Gusto zu spielen") emphasizes elegant, singing tone and briefly compares French, Italian, and German styles in music; he finds the gallant French more playful and frivolous in their music than other nations, though capable of cantabile in instrumental music. The sixth ch. treats thoroughbass for the lute. Part 1 on the history and etymology of the lute is said to be less accurate than similar accounts by Mersenne and Praetorius, and his explanation of technique in Part 2 less detailed than that of earlier lute manuals.

15 BÉRARD, Jean Baptiste (1710-1772)

L'art du chant, dédiér à Madame de Pompadour.
Paris: Dessaint et Saillant, Prault fils, Lambert, 1755; [18]+158+[6]+34p.
*Facs. reprint, Genève: Minkoff, 1972; 228p.
Facs. reprint, New York: Broude Bros., 1967 (MMMLF 75).
English transl. by Sidney Murray. Milwaukee: Pro Musica Press, 1969. (See also his Ph.D. dissertation, University of Iowa, 1965.)

This singing manual treats the physiology of voice production, declamation, correct intonation, and ornamentation. Part 3, ch. 4-9 (pp. 112-54) on ornamentation describe the Cadence (appuyée, precipitée, molle, double), Demi-cadence ou coup de gorge, Port de voix (entier, feint), Accent, Coulé, Flatté or Balancé, and Son filé (entier, demi-filé) and provide a system of ornament symbols. Brief remarks on the vocal production of each ornament concern regulation of air, pitch, volume, and expression. A 34-page musical appendix presents airs of different character with suitable ornamentation, indicated by signs and verbal instructions regarding breathing and diction appropriate to the character of the air (e.g. *majestueux, violent, entrecoupé, tendre, léger, manieré*). Authorship of the treatise was disputed by Abbé Joseph Blanchet (q.v.), who claimed Bérard plagiarized part of his own manuscript treatise.

16 BÉTHIZY, Jean Laurent de (1709-1781)

Exposition de la théorie et de la pratique de la musique, suivant les nouvelles découvertes.
*Paris: Michel Lambert, 1754; xvi+296+60p.
2nd ed., Paris: E. G. Deschamps, 1764; xvi+331+60p.
Facs. reprint, Genève: Minkoff, 1972.

This harmony and composition manual attempts to simplify Rameau's ideas for the musician. Portions devoted to composition in 2, 3, 4, and more parts describe a harmonic, melodic, and textural practice similar to Rameau's. The musical examples (at the end), though not given dance titles, resemble dances in rhythm and texture, with Gavotte, Bourrée, and Chaconne patterns especially frequent. Of greatest interest is the section on voices and instruments (Part 2, ch. 18). With reference to the instrumental accompaniment in stage works (or large works in general), Béthizy lists the instruments making up the typical accompanimental ensemble. He describes the expressive character, range, and role in the ensemble associated with each one, including the flute, oboe, violin, viola, bassoon, violoncello, bass viol, and harpsichord. The bassoon receives the most enthusiastic treatment; the author describes at length the instrument's capacity for tender expression, its surprising aptness for solo lines in plaintive or gracious pieces, and its beautiful effect when combined with the flute and violin. Béthizy credits Rameau and Mondonville for revealing the expressive possibilities of the bassoon. Temperament is discussed in Part 2, ch. 5. Béthizy describes the old type (mean tone) and Rameau's (equal temperament), with tuning instructions for keyboard instruments.

17 BLAINVILLE, Charles Henri de (ca. 1710-ca. 1777)
L'esprit de l'art musical, ou refléxions sur la musique, et ses différentes parties.
*Genève: 1754; 126p.
  Facs. reprint, Genève: Minkoff, 1975.

The essay treats various aspects of vocal composition. While not very specific, chapters on accompaniment ("Des accompagnemens syllabiques," "Des accompagnemens coupés," "De l'accompagnement de caractère") distinguish a French from an Italian type, the French being simple, chordal, and syllabic in setting. Blainville's somewhat eclectic taste has him at times echoing the criticism of Rousseau, Algarotti, and d'Alembert, while simultaneously espousing the musical unity of Lully and Corelli. Passages pertaining to unity, variety, and proportion in music may be found in his chapters on the unity of melody, on style in music, and on truth, variety, and proportion in music.

18 BLAINVILLE, Charles Henri de (ca. 1710-ca. 1777)
Histoire générale, critique et philologique de la musique, dédiée à Madame la duchesse de Villeroy.
*Paris: Pissot, 1767; xi+189p.+69pl.
  Facs. reprint, Genève: Minkoff, 1972.

Part 4, section 2, ch. 3-5 deal with harmonic theory, distinguishing between the older counterpoint-based harmony of Lully, Campra, and Delalande and the more recent "basse fondamentale" theory (of Rameau). Blainville prefers the older system, believing that Rameau's music lacks the purity, simplicity, and unity of Lully's. To demonstrate, he examines in detail a "Gavotte gai et gracieuse" by Rameau (pp. 174-76) in order to show its stylistic discrepancies, and rewrites the bass line for offending passages. He continues the demonstration with an operatic air. His analysis provides useful advice for harmonizing and contriving a bass to a given melody in the style of Lully.

19 BLANCHET, Joseph (1724-1778)
L'art ou les principes philosophiques du chant par M. Blanchet. IIe édition, corrigée et augmentée.
*Paris: Augustin Martin Lottin, Michel Lambert, Nicolas B. Duchesne, 1756; xlviii+148p.

While this singing treatise focuses upon the physiology of voice production, vocal training, and diction, it is of interest here on account of the chapter on ornaments. Part 3, ch. 5, pp. 113-38, provides brief but detailed description of the physical production of each ornament, commenting on regulation of air, pitch, volume, and expression. Included are the Port de voix entier, Port de voix feint, Accent, Flatté ou Balancé, Son filé entier, Son demi-filé, Cadence (appuyée, précipitée, molle, double), Demi-cadence ou Coup de Gorge, Coulé, and Roulade. Portions of the work resemble Bérard's *L'art du chant* (q.v.), which Blanchet considered to be a plagiarism of his own manuscript (an accusation discounted by La Borde, q.v.).

20 BOLLIOUD DE MERMET, Louis (1709-1794)

De la corruption du goust dans la musique françoise.
*Lyon: Aimé Delaroche, 1746; 53p.
    Facs. reprint, New York: AMS Press, 1978.
German transl. with commentary by F. G. Freytag as *Abhandlung von dem Verderben des Geschmacks in der französischen Musik.* Altenburg: Paul Emanuel Richter, 1750; 78p.
German transl. in F.W. Marpurg, *Des critischen Musicus an der Spree erster Band.* Berlin: A. Haude und J. C. Spener, 1750; pp. 321ff.
    Facs. reprint, Hildesheim: Georg Olms, 1970.

In discussing corruption of taste in the composition of music (Part 1) and in the performance of music (Part 2), the author tries to distinguish between the good taste of Lully, Delalande, Couperin, Marais, and others of the Lully period, and the poor taste of the present. He attributes the recent decadence in French music to attempts at imitating foreign styles, especially the Italian (though the French conception of the Italian is erroneous, he says). His railing against modern style and its abuses is specific enough to bring into relief some differences between the Lully and Rameau eras. He inveighs against the lust for excess in length, speed, virtuosity for its own sake, embellishment, unnatural modulation, and unnaturally high and low tessitura, resulting in the abandonment of simplicity and sensitive expression. Comments on the denaturing of the character of individual instruments invoke the pastoral associations of musette and vielle and argue against the evil acoustic consequences of overly taut violin strings. He laments that the older legato manner of playing the harpsichord has given way to a detaché style quite dry in effect. With regard to composition, he decries the indiscriminate repetition of sections as boring; the neglect of rules of composition; the distortion of the verbal text caused by highlighting a word at the expense of the sense of the entire phrase; and the supposed embellishment of a melody that in effect disrupts its unity or integrity.

21 BONNET, Jacques (1644-1724)

Histoire de la musique et de ses effets, depuis son origine jusqu'à présent, et en quoi consiste sa beauté.
Paris: Jean Cochart, Etienne Ganeau, Jacques Quillau, 1715; 487p.
>   Facs. reprint, Genève: Minkoff, 1969.
>   Facs. reprint, Genève: Slatkine, 1969.
Amsterdam: Jeanne Roger, [1721]; 4 v., 333p., 175p., 322p., 230p.
Amsterdam: M. Ch. Le Cène, 1725.
>   *Facs. reprint, Graz: Akademische Druck- und Verlagsanstalt, 1966.
Amsterdam: M. Ch. Le Cène, 1726.
*Den Haag, Frankfurt am Main: Compagnie, 1743. Entitled *Histoire de la musique depuis son origine, les progrès successifs de cet art jusqu'à présent, et la comparaison de la musique italienne et de la musique française par Mr. Bourdelot.*

This history of music was begun by Pierre Bonnet and Pierre Bourdelot, but completed and published by Jacques Bonnet in 1715. The 1721 and subsequent editions added (as volumes 2-4) a reprint of the *Comparaison de la musique italienne et de la musique française* by J. L. Le Cerf de la Viéville (q.v.), written in reply to F. Raguenet's *Parallèle des Italiens et des François* (q.v.). Volume 1, ch. 10 ("De l'établissement de la musique et des spectacles en France, depuis les premiers Gaulois, jusqu'à présent") devotes two pages to Louis XIII and eleven pages to Louis XIV in tracing the growth of music and spectacle in France. Essentially a flattery of Louis XIV, this brief historical sketch lauds the perfection and grandeur he brought to music by means of the institutions he established, the entertainments he ordered or conceived, his own example in dancing, etc. It describes festivals and other entertainments at Fontainebleau and elsewhere, e.g. the Louvre 1663, Vaux-le-Vicomte 1660, Sceaux 1673. Observations touch upon highlights in singing, dancing, instrumental ensemble playing, and spectacle.

22 BORDET, Toussaint (ca. 1730-after 1783)

Méthode raisonnée, pour apprendre la musique d'une facon plus claire et plus précise, à laquelle on joint l'étendue de la flûte traversière, du violon, du pardessus de viole, de la vielle et de la musette; leur accord, quelques observations sur la touche desdits instruments et des leçons simples, mesurées et variées, suivies d'un recueil d'airs en duo faciles et connus pour la plus-part. Ouvrage fait pour la comodité des maîtres et l'utilité des écoliers, dedié à Monsieur le Marquis de Monpesat . . .
*Paris: auteur, Bayard, Le Clerc, Castagnery, [1755]; 75p.
Paris: auteur, Lyon: Brotonne, [ca. 1758]; 79p.
Paris: auteur, aux adresses ordinaires, [1765]; 79p.

This elementary instruction book contains 15 pages demonstrating the rudiments of music, followed by 10 pages of charts showing ranges and trill fingerings for the flute, violin, vielle (hurdy-gurdy), and musette, and 55 pages of dance tunes and airs in two parts by various French composers from operas and comic operas. The section on *agréments* offers brief but concise illustration of ornaments and articulation signs, including Cadence (simple, double, coupée), Port de voix, Coulé, Nottes perlées, Nottes detachées, Nottes piquées et coupée. Bordet defines two types of *prélude* and provides rules and recommendations for improvising preludes, with emphasis on modulation. The music section contains Allemandes, Airs, Ariettes, Barcarolles, Chasses, Contredanses, Entrées, Fanfares, Gavottes, Gigues, Marches, Menuets, Musettes, and Tambourins. Composers include Arnoult, Borderi, Bordet, Braun, Chinzer, Couperin, Danguy, Daquin, Dauvergne, Exaudet, Francoeur, Gaviniés, Gianotty, Handel, Lavaux, Lefèvre, Lully, Mondonville, Naudot, Rameau, Rebel, Rousseau, Senaliés, and Tolou.

23 BORDIER, Louis Charles (1700-1764)

Traité de composition, par feu M. Bordier, maître de musique des Sts. Innocents. Mis au jour par M. Bouin . . .
*Paris: l'éditeur et Melle. Castagnery; Lyon: M. Castaud; Toulouse: M. Brunet, [1770]; 86p.

While this is strictly a thoroughbass manual, it could be considered a useful guide to conservative chord progression and voice leading as demonstrated by "one of the best teachers in Paris" (according to the self-advertisement). Pages 50-53 give examples of *basse figurée*, in which the bass line is enlivened by means of rhythmic divisions and melodic embellishment in the form of scalar, arpeggiated, or other patterned motion. All examples are in duple meter, with no specific reference to dance.

24 BORJON DE SCELLERY, Pierre (1633-1691)

Traité de la musette, avec une nouvelle méthode, pour apprendre de soy-mesme à jouer de cet instrument facilement, et en peu de temps.

*Lyon: Jean Girin et Barthélemy Rivière, 1672; 39+19p.
   Facs. reprint, Bologna: Arnaldo Forni, 1969.
Paris: Louis Vendosme père, 1678.
   Facs. reprint, Genève: Minkoff, 1972.

This is probably the most important treatise on the musette (bagpipe) next to Hotteterre's (q.v.). The author claims it to be the first, since previously the instrument received only brief mention, even by Mersenne. The 39-page essay touches on origins and etymology of the musette, its former status among people of quality, necessary qualities for learning to play, two types of trill (above and below), construction of the instrument (with three beautifully engraved plates showing the components), playing technique, the types of pieces appropriate for the musette (gavotte or bransle, aubade) and those playable on it even if not of characteristic rustic naïveté and simplicity (courantes, sarabandes, ballets, some allemands), the use of the musette in ensembles, care of the instrument, tips for practicing, and famous makers and players (Hotteterre, Descouteaux, Philidor, Doucet, Lissieux of Lyon, François, Lambert, Ponthus). The treatment is quite brief, with frequent references to Greek and Roman times. The second part consists of 19 pages of music in both number tablature and score notation on facing pages, including 8 Bransles, a Bergeronette, and 2 Airs à chanter.

25 BORNET l'ainé (fl. 1762-1790)

Nouvelle méthode de violon et de musique dans laquelle on a observé toutes les gradations nécessaires pour apprendre ces deux arts ensembles. . .

Paris: auteur, [1786]; 82p.
Paris: Mercier, 1786.
Paris: Mercier, [ca.1795]; 35p. *Suivie de nouveaux airs d'opéras.*

Paris: veuve Bornet, [ca.1799]; 82p.

*Paris: Janet et Cotelle, [18—]; 131p. *Nouvelle édition, revue, corrigée, augmentée de plusieurs nouveaux airs et de six duos avec le coup d'archet.*

Clear and orderly instruction in the rudiments of music and violin technique preface some 55 pages of pieces in two parts, with carefully marked articulation and dynamics. These include a Vaudeville, Marches, Rondeaux, Menuets, a Gavote, and Air de Danse, mostly by Gluck, in addition to numerous airs, chansonettes, etc., from recent operas by Grétry, Rousseau, et al. Bornet's most original contribution is said to be a precise description of how to produce good tone on the violin.

26 BOÜIN, Jean François

La vielleuse habile ou nouvelle méthode courte, très facile, et très sure pour apprendre à joüer de la vielle. Dediée à Madame la Comtesse de la Vieuville. Par Mr. Boüin, maître de vielle. Gravée par Joseph Renou. Oeuvre IIIe.

*Paris: aux addresses ordinaires; Lyon: les frères Le Goux, [1761]; 42p.

Paris: veuve Boivin, Dufour, Bayard, etc. [s.d.]; 40p. *Nouvelle ed.*

    Facs. reprint, Genève: Minkoff, 1985.

Much of the instruction in this hurdy-gurdy treatise seems to derive from the earlier work by Dupuit (q.v.). Boüin discusses wheel technique for each meter, grouping the various *airs de caractère* into six metric categories. Describing different sorts of vielles, he distinguishes those with lute bodies from those with guitar bodies, with reference to their respective volume and resonance. (The lute type is louder and more resonant, the guitar type sweeter and softer.) After treating technique and fingering, he describes the wheel technique appropriate to various types of pieces, singling out the Musette as having no fixed number of wrist movements per bar. Ornaments discussed include the Cadence (liée, appuyée, double fermée), Port de voix, Pincé, and Couler. Boüin advises on the selection and care of instruments and the pricing of instruments and strings. A final section touches on how to play pieces with chords. The exercises and lessons include 2 Fanfares, 4 Gavottes, 2 Marches, 24 Menuets, 6 Musettes, and a Tambourin, plus airs, vaudevilles, etc.

27 BRIJON, C. R. (b. ca. 1720)

L'Appolon moderne, ou le développement intellectuel par les sons de la musique. Nouvelle découverte de première culture, aisée et certaine pour parvenir à la réussite dans les sciences, et nouveau moyen d'apprendre facilement la musique.
*Lyon: auteur, 1780; xxxii+264+7+64p.
Lyon: 1782; xxxii+264+7+64p.

This essay on the musical education of the young contains some practical information on French rhythmic and ornamentation practice. Part 2, on teaching the rudiments to children, makes *notes inégales* an important part of the discussion of meter (pp. 184ff.). For each meter, Brijon indicates which note values are to be played unequally; examples in the musical appendix use verbal indications *(égaux, inégales)* over appropriate notes. Various ornaments are realized in the musical appendix, pp. 50-54: Cadence (jettée, doublée, feintes, coupée, finalle, brisée), Pincé, Cadence (on main note with a turned close), Martelement, and Port de voix (simple, feint, coulé). Diction and vocal articulation are also treated, in Parts 1 (p. 107f.) and 2 respectively.

28 BRIJON, C. R. (b. ca. 1720)

Réflexions sur la musique et la vraie manière de l'exécuter sur le violon.
Paris: auteur, 1763; 32p.
*Facs. reprint, Genève: Minkoff, 1972.

An essay in support of French music and the French manner of playing introduces these instructions for playing the violin, which are illustrated by 5 plates and 11 pages of examples and lessons. Remarks on the importance of phrasing and expression stress the need to articulate phrases rhythmically, with tiny pauses between adjacent ones. Brijon treats the rudiments of music and violin playing. The section on bowing is especially detailed; he describes the direction and amount of bow used for playing successions of *notes inégales*. In discussing bowing for continuous quarter notes in triple time, he cites the minuet as an example of music that requires a six-beat bowing pattern, comparable to the minuet step itself, and resembling bowing for common time, except in duration. Brijon insists upon uniform bowing in ensembles and treats specific bowing problems arising in conventional phrasing.

29 BROSSARD, Sébastien de (1655-1730)

Dictionnaire des termes grecs, latins et italiens, dont on se sert fréquement dans toutes sortes de musique, et particulièrement dans l'italienne . . .
Paris: Christophe Ballard, 1701; 344p.
Dictionaire de musique, contenant une explication des termes grecs, latins, italiens, et françois les plus usitez dans la musique. À l'occasion desquels on rapporte ce qu'il y a de plus curieux, et de plus nécessaire à sçavoir; tant pour l'histoire et la théorie, que pour la composition, et la pratique ancienne et moderne de la musique vocale, instrumentale, plaine, simple, figurée, etc. Ensemble, une table alphabétique des termes françois qui sont dans le corps de l'ouvrage, sous les titres grecs, latins, et italiens pour servir de supplément. Un traité de la manière de bien prononcer, surtout en chantant, les termes italiens, latins, et françois. Et un catalogue de plus de 900 auteurs qui ont écrit sur la musique, en toutes sortes de temps, de pays, et de langues.
Paris: Christophe Ballard, 1703; 56p.
*Facs. reprint, Amsterdam: Antiqua, 1964.
2nd ed. Paris: Christophe Ballard, 1705; 380p.
*Facs. reprint, Hilversum: Frits Knuf, 1965.
3rd ed. Amsterdam: Estienne Roger, [ca. 1708]; 388p.
6th ed. Amsterdam: Pierre Mortier, [ca. 1710]; 388p.
*English transl. by Albion Gruber as *Dictionary of music.* Henryville, PA: Institute of Mediaeval Music, 1982.

The first extensive dictionary of musical terms in France, Brossard's famous work provided much material for later musical dictionaries by Walther (q.v.) and J. J. Rousseau (q.v.). The first version (1701), based on a glossary of terms Brossard appended to some of his music, was augmented in the 1703 publication by a 900-item list of writers on musical subjects. The ed. of 1705 (probably the last under Brossard's supervision) had new entries and a change in format, whereby Italian and French terms appeared in separate lists. This 1705 version begins with the main list of primarily Italian terms with definitions, representing both antiquity and the modern period. The subsequent list of French terms provides new definitions when appropriate or cross-reference to the Italian list when not. An essay on pronouncing Italian precedes the section devoted to writers on music, a listing of authors and titles classified by language and period. Much of Brossard's dictionary appears in translation in Grassineau's *Musical dictionary* (q.v.), though with revisions and additions by Grassineau. Gruber's translation follows the 1703 edition, with practical modifications for the English-speaking reader. The 1703 ed. contains many items pertinent to (1) dance (Balletto/Ballet, Ciacona/Chacone, Forlana, Gagliarda/Galliarde, Gavotta/Gavotte, Tempo de Gavotta, Giga/Gigue, Intrada/Entrée, Mascharada/Mascharade, Minuetto/Menuet, Passacaglio/Passacaille, Pastorale/Pastoral, Preludio/Prélude, Saltarella, Volta/Volte); (2) musical instruments (Guitarra/Guittare, Leuto/Luth, Spinetto, Theorba/Théorbe, Tromba, Tombone, Tympano/Tambour, Viola, Violino, Violoncello, Violone), and (3) musical performance (Harpeggiato/Harpegé, Hemiola, Legato/Lié, Obligato/Obligé, Ripieno/Parties du Grand Choeur, Ripresa/Reprise, Stile, Tabulatura/Tablature, Temperamento/Temperament, Tempo/Temps, Tenor/Taille, Thesis, Tirata/Tirade, Tremolo, Trillo, Tripla, Tutti/Tous, Variatio/Variation). The 1705 ed. adds Allemanda, Courante, Loure, Lourer, Passe-pied, Sicilienne, Sarabande, Opera, and Suonata di camera.

30 BURNEY, Charles (1726-1814)

A general history of music from the earliest ages to the present period. To which is prefixed a dissertation on the music of the ancients. 4 v.
London: for the author by T. Becket, J. Robson, G. Robinson (v. 1) 1776, 522p.; (v. 2) 1782, 597p.; (v. 3-4) 1789, 622p., 688p. 2nd ed., London: for the author by Payne & Son, Robson & Clark, G. G. J. & J. Robinson, 1789 (v. 1; v. 2, with 1782 on the titlepage).
*Ed. by Frank Mercer. London: G. T. Foulis, New York: Harcourt Brace, 1935; 2 v.
Facs. reprint, New York: Dover, 1957.

The first substantial music history in English (after Hawkins') owes its significance in large part to the first-hand experience of the author with the music of his own time. His travels through Europe for the purpose of seeking out library materials, musicians, and the musical trends in various regions provided raw material for much detailed information on composers, performers, authors, scores, and performances described in the history. Volume 3, ch. 11, "Of the state of music in France during the 17th century," is a concise historical sketch providing Burney's opinion on many composers, productions, authors, patrons, and performers. It includes an overview of Mersenne's *Harmonie universelle* (q.v.), speculation on the Italian origins of French opera, and a biographical sketch of Lully. Among the singers in Lully's operas, Burney singles out La Maupin for most extensive biographical treatment (drawn from La Borde's *Essai,* q.v.; her lifestory must be one of the most unusual after that of the Chevalier St. George). Famous organists and lutenists of the period are named, and La Borde's editing of musical examples is severely criticized. Volume 4, ch. 6, "Origin of the Italian opera in England, and its progress there during the present century," notes that in the last 10 years (prior to 1789?) "dancing seems to have encroached upon music, and instead of being a dependent or auxiliary, is aiming not only at independency, but tyranny." Burney describes the audience reception of French trained dancers, including the elder Vestris (1781), the younger Vestris, Le Picq, and dancers in Noverre's *Cupid and Psyche* (performed with a revived Cimarosa opera): Vestris, Hilligsberg, Chevalier, Didelot, and Coulon. Book 4, ch. 11, "Of the music of France during the present century," mentions Colasse and other composers between Lully and Rameau, and provides a summary of Raguenet's *Paralèle* (q.v.). In his extensive treatment of Rameau, Burney admits to the composer's influence on himself, despite his earlier prejudices against French opera. His biographical sketch of Rameau includes a description of *Castor et Pollux* (1737), after the score and a revival performance seen by Burney. While not sympathetic to the vocal music of the work, he praises the dance numbers for their "genius and invention," which he attributes to "a necessity for motion, measure, and symmetry of phrase" that characterize them (p. 968 in Mercer's ed.). He attempts to describe the substance of Rameau's theoretical writings and to place his theory with respect to historical and contemporary thought on fundamental bass, etc. He then describes the effects of Italian comic opera on French thought and music, noting the contributions of Rousseau, Duni, and later, Gluck. A ballet by Noverre is mentioned: *Les fêtes chinoises* (1755). A biographical section provides brief remarks on a number of distinguished performers and authors (relying heavily on Marpurg and La Borde), including organists and keyboard players Bernier, Marchand, Calvière, Bousset the younger, Couperin, Balbastre; violinists Le Claire, Guignon, Gavignié; flutists Blavet, Rault; bassoonists Blaise, Cugnier; composers Gossec, Grétry, Salieri; and authors Brossard, Masson, Affilard, Romieu, Béthisy, d'Alembert, Serre, Blainville, Gianotti, Morelet, Balliere, Jamard, Roussier, Dubreuil, Rousseau, Marmontel, Chabanon, de La Cépède, and de La Borde.

31 BURNEY, Charles (1726-1814)

The present state of music in France and Italy, or the journal of a tour through those countries, undertaken to collect materials for a general history of music.

London: T. Becket & Co., 1771; 396p.

2nd ed., London: T. Becket & Co., J. Robson, G. Robinson, 1773; 409p.

Facs. reprint, New York: Broude Bros, 1970 (MMMLF 70).

Facs. reprint, New York: AMS Press, 1978.

Ed. by Cedric Howard Glover (selections, plus additional material from Burney's travel diary in the British Library, Additional manuscript 35122) as *Dr. Burney's continental travels.* London: Blackie & Son, 1927.

*Ed. by Percy A. Scholes, with additional material from Burney's travel diary in the British Library, Additional manuscript 35122, as *Dr. Burney's musical tours in Europe, volume 1: an eighteenth century musical tour in France and Italy, being Dr. Charles Burney's account of his musical experiences as it appears in his published volume with which are incorporated his travel experiences according to his original intention.* London: Oxford University Press, 1959.

German transl. by Christoph D. Ebeling and Johann J. Christoph Bode as *Carl Burney's der Musik Doctors Tagebuch einer musikalischen Reise durch Frankreich und Italien welche er unternommen hat um zu einer allgemeinen Geschichte der Musik Materialen zu sammeln.* Hamburg: Bode, 1772-73.

Facs. reprint, Kassel: Bärenreiter, 1959. Ed. by Richard Schaal.

Ed. by Eberhardt Klemm. Leipzig: Philipp Reclam jun., 1968.

French transl. by Charles Brack as *De l'état présent de la musique en France et en Italie . . .* Genoa: J. Giossi, 1809-10.

Though somewhat prejudiced against French music, Burney was nevertheless a keen musical observer with a professional's interest in communicating both facts and value judgments. His trip to France in 1770 provides us with a first-hand account of the contemporary musical scene. He describes places of public diversion in Paris, including the new Vauxhall where people dance minuets, allemandes, cotillons, and contredanses (pp. 13 and 33 of Scholes's ed.). His attendance at a revival of the *ballet-héroique, Zaide,* by J. N. P. Royer, elicits positive judgment on the dancing (pp. 18-20 in Scholes's ed.), though he condemns the music as too old-fashioned and regrets the French stress on dancing and decoration at the expense of drama and music. He recalls an anti-French theater riot in London that ruined a dance program by Noverre (p. 22). A Ruckers harpsichord and several organs played for him by the organist Balbastre are described (p. 24). A remarkably clear distinction between sacred and secular style of keyboard playing emerges from Burney's observations on the organ playing of Armand-Louis Couperin (pp. 26-27): he notes that while Couperin has a "true organ touch, smooth and connected," he nevertheless occasionally injects into his playing "mere harpsichord passages, smartly articulated and the notes detached and separated." Burney observes the mixing of sacred and secular styles in the organ playing of Balbastre as well (p. 24): "When the Magnificat was sung, he played likewise between each verse several minuets, fugues, imitations, and every species of music, even to hunting pieces and jigs, without surprising or offending the congregation, as far as I was able to discover." Later, after hearing an oratorio in Rome (G. B. Casali's *Abigail),* he criticizes the rapid tempo of the finale to the overture (p. 290), a "minuet degenerated into a jigg of the most common cast. This rapidity in the minuets of all modern overtures renders them ungraceful at an opera, but in a church they are indecent."

32 BURNEY, Charles (1726-1814)

The present state of music in Germany, the Netherlands and United Provinces. Or, the journal of a tour through those countries, undertaken to collect materials for a general history of music. 2 v.
London: T. Becket, J. Robson, G. Robinson, 1773; 376p., 352p. 2nd ed., London: T. Becket, J. Robson, G. Robinson, 1775; 380p., 352p.

Facs. reprint, New York: Broude Bros., 1970 (MMMLF 117). *Ed. by Percy A. Scholes, with additional material from Burney's travel diary in the British Library, Additional manuscript 35122, as *Dr. Burney's musical tours in Europe, volume II: an eighteenth century musical tour in central Europe and the Netherlands, being Dr. Charles Burney's account of his musical experiences.* London: Oxford University Press, 1959.
German transl. by D. C. Ebeling and J. J. C. Bode as *Carl Burney's, der Musik Doctors, Tagebuch einer musikalischen Reise* . . . Hamburg: Bode, 1772-73; 311p., 272p., 314p.

Facs. reprint, Kassel: Bärenreiter, 1959.
Dutch transl. by Jacob Wilhelm Lustig as *Rijk gestoffeerd verhaal van de eigenlijke gesteldheid der hedendaagsche toonkunst, of Karel Burney's* . . . *Dagboek van zyne onlongs gedaane musicale reizen door Frankrijk, Italië en Duitschland.* Groningen: J. Oomkens, 1786; 472p. Utrecht: W. van Yzerworst, 1790; 472p.
French transl. by Charles Brack as *De l'état présent de la musique* . . . Genoa: J. Giossi, 1809-10.

A few references to French music appear in Burney's comments on musical life in Germany and the Netherlands during his 1772 tour. He admits that "upon keyed-instruments, particularly the harpsichord, the French, in point of neatness, precision, and brilliancy of execution, are not excelled by the people of any other country in Europe; and it is but just to observe likewise, that the French military music is now not only much better in itself, but better performed than it was a few years ago" (p. 4 of Scholes's ed.). While allowing the superiority of French serious opera as spectacle, with respect to the dances and decorations, he nevertheless denigrates its music as "still in the trammels of Lulli and Rameau" (p. 18). In Vienna, Burney saw a German comedy followed by a ballet by the celebrated ballet master Noverre, described by Burney as "a very spirited and entertaining dance" with four principal performers notable for their grace, activity, and precision (p. 78). Upon hearing Gluck's *Iphigénie,* he remarks on Gluck's ability to accommodate himself to the older French style rooted in the music of Lully and Rameau (p. 91). He records the flutist Quantz's reminiscences of French music in 1726; upon returning to Paris after a trip to Italy in that year, Quantz was displeased with French taste and found the affected manner of singing, especially of female singers, most offensive (p. 192).

33 BUSBY, Thomas (1755-1838)

A complete dictionary of music. To which is prefixed a familiar introduction to the first principles of that science.
London: Richard Phillips, [ca.1786]; xxxiiip.+294f.
London: Richard Phillips, [1801]; xxxiiip.+[149f.].
London: Richard Phillips, 1806; xxxiii+299p.
*3rd ed., London: Richard Phillips, 1811; 330p.
4th ed. as *A Dictionary of music, theoretical and practical. To which is prefixed a familiar introduction to the first principles of that science.* London: Richard Phillips, 1813.

*London: Richard Phillips, 1817; xxxiv+330p.

1st American ed., Philadelphia: G. M. & W. Snider, 1826; xxx-iip.+136f. (Similar to London: R. Phillips [1801].)

Philadelphia: G. M. & W. Snider, 1827; xxxii+272p.

Busby's dictionary first appeared in installments in the *New musical magazine* as "An universal dictionary of music" (London, ca.1783-86), presumably with assistance from Samuel Arnold for the musical portions. The subject matter of the dictionary ranges widely over theory, history, and practice. It may be considered useful for English translations of French terms and expressions. Articles among the various editions include Allemande (as a suite movement now obsolete; as a German and Swiss folk dance), Ballet, Ballet Master, Balli, Bourée, Boutade, Canaries, Chacone/Passacaille (2 entries, one as a musical composition with a ground bass of 4 or 8 measures in 3/4 time, etc., the other as an old French dance), Chorus, Contre-Danse, Coryphoeus, Cotillon, Country Dance, Courante, Dances, Danceries, Divertisement, Entries, Fandango, Galliard, Gavot, Giga/Gigue/Jig, Histrio, Hornpipe, Interlude/Intermezzi, Lavolta/La Volte/Volta, Loure, Louvre ("a term applied singly to a well-known French air, otherwise called *L'aimable vainqueur,* for which Lewis the Fourteenth had a remarkable predilection. This air has since formed a well-known dance"), Mascharada, Masque, Mimes, Minuet, Morrice-Dance, Morisco, Musette, Opera, Orchestra, Pantomime, Passacaglio/Passecaille, Passepied, Passomezzo, Pavane, Polonoise, Pyrrhics, Reel, Ridotto, Rigadoon, Rondo/Rondeau, Saltarella, Sarabande, Siciliana, Suite, Tambourin, Tarantula Dance, Tempo de Ballo/Gavotta/Minuetto, and Waltz. Also useful for style study are articles on Contrast, Phrase, and Phrases manquées, in the spirit of but not identical to Rousseau's.

34 CHOQUEL, Henri Louis (d. 1767)

La musique rendue sensible par la méchanique, ou nouveau système pour apprendre facilement la musique soi-même. Ouvrage utile et curieux approuvé par l'Académie Royale des Sciences.
Paris: Ballard, Duchesne, 1759; xiv+213p.
*Paris: Christophe Ballard, 1762; xiv+213p.

  Facs. reprint, Genève: Minkoff, 1972.

Paris: Lamy, 1782. Entitled *Méthode pour apprendre facilement la musique soi-même, ou la musique rendue sensible par la méchanique.* Paris: Leroy et Moureau, 1787.

Choquel's discussion of meter (Part 4, ch. 1-8) exceeds that in most introductions to music in indicating not only the quantity but the quality of movement denoted by each metric signature (in terms of tempo and character). Several sections list French dance types for which the meter is appropriate, although musical examples derive primarily from operas and cantatas by Lully, Campra, Clérambault, Delalande, Rousseau, and others. Remarks on relative tempo of pieces in a particular meter distinguish dance types from other music (cf. 3, 3/8, 2). He interprets 6/8 and 9/8 to mean respectively 2 and 3 slurred beats per measure, with implications for bowing or vocal articulation. Instruction on beating the measure (ch. 6) urges use of a pendulum, indicating how long to make the string to obtain the proper tempo for various metric signs. His use of the pendulum as a time-keeping device follows earlier writings on the subject by Mersenne, Loulié, L'Affilard, and Tans'ur; see Rosamond Harding, *Origins of musical time and expression*, p. 18.

35 CHRISTMANN, Johann Friedrich (1752-1817)

Elementarbuch der Tonkunst zum Unterricht beim Klavier für Lehrende und Lernende mit praktischen Beispielen. Eine musikalische Monatschrift.
*Speyer: H. Ph. C. Bossler, 1782-89; 2 v., xxvi+330p., 179+80 ("Beiträge") p.

In this music magazine for keyboard teachers and their pupils, each issue takes the form of a dialogue between the teacher and pupil Karl, touching on music history, theory, and general background. Volume 1, pp. 270-74, treats pieces of particular character, offering concise but detailed descriptions of the Allemande (2 types), Bourrée, Burlesko, Canarie, Chaconne, Capriccio, Courante, Couplet, Divertimento, Englische Tänze, Folie d'Espagne, Forlane, Fantasie, Gagliarda, Gavotte, Gigue, Loure, Musette, Passacaille, Passepied, Rigaudon, Sarabande, Siciliano, and Tambourin. The Menuet is described on p. 46; on pp. 196-202 teacher and pupil discuss a minuet with 6 variations, pointing out the variation technique and performance problems such as fingering and ornamentation. The 80-p. *Praktische Beiträge zu dem Elementarbuch der Tonkunst* (Speier 1782) provides music examples and lessons to accompany the *Elementarbuch*. It includes 18 minuets (2 cancrizans; 1 with 6 variations), 5 alla Polacca, 1 Contredanse, 4 Allemandes (Schwäbischer Tänze or Schleifer), 3 Marches (Marcia), and 2 Inglesi.

36 CORRETTE, Michel (1709-1795)

La belle vielleuse, méthode pour apprendre facilement à jouer de la vielle. Contenant des leçons où les doigts sont marqués pour les commençans; avec des jolis airs et ariettes en duo, deux suittes avec la basse et des chansons.
*Paris: les marchands assortis, Mlle Castagnery, [1783]; 50p.
Facs. reprint, Genève: Minkoff, 1984.

This beginning instruction manual in hurdy-gurdy playing treats tuning, position, wheel technique, fingering, wrist action, and ornaments (Cadence, Pincé), and offers technical advice. The lessons (pp. 14-50) include 4 Allemandes (2/4 meter), 1 Badine, 1 Chaconne, 7 Cotillons, 2 Fanfares, 23 Menuets, 6 Musettes, 2 Pastorales, 2 Tambourins, and 17 Vaudevilles and Contre-Danses.

37 CORRETTE, Michel (1709-1795)

L'école d'Orphée, méthode pour apprendre facilement à jouer du violon dans le goût françois et italien; avec des principes de musique et beaucoup de leçons à I et II violons. Ouvrage utile aux commençants et à ceux qui veulent parvenir à l'exécution des sonates, concerto [sic], pièces par accords et pièces à cordes ravallées . . . Oeuvre XVIIIe.
Paris: auteur, Boivin, Le Clerc, 1738; 43p.
*Facs. reprint, Genève: Minkoff, 1973.

Ch. 4 (pp. 3-5) of this violin tutor identifies common types of musical movement (tempo or character) by associating each metric signature with specific genres, including dance types: 2 for Rigaudons, Bourrées, Gavottes, Branles, Gailliardes, Villageoises, Cotillons; 3 for Menuets, Sarabandes, Courantes, Passacailles, Chaconnes, Folies d'Espagne; 6/8 for Canaries, Gigues; 12/8 for Gigues; 3/4 for Courantes; 3/8 for Passepieds; 6/4 for Loures, Forlannes; 3/2 for Italian Sarabandes; 9/8 for Italian Gigues. For each metric signature, Corrette indicates which notes are to be played unequally. He distinguishes between the Italian and French manner of holding the bow (p. 7). Ch. 5 (pp. 11-36) treats ornaments (Cadence, Double cadence), then offers pieces for learning to play the violin in the French manner (15 Menuets, 1 Rigaudon, 1 Entrée, 1 Gigue, 1 Forlanne, 1 Sarabande, 1 Loure, 1 Chaconne) and in the Italian manner (1 Gavotta, 1 Corrente, 1 Sarabanda, 2 Menuets). The lessons provide bowing indications and articulation, as well as occasional fingering and remarks on performance practice. Ch. 6 (pp. 37-40) on positions contains shifting exercises and 2 scordatura minuets.

38 CORRETTE, Michel (1709-1795)

Le maître de clavecin pour l'accompagnement, méthode théorique et pratique. Qui conduit en très peu de tems à accompagner à livre ouvert. Avec des leçons chantantes où les accords sont notés pour faciliter l'étude des commençans. Ouvrage utile à ceux qui veulent parvenir à l'excelence de la composition. Le tout selon la règle de l'octave et de la basse fondamentale.
Paris: auteur, Bayard, Le Clerc, Mlle. Castagnere, 1753; 94p.
  Facs. reprint, Bologna: Arnaldo Forni, 1969.
  Facs. reprint, Hildesheim: Georg Olms, 1973.
  Facs. reprint, Genève: Minkoff, 1976.
  *Facs. reprint, New York: Broude Bros., 1976 (MMMLF, 13).

Corrette's thoroughbass manual presents exercises in accompaniment as models for practice and imitation, with chords to a figured bass completely written out. His method derives from François Campion's *Traité d'accompagnement* (Paris 1716), with the addition of Rameau's concept of the *basse fondamentale.* While Corrette prefers the music of French imitators of Italian composition (Rebel père, Morin, Dandrieux, and others), he takes pains to differentiate the French from the Italian manner of figured bass notation (ch. 20). To illustrate French usage, he briefly discusses chords employing augmented and diminished intervals used by French composers of the previous generation, citing Lully's operas (specifically *Armide),* Clérambault's cantatas, and Senallié's violin sonatas. Ch. 11 on *point d'orgue* has examples of both chordal and improvisational melodic realizations over tonic and dominant pedalpoints. Among the various complete examples, called *leçons chantantes,* appear two Gigas and one Rondeau; most of the other pieces are Italian in style. (Additional examples are to be found in Corrette's supplemental volume entitled *Prototipes contenant des leçons d'accompagnement par demandes et par reponses; pour servir d'addition au livre intitulé Le maître de clavecin pour l'accompagnement. Avec des sonates pour le violon, la flûte, le pardessus de viole où les accords sont notés sur la basse* [Paris: auteur, 1754; enlarged 1775; facs. reprint 1976].) Ch. 21-22 cover the practical matters of stringing and tuning harpsichords and spinets. The discussion of string sizes and materials in ch. 21 provides an 18th- c. counterpart to Mersenne's treatment; Corrette's chart of string lengths compares French and German instruments with those of the Flemish maker Jean Ruckers, naming several French makers. Instructions for tuning harpsichords and organs in ch. 22 recommend meantone tuning *(partition)* as "the most widely used by the best makers for the last 200 years;" equal temperament is presented as new and controversial, along with another variety of tempered tuning demonstrated earlier by the English author Gottfried Keller. According to a note in the Broude Bros. facsimile reprint, existing copies of this book show a mixture of states, even within a copy. The Broude reprint "reproduces the latest state of each plate; it presumably reflects, therefore, ideal copy for the latest issue." The most noteworthy variants include a 3-page preface not found in earlier copies; two new pages of examples (pp. 66-67, with renumbering of all subsequent pages and corresponding alteration of the page numbers in the table of contents); two completely revised pages (pp. 76-77) adding explanatory notes and examples, while deleting or compressing other examples, in a section comparing the usual continuo bass with the *basse fondamentale* (chord root bass) in passages of root position and first inversion chords; and some details of the figured bass notation.

39 CORRETTE, Michel (1709-1795)

Méthode pour apprendre aisément à joüer de la flûte traversière. Avec des principes de musique, et des brunettes à I. et II. parties. Ouvrage utile et curieux, qui conduit en très peu de tems à la parfaite connoissance de la musique à joüer à livre ouvert les sonates et concerto.

Paris: Boivin, Le Clerc, [ca. 1740]; 51p.

Facs. reprint, Hildesheim: Georg Olms, 1975.

Facs. reprint, Buren: Frits Knuf, 1978.

Paris: auteur, 1753; 50p.

Paris: adresses ordinaires, [1773]; 66p. *Nouvelle édition, revue, corrigée et augmentée de la gamme du hautbois et de la clarinette.*

Facs. reprint, Genève: Minkoff, 1978.

Paris: 1780.

Facs. reprint, Hildesheim: George Olms, 1970.

*English transl. by C. R. Farrar as *Michel Corrette and flute playing in the 18th century.* Brooklyn, NY: Institute of Mediaeval Music, 1970.

This is the first known independent flute method after Hotteterre's *Principes* (q.v.), since others were largely derived from Hotteterre's. In Part

1, devoted to the rudiments of music, ch. 5 on meter indicates the types of dance tunes and other pieces associated with each metric signature, distinguishing between French and Italian usage with regard to choice of time signature. *Notes inégales* are indicated for each meter. Corrette declares that slurred articulation in 12/8 time commonly encompasses either two eighth-notes or three. Part 2 on flute playing contains a chapter on tonguing (ch. 5), in which the author says that the tonguing syllables "tu, ru" are no longer used by modern flutists. Ch. 6-7 on trills and turns illustrate the Cadence and Double cadence, requiring the upper auxiliary note and accelerating speed of repercussion. In his fingering charts for trills, Corrette is the first to show a trill on F#‴-E‴, G‴-F#‴, and D#″-C#″. Ch. 8 describes the finger vibrato (Flattement), ch. 9-11 the Battement, Port de voix, Accent, Martellement. Ch. 13 concerns the improvisation of simple preludes. The final 2 chapters discuss transposition and adapting violin music for the flute. Lessons and examples include 1 Allemande, 1 Brunette, 2 Fanfares (by Dandrieu), 1 Gavotte from *Dardanus,* 29 Preludes emphasizing various intervals and rhythms, 3 Menuets, 2 Rondeaux, 2 Sarabandes, and 2 Vaudevilles.

40 CORRETTE, Michel (1709-1795)
Méthode théorique et pratique pour apprendre en peu de tems le violoncelle dans sa perfection . . . XXIVe ouvrage.
*Paris: auteur, Boivin, Le Clerc; Lyon: Brotonne, 1741; 46p.
  Facs. reprint, Genève: Minkoff, 1972.
2nd ed. 1783.
English transl. by Charles D. Graves as *The theoretical and practical method for cello by Michel Corrette: translation, commentary, and comparison with seven 18th-century cello methods.* Ph.D. dissertation, Michigan State University, 1972.

Part 1, devoted to the rudiments of music, cites French and Italian composers frequently. Ch. 5 on meter indicates which dance types are associated with each metric signature, distinguishing between French and Italian usage. Remarks on *notes inégales* refer to well known examples, e.g. Lully's chaconne from *Phaëton.* Part 2, the violoncello method, offers some of the earliest printed instruction in 'cello technique, covering tuning, French bowing, fingering, positions, string crossing, articulation (gigue eighth notes are bowed 2 plus 1), double stops, arpeggios, thumb positions, half position, and ensemble playing and accompaniment. A comparison of the viol and the 'cello contrasts their fingerboards and ranges.

41 CORRETTE, Michel (1709-1795)

Le parfait maître à chanter, méthode pour apprendre facilement la musique vocale et instrumentale où tous les principes sont dévelopés nettement et distinctement.
Paris: auteur, [1758]; 56p.
*Paris: auteur, [1782]; 61p. *Nouvelle édition augmentée de nouveaux signes de musique et d'airs à chanter.*

This elementary singing manual illustrates the various dance airs in a series of musical examples without further commentary. Represented are the Chaconne, Courante, Entrée, Forlanne, Gavotte, Gigue, Loure, Menuet (françoise, italienne), Passepied, Rigaudon, Rondeau, Tambourin, and Vaudeville. Ch. 15 on ornaments describes quite briefly the Cadence (appuyée, precipitée ou subite, coupée, feinte ou brisée, double, fermée, italienne), Martellement ou Pincé, Coulé, Port de voix (simple, double), Accent, Flaté, Chûte, Balancement, and Son filé. Also of interest is a chart showing the tuning of string instruments, including the viols, viola d'amore, hurdy-gurdy (vielle), guitar, lute, archlute, theorbo, and pardessus de viol both of 6 and of 5 strings, as well as the violin, viola, violoncello, and bass. Another chart compares the ranges of various voices and orchestral instruments.

42 COUPERIN, François (1668-1733)

L'art de toucher le clavecin.
Paris: auteur, 1716; 65p.
Paris: auteur, 1717; 71p.
    Facs. reprint, New York: Broude Bros., 1969 (MMMLF, 23).
    Facs. reprint, Genève: Minkoff, 1986.
*Ed. with German transl. by Anna Linde, English transl. by Mevanwy Roberts. Wiesbaden: Breitkopf & Härtel, 1933.
Japanese transl. by Mitsugu Yamada as *Clavecin sôhô.* Tokyo: Sinfonia, 1976.

Couperin's instruction manual for the harpsichord is not a complete method (such as St. Lambert's attempts to be), but a commentary on some aspects of teaching and performing, with specific reference to his own published harpsichord pieces. His sensitive remarks on the harpsichord as a medium, its capabilities, and the music best suited to it, as well as idiosyncracies of French style, have made this the most frequently quoted treatise on French instrumental music. It begins with the position of the body and hands and proceeds with fingering, especially of ornaments. Couperin still crosses the third finger over the second and fourth in scale passages, but he eagerly recommends new practices such as changing fingers on the repeated note of a prepared port-de-voix and legato fingering of double thirds. Attentive to the expressive capabilities of the instrument, he introduces the *aspiration* and *suspension* (agogic accents) and discusses the importance of *notes inégales* and *mouvement* or spirit in French music. Chord arpeggiation should be used with discretion. He comments on the rhythmic flexibility and improvisational character required in the performance of preludes, of which he provides 8 original examples for use as etudes and as introductory pieces for his keyboard suites. Pieces from these suites here discussed for fingering and articulation include a Courante, Gigue, and Passacaille. Best known today is the table of ornaments and articulation, including Pincé (simple, double, diésés et bémolisés, continu), Port de voix (simple, double, coulée), Tremblement (appuyé et lié, ouvert, fermé, lié sans être appuyé, détaché, continu), Accent, Arpègement, Coulés, Tièrce coulée, Aspiration, Suspension, and Double (turn). The discussion of fingering incorporates detailed remarks on the performance of appoggiaturas and trills.

43 CRAMER, Carl Friedrich (1752-1807)
Kurze Uebersicht der Geschichte der französischen Musik.
*Berlin: Rellstab, 1786; xxiv p.

Articulate sketch of the history of French theater music, with digests of the literature pertaining to major figures and controversies, e.g. Lully, Rameau, the *guerre des bouffons,* etc. Raguenet's *Paralèle* (q.v.) appears in a German précis.

44 CROME, Robert
The fiddle new model'd, or a useful introduction for the violin, exemplify'd with familiar dialogues.
*London: J. Tyther, [ca. 1750]; 70p.
London: David Rutherford, [ca. 1760].
London: John Rutherford, [ca. 1775].
London: S. A. and P. Thompson, [ca. 1785].

This elementary music instruction book presented as a teacher-pupil dialogue uses a contrived minuet and jigg to illustrate elements of pitch,

rhythm, and meter. To compare various triple meters, Crome shows the
original 3/4 time minuet tune successively in 3/8, 6/8, and 6/4. Scholar:
"I see these mark'd 6/4 and 6/8 have two bars in one." Master: "Yes,
they have double the quantity of the 3/8 and in minuets for dancing they
generally beat every other bar of single time or 3 units in a bar. . . ."
Simple bowing and articulation rules include slurring eighth notes in
twos or threes in Jiggs. The lessons (pp. 64-70) include 6 Minuets, 3
Jiggs, and a Gavotte.

45 CUPIS, François (1732-1808)

*Méthode nouvelle et raisonnée pour apprendre à jouer du violon-
celle où l'on traite de la manière de l'accorder, de placer cet
instrument et de tenir l'archet, de la position de la main sur la
touche, du tact, de l'étendue du manche, du doigter dans tous les
modes majeurs et mineurs, du tirer et du pousser, avec un nombre
de leçons, romances, ariettes et menuets variés, etc.*
*Paris: Le Menu, aux adresses ordinaires, [1772]; 43p.

   Facs. reprint, Bologna: Forni, 1974. Misattributed to Cupis'
   brother.

Although this 'cello method was influential in the late 18th and early
19th c., it has less relevance for French dance music than Corrette's.
Scales and intervals are emphasized; musical examples show possibilities for bowing and articulation. The 35 exercises include several minuets.

46 D'ALEMBERT, Jean le Rond (1717-1783)

*Élémens de musique théorique et pratique, suivant les principes
de M. Rameau.*
Paris: David l'aîné, Le Breton, Durand, 1752; xvi+171p.
   Facs. reprint, New York: Broude Bros., 1966 (MMMLF, 19).
Paris: Charles-Antoine Jombert; Lyon: Jean-Marie Bruysset,
1759.
Lyon: Jean-Marie Bruysset, 1762; xxxvi+236p.
Lyon: Jean-Marie Bruysset, 1766; xxxvi+236p.
Lyon: Jean-Marie Bruysset, 1772; xxxvi+236p.
*Lyon: Jean-Marie Bruysset père et fils, 1779; xxxvi+236p.
German transl. by F. W. Marpurg as *Systematische Einleitung in*

die musikalische Setzkunst, nach den Lehrsätzen des Herrn Rameau. Leipzig: Johann Gottlob Immanuel Breitkopf, 1757; 136p.

Book 2, ch. 16 (pp. 2C°-10 in the 1779 ed.) offers the composition student very brief description of the character of various airs given special names: Chaconne, Vilanelle, Passacaille, Menuet, Sarabande, Courante, Passepied, Loure, Gigue, Forlane, Rigaudon, Bourrée, Gavotte, Tambourin, Musette. Tempos are indicated relative to one another, e.g. the courante is considered to be a slow sarabande.

47 DANOVILLE (fl. 1687)

L'art de toucher le dessus et basse de violle, contenant tout ce qu'il y a de nécessaire, d'utile, et de curieux dans cette science. Avec des principes, des règles et observations si intelligibles, qu'on peut acquérir la perfection de cette belle science en peu de temps, et mesme sans le secour d'aucun maistre.
*Paris: Christophe Ballard, 1687; 47p.
Facs. reprint, Genève: Minkoff, 1972.

This method book for viol playing in some ways supplements the *Traité* of Jean Rousseau (q.v.). Its first 3 parts on elementary technique cover bowing, scales, fingering, clefs, tablature, notation, and tuning. The fourth part purports to illustrate all ornaments practical for the instrument, including Tremblement, Supposition, Battement, Pincé, Port de voix, Coulé de doigt, Balancement de main, and Couché du doigt.

48 DARD (fl. 1761-1779)

Nouveaux principes de musique, qui seuls doivent suffire pour l'apprendre parfaitement. Auxquels l'auteur à joint l'histoire de la musique et de ses progressions, depuis son origine jusqu'à présent dédiés à M. Duvaucel.
*Paris: auteur, gravés par Melle. Girard, [1769]; 149+19p.
Paris: auteur, [s.d.]; 149+19p. *Nouveaux principes de musique suffisant pour. . . .*

Fundamentals are treated in more than usual detail in this introduction to music by a little known bassoonist. Remarks on clefs indicate which of several F, G, and C clefs are appropriate to individual vocal and instrumental parts. The discussion of meters includes the signatures 2/16, 4/16, 6/16, 3/16, and 12/8 in addition to the more common ones. For each signature, Dard indicates which notes are to be played *inégales,* including 64th notes in 2/16 meter, etc. The ornaments described include Cadence (appuyée, subite ou jettée, brisée, double, molle), Coulé, Port de voix, Accent, Tremblement d'orgue (for voice, strings, or winds), Martellement. The lessons (pp. 32-147) include an Allemande, 2 Gavottas, 3 Gigues, 8 Minuettos, 1 Polonoise, 1 Siciliana, and 2 Tambourins, either solo or duet. A collection of *petites ariettes* (p. 149 and the additional 19 pages), songs with flute or violin accompaniment, include a Musette and a Barcarolle.

49 DAUBE, Johann Friedrich (ca. 1730-1797)

Anleitung zur Erfindung der Melodie und ihrer Fortsetzung.
*Wien: Christian Gottlob Täubel, 1797-98; 2 v., 51p., 68p.
Wien: J. Funk, 1798; 2 v., 51p., 68p.
Wien: Schaumburg in Kommission, 1798; 2 v., 51p., 68p. Entitled *Anleitung zum Selbstunterricht in der musikalischen Komposition sowohl für die Instrumental- als Vocal-Musik.*
Wien: Binz, 1798; 2 v., 51p., 68p.
Linz: Commission der Akademischen Buchhandlung, 1798.

This treatise derives its theory of melody (treating melodic construction, extension, and phrasing) from music other than that influenced by French Classicism. It is nevertheless noteworthy here owing to its naive affirmation of regular (symmetrical) phrasing as the only correct phrasing, especially in dance music. Daube declares on p. 38 that only ignorance of regular 2-plus-2 and 4-plus-4 phrasing produced so many undanceable minuets with irregular phrasing, such as those in symphonies.

50 DAVID, François

Méthode nouvelle ou principes généraux pour apprendre facilement la musique, et l'art de chanter.
*Paris: Boivin, Le Clerc; Lyon: Desbretonnes, auteur, 1737; 142p.
*Paris: de la Chevardière; Lyon: les frères le Goux, [1763]; 142p.

This elementary singing manual has a brief but informative section (pp. 131-36) on vocal ornamentation. David comments not only upon the vocal technique required to produce the specific ornament, but on its timing and rhythm. The appropriate melodic context is also described. Ornaments so discussed and presented in musical examples include the Cadence (preparée, coulée, jettée, subite, par redoublement, etc.), Port de voix (préparé, doublé, par intervalle en descendant), Coulé, Accent, Pincé, Plainte, Frémissement, etc. (Several of the so-called ornaments are actually compounds described as expressing specific feelings.) A list indicating the general tempo and meter of various characteristic airs includes the Ouverture or Prélude, Gavotte, Bourrée, Branle, Rigaudon, Forlana; Sarabande, Passacaille, Courante; Menuet, Chaconne; Gigue; Loure; Canarie, Passepied; Alemande; Marche.

51 DELAIR, Étienne Denis (d. after 1727)

Traité d'accompagnement pour le théorbe, et le clavessin. Qui comprend toutes les règles nécessaires, pour acompagner sur ces deux instrumens. Avec des observations particulières touchant les différentes manières qui leurs conviennent. Il enseigne aussi à accompagner les basses qui ne sont pas chifrées.
*Paris: auteur, 1690; 61p.
   Facs. reprint, Genève: Minkoff, 1972.
Paris: auteur, Boivin, [1724]; [24]+72p. *Nouveau traité. . . .*

Considered to be one of the best French accompaniment methods before Saint-Lambert's *Nouveau traité* (q.v.), Delair's is a treatise on harmony with emphasis on the irregular resolution of dissonance. He provides an introduction to both theorbo and harpsichord. Other sections treat modulation and transposition, figural (i.e. florid) bass lines, and accompanying from an unfigured bass. The 1724 ed. has several supplementary sections and additions, mainly rules of harmony.

52 DENIS, Claude (late 17th c.-ca. 1752)

Nouvelle méthode pour apprendre en peu de tems la musique et l'art de chanter, avec un nombre de leçons dans plusieurs genres . . . deuxième édition revüe et corrigée.
Paris: Le Clerc, [1757]; 70p.
*Paris: de la Chevardière, [1759]; 72p.

Treatment of the rudiments of music is brief and rather simplified, but the descriptions of meters indicate dances to which each metric sign is appropriate: 3 is exemplified by the Passacaille, Sarabande, and "Aimable vaincoeur" from Lully's *Hesione* (a loure); 3/2 by the slow Passacaille and Sarabande; 3/4 by the Chaconne and Menuet. Note values to be played unequally are indicated. Ornamentation receives only brief treatment without examples; Denis defines the Cadence (preparée, feinte, subite), Coulé de tièrce, Port de voix, Martellement, and Accent. The lessons (which take up 50 of the 70 pages), all for one voice, include 1 Bourrée, 2 Canaries, 1 Chaconne, 3 Courantes, 1 Fanfare, 1 Forlane, 3 Gavottes (1 en musette), 9 Gigues, 3 Loures, 3 Marches, 5 Menuets, 1 Musette, 3 Passepieds, 7 Preludes, 1 Rigaudon, 3 Sarabandes, 1 Sauterelle, and 5 Tambourins.

53 DENIS, Jean (ca. 1600-1672)

Traitté de l'accord de l'épinette, avec la comparaison du clavier d'icelle, à la musique vocalle.
Paris: 1643; 24p.
*Paris: Robert Ballard, 1650; 40p. *Traité de l'accord de l'espinette, avec la comparaison de son clavier à la musique vocale. Augmenté en cette édition des quatre chapitres suivants. I. Traité des sons et combien il y en a. II. Traité des tons de l'église et de leurs estenduës. III. Traité des fugues et comme il les faut traiter. IV. La manière de bien jouër de l'espinette et des orgues. Dédié à Monseigneur le Marquis de Mortemart.*
  *Facs. reprint, New York: Da Capo Press, 1969. Introduction by Alan Curtis.

Denis defends meantone temperament for keyboard instruments (organ and harpsichords of all types) against the newly favored tempered tuning. The last two chapters (1650 ed.) treat keyboard technique. Like Couperin later on, Denis recommends a hand position with the wrist level and the use of stronger fingers for trills. Comments on fingering extend to the fingering of cadential trills and the use of the thumbs. He discusses three types of ornaments (Pincements, Fredons, Cadences parfaites). In passages of four notes of equal value, he suggests playing Pincements on only two notes (1 and 3, or 2 and 4) to avoid melodic confusion. While there are no musical examples, he seems to describe an inverted mordent (Pincement au dessus) to be used in descending passages.

54 DENIS, Pierre (early 18th c.-after 1777)

*Méthode pour apprendre à jouer de la mandoline sans maître,
avec six caprices.*
*Paris: auteur, [1768]; 23p.
   Facs. reprint, Genève: Minkoff, 1982.
Paris: Boyer, [1792]; 53p.
*Seconde partie de la méthode pour apprendre à jouer de la man-
doline sans maître, avec des variations sur douze petits airs de la
comédie italienne, et six menuets pour danser, six allemandes et
un prélude d'arpegio sur chaque ton de musique.* Paris: auteur,
[1769]; 29p.
   Facs. reprint, Genève: Minkoff, 1982.

As an introduction to mandoline technique for trained amateur violinists,
this is less detailed and well-ordered than Leone's mandolin treatise
(q.v.). It is notable here only for its inclusion of several Allemandes in
2/4 meter (pp. 12-15).

55 DESPRÉAUX, Louis Félix (1746-1813)

*Cours d'éducation de clavecin, ou pianoforte. Seconde partie
contenant les principes du doigté de clavecin suivis de 50. leçons
composées de musettes, menuets, contredanses, allemandes, tambourins, airs de balets et ouvertures d'opéras, etc. le tout ar-
rangé d'une difficulté graduelle par L. Félix Despréaux.*
*Paris: Le Duc, [ca. 1785]; 59p.
2nd ed. Paris: Le Duc, [s.d.]; 53p.
*Paris: Naderman, [ca. 1800]; 59p.

The modern keyboard fingering taught in Despréaux's piano method
makes the thumb equal to other fingers. Trill-fingering exercises show
only the trill beginning on the upper auxiliary. The lessons are noteworthy for their inclusion of older dance types, especially Allemandes in 2/4
meter with drone-like basses (numbers 4 and 14) and dances from operas
by Grétry and Gluck. Among these are 2 Allemandes (numbers 4 and
14), a Contredanse in 6/8 (20), a Fanfare (35), a Gavotte from *Iphigénie
en Tauride* (28), a Marche (32), 7 Menuets (2, 10, 12 [Grétry], 15, 25
[d'*Iphigénie*], 41 [Gluck, *Alceste*], 43), a Musette (1), 4 Tambourins
(22, 45, 46, 47), and a Valzer (30).

56 DREWIS, F. G.
Freundschaftliche Briefe über die Theorie der Tonkunst und Composition.
*Halle: J. C. Hendel, 1797; 88p.

Letters by a self-proclaimed dilettante respond to the wish of a "liebe Freundin" for musical instruction. Drewis relies primarily on German theoretical literature, with references to Reichardt, Türk, Marpurg, Kirnberger, and Sulzer (i.e. Schulz). The sixth letter, on the composer's need to take account of the character and genre of both the poetic text and its musical setting, treats selected dance types (pp. 65-68). The Polonaise, Menuet, and Marsch are described in detail with reference to character, appropriate instrumentation and texture, internal modulation, length of sections, placement of caesuras, and rhythmic activity of the melody as contrasted with that of the bass.

57 DUPONT, Pierre (d. 1740)
Principes de musique par demandes et par réponçes avec de petits exemples.
*Paris: Ch. Ballard, 1713; 73p.
Principes de musique, par demande et par réponçe, par lequel toutes personnes, pouront aprendre d'eux même à connoître toutte la musique. *Paris: auteur, Boivin, Le Clerc, 1718; 48p.
Paris: auteur, Foucault, 1718; 46p.
Principes de musique, par demandes et par réponçes, avec différents exemples, tirez des meilleurs auteurs, à l'usage des enfans.
Paris: J. B. C. Ballard, 1719; 81p.
Principes de musique . . . par lequel toutes personnes . . . la musique. Paris: auteur, veuve Boivin, Le Clerc, 1740; 46p.

This introduction to music in dialogue form comments on the character implied by metric signatures, using dance types to define each. A gavotte with the signature 2 is to be sung graciously; a 6/4 loure must be sung gravely, but a 6/4 gigue must be light and quick. In certain situations signatures may indicate faster tempo, especially 2/4 and 6/8. Courantes in 3/2 are played very gravely, detaching quarter notes. Dupont indicates *notes inégales* for some meters, e.g. in 3 time eighth notes are played unequally. Suggested articulation contrasts strikingly with later 18th-c. recommendations. In gigues, canaries, and 6/8 meter in general, dotted eighth notes are stressed while sixteenth notes are passed

over lightly; series of eighth notes must be played detached or even
staccato in 9/8, 6/8, and 3/8 meter. (Many later treatises recommend
slurring such eighth notes.) A table of ornaments appears without commentary. Questions of absolute tempo are answered with reference to
the ringing of a typical church bell.

58 DUPONT, Pierre (d. 1740)

*Principes de violon par demandes et par réponçe par le quel
toutes personne, pouront aprendre d'eux mêmes à jouer du dit
instrument.*
*Paris: auteur, Foucault, 1718; 15p.
Paris: auteur, Boivin, Le Clerc, 1740; 18p.

Pages 6-8 of this violin tutor explain in words and complete examples
how to bow a Prélude, Sarabande, Bourée, Paspied, Menuet, Rigodon,
Musette, Gigue or Canarie, and Entrée. The bowing adheres to the rule
of downbow on every downbeat, resulting in successive downbows at
times. The examples are useful for articulation suggestions as well; notable are the eighth notes slurred in pairs in the musette.

59 DUPUIT, Jean Baptiste (fl. 1741-1757)

*Principes pour toucher de la viele avec six sonates pour cet in-
strument qui conviennent aux violon, flûtes, clavessin, etc. . . .
Oeuvre I.*
*Paris: auteur, Mme Boivin, Le Clerc, [1741]; xi+35p.
Facs. reprint, Genève: Minkoff, 1984.

Dupuit is considered to be one of the most capable advocates of the
pastoral style cultivated in middle and upper class circles of Louis XV's
time. His method for the hurdy-gurdy is probably the best 18th-c. technical manual for this instrument. In addition, it treats ornamentation and
the interpretation of music of a pastoral character. Ornaments include
Cadences (pincé, liée, apuiée, double, fermée), Port de voix, and
Couler. He recommends playing a 16th-note rest before and sometimes
after an ornament, playing legato unless another manner is indicated.
Wrist motions and wheel technique depend upon meter, prevailing note
values, and the character of the piece; the tambourin and musette have
special instructions. On page x, the author discusses proper articulation
and other performance details for each of the demonstration pieces,

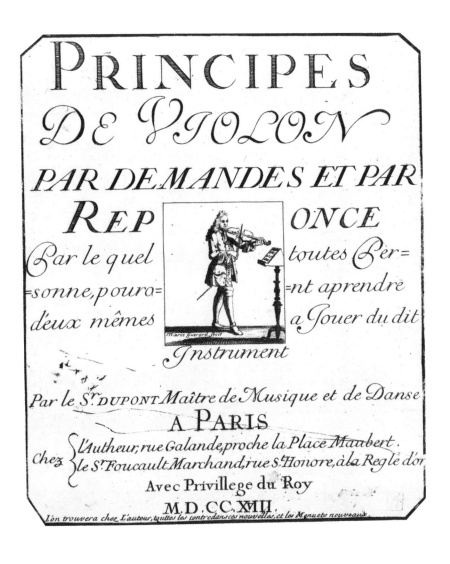

II-58 Pierre DUPONT, *Principes du violon par demandes et par reponçes* (Paris: auteur, Foucault, 1718). The title page shows a violinist and advertises new contredanses and minuets available from the author. [Chicago, The Newberry Library, Case 5A-208]

II-58 Pierre DUPONT, *Principes du violon par demandes et par re-*
ponçes (Paris: auteur, Foucault, 1718), pp. 6-7. Examples with text for
bowing a prelude, sarabande, bourrée, passepied, minuet, rigaudon, musette, gigue or canarie, and entrée. [Chicago, The Newberry Library, Case
5A-208]

130

Explication du coup d'archet, du Menuet.

D Qu'elle remarque faite vous du coup d'archet du Menuet.

R Lorsqu'il y a vne blanche et vne noire, dans vne mesure, il faut tirer la blanche et pousser la noire et lorsqu'il y a 2. croches entre 2. noires, il les faut pousser toutes 2. lorsqu'il y a 3. noires, il faut tirer la pre et pousser les 2. autres. lorsqu'il y a vne noires et 4. croches, il faut tirer la noire et pousser les 2. pre croches.

D Que signifie ces petites + qui sont audessus des notes

R C'est le signe de la cadanse, ou tremblement, voyez mon Livre de principe de Musique, page 24.

Explication du coup d'archet, du Rigôdon.

D Qu'elle remarque faite vous du coup d'archet, du Rigôdon.

R Je remarque que c'est le même que celuy de la Bourée, excepté que lors qu'il est marqué par un 4. et 8. l'on joüe les croches du Rigôdon, comme les noires de la Bourée et les doubles croches a proportion

D Quel est le gout du Rigôdon.

R Voyez mon Livre de principe de Musique, page 37.

Explication du coup d'archet, de l'air de Musette.

D Quel est le coup d'archet, de l'air de Musette.

R Le petit croissant qui lie les 2. pre croches vous avertit de faire le mi et le fa, du même coup d'archet ainsi des autres et l'on détache les noires, en tirant et poussant alternativem't si le t. et le p. ne vous marque le contraire, par les raisons que vous avons dite sidevant, sur tout jouez tendrement les Musettes.

D Ne doit on pas scavoir bâtre la mesure de tout les airs que l'on joüe

R Ouy et ceux qui voudrons scavoir les principes a font comme il doivent, car ons recoirs côme j'ay dit au Livre de principe, ou je traite de tout emplement, j'antant que ceux qui aprênent a chanter doivent marquer les temps avec la main, et ceux qui aprênent a jouer la marque avec le pied.

Menuet.

Rigôdon.

Musette rôdeau.

which include an Allemande, 2 Badines en rondeau, 1 Corrente, 1 Giga, 2 Minuettos, 2 Pastorellas (gavottes?), 1 Siciliena, and 2 Tambourins.

60 DURIEU

Nouvelle méthode de musique vocale; concernant les principes de cet art, démontré par des leçons, et accompagné d'examples qui en applanissent toutes les difficultés. Adoptée par l'Institut National de Musique, Chant et Declamation. Dediée au Citoyen Gossec, et aux professeurs ses collègues, par le Citoyen Durieu. *Paris: auteur, [1793]; 107p.

While the style taught in this singing manual is more nearly Italian than French, the section on ornaments is of interest for its attempt to describe the dynamic inflection of typical embellishments. Article 15 (pp. 59-65) provides concise descriptions with clear examples and realizations for the Port de voix, Accent, Notes de goût, Cadences (préparée, subite ou non préparée, feinte, double), Aspiration, and Martellement. Dynamic indications show that the Accent may be heard as the extension of a Son filé (decrescendo), and that *notes de goût* (passing appoggiaturas) should be part of decrescendos encompassing the surrounding main notes. (That this may reflect only late 18th-c. practice must be considered; Durieu's chief example of the trill begins without an upper auxiliary.)

61 DUVAL, Pierre (d. 1781)

Principes de la musique pratique par demandes et par réponses. *Paris: Cailleau, veuve Valeyre, 1764; 66p.

This concise elementary instruction manual provides some exceptional detail in areas of performance practice customarily vague in 18th-c. musical tutors, notably the use of *notes inégales* and triplets. Article 19 defines the triplet, then explains its use as a substitution for a pair of unequal notes, strongly implying that the long-short relation of the *notes inégales* is as 2:1, corresponding to the triplet rhythm. On p. 43 Duval says that notes meant to be an exception to the rule of unequal notes bear either verbal instructions or dots or strokes above them to indicate their rhythmic equality. On p. 52 he formulates a rule governing the use of unequal notes in various meters, to the effect that all notes of value smaller than that indicated by the lower number in the metric signature must be played unequally, except in 2/4 and 3/4, in which only the 16th and 32nd notes are unequal. Article 23, pp. 53-56, treats ornaments, with brief but articulate definitions and examples, including Martellement, Port de voix (ordinaire, feinte), Coulé, Accent, Son filé, and Cadence (préparée, subite, doublée, feinte).

62 ENGRAMELLE, Marie Dominique Joseph (1727-1805)
La tonotechnie ou l'art de noter les cylindres, et tout ce qui est susceptible de notage dans les instrumens de concerts méchaniques. Ouvrage nouveau, par le père Engramelle, religieux augustin de la Reine Marguerite.
Paris: P. M. Delaguette, 1775; xxviii+236p.+5pl.
*Facs. reprint, Genève: Minkoff, 1971.

Engramelle's description of his new means for determining stud placement on the barrels of mechanical musical instruments provides extraordinary information on musical performance practice among conservative French musicians of the later 18th century. By way of presenting his special notation signs (ch. 3-4, pp. 15-61), he discusses in detail the fine distinctions in articulation, rhythm, and ornament to which the musical mechanic must be alert. A table of notation signs (pp. 43-50) distinguishes between 8 degrees of note articulation (note duration plus silence of articulation), 12 types of Martellement, 4 Ports de voix, 4 Accents, 2 Coulés, 4 Flattées, 4 Pincées, and 26 varieties of Cadence. This and the detailed discussion of specially notated examples in plates 3, 4, and 5 (ch. 24-25, pp. 207-36) provide evidence for fluctuating tempos and retards; the prevalence of detached articulation, with subtle gradations of detachment; variable proportion for the inequality of *notes inégales,* ranging from 3:1 to 9:7; accelerating trills; and on-the-beat performance of appoggiaturas, short and long. The 12 examples include La Marche du Roy (with a variation), Badine d'Alarius (gigue), Menuet de Zelindor, Romance, Menuet, Le Bucheron (gavotte), La Fontaine de Jouvence (gavotte), Allemande (2/4 meter), Marche, Menuet du Roy de Prusse, and Les Portraits à la Mode (gigue).

Further description of Engramelle's system occurs in Dom François Bédos de Celles, *L'art du facteur d'orgues, quatrième partie* (Paris: L. F. Delatour, 1778); plate 119 contains elaborate tabular notation for a movement from a sonata by Claude Balbastre, there entitled Romance (actually a gavotte en rondeau). This plate appears in facsimile in Hans Peter Schmitz, *Die Kunst der Verzierung im 18. Jahrhundert* (Kassel: Bärenreiter, 1965) and in David Fuller, *Mechanical musical instruments as a source for the study of notes inégales* (Cleveland, OH: Divisions,

⸬ *Tenue simple*, suivie d'un silence de cinq doubles croches ; (elle ne peut convenir qu'aux rondes & aux blanches pour les reprises d'haleine).

Quant aux autres *silences*, on emploiera ceux usités dans la musique, ou bien l'on augmentera le nombre de points pour chaque valeur de doubles croches.

TENUES COMPOSÉES.

MARTELLEMENS.

ᚼ Martellement simple de deux *modules*, du dessus au-dessous, avec une petite *tenue* à fin.

↘ Martellement simple de deux *modules*, du dessous au-dessus, avec une petite *tenue* à la fin.

Λ Martellement de trois *modules*, cadencé avec la note de dessus, & une petite *tenue* à la fin.

V Martellement de trois *modules*, cadencé avec la note de dessous, & une petite *tenue* à la fin.

↘— Martellement d'un *module* & une grande *tenue* à la fin, cadencé du dessus au-dessous.

II-62 Marie Dominique Joseph ENGRAMELLE, *La tonotechnie ou l'art de noter les cylindres* (Paris: P. M. Delaguette, 1775), p. 44. Explanatory table of characters used to notate embellishments in detail. [Chicago, The Newberry Library, V7.266]

II-62 Marie Dominique Joseph ENGRAMELLE, *La tonotechnie ou l'art de noter les cylindres* (Paris: P. M. Delaguette, 1775), plate V. Dance tunes with special notation to indicate details of embellishment and articulation. [Chicago, The Newberry Library, V7.266]

1979), which also includes a computer generated sound recording made from Engramelle's notation.

63 FOUCHETTI, Giovanni or Jean FOUQUET (fl. 1788)

Méthode pour apprendre facilement à jouer de la mandoline à 4 et à 6 cordes dans la quelle on explique les différents coups de plume nécessaire pour cet instrument. On y a joint six sérénades et six petites sonates.

*Paris: adresses ordinaires; Lyon: Castaud, [ca. 1770-80]; 18+15p.

Facs. reprint, Genève: Minkoff, 1982.

The 18-p. introduction to mandoline playing covers tuning, strings, manner of using the pick, conventional use of tremolo on long notes (half or whole notes), and pick technique for ornaments. Several observations have implications for performance practice in general. Fouchetti's assertion that appoggiaturas (coulés) cannot be played on the mandoline and must therefore be written out as *notes de valeur* suggests that the slurring of an appoggiatura to its note of resolution was an important component of the ornament. Trills, according to his description, always begin with the upper auxiliary, accelerate gradually, and then pause briefly (an eighth to a quarter of the written value) on the principal note before moving on to the next note. The tremolo on long notes is supposed to last only one-half to three-quarters of the value of the note. The 15 pages of duets include 5 Allemandes, 6 Marches, and 7 Minuetti, the last one with 3 variations.

64 FRAMERY, Nicolas Étienne (1745-1810), Pierre Louis GIN-GUENÉ (1748-1816), and Jérôme Joseph de MOMIGNY (1762-1842)

Encyclopédie méthodique. Musique.

V. 1 ed. by Framery and Ginguené. Paris: Panckoucke, 1791; 760p.

V. 2 ed. by Framery, Ginguené, and Momigny; Paris: veuve Agasse, 1818; 558+74+114p.

*Facs. reprint, New York: Da Capo Press, 1971.

Facs. reprint, Genève: Minkoff, 1984.

Part of a large general encyclopaedia, these volumes on music are based on articles by J. J. Rousseau taken from his dictionary or from the Diderot-D'Alembert encyclopedia (q.v.). For most subjects, additional commentary appears, signed either by Framery, Ginguené, or Abbé Feytou (v. 1) or Momigny (v. 2). Dance related items include Allemande, Angloise, Ballet, Ballet-Opéra, Bergamasque, Bourdon, Bourrée, Camergo, Chaconne, Contredanse, Cotillon, Courante, Divertissement, Ecossoise, Entrée, Fandango, Fanfare, Folies d'Espagne, Forlane, Gaillarde, Gavotte, Gigue, Loure, Marche, Menuet, Musette, Passacaille, Passe-pied, Pavane, Prélude, Rigaudon, Rondeau, Saltarella, Sarabande, Suite (especially Handel's, describing the Prélude, Allemande, Courante, and Gigue), and Volte. The second musical supplement contains part of the Marche des Mousquetaires du Roi de France (p. 106) to illustrate the article Marche.

French ornamentation practice is described in the articles Accent, Accent double, Acciacatura, Accolades, Agréments du chant, Appuyé, Balancement, Battement, Batterie, Broderie, Cadence, Chevrotter, Chûte, Coulé, Détaché, Double, Filer, Flatté, Fredon, Fusée, Liées, Lourer, Martellement, Pincé, Pointer (notes inégales), Port de voix, Roulade, Tirade, Tremblement, and Variation. The first musical supplement contains realized notated examples of the Accent, Cadence pleine, Cadence brisée, Coulé, Martellement, Flatté, and Port de voix (p. 5), as well as various Chûtes (p. 38).

Items pertaining to instruments include Basse de viole, Castagnettes, Clavecin, Cor et cor-de-chasse, Cornets (organ stop), Flûte, Forte-Piano, Guittare, Harpe, Hautbois, Loure, Luth, Mandoline, Mandore, Piano, Poche, Ravalement, Serpent, Tambour, Tambourin, Tropette, Viole, Violon, Violoncelle, Voix. The first musical supplement shows the ranges of voices and instruments (pp. 64-65).

Other articles relevant to performance include Accent (rhetorical and musical), Accompagnement figuré, Basse fondamentale, Basse continue, Bâton de mesure, Battre la mesure, Chiffre (with table of bass figures), Choeur (petit-choeur), Chronomètre, Doigter (fingering), Goût, Goût du chant, Maître de musique, Orchestre, and Tempérament. French tempo and character markings are distinguished from Italian counterparts in the entries for Gaiment, Gracieusement, Gravement, Légèrement, Lentement, Vite, etc.

65 FRANCOEUR, Louis Joseph (1738-1804)

Diapason général de tous les instrumens à vent avec des observations sur chacun d'eux. Auquel on a joint un projet nouveau pour

simplifier la manière actuelle de copier.
Paris: Le Marchand, [1772]; 85p.
  Facs. reprint, Genève: Minkoff, 1972.
*Paris: Des Lauriers, [ca. 1782]; 83p.

Best known as a conductor and arranger for the Paris opera orchestra under Louis XVI and after the revolution, Francoeur revealed his technical expertise in this instrumental guide for composers and arrangers. Chapters treat respectively flutes (flute, piccolo, recorder, fife), oboe, clarinets (G, A, B^b, B, C, D, E, F), natural horns (C, D, E^b, E, F, G, A, B^b, B), bassoon, and trumpet. For each he indicates ranges, the character of each portion of the range, the best or most characteristic tones for the instrument, difficult trills, notes or progressions to avoid in fast passage work owing to their difficulty, and intervals especially easy or hard to play as leaps. Appropriate transposition for clarinet and horn is explained. Francoeur distinguishes the high solo horn range (with lipped notes) from the low or accompanimental second horn range, with examples of different kinds of horn writing.

66 FREILLON-PONCEIN, Jean Pierre

La véritable manière d'apprendre à jouer en perfection du hautbois, de la flûte et du flageolet, avec les principes de la musique pour la voix et pour toutes sortes d'instrumens.
Paris: J. Collombat, 1700; 74p.
  *Facs. reprint, Genève: Minkoff, 1974.
English transl. by Catherine P. Smith as *The true way to learn to play perfectly the oboe, recorder, and the flageolet.* Brooklyn, NY: The Translation Center, Brooklyn College, 1969; xi+115p.

This oboe and flute (recorder) tutor emphasizes tonguing, using the syllables "tu-ru." Tu-ru patterns suitable in each meter appear with musical illustration. The author singles out the typical minuet rhythm of four eighth notes plus a quarter note for a special articulation pattern: tu-tu ru-tu ru. A section on tonguing ornaments treats the Port de voix, Accent, Battemen or Pincé, and Cadence (parfaite, imparfaite, rompuë). A number of preludes for oboe and for recorder appear on pp. 29-38. Instructions for trills are given on pp. 39-47. A unique feature is the section on learning to compose characteristic pieces, pp. 54-64. There are brief instructions, chiefly concerning rhythmic and metric details, for composing Ouvertures, Gigues, Canaries, Chaconnes, Passacailles,

Sarabandes, Menuets, Passepiez, Rigaudons, Bourées, Gavottes, Courantes, and Folies d'Espagne. A suite entitled *Bruits de guerre* contains minuets and a passecaille scored for wind, string, and drum ensemble.

67 GERVAIS, Laurent (fl. 1725-1745)

Méthode pour l'accompagnement du clavecin, qui peut servir d'introduction à la composition et apprendre à bien chiffrer les basses.
Paris: veuve Boivin, [1733]; 28p.
  *Facs. reprint, Bologna: Arnaldo Forni, 1970.

Gervais captured the lightness, charm, and grace of the Louis XV era in his music, largely chamber cantatas. His method for accompaniment at the keyboard deals mainly with thorough-bass, but a section on other aspects of accompaniment distinguishes between the lively and the gracious styles of accompaniment, the former characterized by full harmony and sharp attack, the latter by arpeggiated chords and softer effects.

68 GRASSINEAU, James (ca.1715-1767)

A musical dictionary; being a collection of terms and characters, as well ancient as modern; including the historical, theoretical, and practical parts of music: as also, an explanation of some parts of the doctrine of the antients; interspersed with remarks on their method and practice, and curious observations on the phoenomena of sound mathematically considered, as it's [sic] relations and proportions constitute intervals, and those again concords and discords. The whole carefully abstracted from the best authors in the Greek, Latin, Italian, French, and English languages.
London: J. Wilcox, 1740; xii+348p.
  *Facs. reprint, New York: Broude Bros., 1966 (MMMLF 40).
London: J. Robson, 1769; xii+347+52p. Entitled *A musical dictionary: containing a full explanation of all the terms made use of in . . . music: also explanations of the doctrines of ancient music, and . . . inquiries into the nature of sound . . . together with a full description of all the various kinds of musical instru-*

139

ments . . . abstracted from the best authors in the Greek, Latin, Italian, French, and English languages . . . new edition, to which is added an appendix, selected from the Dictionnaire de musique of M. Rousseau.

This was the most important British dictionary of music before the English transl. of Rousseau's (ca. 1779). Long considered a mere transl. of Brossard's dictionary, Grassineau's is actually a revision of it, enlarged with new articles and added information. The additional material may derive from Ephraim Chambers' *Cyclopaedia* (London, 1728, etc.) or from *A short explication of such foreign words, as are made use of in musick books* (London: J. Brotherton, 1724; possibly by Dr. J. C. Pepusch, Grassineau's sometime employer, from whom Hawkins, in his *General History* [q.v.], p. 30, says Grassineau obtained the information). It is in turn identical to the glossary of the anonymous *Rules; or a short and compleat method* (q.v.). The 1769 ed. of Grassineau's work is a posthumous reissue with anonymously edited articles translated from Rousseau's dictionary (q.v.).

Among dance related entries, Grassineau adds Burre/Bouree/Boree, Pavan, Rigadoon, and Rondeau to those already represented in Brossard (Allemand, Chacone, Balletto, Corrente/Courant/Currant, Forlana, Galliard/Galliarda, Gavotta/Gavotte, Tempi di gavotta, Giga/Gigue, Jigg, Mascharada/Masquerade, Minuet/Menuet, Passepied, Passacaglio, Pastoral, Prelude, Saltarello, Sarabande, Sicilian, Sonata da camera, and Volta).

Relevant to performance practice are entries for Appoggiatura, Port de voix, Prelude, Quavering, Repeat (signs), Trillo, Tremolo, and Variation. The article Harpsichord contains an essay on playing, with explication of ornaments including the Shake, Beat, Forefall, Backfall, Plain note and shake, Turn, and Shake turned. The article Singing illustrates an accelerating trill and describes its melodic usage. Musical instruments entered include the Bagpipe, Bassoon, Bass violin, Bell, Bombarda, Bridge (of string instruments, including lute and harpsichord), Castanets, Clarichord (sic), Clarino, Clarion, Cornet, Cornettino, Curtail, Cymbal, Drum, Dulcimer, Fagottino, Fagotto, Fife, Flageolet, Flute, Guitarra, Harp, Harpsichord, Hautboy, Lute, Manichord, Octavina, Organ, Posaune, Sacbut, Serpent, Spinette, Soundboard (organ), Tabor, Theorbo, Trumpet, Tympanum, Viola, Viola da gamba (etc.), Violin, Violoncello, and Violone. ("The style and sound of the violin is the gayest, most lively, and sprightly of all instruments; and hence it is of all others the fittest for dancing" [p. 327].)

69 HAWKINS, John (1719-1789)

A general history of the science and practice of music.
London: T. Payne and Son, 1776; 5 v., lxxxiv+465, 544, 535, 548, 482p.
London: J. Alfred Novello, 1853; 2 v., xlii+967p. With author's emendations drawn from posthumous notes in his own copy.
  *Facs. reprint, New York: Dover, 1963; 2 v. with introduction by Charles Cudworth.
London: J. Alfred Novello, 1875. Reprint of the 1853 ed.
  Facs. reprint, Graz: Akademische Druck- und Verlagsanstalt, 1969. Ed. by Othmar Wessely.

Book 16, ch. 148 (pp. 703-5 in the 1853 ed.) describes as "old [suite dance] airs" the Passamezzo, Galliard, Allemand, Coranto, Chacone, Passacaglio, and Jigg. The "airs of the moderns" include the Gavot, Minuet, Paspy/Passe-pied, Bourée, Siciliana, Louvre (i.e. *L'aimable vaincoeur),* Hornpipe, Canaries, Trenchmore, and Country-Dance. Each term stimulates erudite inquiry into etymology and origin of the dance type. Hawkins describes the musical structure with reference to its strains, number of measures, rhythm of the upbeat, and type of medial cadence, referring to authorities both musical and linguistic (e.g. Furetière), as well as to representative examples in the works of Handel, Lully, Vivaldi, et al. In the appendix of musical examples, an example of a Trenchmore appears as number 14. Examples in the text include a Hornpipe by Ravenscroft (p. 894), Allemande by F. Couperin (p. 780), and Allemande by T. Baltzar (p. 682), as well as a Coranto and Moresca.
   References to dancers and dancing appear in the 1853 ed. on pp. 853 (an anecdote about Harry Bishop, English dancing master to the French queen), 685 (concerning French dancers in English theatrical productions; see the footnote), and 936 (musical example appendix number 27, Mademoiselle Subligny's Minuet, with a biographical note on her career in England).
   Hawkins' history is famous for its summaries and extensive translations into English of portions of early treatises on music. Relevant treatises summarized or exerpted include Bonnet's *Histoire de la musique et de ses effets* (pp. 832ff.), Raguenet's *Parallèles* and Le Cerf de la Viéville's *Comparaison* (pp. 781-84), Mersenne's *Harmonicorum libri XII* (pp. 600-16), Kircher's *Musurgiae universalis* (pp. 635-42), Ménéstrier's *Des représentations en musique* (pp. 632-33), Mace's *Musick's monument* (pp. 726-33), Playford's *Introduction to the skill of musick*

(pp. 733ff.) and other writings, and Malcolm's *Treatise on musick* (pp. 838ff.).

French musicians whose lives and works are discussed (pp. 776ff. and 899ff.) include Dumont, Lambert, Gauthier, Loulié (with translated excerpts from his *Principes)*, Moreau, Charpentier, Lully's sons, Colasse, Allouette, Minoret, Campra, Gilles, de Lalande, Théobalde, Lalouette, Marais, de la Guerre, Salomon, Couperin family, Bernier, Montéclair, Mouret, Dandrieu, Desmarets, Gervais, Destouches, Clérambault, Royer, de Blamont, Leclair, Rameau, and Lully (pp. 646ff.). Hawkins names authors of musical writings in France (p. 902). Portraits of famous musicians include those of Mersenne, Lully, Playford, Purcell, and Handel.

Numerous passages concerning the establishment of the violin family of instruments in England attest to French preeminence in violin playing, on account of the 24 Violons du Roi. (See p. 703 on the attempt of Charles II to imitate Louis XIV in this regard.)

70 HAYN, Friedrich Gottlob (ca.1771-1804)

Anleitung Angloisen mit Würfeln zu komponiren. Beytrag zur Unterhaltung für Musikliebhaber.
*Dresden: K. A. Kirmse, [ca. 1798]; 5p.

Players of this dice game produce 8+8 measure contredances (2/4 meter) in F major in keyboard score. A roll of one die for each measure of the piece yields a number that coordinates, by means of a numerical table for each of the two reprises of the dance, with the number of a particular measure in the table of 96 musical measures. The method is essentially similar to that employed by Kirnberger in his *Allezeit fertige Polonoisen- und Menuettenkomponist* (q.v.).

71 HECK, John Caspar (1740?-1791)

The art of fingering. Or, the easiest and surest method how to learn to play on the harpsichord with propriety and expedition, being exemplified by a gradation of fine lessons from the easiest to the more difficult compositions, by some of the most eminent masters, each lesson being mark'd with the most proper manner of fingering. To which is added a table of all the different keys, shewing the different manner of fingering the same. As also an explanation of all graces, shakes, etc. and the several marks re-

ferring thereto, a work that will prove very usefull to all young beginners. And such as have accustomed themselves to a wrong way of fingering may by this means be restored to the right method. The manner of fingering, as well as the explanation of graces, is entirely regulated after the rules and method of the celebrated C. P. E. Bach of Berlin.
*London: W. Randall & J. Abell, [ca. 1766]; 35p.
London: for Wright and Wilkinson, [ca. 1782].

While the manner of fingering and realization of ornaments comes from C. P. E. Bach's *Versuch* (q.v.), this is most notable for the lessons, pp. 8-35. Complete fingering for both hands appears in the 12 Menuets, Passepied, Gavotte, Tempo di minuetto, Chaconne, and Gigue, in addition to pieces by C. P. E. Bach.

72 HEINICHEN, Johann David (1683-1729)
Neu erfundene und gründliche Anweisung, wie ein Music-liebender auff gewisse vortheilhafftige Arth könne zu vollkommener Erlernung des General-Basses, entweder durch eigenen Fleisz selbst gelangen, oder durch andere kurtz und glücklich dahin angeführet werden, dergestalt, dass er so wohl die Kirchen als theatralischen Sachen, insonderheit auch das Accompagnement des Recitativs-Styli wohl verstehe, und geschickt zu tractiren wisse. Wobey zugleich auch andere schöne Vortheil in der Music an die Hand gegeben, und alles mit vielfachen Exempeln, und hierzu mit Fleisz auserlesenen nützlichen Composition-Regeln erläutert worden. Nebst einer ausführlichen Vorrede.
*Hamburg: Benjamin Schiller, 1711; 284p.
Der General-Bass in der Composition, oder: Neue und gründliche Anweisung, wie ein Music-Liebender mit besonderm Vortheil, durch die Principia der Composition, nicht allein den General-Bass im Kirchen- Cammer- und theatralischen Stylô vollkommen, & in altiori Gradu erlernen; sondern auch zu gleicher Zeit in der Composition selbst, wichtige Profectus machen könne. Nebst einer Einleitung oder musicalischen Raisonnement von der Music überhaupt, und vielen besondern Materien der heutigen Praxeos.
*Dresden: Autor, 1728; 960+[28]p.
Facs. reprint, Hildesheim: Georg Olms, 1969.

143

While Heinichen's duly famous thoroughbass manual represents the experience of a German heavily influenced by Italian opera, it is noteworthy here on account of its exceptional detail on topics of interest to all accompanists of early 18th-c. music, as well as for its agreement with French instruction in some topics. Compared to the first edition, the edition of 1728 is a thorough revision, with new chapters, extensive footnotes reflecting upon many subjects, and many additional musical examples. The 1728 edition shows greater awareness of Italian opera and sympathy for the galant aesthetic. Heinichen describes the general characters of French, Italian, and German music, envisioning a new style that combines French *tendresse* with Italian *vivacité* (p. 10, 1728 ed.). His discussion of taste or *goût* in music (pp. 23-27) resembles that of Michel de Saint-Lambert in ch. 9 of his *Nouveau traité de l'accompagnement du clavecin* (Paris 1707). Heinichen's table of bass figures assembles a variety of signs used in different countries for expressing the same chords (pp. 112-13). A study by George J. Buelow *(Thoroughbass accompaniment according to Johann David Heinichen,* Berkeley, CA: University of California Press, 1966) brings into relief these and other differences in practice among selected French, Italian, and German authors of thoroughbass and accompaniment manuals. Heinichen, not yet affected by Rameau's theory of fundamental harmony, still groups chord structures according to their common dissonant intervals (2nd, 4th, 5th, 7th, 9th, etc.). Unique, however, is his chapter on accompanying fast-moving bass lines. Organized according to meter, this chapter offers advice for recognizing non-harmonic bass notes. The section on "overture meter," or pieces using the metric sign 2 or $\mathbb{Z}$ (pp. 348ff.), apparently refers to the French suite, or *ouverture.* Such music, says Heinichen, would be accompanied by a harpsichord *(clavecin)* rather than an organ, and thus more frequent chord repercussions per bass note are appropriate.

Heinichen confirms the views of earlier French authors by emphasizing simplicity in accompaniments, avoiding interference with the solo line, and shunning displays of musical vanity. For the sake of appropriate embellishment of chords, however, he does discuss embellishments such as the Trill, Passing tone *(Transitus),* Appoggiatura *(Vorschlag),* Slide *(Schleiffung),* Mordent, and Acciaccatura. Like his French predecessors Étienne Delair (q.v.) and Saint-Lambert, Heinichen offers instruction in full-voiced accompaniment (better suited to the harpsichord than to the organ, p. 132 fn.) and a system for deriving figures for an unfigured bass accompaniment, with or without an orchestral texture (pp. 725ff.). Excellent musical examples (transcribed in Buelow's study) illustrate, among other topics, different numbers of voices and degrees of rhythmic-melodic embellishment over a given bass.

73 HELY, Benjamin (fl. 1680-1690)

The compleat violist. Or an introduction to ye art of playing on ye bass viol wherein the necessary rules and directions are laid down in a plain and familiar method. With a collection of the psalm tunes set to the viol, as they are now in use in the churches where there are organs. To which are added some select airs and tunes, set according to ye divers manners of playing by the G sol re ut cliff, the C sol fa ut cliff, and ye fa ut cliff, also several lessons, viz. almans, sarabands, courants, Iiggs, etc. compos'd for that instrument by ye late famous master Mr. Benjamin Hely.
*London: for & sould by I. Hare, [1699]; 16f.

The pedagogical text of this bass viol tutor is quite rudimentary, but the collection of tunes (presented on a single staff using variously the G, C, or F clefs) includes an Allemande, 3 Almands, 6 Ayres, a Boree, 3 Courants, Forlane, Hornpipe, 4 Jiggs, 6 Minuets, Rigadoone, 3 Sarabands, New Canaries, New Morris Round, New Rigadoon, and "The Princes: a new Dance at the Ball at St. James's" (Minuet?).

74 HILLER, Johann Adam (1728-1804)

Wöchentliche Nachrichten und Anmerkungen die Musik betreffend. 4 v.
Leipzig: Zeitungsexpedition, 1766-1770; 408p. (July 1766-June 1767); 406p. (June 1767-June 1768); 408p. (July 1768-June 1769) and 206p. (July 1769-December 1769); 208p. (January 1770-December 1770).
*Facs. reprint, Hildesheim: Georg Olms, 1970.

Hiller wrote most of the articles himself in what is probably the first specialized musical periodical, dealing variously with aesthetics, history, theory, pedagogy, criticism, and current events. Dance receives attention only in relation to music, as in reviews of opera performances (Mondonville's *Theseus* at Fontainebleau, v. 1, p. 56; works by Lully, Mondonville, and Rameau in Paris, v. 2, p. 205) and notices of musical activity in Paris, Amsterdam, Leipzig, Hamburg, Vienna, Augsburg, or Brussels (e.g. "Der Tanz" in Italy, v. 4, p. 271). Hiller remarks on the misuse of ballet in opera (v. 3, p. 7) and the coordination of dance and dramatic action in French opera (v. 4, p. 371). He offers examples of dance music by Adam, said to be the best composer for dance (v. 1, p.

375), and Weinlich (v. 2, pp. 173, 182); minuets by Miller (v. 1, p. 321), Benda (with variations, v. 2, p. 242), and Sieg (v. 2, p. 13); a polonoise (v. 4, p. 236); and a tongue-in-cheek "recipe" for creating German dance melodies equally as insipid as those in the Spies and Späth collection under review (v. 1, p. 133). Among Hiller's discussions of French writings on music appear translations of articles from Rousseau's dictionary of music (q.v.), including "Ballet" (v. 3, pp. 208-11), and reviews of Blainville's *L'esprit* (q.v.; v. 1, pp. 212, 308), *Essai sur l'union de la poésie* (v. 1, pp. 379, 387), and *Histoire générale . . . de la musique* (q.v.; v. 2, p. 329), Lacassagne's *Traité générale* (q.v.; v. 2, p. 237), and Roussier's *Traité des accords* (v. 1, p. 245). For their innovations in combining expressivity and the *galant* idiom, he eulogizes Lully (v. 1, p. 324; v. 2, pp. 46, 193, 233) and Rameau (v. 1, pp. 325, 268). He reviews Kirnberger's collection of keyboard dances (v. 1, p. 116). A description of the French "tambourin" (v. 4, p. 203) refers only to the instrument (drum) of that name.

75 HOEGI, Pierre

A tabular system whereby the art of composing minuets is made so easy that any person, without the least knowledge of musick, may compose ten thousand, all different, and in the most pleasing and correct manner.
*London: Welcker, [1763]; 8p.

Hoegi's system is comparable to Kirnberger's earlier dice game *(Der allezeit fertige Polonoisen- und Menuettenkomponist,* q.v.), even though Hoegi uses no dice. To construct a 16-measure minuet for one treble instrument, the "composer" randomly chooses for each measure a number from 8 to 48, corresponding to one of the 41 possibilities offered for that particular measure. The 41 choices, consisting of one-measure musical figures, appear consecutively on one staff. Eight such staves in vertical alignment represent the 8 measures of the first reprise. On pp. 5-8, a second table of 8 staves, each with 41 choices of figure, represents the final 8 measures or second reprise. In essence, the system offers a pre-fabricated harmonic structure with 41 rhythmic-melodic variations of each chord or progression. One need only pick the variation and write it down.

76 HOTTETERRE, Jacques Martin "le Romain" (1674-1763)

L'art de préluder sur la flûte traversière, sur la flûte-à-bec, sur le hautbois et autres instrumens de dessus. Avec des préludes tous faits sur tous le tons dans différens mouvemens et différens caractères, accompagneés de leur agrémens et de plusieurs difficultées propres à exercer et à fortifier. Ensemble des principes de modulation et de transposition; en outre un dissertation instructive sur toutes les différentes espèces de mesures, etc. Oeuvre VIIe.

*Paris: auteur et Boivin (auteur et Boucault), 1719; 65p.

*Facs. reprint, Paris: A. Zurfluh, [ca. 1966].

Facs. reprint, Genève: Minkoff, 1978.

Ed. by Erich Doflein and Nikolaus Delius as *48 Préludes in 24 Tonarten aus Op. 7, 1719.* Mainz: B. Schött's Söhne, 1972.

The first great French flute virtuoso and founder of the French school of flute playing before Blavet here offers instruction for improvising preludes on the flute, recorder, and oboe. It is the only important work on the improvisation of flute preludes to have appeared in France. Hotteterre discusses form and modulation. Examples of preludes in every key serve as models, illustrating different tempos *(mouvements)* and styles *(caractères)*. He discusses the function of the leading tone and cadences in modulation and describes the distribution of cadences in a prelude. He shows how to recognize the key of a piece from its opening and how to transpose in all clefs and keys. Ch. 11 deals with metric signatures and their implications for rhythmic inequality. He notes which dances and other genre pieces are associated with each meter and illustrates the metric signature with musical examples from operas and cantatas by Lully, Clérambault, Bernier, Corelli, Campra, et al. Two examples of an extended prelude feature cadences on each scale degree, one major and one minor. A large portion of the treatise is devoted to examples of *traits*, improvisatory fragments in the manner of caprices, as exercises for each of the three instruments in both major and minor keys.

77 HOTTETERRE, Jacques Martin "le Romain" (1674-1763)

Méthode pour la musette, contenant des principes, par le moyen desquels on peut apprendre à joüer de cet instrument, de soy-même au défaut de maître. Avec un nouveau plan pour la conduite du souflet, et plusieurs instructions pour le toucher, etc. Plus un recueil d'airs, et quelques préludes, dans les tons les plus convenables. Oeuvre X.

Paris: J. B. Chr. Ballard, 1737; 8+84+32p.
*Paris: J. B. Chr. Ballard, 1738; 8+86+32p.
Facs. reprint, Genève: Minkoff, 1978.

Probably the best method for the musette to appear in the 18th c., this instruction manual for playing the bagpipes describes the construction of the instrument, sound production, and technique. Fingering of accidentals and trills is given for each of the chalumeaux. Remarks on note values (p. 35) suggest that détaché playing is stylistically and technically important for quick dances such as menuets, passepieds, and bourrées. Lessons found in the text include a Rigaudon, Marche, Menuet du Ballet du Roy 1721, [Menuet] du Ballet de la Grotte de Versailles, Bourée de *Bellerophon,* and Gavotte de *Cadmus.* Ch. 15 treats the fingering of ornaments, including Ports de voix, Flattements, and Battements. A description of the bourdon (drone) precedes the final section on the care of the instrument. The 32 pages of music constituting the second part include 2 Allemandes, a Bransle, Brunettes, 3 Bourées, Contredanses, a Gavotte, 3 Marches, 9 Menuets, 10 Musettes, and 4 Rigaudons, as well as airs, vaudevilles, and chansons.

78 HOTTETERRE, Jacques Martin "le Romain" (1674-1763)

Principes de la flûte traversière, ou flûte d'Allemagne, de la flûte à bec, ou flûte douce, et du haut-bois, divisez par traitez.
Paris: Chr. Ballard, 1707.
Amsterdam: Estienne Roger, [1710]; 33+46p.
    *Facs. reprint, Kassel: Bärenreiter, 1941.
Paris: Christophe Ballard, 1713.
Paris: J. B. Christophe Ballard, 1720.
Paris: J. B. C. Ballard, 1721.
    Facs. reprint, Genève: Minkoff, 1973.
Paris: J. B. C. Ballard, 1722.
Amsterdam: Michel Charles Le Cène, [s.d.].
Paris: J. B. C. Ballard, 1741.
Paris: Bailleux, [ca. 1765]; 79p. Entitled *Méthode pour apprendre à jouer en très peu de tems de la flûte traversière, de la flûte à bec et du haut-bois divisée en differents traités par M. Hotteterre, le Romain . . . Nouvelle édition augmentée des principes de la musique et des tablatures de la clarinette et du basson suivi d'un recueil d'ariettes choisies dans les plus beaux opéras comiques,*

menuets et autres jolis airs ajustés pour deux flûtes traversières, violons ou pardessus de viole . . .

Dutch transl. by Abraham Moubach as *Grond- beginselen over de behandeling van de dwars-fluit. In een duidelyke verhandeling over het recht gebruik, in een korte leeroeffening van dien vervat.* Amsterdam: Michel Charles Le Cène, 1728; 47p.

German transl. by Hans Joachim Hellwig. Kassel: Bärenreiter, 1941.

English transl. as *The rudiments or principles of the German flute. Explaining after an easy method every thing necessary for a learner thereon, to a greater nicety than has been ever taught before. Wrote in French by the sieur Hotteterre le romain . . . and faithfully translated into English. To which is added a collection of familiar airs for examples.* London: J. Walsh and Joseph Hare, [1729]; 36f.

*English transl. by Paul Marshall Douglas as *Rudiments of the flute, recorder and oboe.* New York: Dover, 1968.

English transl. by David Lasocki as *Principles of the flute, recorder and oboe.* New York: F. A. Praeger, 1968.

The first known treatise on playing the transverse flute contains as well separate "treatises" devoted to the recorder and the oboe. The 9 concise chapters cover posture, embouchure, fingering of notes and trills, tonguing, and ornamentation. Of special interest are ch. 8 on articulation (with tonguing syllables "tu-ru" and a brief remark on *notes inégales),* Ports de voix, Accents, and Doubles cadences, and ch. 9 on Flattements (Tremblements mineur) and Battements. Fingering charts are augmented by the author's description of the technique for obtaining each pitch, trill, and finger vibrato available on the instrument. A beautiful engraving illustrating stance and embouchure presumably depicts Hotteterre himself. The treatise on the recorder discusses in 4 chapters posture, fingering, trills, and Flattements and Battements. The method for the oboe treats in 2 pages posture, embouchure, and fingering.

79 HOYLE, John (ca. 1744-1796) [pseudonym for John BINNS]
Dictionarium musica, being a complete dictionary, or treasure of music. Containing, a full explanation of all the words and terms made use of in music, both speculative, practical and historical. All the words and terms made use of by the Italians, are also

inserted. The whole compiled from the best antient and modern authors who have wrote on the subject.
London: the author and S. Crowder, 1770; 112p.
  Facs. reprint, New York: Broude Bros., 1976 (MMMLF 83).
A complete dictionary of music, containing a full and clear explanation, divested of technical phrases, of all the words and terms, English, Italian, etc., made use of in that science, speculative, practical, and historical. The whole compiled from the best ancient and modern authors, and particularly adapted to scholars, as well as proficients. London: for H. D. Symonds, J. Dale, Miller, J. Sewell, 1791; iv+160p.
  *Facs. reprint, Genève: Minkoff, 1975.

This dictionary of music is said to derive largely from those of Grassineau and Rousseau (q.v.). Articles on dances mention only the most superficial aspects of musical character and structure, with virtually nothing on dancing. There are entries for the Allemanda, Bourée, Ciacona/Chacoon, Corant, Entrée, Forlana, Galliarda, Gavotta/Gavot, Gigg/Giga/Gigue/Jig, Lovre, Minuet, Passacagatio ("something like a Chacoon"), Passepied, Rigadoon, Rondeau, Saltarella, Sarabande, and Siciliane.

80 JONES, William "of Nayland" (1726-1800)

A treatise on the art of music; in which the elements of harmony and air are practically considered, and illustrated by an hundred and fifty examples in notes, many of them taken from the best authors, the whole being intended as a course of lectures, preparatory to the practice of thorough-bass and musical composition.
Colchester: for the author, W. Keymer, 1784; xii+61p.+40pl.
  *Sudbury: Fulcher; London: Longman, 1827; xii+61p.+40pl.

This genteel introduction to music and composition associates strict regular phrasing with dance music. A paragraph in ch. 8 on the analysis of air and the conduct of subject (p. 45) identifies minuets, gavotts, gigs, etc., as movements in which an established measure "restrains the air to a certain number of bars . . . on which account all music of this class, being most easily understood, gives most pleasure to unlearned hearers. . . . The whole number of bars in such movements is divisible by 4, and the leading air is comprehended within 2 or 4 bars: and as the air has a mechanical harmony of commensuration, the regular motions of the dance may be accommodated to it.'' Because of its strong associations with dancing, observes Jones, this sort of regulated measure is not suited to sacred music.

81 KELLNER, David (ca. 1670-1748)

Treulicher Unterricht im General-Bass, worinne alle Weitläufftigkeit vermieden, und dennoch gantz deutlich und umständlich allerhand sothane neuerfundenen Vortheile an die Hand gegeben werden, vermöge welcher einer in kurtzer Zeit alles, was zu dieser Wissenschaft gehöret, sattsam begreiffen kan. Zum Nutzen, nicht allein derer, so sich im General-Bass üben, sondern auch aller andern Instrumentisten und Vocalisten welche einen rechten Grund in der Music zu legen sich befleissigen, herausgegeben von D. K.

Hamburg: Kissner, 1732; 93p.

2nd ed., Hamburg: Christian Herold, 1737; 99p. Foreword by Telemann.

3rd ed., Hamburg: Christian Herold, 1743; 98p. Foreword by D. Solanders.

4th ed., Hamburg: 1749.

*4th ed., Hamburg: Christian Herold Witwe, 1767; 98p.

5th ed., Hamburg: Christian Herold Witwe, 1773; 98p.

*6th ed., Hamburg: Christian Herold Witwe, 1782; 98p.

7th ed., Hamburg: J. G. Herold, 1787; 64p. With additional music by C. P. E. Bach.

Hamburg: J. G. Herold, 1796; 64p.

Swedish transl. as *Trogen underrättelse uti general-basen* . . . Stockholm: Benj. Gottl. Schneider Enckia, 1739; 98p.

Dutch transl. by G. Havingha as *Korte en getrouwe onderregtinge van de generaal bass of bassus continuus* . . .

Amsterdam: G. F. Witvogel, 1741; 171p.

Amsterdam: J. Covens junior, 1751; 171p.

This manual of thoroughbass and intervallic harmony by a lutenist-composer of lute dances has one short reference to dance pieces. Kellner mentions on p. 43 the use in figured bass of a horizontal line to indicate harmony sustained from the previous figure over a moving bass, a symbol much clearer than repeated figures. He notes that the French have always used the line in this manner, whereas the Italians persist in repeating figures. In this connection he mentions the indication *tasto solo* as used in musettes (6th ed.: and pastorellas) often found in French music, in which the bass must often suffer much restraint.

82 KIRNBERGER, Johann Philipp (1721-1783)

Der allezeit fertige Polonoisen- und Menuettenkomponist.
*Berlin: Georg Ludewig Winter, 1757; 10+xxix p.
L'art de composer des menuets et des polonoises sur le champ.
Berlin: Georg Ludwig Winter, 1757; 10+xxix p.

This is the first of more than a dozen different musical games known to have appeared in print between 1757 and 1813. By rolling dice and using numerical and musical tables, the player can "compose" polonaises of 6 plus 8 measures and minuets and trios of 8 plus 8 measures, all scored for two violins and keyboard instrument. The harmonic progressions are fixed, such that all the resulting minuets would have the same chord structure. But for each measure there are 11 possible melodic variants, corresponding to the 11 numbers yielded by throwing two dice. These are selected by coordinating the number of the throw (i.e. measure number) with the number turned up by the dice in the numerical table provided for the appropriate reprise (first or second half) of the piece. The resultant number indicates the measure in the musical table to be copied out for the new piece. The pieces constructed by means of such games are said to be typical of 18th-c. popular idioms without revealing their mechanical origin; see Leonard Ratner, *"Ars combinatoria:* chance and choice in eighteenth-century music," in *Studies in eighteenth-century music: a tribute to Karl Geiringer on his seventieth birthday,* ed. by H. C. R. Landon and R. E. Chapman (New York: Oxford University Press, 1970), pp. 343-63. A review of Kirnberger's game and a discussion of *ars combinatoria* appear in F. W. Marpurg's *Historisch-kritische Beyträge zur Aufnahme der Musik,* v. 3 (Berlin 1757), pp. 135-54.

83 KIRNBERGER, Johann Philipp (1721-1783)

Recueil d'airs de danse caractéristiques, pour servir de modèle aux jeunes compositeurs et d'exercice à ceux qui touchent du clavecin, avec une préface par J. Ph. Kirnberger. Partie I. Consistant en XXVI pièces.
*Berlin, Amsterdam: Jean Julien [Johann Julius] Hummel, [ca. 1777]; 4+27p.

*English transl. of the preface by Newman W. Powell in "Kirnberger on dance rhythms, fugues, and characterizations," *Festschrift Theodore Hoelty-Nickel: a collection of essays on church music,* ed. by N. W. Powell (Valparaiso, IN: Valparaiso University, 1967), pp. 66-76.

The celebrated theorist and Bach pupil Kirnberger here offers a collection of dance tunes and other character pieces for keyboard instruments to serve as models for composers and performers. In the 4-p. preface he fervently advocates the playing of characteristic dances as a necessary prerequisite to expressive, stylistically correct performance and to good composition. The various dance melodies offer a range of phrasing, rhythmic patterns, and emphases that constitute a language basic to all types of music. The playing of fugues, for example, requires perception of these various rhythms and characters. Further, one should be alert to national or regional difference among dances of the same type. A practiced ear can distinguish a Viennese minuet from a Prague or Dresden minuet; Dresden minuets are the best, while French ones are the worst (!). Kirnberger wishes that systematic collections of national dance melodies and characteristic pieces were available in Germany and elsewhere. These would aid the composer of pantomimic ballets, such as those of Noverre. As models of this sort of composition he points to the works of Starzer in Vienna.

The 27 pages of music contain dances and other character pieces, mostly by Kirnberger. "Les Caractères des Danses" includes an Entrée, Courante, Menuetto, Bourrée, Chaconne, Sarabande, Forlane, Rondeau, Fanfare, Passepied, Gavotte, Gigue, Loure, Musette, Rigaudon, Polonoise, Canarie, Souabe (2), Marche, Corente, Les Carillons, Les Tambourins, and Menuet Allemande.

84 KOCH, Heinrich Christoph (1749-1816)

Versuch einer Anleitung zur Composition. 3 v.
Rudolstadt: Löwe Erben und Schirach, 1782 (v. 1); Leipzig: Adam Friedrich Böhme, 1787 (v. 2), 1793 (v. 3); 374p., 464p., 454p.
*Facs. reprint, Hildesheim: Georg Olms, 1969.
Partial English transl. as *Introductory essay on composition. The mechanical rules of melody. Sections 3 and 4* by Nancy Kovaleff Baker. New Haven: Yale University Press, 1983; xxv+259p.

The third volume of Koch's composition manual concerns itself with phrase and period structure in common musical forms of the classic period. In examining the nature of thematic connection in small forms, Koch devotes section 4, ch. 2, paragraph 18 to dance types in common usage: Gavotte, Bourée, Polonoise, Angloise or Contertanz, Menuet, and March. Koch's descriptions are among the most thorough for stylized dance music seen from the composer's point of view. For each dance type, he remarks on current usage (the gavotte is said to be less well known than the others), metric and rhythmic characteristics, and formal structure (length of phrases, number and length of sections, timing and quality of cadences). Complete examples appear for the gavotte and bourrée. Incidental reference to dance music occurs elsewhere in the volume. Koch believes the best and most frequently heard type of phrase for dance music is the four-measure phrase (p. 52, par. 20). Among his examples of various ways to compress, overlap, and extend phrases are several minuets, including ones by Stamitz (p. 70) and Haydn (p. 133).

85 KOLLMANN, August Friedrich Christoph (1756-1829)

An essay on practical musical composition, according to the nature of that science and the principles of the greatest musical authors. 2 v.

London: author, 1799; xx+106p., 167p.

*Facs. reprint, New York: Da Capo Press, 1973.

2nd ed. 1812. (Much revised; see Jamie C. Kassler, *The science of music in Britain.*)

Kollmann's presentation to the English public of a German method of teaching composition contains articulate treatment of dance music. In ch. 12, part 2, pp. 102-6 on "national music," he elaborates upon Kirnberger's argument that a knowledge of dance characters is a stimulus to the composer. His description of characteristic national pieces touches on aspects of musical form (meter, length of upbeat, phrasing), expression or character, manner of performance, and relative tempo. References to examples among the works of Bach and Handel accompany most of the definitions. He often refers to the definitions in Sulzer's *Allgemeine Theorie* (q.v.). Dances discussed include the Allemande, Bourée, Ciaconne or Chaconne, Courante or Corrente, Gavotte, Gigue or Jig, Loure, Passacaille, Passepied, Pastorale (Musette), Polonoise, Rigaudon, Sarabande, Siciliano, and Walzer.

86 L'ABBÉ le fils, Joseph Barnabé Saint Sevin (1727-1803)

Principes du violon pour apprendre le doigté de cet instrument, et les différens agrémens dont il est susceptible . . . par M. l'Abbé le fils . . . Ces principes sont suivis de deux suites d'airs d'opéra à deux violons, dont le choix lui a paru le meilleur, de plusieurs leçons dans le genre de sonates avec la basse chiffrée pour le clavessin, d'examples analogues à ces leçons, de préludes dans les tons majeurs et mineurs, et d'une suite de jolis airs variés pour un violon seul.

Paris: auteur, Le Clerc, [1761]; 81p.

*Facs. reprint, Paris: Centre de Documentation Universitaire, 1961.

Paris: Des Lauriers, [ca. 1772]; 81p.

Facs. reprint, Genève: Minkoff, 1976.

An advanced technique manual for the violin, this treatise combines the old French dance tradition with the newer Italian sonata tradition and a progressive attitude towards technical innovation (see David Boyden, *History of violin playing,* p. 365). Sophisticated bowing, articulation, and use of both natural and artificial harmonics reflect professional violin playing in mid-century France, while the emphasis on ornamentation and the numerous dances among the examples and exercises suggest retention of French traditions. Ornaments illustrated include the Cadence (appuyée, subite, feinte, tournée), Martellement, Port de voix, Accent, and Coulé. *Notes inégales,* while not discussed separately, are implied in several bowing exercises (e.g., "Leçon pour piquer les brèves"). The suites for two violins include a Chaconne, Gavottes, Gigue, Menuet, Ouvertures, Rondeau, and Sarabande. Other lessons provide 4 Menuets and a Vaudeville completely bowed, a Rondeau for learning coulés, and over a dozen Menuets and other airs illustrating bowing and articulation, including one Menuet completely in harmonics.

87 LA BORDE, Jean Benjamin de (1734-1794)

Essai sur la musique ancienne et moderne. 4 v.

*Paris: Eugène Onfroy (printed by Philippe Denys Pierres), 1780; xx+445+59p., 444+178p., 702+59p., 475+59p.

Facs. reprint, Paris: 1972.

Facs. reprint, New York: AMS Press, 1978.

The first French musical encyclopaedia, this singular work ranges
widely in subject matter and organization from volume to volume. In v.
1, part 2, ch. 14-16 deal respectively with modern wind, percussion,
and string instruments. Comments bear upon construction, range, best
notes and keys for the instrument, and playing technique for the Clarinet, Cor de chasse, Cornemuse, Cornet, Courtaut, Fifre, Flageolet,
Flûte traversière, Petite flûte, Hautbois, Loure, Musette, Saquebute,
Serpent, Taille de hautbois, Tromboni, Trompete (with martial signals),
Basson (tonguing); Castagnettes (usage and notation), Cymbales, Tambour ou Caisse (military signals with tunes), Tambourin, Tymbales; Ar-
chilute, Contrebasse (3, 4, or 5 string tunings), Guittare, Harpe, Luth,
Mandoline, Quinte (viola), Théorbe, Vielle, Viole, Viole d'amour, Viola, Violoncelle (bowing and technical exercises, bowing of ornaments), Clavecin, Epinette, and Violon. In several instances instruction
manuals are mentioned. Ch. 20 sketches the history and current status of
musical institutions in Paris, including the Opéra, Opéra Bouffon, Opéra
Comique, and Concert Spirituel. A comparison of Opéra orchestral personnel in 1713 and 1778 details the size and make-up of the Opéra
orchestra, as well as the chorus, corps de ballet, and stable of singers.

In v. 3, part 5 is a biographical dictionary with sections devoted to
French composers, performing musicians in the King's service, poets,
and authors of musical writings. Among composers cited are Alexandre,
d'Aquin, Aubert, d'Aubergne, Bacilly, Balbastre, de la Barre, Batistin,
Beaujoyeux, Beaulieu, le Bègue, Bernier, Bertin, Berton, Blaise, Bla-
mont, Blanchard, Boesset, Boismortier, Bourgeois, Bousset, Brossard,
Bury, Calvière, Cambert, Campra, Candeille, Charpentier, Cheron,
Clairembaut, Clément, Colasse, la Coste, Cottereau, Couperin,
Desbrosses, Desmarets, Desormery, Destouches, Dumont, Duni,
Duphly, Floquet, Francoeur, de la Garde, Gaviniés, Gautier, Gervais,
Gluck, Gossec, Grétry, de la Guerre, Kohaut, Lalande, Langlé, Légat
de Furcy, Lully, Marais, Marchande, Mondonville, Montéclair,
Mouret, Philidor, Rameau, Tarade, and Vachon.

88 LACASSAGNE, Joseph (ca. 1720-1780)

Traité général des élémens du chant.
*Paris: auteur, veuve Duchesne; Versailles: Fournier, 1766;
188p.
  Facs. reprint, New York: Broude Bros., 1967 (MMMLF, 27).
  Facs. reprint, Genève: Minkoff, 1972.

This treatise on the rudiments of music is most notable for its attempt to reform metric signature notation. Lacassagne recommends (pp. 98-101) reducing the conventional variety of time signatures to three: 2, 3, and 2/3. The last one is to be used for compound meter with ternary subdivisions. Lacassagne's musical examples showing metric equivalence between the old and new time signatures is one of few clues to interpretation of the puzzling 2/3 time signature used in two choreograhic courante sources ("La Dombe," "La Bocanne;" see Meredith Little's catalogue of choreographic sources). For a discussion of Lacassagne's role in time signature reform, see George L. Houle, *The musical measure as discussed by theorists from 1650 to 1800* (Ph.D. dissertation, Stanford University, 1960), pp. 108-9. Very brief definitions appear on pp. 145-49 for Chaconne, Bourrée, Forlane, Gigue, Gavotte, Menuet, Musette, Loure, Passepied, Rigaudon, Sarabande, Passacaille, and Tambourin, remarking on the presence of strict 4-measure phrasing in the chaconne, menuet, rigaudon, and tambourin. A section on ornaments offers brief definitions of the Cadence, Accent, Martellement, Port de voix, Filé, Coulé, and Pincé.

89 LACÉPÈDE, Bernard Germain Etienne Médard de la Ville-sur-Illon, comte de (1756-1825)

La poétique de la musique. 2 v.
*Paris: imprimerie de Monsieur, 1785; xii+385p., iv+252 [recte 352]p.
3rd ed., 1797.
Paris: 1826. In *Oeuvres complètes.*

Emphasizing the importance of symmetry in music (especially pp. 71-77 in "De la nature de la musique;" relevant portion translated in *Music and aesthetics in the eighteenth and early-nineteenth centuries,* edited by Peter le Huray and James Day [Cambridge: Cambridge University Press, 1981], pp. 179-81), Lacépède mentions dance music as the source of conventional symmetry in the phrase structure of both instrumental and vocal music. In a later chapter on the use of choruses and ballet music in opera ("Des choers & des airs de ballets de la tragédie lyrique," especially pp. 270-78), the acknowledged admirer of Gluck discusses airs de ballet as vehicles for dramatic expression. Arguing that every aspect of the production can further the drama, he specifically affirms the possibility of depicting images in the dance music.

Il est besoin presentement de connoitre les signes principaux qui serventaux agréments, et à la propreté du Chant, pour s'habituer peu à peu à Chanter les leçons auec gout, quand il sera tems di joindre la parolle, j'en parleray dans son lieu. Exemple des figures.

Port de voix - Port de voix double - Coulements - Coulements double. Coulem.ᵗ triple

Coulements double triple - Accent - Accent double. Cadence tremblé. Cadence coupeé

La liaison mise au dessus, ou au dessous des pelittes nottes postiches, ou meme des grosses qui servent aux agremens, soit des ports de voix, soit des Coulements, la premiere Notte ou est attachée la liaison, est celle ou il faut donner le coup de langue, qui doit seruir pour touttes celles que la Liaison en chaine.

Demonstrations pour en conceuoir l'execution

Port de Voix — mi mi fa mi fa mi fa — port de voix double — re re mi fa re fa fa re fa

Coulement — Sol fa mi re ut Sol mi ut Sol mi ut Sol mi ut — coulement double — Sol fa mi re

mi re ut si Sol re mi si Sol re mi si — coulement triple redouble triple — Sol Sol fa Sol ut

ut si la si si Sol Sol ut ut si Sol Sol ut ut si — Accent — Sol la re Sol re

Sol re Sol la fa mi Sol mi Sol mi — accent double — coulement coupé — Sol sol fa mi re Sol fa mi re Si fa mi re

La maniere de faire auec regularité la Cadence marquée par vne Croix, auec le nombre de batemens que l'on doit faire à chaque differente valeur de notte : pour la valeur de la ronde sans étre preparée à la mesure du double Majeur, l'on doit faire vingt batements, dont les premiers doivent étre batus plus lentements que les derniers.

II-90 Jacques Alexandre de LA CHAPELLE, *Les vrais principes de la musique* (Paris: auteur, veuve Boivin, Le Clerc, 1736-52), Livre 2, pp. 14-

voila à peu prés la
maniere de la faire.

Lors qu'on la prépare de la moitié, Soit pour la ronde, ou pour
les autres Nottes, ou il faut qu'elle soit préparée, l'on doit diminuer
les batements à proportion : pour la valeur de la blanche, vnze,
les quatre prémiers lents, pour la valeur d'une Noire, six, les deux
prémiers un peu lents, pour la valeur d'une Croche, quatre, pour
la valeur d'une double croche, trois precipités, On se reglera à propor
=tion selon les autres mouvements de mesure, ou les Nottes ont plus
ou moins de durée.

   On croira peu être Selon la quantité des batements de la ronde,
que le nombre pour les autre valeurs de Notte n'est plus pro-
portioné par l'inegalité; mais lors que l'on fera attention, que
Selon la durée de chaque notte, le nombre des batemens lents ne peu-
=vent se partager que Selon la durée de la notte ou la Cadence
est marquée, l'on vera que le nombre des batemens est jnegal
Selon les differentes valeurs des Nottes.

   Jl y à vn grand nombre de personnes qui pratique la musique, tant pour les jnstruments, que pour la Vocalle, qui font des
Cadences Sans observer cette regularité, qui est cependent vn des
beaux agrements de la Musique, ils battent leurs Cadences
aussi vitte en la commencant qu'en la finissant, ce qui ne se doit
pas, Sur tout quand la durée de la notte le permet, et principalement
Sur les finalles ou l'on est jamais borné, S'il etoit vrai
que l'on du faire les batements egaux, au lieu de vingt que
vous voiés à la valeur de la ronde, il en faudroit faire trente
deux, à la valeur de la blanche, Seize, et aux autres nottes
à proportion, Mais cela ne doit pas être.

   Les Auteurs de methodes, ont passé Sur cet article, Sans
donner aucun principe certin, pour moy, je prouue qu'il est
necessaire que l'ecolier soit fondé Sur des principes sertins, suivis de
demonstrations qui soient intelligibles, et faciles, pour en acquerir la con=
=naissance, et la pratique, non seulement pour cet article Seul. mais pour
tous en general. Jl y à aussy vn àgrement, qui se fait en enflant et en
diminuant, le Son d'une Notte, on ne se sert d'aucun Signe pour distinguer
cette notte d'avec vne autre, mais moy, je lay distingué, par le
moyen d'une petitte barre paralelle, que j'ay mise audessus ou audessous

15. Musical embellishments described and illustrated. [Paris, Bibliothèque
de l'Arsenal, 51147 M497 (2)]

On colera sur une planche de quatre pieds de longueur sur un pied de large un papier ou parchemin large d'un pouce et sera de la longueur de la planche placé dans le milieu.

En suite on tracera sur le milieu de ce parchemin des distance de pouce en pouce par lignes transuersalle. il faut remarquer qu'on ne doit commencer la premiere diuision des lignes quà l'endroit ou le cordon qui suspend le globe passe par le trou de la lame de cuiure dont il est parle ci dessus, et marquer par chiffre à colé de chaque ligne le nombre des pouces, à la premiere ligne 1 à la seconde 2 ainsi de suite iusque en bas -ainsi que le dessin

On fera entrer le porte pouli marqué AA perpendiculai-ment dans le haust de la planche au point A.

Le piton C sera placé aussi perpendiculairement au point C.

La cheuille D sera placé de mesme dans le gros trou D. il faut qu'elle soit grosse pour tirer ou lacher plus vite le cordon qui se roulera dessus.

Le globe F pessera quatre onces sans le cordon ni plus ni moins.

Cette planche sera faite ainsi et aura quatre pieds de longueur depuis la ligne H iusque en bas diuisé en quarante huit pouces cette planche sera large d'un pied, à la quelle on ajoutera vne autre planche au coté du quelle procederont les vibrations coupée obliquement sur la quelle on se reglera pour l'eloignement de l'aplom. le premier eloignement se prendra d'un pouce et le dernier d'un pied et demi en suivant le plan de la planche. la poulie B peut auoir deux pouce de diametre le cordon pasera a trauer le fer qui porte la poulie au point E et sera placé directement au milieu de la premiere ligne H. il faut à laxe du globe un cercle horisontal à la ligne r.

II-90 Jacques Alexandre de LA CHAPELLE, *Les vrais principes de la musique* (Paris: auteur, veuve Boivin, le Clerc, 1736-52), Livre 2, pp. 43-

160

le globe dans son aplom sera eloigné de trois pouces aux lignes
de division à fin que les vibrations se fasse librement sans
toucher à la planche. dans cet éloignement il sera bon d'avoir
vne éguere plate qu'on placera au point designé des pouces
comme 4. 6. 10. &c affin que le haust de l'éguere touche égalem.t
la ligne marquée et le milieu du globe designé par la ligne P P.

Mais comme plusieurs Musiciens de marque ont deja auan
ce' qu'il etoit facile de faire vn retranchement considerable dans
le nombre des Signes des Mesures, Je prouve qu'en àdoptant
la pratique de ce Pendule, on peut se restraindre au double
ordinaire marqué par un 2. au triple ordinaire marqué par un 3,
et au Six quatre 6/4 Et au lieu de mettre au commencement des
pieces Ces mots vite, lentement &c. l'on y mettroit simplement
vn chiffre qui indiquera la distence à la quelle on mettra
l'aplom, et par ce moyen l'on ne poura manquer de parvenir
à vne connoissance parfaitte des differents mouvements. meme
par la memoire pourvu que l'on ait fait attention quelques fois
au mouvement du Pendule.

Leçons pour pratiquer les Airs de dance selon leurs mouvements reglé sur le Pendule.

les chiffres mis au
comencement des
leçons jndiquent le
mouvement qu'on
poura voir au pa=
reil chiffre du pendule

44. Regulating the tempo of dance tunes by means of a pendulum. [Paris,
Bibliothèque de l'Arsenal, 51147 M497 (2)]

90 LA CHAPELLE, Jacques Alexandre de

Les vrais principes de la musique exposéz par une gradation de leçons distribuéez d'une manière facile et sûre pour arriver à une connoissance parfaite et pratique de cet art dédié à Mgr. le comte d'Argenson par le Sr. de La Chapelle. 4 v.

*Paris: auteur, veuve Boivin, le Clerc, (v. 1) 1736, 31p.; (v. 2) 1737, 56p.; (v. 3) 1739, 82p.; (v. 4) 1752?, 84p.

Book 2 of this introductory treatise on singing contains extraordinarily explicit treatment of ornaments and tempo. In the section on ornaments (pp. 14-15), especially lucid three-stage examples demonstrate execution of the Port de voix, Coulement, Accent, Cadence coupé, and Cadence. La Chapelle emphasizes the importance of accelerating the trill and even proscribes the exact number of repercussions at each level of speed during the acceleration, with appropriate examples for trills on half, quarter, eighth, and sixteenth notes. Similar treatment of the Son enflé, Son diminué, and Balancement indicates for example 16 pulsations per whole note in a balancement and proportionately fewer for shorter notes. An ornament combining the Son enflé and Balancement is shown on a whole note as a half-note crescendo plus 16 tremolo pulsations. A general rule for *notes inégales* is applied in 3/2 meter, but suitable note values are not specified for other meters. On pp. 41-44 of Book 2, La Chapelle describes a pendulum devised as a musical time keeping aid (a simplification of the mathematician Sauveur's original invention). The subsequent lessons (pp. 44-48) present dance melodies with their tempos regulated by the pendulum: a number at the beginning of each tune indicates the length of the swinging pendulum according to a scale on the machine ranging from 1 to 28 (inches?). The tunes include an Allemande, Bourée, Branle, Canarie, Chaconne, Entrée de ballet, Gavotte, Gigue, Gaillarde, Loure, Marche, Menuet, Musette en rondeau, Passecaille, Pavane, Rigaudons, Sarabande, and Tambourin. Pendulum markings are also placed over the subsequent vocal exercises and the pieces in Book 3. Book 3, in which lessons for 2 voices and for voice with instruments demonstrate Church music, French theatrical music, and Italian airs, offers a pronunciation guide for singers, especially those not used to singing in French. Book 4 presents more advanced pieces and instruction in harmony and thoroughbass.

91 L'AFFILARD, Michel (ca. 1656-1708)

Principes très faciles pour bien apprendre la musique qui conduiront promptement ceux qui ont du naturel pour le chant jusqu'au point de chanter toutes sortes d'airs proprement et à livre ouvert.

*Paris: Christophe Ballard, 1694; 100p.

2nd ed., Paris: Christophe Ballard, 1697; 133p.

3rd ed., Paris: Christophe Ballard, 1700; 133p.

3rd ed., Paris: Christophe Ballard, 1701; 133p.

4th ed., Paris: Christophe Ballard, 1702; 139p.

5th ed., Paris: Christophe Ballard, 1705; 181p.

   *Facs. reprint, Genève: Minkoff, 1971.

6th ed., Paris: Christophe Ballard, 1705; 176p.

7th ed., Amsterdam: Estienne Roger, [1710]; 173p.

Paris: J. B. Chr. Ballard, 1716; 182p.

Paris: J. B. Chr. Ballard, 1717; 175p.

Paris: J. B. Chr. Ballard, 1717; 176p. *Nouvelle édition à l'usage des dames religieuses.*

Paris: J. B. Chr. Ballard, 1722; 176p.

Paris: J. B. C. Ballard, 1747; 185p. *Très nouvelle édition à l'usage du monde.*

L'Affilard, composer and performer at the court of Louis XIV, here offers instruction in sight-singing, particularly of dance music or *pièces de mouvements.* An anthology of dance tunes forms the second part; monophonic in earlier editions, the dances appear in a two-part (treble and bass) setting in the 5th and subsequent editions, supplied with either sacred or secular poetic texts, depending on the issue and edition. (Concerning editions and their variance, see Erich Schwandt, "L'Affilard on the French court dances," *Musical quarterly,* v. 60 [1974], pp. 389-400.) The dance tunes composed by the author were made purposely regular in structure in order that they might serve either for dancing or as models for composition of dance music. Some editions have breath marks in the score indicating phrasing in an unusually clear manner. Pieces in the 5th edition include a Bourée, Branle, Courante, Chaconne, Canaries, Gavotte, Gigues, Marches, Menuets, Pavanne, Passacaille, Passepied, Rigaudon, and 3 Sarabandes. A table of ornaments shows realizations without comment for the Accent, Port de voix (simple, doublé), cadence (coupée), Double cadence (coupée, battuë, soutenue, appuyée), Martellement, Feinte, Pincé, Tremblement subit, Balancement, Coulement, and Hélan. L'Affilard is best known for the absolute tempo indications he provides in the scores (5th and subsequent editions). Referring to Joseph Sauveur's system of measuring the swing of a pendulum, he provides instructions for making and using one in connection with the dance tunes. (The description appears in facsimile in Rosamond Harding, *Origins of musical time and expression;* metronomic equivalents have been worked out most satisfactorily by Erich Schwandt in the article cited above and in *The new Grove dictionary* article on L'Affilard.) Remarks concerning over-dotted rhythm and *notes inégales* are unusually explicit, though brief.

92 LANGE, Hermann François de (ca. 1717-ca. 1781)

Le tôton harmonique ou nouveau jeu de hazard, par lequel toutes personnes pourront composer une infinité de marches en trio, en faisant tourner un tôton, et cela sans sçavoir la composition ni même la musique. Ces marches pourront se jouer sur toutes sortes d'instruments à cordes et à vent. Mis au jour par Mr. de La Chevardière.
*Paris: de La Chevardière, [1762]; 25p.
Liège: F. J. Desoer, [1768]; 27p.

This musical game employs a nine-sided spinning top and two sets of charts, one numerical and one musical, to produce pairs of marches in three parts (two violins and bass), one in D major and one in D minor. Each 16-measure march requires 16 spins. The number resulting from each spin, coordinated with the number of the spin, provides a cue to the proper measure in the musical chart, which is then copied out. For the significance of such games for musical composition and theory, see Leonard G. Ratner, *"Ars combinatoria:* chance and choice in eighteenth-century music."

93 LANGLÉ, Honoré François Marie (1741-1807)

Traité de la basse sous le chant, précédé de toutes les règles de la composition.
*Paris: Nadermann, [ca. 1798]; 304p.

While this manual for accompaniment appeared rather late, it is the work of a teacher active in Paris during the 1780s and 1790s. It is of interest here primarily on account of the section (article 14, pp. 46-50) on how to compose a bass to a given melody. Langlé's 5 rules admonish the composer to (1) avoid duplicating treble notes except at cadences or the beginning and end; (2) create regular and natural melodic motion, mostly in fourths, fifths, and octaves, in descending thirds or ascending sixths, or in conjunct motion contrary to the treble; (3) keep the bass within three octaves of the melody; (4) possibly vary the harmony under a note that can be interpreted as part of more than one triad, especially a held note; and (5) avoid doubling a note functioning as a leading tone.

94 LA VOYE MIGNOT, de (fl. 1649-56, d. 1684)

Traité de musique, pour bien et facilement apprendre à chanter et composer, tant pour les voix que pour les instruments. Divisé en trois parties. Où se voyent tous les exemples des principales règles et observations pratiquées par les plus excellens autheurs.
Paris: R. Ballard, 1656; 115p.
Paris: R. Ballard, 1659; 107p.
*2nd ed., Paris: Robert Ballard, 1666; 115+36p. *Reveu et augmenté de nouveau d'une quatriesme partie.*
   Facs. reprint, Genève: Minkoff, 1972.
English transl. by Albion Gruber as *Treatise on music,* based on the 1656 ed. Brooklyn, NY: Institute of Mediaeval Music, [1972]; 90p.

The author of this counterpoint treatise may have been the composer of the allemandes and courantes identified with the name "De la Voys" in the Cassel and Uppsala manuscript dance music collections (published in Jules Ecorcheville's *Vingt suites d'orchestre du XVIIe siècle français* [Paris: L. Marcel Fortin; Berlin: L. Liepmannssohn, 1906; reprint New York: Broude Bros., 1970], v. 1, pp. 10 and 55). His brief discussion of meter is noteworthy for its inclusion of metric signs that gradually fell out of use during the 17th c. Those he characterizes as already fallen out of use include O or Θ and O_3^2 or $\emptyset_3^2$. Signs then currently in use include C or 2, $\mathcal{C}$ or 2, C3 or 3, and $\mathcal{C}_3^2$ or 3. In the chapter on note values, he distinguishes between several types of triple meter, three using white notation and two black, the first white type illustrated with the signature $\mathcal{C}_3^2$. This use of $_3^2$ is one of a few that might have bearing on the use of that sign in two choreographic sources for the courante. (In his English transl., Gruber considers the sign a misprint for $_2^3$.)

95 LE BLANC, Hubert (fl. early 18th c.)

Défense de la basse de viole contre les entreprises du violon et les prétentions du violoncel.

*Amsterdam: Pierre Mortier, 1740; 148p.

   Facs. reprint, Genève: Minkoff, 1975.

   Ed. serially in the *Revue musicale,* v. 9 (1927-28).

   German transl. by Albert Erhard as *Verteidigung der viola da gamba.* Kassel: Bärenreiter, 1951; 148p.

   English transl. by Barbara Jackson as "Hubert Le Blanc's Defense de la viole: a translation and commentary," *Journal of the viola da gamba society of America,* v. 10 (1973), pp. 11-28, 69-80; v. 11 (1974), pp. 17ff.; v. 12 (1975), pp. 14ff.

This wry defence of the viola da gamba at a time of declining usage in France compares the noble instrument with its rivals, the violin and violoncello, considering its aesthetic and functional appropriateness for various musical purposes and answering arguments against its continued use. The essay not only offers glimpses of Parisian concert life, but gives evidence for the vast difference in technique and manner of playing the viola da gamba and the violoncello.

96 LÉCUYER (18th c.)

Principes de l'art du chant, suivant les règles de la langue et de la prosodie françoise. Ouvrage utile aux amateurs du vrai et du beau chant, aux personnes qui se destinent au théâtre et aux jeunes compositeurs.

Paris: auteur, 1769; 24p.

   *Facs. reprint, Genève: Minkoff, 1972.

This modest vocal instruction manual treats various aspects of articulation, diction, and ornamentation as means to expressive singing. Briefer and less well illustrated than Montéclair's *Principes* (q.v.), it is useful for its rules concerning the emphatic pronunciation of certain types of words for expressive purposes. A brief section on meter (pp. 22-24) cautions the singer never to take rhythmic freedoms in airs of character, except possibly at cadences; a loure from Rameau's *Indes galantes* is cited, along with other similar airs, as examples that can only be ruined by applying to them the diction suited to recitative. Ornaments, described verbally with few examples, include Cadence (parfaite, feinte ou brisée, subite, jettée, double, molle), Port de voix (feint, appuyé, achevé), Accent, Martellement, Coulé, and Sons filés.

97 LÉGAT DE FURCY, Antoine (b. ca. 1740-d. after 1790?)

Seconds solfèges, ou principes de musique clairs et faciles; suivis de 99 leçons sur toutes les clefs, dans tous les tons et dans tous les genres, de 12 duo, et de plusieurs airs de maîtres, les plus célèbres, le tout avec basse chiffrée pour la facilité des personnes qui apprennent l'accompagnement.
*Paris: Boyer, [1784]; 117p.

The only relevant portion of the brief 9-page essay on rudiments of singing preceding this collection of vocal exercises is the section on vocal ornaments, pp. 7-9. Very brief definitions and good realization of examples appear for the Coulé, Port de voix, Martellement, Flatté, Accent, Cadence parfaitte ou appuyée, Cadence subitte ou jettée, Cadence feinte ou brisée, Grouppe, Son enflé et diminué, Trille elevé, and Trille abaissé.

98 LEONE, Pietro (18th c.)

Méthode raisonnée pour passer du violon à la mandoline et de l'archet à la plume ou le moyen seur de jouër sans maître en peu de temps par des signes de convention assortis à des exemples de musique facile. Contenant XXIV. airs dansants à deux mandolines, VI. menuets avec accompagnement, II. duo, I. sonate avec la basse et plusieurs airs connus variés par Mr. Leone de Naples maître de mandoline de S. A. S. Monseigneur le Duc de Chartres Prince du Sang.
*Paris: gravée par Mme. Vendôme, imprimé par Montutai, [1768]; 67p.
   Facs. reprint, Genève: Minkoff, 1982.
Paris: imprimé de Montutai, gravée par Mme. Vendôme, [ca. 1770]; 67p.
Paris: Bailleux, [1773]; 67p.
English transl. as *A complete introduction to the art of playing the mandoline. Containing the most essential rules and examples for learners to obtain a proficiency. To which are added a pleasing variety of airs, lessons, duets and sonatas. Composed, and judi-*

ciously arranged for that instrument by sigr. Leoni of Naples.
London: Longman and Broderip, 1785; 64p.

Instruction in mandoline technique for the trained amateur violinist precedes a collection of French dances for two mandolines, plus other music. The technical exercises are of interest for their variety of articulation and arpeggiation patterns. The dance melodies (pp. 21ff.) include 24 Allemandes in 2/4 time with French descriptive titles and 6 menuetti with Italian descriptive titles or character designations. Six examples of simple cadenzas 5 to 7 measures in length (p. 47), comprised of scales, sequences, characteristic figuration, etc. demonstrate the *point d'orgue ad libitum* (probably intended for Italian sonata movements, although one of the menuetti has a fermata).

99 LE PILEUR D'APLIGNY
Traité sur la musique, et sur les moyens d'en perfectionner l'expression.
Paris: Demonville, Monory, l'auteur, 1779; viii+174p.
*Paris: Demonville, Saugrain et Cie, l'auteur, 1779; viii+174p.

A dramatist's critique of music and opera in abstract compares French and Italian music as emanations of different national personalities expressed through differing media. The chapter on French recitative ends with an articulate description of the French national character as it reveals itself in the Frenchman's manner and music. Chapters on the musical period (pp. 131-32) describe for airs in general and for vaudevilles in particular the nature of their typical phrase and period structure.

100 LORENZONI, Antonio
Saggio per ben sonare il flauto traverso con alcune notizie generali ed utili per qualunque strumento, ed altre concernenti la storia della musica.
*Vicenza: Francesco Modena, 1779; 91p.
  Facs. reprint, Bologna: Arnaldo Forni, 1969.

Lorenzoni's flute treatise relies heavily on Quantz's. In ch. 16 on proper expression, he briefly describes as "pieces of fixed character" the Minuetto, Trio, Giga, Ciaccona, Villanella, Passagallo, Serrabanda, Corrente, Passapiede, Furlana, Rigadon, Alla Siciliana, Tamburrino,

Gavotta, Preludio, Pastorale, Allemanda, Contradanza, Rondo, and Marchia. Remarks concern tempo, meter, length of upbeat, and sometimes affect and origin as well, without distinguishing between Italian and French types.

101 LOULIÉ, Étienne (ca. 1655-ca. 1707)

Éléments ou principes de musique, mis dans un nouvel ordre. Très-clair, très-facile, et très-court et divisez en trois parties. La première pour les enfans. La seconde pour les personnes plus avancez en âge. La troisième pour ceux qui sont capables de raisonner sur les principes de la musique. Avec l'estampe, la description et l'usage du chronomètre ou instrument de nouvelle invention, par le moyen duquel, les compositeurs de musique pourront désormais marquer le véritable mouvement de leurs compositions, et leurs ouvrages marquez par rapport à cet instrument, se pourront exécuter en leur absence comme s'ils en battoient eux-mesmes la mesure.

Paris: Christophe Ballard et l'auteur, 1696; 96p.

  Facs. reprint, Joachimsthal: Knuf, 1969.

  Facs. reprint, Genève: Minkoff, 1971.

*Amsterdam: Estienne Roger, 1698; 110p.

English transl. by Albert Cohen as *Elements or principles of music.* Brooklyn, NY: Institute of Mediaeval Music, 1965.

This introduction to music describes the usage of *notes inégales* in a manner unusually articulate for its time. Loulié relates equality to melodic motion: disjunct half-beats must be played equally, conjunct ones somewhat unequally, and dotted patterns with an even greater contrast of long and short. Loulié's description of his *chronomètre*, frequently referred to in musical books of the 18th c., was the most celebrated attempt to introduce a machine for counting musical time before that of Mälzel. Rosamond Harding, *Origins of musical time and expression*, reproduces his entire description in facsimile.

102 LUSSE, Charles de (b. ca. 1720-d. after 1774)

L'art de la flûte traversière.

Paris: adresses ordinaires de musique et chez l'auteur, 1761; 38p.

  *Facs. reprint, Genève: Minkoff, 1973; 34p.

This flute manual without text presents its information in charts, beginning with the basics of fingering and notation. A table of expressive ornaments (p. 9) includes the Cadence (accelerating), Tremblement (simple, tourné, composé superieur, composé inferieur), Pincé, Port de voix (superieur, inferieur), Tenuë, Tremblement flexible, Gradation du son, Dégradation du son, and Martellement. Exercises in articulation (p. 10), using patterns of syllables, feature Coups de langue perlés, Tacs aspirés, Doubles coups de langue, and Syncopes. Other charts show the notation for harmonics and the fingering for Martellements. A series of lessons in two parts (flute and bass) contains largely Italianate movements, one a minuet; preludes and solo pieces (p. 25ff.) use advanced technique.

103 LUSTIG, Jacob Wilhelm (1706-1796)

Muzykaale spraakkonst; of duidelyke aanwyzing en verklaaring van allerhande weetenswaardige dingen, die in de geheele muzykaale practyk tot eenen grondslag konnen verstrekken.
*Amsterdam: A. Olofson, 1754; 206p.+11pl.

Sections on varieties of composition (including dance types), ornamentation, and poetic and musical meter derive almost verbatim from Mattheson's *Vollkommene Capellmeister* (q.v.). Remarks concerning accentuation of beats in the measure, though derived from Mattheson's, contain an unusual musical example using the time signature C_3^2 with three half notes per measure (p. 110); in later examples the usual $\frac{3}{2}$ signature is used. (See Lacassagne and La Voye Mignot.)

104 MACE, Thomas (1612/13-1706?)

Musick's monument; or a remembrancer of the best practical musick, both divine and civil, that has ever been known, to have been in the world. Divided into three parts. The first part, shews a necessity of singing psalms well, in parochial churches, or not to sing at all, directing, how they may be well sung, certainly; by two several ways, or means; with an assurance of a perpetual national-quire; and also shewing how cathedral musick may be much improved, and refined. The second part, treats of the noble lute, (the best of instruments) now made easie; and all its occult-lock'd-up-secrets plainly laid open, never before discovered;

whereby it is now become so familiarly easie, as any instrument of worth, known in the world; giving the true reasons of its former difficulties; and proving its present facility, by undeniable arguments; directing the most ample way, for the use of the theorboe, from off the note, in consort, &c. Shewing a general way of procuring invention, and playing voluntarily, upon the lute, viol, or any other instrument; with two pritty devices; the one, shewing how to translate lessons, from one tuning, or instrument, to another; the other, an indubitable way, to know the best tuning, upon any instrument: both done by example. In the third part, the generous viol, in its rightest use, is treated upon, with some curious observations, never before handled, concerning it, and musick in general.

London: author & John Carr (T. Ratcliffe & N. Thompson), 1767; 272p.

*Facs. reprint, Paris: Centre National de la Recherche Scientifique, 1958.

Facs. reprint, New York: Broude Bros., 1966 (MMMLF, 17).

In the second part, on the lute (pp. 128-34), Mace names and describes the various sorts of pieces included in the lessons, including Preludes, Fancies and Voluntaries, Pavines, Allmaines, Ayres, Galliards, Corantoes, Serabands, Tattle de moys, Chichonas, Toyes or Jiggs, Common Tunes, and Grounds and Divisions upon them. The work is otherwise a defense of English musical tradition against the incursion of French style in England. It has much useful information about the lute and viol concerning construction, care, and performance practice; continuo accompaniment on the theorbo; and ornamentation.

105 MAHAUT, Antoine (ca. 1720?-ca. 1785?)

Nieuwe manier om binnen korten tijd op de dwarsfluit te leeren speelen; tot gebruik van aanvangers en meer gevorderden opgesteld door A. Mahaut. Nieuwe druk, voorzien met 12 nooten tabula's.

Amsterdam: J. J. Hummel, [1759]; 36p.

Facs. reprint, Buren: Frits Knuf, 1981.

Nouvelle méthode pour aprendre en peu de tems à jouer de la flûte traversière, à l'usage des commençans et des personnes plus avancées, suivie de petits airs, menuets, brunettes etc. accom-

*odés pour deux flûtes, violons et pardessus de viole . . . Par M.
Mahaut . . . IIe recueil.*
*Paris: La Chevardière, [1759]; 63p.
  Facs. reprint, Genève: Minkoff, 1972.
  Facs. reprint, Buren: Frits Knuf, 1981.

Mahaut goes beyond Hotteterre, Corrette, and other earlier authors of
French flute treatises in his comprehensive treatment of articulation,
ornaments, and fingering. He recommends using the tonguing syllables
"tu-ru," or "di-del" for double tonguing. A completely marked movement illustrates a variety of articulation patterns. Ornaments defined and
illustrated include Cadences ou Tremblemens, Flattements, Battements,
Martellement, Port de voix, and Accents. Mahaut distinguishes the
French trill from the Italian as having a sustained preparatory note and
accelerating repercussions, rather than a short preparatory note and
equal repercussions. Fingering is discussed in detail; charts placed directly below each note show the exact fingering for two minuets and a
contredanse. Four musettes also appear among the lessons.

106 MARCOU, Pierre (d. ca. 1820)
Élémens théoriques et pratiques de musique.
London, Paris: veuve Ballard et fils, 1782; 58p.
*Paris: veuve Ballard et fils, Versailles: Blaisot, 1782; 58p.

Only the rudiments of music are treated here; the ornament table derives
from Rousseau's. Remarks on *notes inégales* attest to disagreement
among musicians concerning the application of the principle, both as to
the degree of inequality and its appropriateness if not explicitly indicated
by dotted notes.

107 MARPURG, Friedrich Wilhelm (1718-1795)
*Clavierstücke mit einem practischen Unterricht für Anfänger and
Geübtere.* 3 v.
*Berlin: Haude und Spener, 1762-63; 10+xvi p., 30p., 30p.

The three short collections of keyboard pieces are each accompanied by
an essay providing background to the pieces as individual works and as
types. The first discusses fingering for the Chaconne as well as keyboard
technique and fingering required in each of its variations. Marpurg then

defines the suite as distinct from the sonata, defines rondeau and chaconne, and distinguishes between the Chaconne and the Passecaille. A
discussion of phrase and period structure in music is illustrated by means
of reference to Clérambault's rondeau *La Jeannette,* a gavotte (though
not so labeled). The essay following the second collection continues
with an extensive description of the Allemande as a member of the suite,
distinct in style from the allemande as a dance. The latter is typified by
Campra's music to Pécour's choreograhy of 1702, which Marpurg
quotes. He also discusses the Gavotte, Rigaudon and Bourrée, Vielle,
Musette, Tambourin, Murky, and Masure (as well as fugue). The third
collection is devoted to accompaniment and counterpoint.

108 MARPURG, Friedrich Wilhelm (1718-1795)

Des critischen Musicus an der Spree erster Band.
*Berlin: A. Haude und J. C. Spener, 1750; 406p.
Facs. reprint, Hildesheim: Georg Olms, 1970.

Of relevance here is a comparison of the French and German personality
in music (p. 217). Marpurg describes French musical character from the
German's point of view as cheerful and light-hearted in contrast to the
passion and melancholy expressed by German music. Examples of
French ornaments in Table 2 derive from Couperin's tables, but Marpurg's use a rhythmically more precise notation.

109 MASSON, Charles (fl. 1680-1701)

Divers traitez sur la composition de la musique. Premier traité.
*Secret de l'harmonie, pour apprendre d'une manière très-sûre et
très-facile à faire une basse à un dessus.*
*Paris: Jacques Collombat, 1705; 12+[6]p.

The instructions for setting a bass line (thoroughbass) to a given melody
combine elementary rules of two-part counterpoint (avoid successive
fifths and octaves; progression of perfect to diminished fifth is permissi-
ble if the melody descends; contrary motion is preferred; avoid repetition of the bass note without reason; do not necessarily set chords to
purely ornamental notes, especially those that fill in a third [e.g. notes
on the second beat of triple or 6/4 meter]) with tips on the recognition
and proper treatment of implied chord progression and modulation. Expressed as intervals below the melody notes, the conventional choice of

bass notes (and implied harmony) is indicated for each note of the major
or minor scale as used in typical melodic progressions. Masson also
shows the conventional harmonization of standard melodic cadences.
While his examples are for the most part abstract melodic fragments, the
three airs offered as exercises on the last page resemble a gavotte and
two minuets, implying that his instructions might be more readily applicable to dance music than those in contemporary composition treatises
oriented to sacred music.

110 MASSON, Charles (fl. 1680-1701)

*Nouveau traité des règles de la composition de la musique par
lequel on apprend à faire facilement un chant sur des paroles; à
composer à 2. 3. et 4. parties, etc. et à chiffrer la basse-continue
suivant l'usage des meilleurs auteurs tant de France que d'Italie.
Ouvrage très utile à ceux qui jouent de l'orgue, du clavessin et du
théorbe.*

Paris: Jacques Collombat et l'auteur, 1697; 80p.

2nd ed., Paris: Christophe Ballard, 1699; 120+7p.

   *Facs. reprint, New York: Da Capo Press, 1967.

Paris: Christophe Ballard, 1700; 120p.

Paris: Christophe Ballard, 1701; 120p.

3rd ed., Paris: Christophe Ballard, 1705; 120p.

   Facs. reprint, Genève: Minkoff, 1971.

4th ed., Amsterdam: Estienne Roger, [ca. 1708]; 148p.

Paris: J. B. C. Ballard, 1738; 127p.

Paris: Ch. Ballard, 1755.

Anticipating Rameau's theories in some respects, this was probably the
most important composition manual used in France before Rameau's
theoretical writings appeared. (The 1694 first edition has not survived.)
Masson was the first theorist to give rules for writing in only two modes
(major and minor). Frequent reference to music by Lully makes this
book a practical guide to French style in the late 17th c. Near the end of
the first chapter of Part 1 on melody, a section entitled "De la mesure et
de la différence de ses mouvements" treats meter from the viewpoint of
the musician beating time. To illustrate duple and triple meters in various related tempi, Masson mentions characteristic dances (Gavotte and
Galliard; Bourrée and Rigaudon; Sarabande, Passacaille, and Courante;
Chaconne, Menuet, Passepied, Loure; Canaries and Gigue), as well as

specific Entrées from Lully's stage works. Masson's tempo comparisons equate the larger duple beats of simple and compound meters (e.g. the Gigue and Bourrée are both beaten in duple time at the same tempo).

Of special significance to the dance historian are Masson's remarks on the minuet and passepied, attesting to the hemiola created by the rhythm of the dance step against that of the music. For the two triple-meter measures of the minuet phrase, the dancing master beats one step in a slow triple, while the musician beats two quicker triple measures ("deux tems inégaux"). The remainder of the treatise provides background useful in reconstructing musical textures of the Lully era. Ch. 5 of Part 1 offers general rules for composing a melody either for the treble or the bass part of a composition. Ch. 6 treats melodic cadences, ch. 7 how to set words to a tune. Part 2 deals with harmony and composition in 2, 3, 4, and more parts of a homophonic texture (with a section on fugue and species counterpoint). Final remarks on the means of achieving agreeable variety within a composition make some reference to instrumental dance pieces.

111 MATTHESON, Johann (1681-1764)

Das neu-eröffnete Orchestre, oder universelle und gründliche Anleitung, wie ein Galant Homme einen vollkommenen Begriff von der Hoheit und Würde der edlen Music erlangen, seinen Gout darnach formiren, die Terminos technicos verstehen und geschicklich von dieser vortrefflichen Wissenchafft raisonniren möge. Durch J. Mattheson, Secr. mit beygefügten Anmerckungen Herrn Capell-Meister Keisers.
*Hamburg: der Autor, Benjamin Schillers Witwe, 1713; 338p.
Hamburg: Benjamin Schillers Witwe, 1713; 338p.

In Part 2 on composition and counterpoint, Mattheson discusses in ch. 4 the composition of different sorts of pieces. In the chamber category, he briefly describes the Allemanda, Bourée, Canarie, Chaconne & Passecaille (distinguishing between them according to the degree of freedom in the bass line), Courante (distinguishing between French and German [!] types), Entrée, Gavotte, March, Menuett, Passepied, Rigaudon, Rondeau, and Sarabanda (pp. 184-99). The comments, primarily on structure and instrumentation, vary from those in his later writings.

112 MATTHESON, Johann (1681-1764)

Der vollkommene Capellmeister, das ist gründliche Anzeige aller derjenigen Sachen, die einer wissen, können, und vollkommen inne haben muss, der einer Capelle mit Ehren und Nutzen vorstehen will: zum Versuch entworffen von Mattheson.
Hamburg: Christian Herold, 1739; 28+484p.
*Facs. reprint, Kassel: Bärenreiter, 1954. Commentary by M. Reimann.
English transl. by Ernst C. Harriss. Ann Arbor, MI: UMI Research Press, 1981. Also Ph.D. dissertation, Georg Peabody College, 1969.
English transl. of excerpts in Hans Lenneberg, "Johann Mattheson on Affect and Rhetoric in Music," *Journal of music theory,* v. 2 (1958), pp. 47-84.
English transl. of ch. 13 by Walter Winzenburger in *Bach; the quarterly journal of the Riemanschneider Bach Institute,* v. 2 (1971), pp. 38-41.

This encyclopedic cumulation of musical knowledge for the music director contains one of the most important descriptions of French dance types in literature outside of France. In Part 2, ch. 13, paragraphs 81-136, Mattheson discusses the character and musical traits of the Menuet, Gavotta, Bourrée, Rigaudon, Marche, Entrée, Gigue (Loure, Canarie, Giga), Polonoise, Angloise (Country-Dance, Ballad, Hornpipe), Passepied, Rondeau, Sarabanda, Courante/Corrente, Allemanda, Aria, Fantasie (Boutade, Capriccio, Toccata, Prelude), Chaconne/Ciacona, and Passecaille/Passagaglio. The minuet and courante receive fullest treatment, with consideration of phrase structure and brief analysis of complete examples. Ch. 12, par. 32, in which Mattheson asserts that even dance melodies express praiseworthy affections, provides a brief summary of the different characters of the various dances.

Mattheson's attempt to apply the doctrines of rhetoric to musical composition results in a remarkable demonstration of dance rhythms (Part 2, ch. 5). By altering metric-rhythmic patterns, he changes familiar chorale melodies into dance tunes in a series of paired examples including a Menuet, Gavotte, Sarabande, Bourée, and Polonoise. Other dance tunes are then changed into chorale melodies (Menuet, Angloise). The ensuing discussion of musical counterparts of classical meters refers to characteristic dance rhythms, e.g. the mixture of iambic and trochaic patterns typical in the minuet.

In defining a relation between functional distinctions (church, chamber, and theater styles) and qualitative distinctions (high, middle, and low styles), Mattheson brings his conclusions to bear upon dance. He cites the minuet among the noblest dances and describes its expressive character (Part 1, ch. 10, par. 14-30). He perceives in the noble art of theatrical dance an independent style to be taken seriously both by dancers and composers. He bears witness to French superiority not just in dancing, but in dance music. Good French dances—especially sung dances combining music, dance, and poetry—provide better compositional models than any Italian counterpart (Part 1, ch. 10, par. 80-81). As a genre in itself with its own singular style, dance music has in turn influenced other genres of composition (ch. 10, par. 113).

113 MERCHI, Joseph Bernard (ca. 1730-1793)

Le guide des écoliers de guitarre ou préludes aussi agréables qu'utiles, sur tous les modes, les positions et les arpégemens avec des airs et des variations. Par M^r. Merchi. V^e. livre de guitarre. Oeuvre VIIE. Gravé par Mad.^{me} Oger.
*Paris: auteur, [ca. 1761]; iv+20p.
    Facs. reprint, Genève: Minkoff, 1980.

Merchi was an Italian guitarist active in France from 1751 on. His instruction and etudes for guitar include a Rondeau, 11 Menuets (3 with doubles), a Gigue, and a Folies d'Espagne with 30 variations, all by Merchi and arranged for guitar. (The dances are not discussed in the text.)

114 MERCHI, Joseph Bernard (ca. 1730-1793)

Traité des agrémens de la musique, exécutés sur la guitarre. Ouvrage qui manquait aux amateurs, et qui est indispensable, pour exécuter, avec goût, les pièces, et les traits de chant qui se trouvent souvent dans les accompagnemens. Contenant des instructions claires et des exemples démonstratifs, sur le pincer, le doigter, l'arpège, la batterie, l'accompagnement, la chûte, la tirade, le martellement, le trill, la glissade et le son filé: suivis de plusieurs airs, la plûpart connus, dont le dernier renferme, dans 19 variations, tous les agrémens. Par M^r. Merchi, maître de guitarre. Oeuvre XXXVE. Gravé par Mad.^{me} Oger.
Paris: auteur, [1777]; 38p.
    *Facs. reprint, Genève: Minkoff, 1982.

After describing how to hold, pluck, and finger the guitar, Merchi discusses arpeggiation (p. 7) and extended broken chord figures *(batteries,* p. 8), then offers advice on thoroughbass realization for accompaniment (p. 10). The remainder deals with the performance of embellishments, specifically the Chûte ou coulé montant (p. 11), Tirade ou coulé descendant (p. 14), Martellement (p. 18), Trill ou cadence (which he equates with the cadence jettée ou subite, p. 18), Glissade (p. 20), Son filé ou flaté (pp. 22-23). While describing the performance technique for each embellishment, Merchi effectively indicates articulation (e.g. notes plucked or not). On p. 17 he discusses alternative patterns of articulation for rapid scalar passages, including long slurs, short slurs, and mixed slurs and staccato marks. Music on pp. 24-38 incorporates all ornaments and articulation described. Along with airs in 2/4 meter, the music includes a Pastorella (p. 26), 3 Allemandes (pp. 26, 27, all in 2/4 meter), 2 Minuetti (pp. 28, 30), a Rondeau (pp. 31-32), and an Air with variations (pp. 34-38).

115 MERSENNE, Marin (1588-1648)

Harmonie universelle, contenant la théorie et la pratique de la musique, où il est traité de la nature des sons, et des mouvements, des consonances, des dissonances, des genres, des modes, de la composition, de la voix, des chants, et de toutes sortes d'instrumens harmoniques, par F. Marin Mersenne de l'ordre des Minimes.

Paris: Sébastien Cramoisy, 1636; 228+36+180+442+412+79+68+28p.

   *Facs. reprint, Paris: Centre Nationale de la Recherche Scientifique, 1963. With marginal notes by the author.

Paris: Pierre Ballard, 1636.

Paris: Richard Charlemagne, 1636.

*English transl. of the books on instruments by Roger Chapman. The Hague: Nijhoff, 1957.

English transl. of the 4th treatise by Robert Fortson Williams. Ph.D. dissertation, University of Rochester, 1972.

The 5 treatises comprising the *Harmonie universelle* offer a store of information about music theory and practice in the early Baroque period. The first on the nature of sounds and movement, including the physics of sound, contains (p. 136) perhaps the earliest attempt to work out the length of a pendulum for measuring musical time (although Mersenne's pendulum was too long for practical use; see Rosamond Harding, *Origins of musical time and expression,* p. 8). The third treatise on the voice and singing has a section describing dance types (pp. 158-80). A brief discussion of dancing and ballet precedes definitions of the Passemezze, Pavanne, Allemande (Vaudeville, Gavote), Sarabande, Volte, Courante, Gaillarde; various Bransles used in ballets and balls, Gavote, and Passepied; and various ballet types including the Canarie, Bocanne, Courante à la reyne, Bohemienne, and Moresque, with musical examples. Mersenne discovers the expressive character or affection of each dance by associating its rhythmic patterning with the cognate Greek poetic meter. This association has been perceived as a derivative of the rhythmic theory of Baïf's Academy (see Herbert Schneider, *Die franzö- sische Kompositionslehre,* pp. 61-63) and as an indication of the growing importance of ballet in the 17th c. (see Robert Isherwood, *Music in the service of the king,* p. 36). The section concludes with discussion of sad versus gay expression and a tabulation of rhythmic formulae characteristic of French airs and dance tunes.

The fourth treatise on consonance and dissonance provides a section on vocal embellishment (pp. 353ff.), illustrating chiefly rhythmic but also a few melodic ornaments. The culminating example shows an *air de cour* by Boësset with four embellished variants of the treble line and two of the bass, all in multiple score.

The fifth treatise on instruments contains 7 books. The first, on string instruments, stresses the practicality of tempered tuning for fretted instruments and discusses the construction of both metal and gut strings. The second treats the lute and theorbo: construction, strings, technique (including ornamentation, pp. 79-82: Tremblemens, Accens plaintifs, Martelemens, Verres cassez, Battemens), tablature, and tuning. The mandor, guitar, cittern, and colaphon are included. Book 3 treats the spinet, harpsichord, harp, psaltery, and régales de bois, including construction and tuning. Book 4 on the violins contains an example of a 5-part fantasy by Henry Le Jeune with an ornamented version of the first 30 measures of the treble violin part, to demonstrate the manner in which violins customarily diminish all sorts of pieces (making reference to the 24 Violons du Roi). The viols, lira viol, hurdy-gurdy, and tromba marina are described.

Book 5 on wind instruments discusses acoustical and technical questions and provides fingering charts as well as musical examples of the range and style suited respectively to flutes, flageolets, trumpets, horns, sackbut, cornetto, serpent, bagpipe, oboe, bassoon, and cornemuse. Book 6 on the organ has examples of keyboard ornamentation. Book 7 on percussion instruments describes castanets, cymbals, and drums, as well as bells.

179

Miscellaneous musical examples in the books on instruments include a Courante by R. Ballard ("old tuning"); Allemandes by Mezangeau, Chancy, Basset, and Martin; a Sarabande; a Courante in cittern tablature; a Gavotte for recorders by Henry Le Jeune; and a Pavane for 6 oboes, as well as numerous fantasies, horn calls, and trumpet calls.

Mersenne considered dance to be a metaphor for life, since both consisted of motion and rest. Indeed, for him God was the "plus grand maître de ballet." He advocated the use of dance as a pedagogical instrument to teach astronomy, mechanics, geometry, architecture, etc. (Book 2, part 2, the section on dance types, pp. 158ff.). For modern evaluation of Mersenne's influence on the ballet de cour, see Christout, *Le ballet de cour,* and Prunières, *Le ballet de cour.* For a comparison with Mersenne's *Harmonicorum libri XII* (1648; Facs. reprint, Genève: Minkoff, 1973), see John Hawkins, *A general history of the science and practice of music.*

116 METOYEN, J. B.

Démonstration des principes de musique ou méthode nouvelle réduite en douze cartes . . . par J. B. Metoyen ordinaire de la musique du roi.
Paris: adresses ordinaires, [s.d.]; 19p.
*Versailles: Fournier, [s.d.]; 19p.

Elementary instruction in music appears in chart form. Chart 11, presenting vocal ornaments, briefly describes the Cadence (appuyée, précipitée, double, molle, feinte ou brisée), Port de voix (entier, feint), Accent, Pincé, and Coulé. Short examples accompany each, but there are no realizations for the Cadences. Chart 12 shows 8 standard ranges, indicating for which voice and instruments each clef is typically used.

117 MEUDE-MONPAS, J. J. O., chevalier de

Dictionnaire de musique, dans lequel on simplifie les expressions et les définitions mathématiques et physiques qui ont rapport à cet art; avec des remarques impartiales sur les poëtes lyriques, les vérificateurs, les compositeurs, acteurs, exécutants, etc.
*Paris: Knapen et fils, 1787; xvi+232p.
Facs. reprint, New York: AMS Press, 1978.
Facs. reprint, Genève: Minkoff, 1982.

This eccentric dictionary serves largely as a vehicle for the author's opinions on singing, national character, etc., despite claims to objectivity and extensive borrowing of articles from Rousseau's dictionary of music (q.v.). Articles pertaining to dance (Ballet, Dance, Entr'acte ["un divertissement pendant un entr'acte est une chose ridicule"], Entrée, Fête, Fragments ["doivent nécessairement revolter le spectateur délicat"], Intermède, Pantomime) offer broad opinion on the role of dance in stage works and the superiority of dance to pantomime. In the author's opinion, ballet is theatrical dance guided by music. Pantomime, he believes, belongs to the realm of action, not to ballet—a view that informs all related definitions.

Most of the articles on individual dance types (Allemande, Bourrée, Chaconne, Contredanse, Gavotte, Gigue, Loure, Musette, Passacaille, Passepied, Pavane, Rigaudon, Sarabande, Sicilienne, Tambourin, Villanelle, Volte [hardly in use]) provide minimal information. A lengthier article on the Menuet emphasizes 4 and 8- measure phrase structure as a necessary counterpart to the rhythmic organization of the dance steps. Comment also touches on the need for marking the beat, not obscuring it with extra notes, and on the declining popularity of the minuet. The Sarabande is said to be no longer in use. The only article to touch on technical aspects of dance is Elévation. The entry Baton de mesure defends the French practice of conducting opera (including chorus and ballet) by audibly beating time with a paper or wooden baton. (Fétis mentions an article by Framéry in the *Mercure de France* of 1788, criticizing Meude-Monpas' dictionary.)

118 MEYER, Philippe Jacques (1737-1819)

Essai sur la vraie manière de jouer de la harpe, avec une méthode de l'accorder. Par Philippe-Jacques Meyer. Oeuvre premier.
*Paris: auteur, 1763; 8+vii+23p.
Paris: impr. de P. Al. Leprieur, [s.d.].
Paris: de la Chevardière, 1772.
Nouvelle méthode pour aprendre à jouer de la harpe avec la manière de l'accorder par P. J. Meyer . . . Mis au jour par M.ʳ Böuin. Oeuvre IX.
*Paris: Bouin, [1774]; 19p.

Meyer's harp tutor is noteworthy for its history of the instrument. Topics treated include hand position, fingering, tuning, accompaniment figures *(harpègemens)*, ornaments with realizations (Tables 2 and 3: trills, mor-

181

dants, and a variety of turn figures), and fingering for specific passages in the lessons to follow (Tables 6 and 7). The 23 pages of lessons contain an aria (chaconne?) with 9 variations, 2 Gavottas (1 with 2 variations), a Giga, Minuetto, and numerous Italianate pieces. The simpler version of the treatise published in 1774 has an extensive fingering chart for ornaments and instructions for tuning the pedal harp.

119 MILANDRE, Louis Toussaint

Méthode facile pour la viole d'amour où l'on traite des différentes gammes, de la double corde, des pincés, des sons harmoniques etc. avec une suite d'airs connus arrangés pour cet instrument seul, d'autres airs avec accompagnement de basse, et deux trio pour une viole d'amour, violon et basse . . . par Mr. Milandre. Oeuvre V.
*Paris: Le Menu, auteur, [1777]; 33p.
   Facs. reprint, Genève: Minkoff, 1979.

Technical instruction for the viole d'amour covers tuning, scales in unisons, sixths, and thirds, alternate fingering for thirds, etc.; fingering of double trills in thirds; hand positions; left hand pizzicato; and harmonics. The various airs and pieces (pp. 14-33) include a Menuet d'Exaudet en sons harmoniques, Musette de Rameau, Musette de Gossec, Allemande (3/8); the Italian trios include 4 Menuettos, a Giga (rondo), and Polonoise. Some pieces are acompanied by a violoncello tuned to the viole; the trios are for violin, viole d'amour, and bass.

120 MILLET, Jean (1618-1684)

La belle méthode ou l'art de bien chanter. Par I. Millet, Chanoine surchantre, en l'insigne église métropolitaine de Besançon. L'on voit à la fin quelques airs, composés par l'auteur.
Lyon: Jean Gregoire, 1666; 65p.
   *Facs. reprint, New York: Da Capo Press, 1973. Commentary by Albert Cohen.

Millet's treatise on vocal ornamentation documents the practice associated with the French *air de cour* in the mid-17th c. The author classifies ornaments into three groups: those that precede the note embellished, those that follow it, and those that combine or elaborate either of the other two. As in many Italian tutors of the time, examples show how to embellish two or three-note groups representing different intervallic combinations and cadence formulas. Ornamented airs appended to the treatise reflect the style of the 17th-c. *air de cour* with lute accompaniment. Comments extend to rhythmic freedom in ornamentation, phrasing (breath-marks are indicated in the score), and ornamentation of the bass line.

121 MONTÉCLAIR, Michel Pignolet de (1667-1737)

Nouvelle méthode pour aprendre la musique par des démonstrations faciles, suivies d'un grand nombre de leçons à une et à deux voix, avec des tables qui facilitent l'habitude des transpositions et la conoissance des différentes mesures. Ouvrage également utile à ceux qui enseignent ou qui aprenent la musique, par le moyen duquel les persones qui en ont déja quelque teinture, soit pour la voix soit pour les instruments, même celles qui savent seulement le plainchant, pouront en cas de necessité s'instruires par elles mêmes.
*Paris: auteur, Foucault, 1709; 64p.

Rudiments and elementary instruction are simplified with the aid of charts and examples. Montéclair's remarks on *notes inégales* admit to the complexity of their application and suggest far less rigidity than other writers perhaps unwittingly imply. He relates their use to the style *(goût)* of the piece, the meter, and the prevailing melodic motion (conjunct or disjunct), indicating that in certain situations the prolonged notes should be almost as long as dotted notes. The lessons include a section entitled "Airs de dance, sur toutes sortes de mouvements," pp. 34-40, containing an Air ou Entrée de ballet, Marche, Rigaudon, Gavotte, Bourée, Pavane, Gaillarde, Branle, Air villageois, Entrée étrangère, Courante,, Passacaille, Chaconne, Sarabande, Menuet, Passepied, Air tendre, Loure, Gigue, Canarie, Sarabande, etc.

122 MONTÉCLAIR, Michel Pignolet de (1667-1737)

Petite méthode pour apprendre la musique aux enfans et même aux personnes plus avancées en âge. Composée par Mr. Montéclair.
*Paris: Boivin, [ca. 1735]; 82p.

Although Montéclair simplifies the presentation of fundamentals by delaying introduction of rhythmic values, *notes inégales* and ornaments form an integral part of the line in his simple melodic exercises. He indicates that the black notes representing passing or weak notes be sung quickly, while the white notes representing main notes be of longer duration, for the sake of taste. Later (p. 42), after introducing rhythmic notation and meter, he specifies the lengths of unequal eighth notes in duple meter as almost as long as a dotted note for the first and almost as short as a sixteenth note for the second. Various tempos and meters, says the author, are best exemplified by a series of dance tunes. With no further definition appear examples of an Entrée de ballet grave, Entrée gay, Musettes, Trompettes—Bruit de guerre, Rigadon, Bourée, Gavotte, Gaillarde, Branle le vilage ou Contredanse, Tambourin, Courante, Passacaille, Sarabande (grave; legère), Chacone, Menuets, Passepied, Canarie, Air infernal, Vents—vitte, Loure, Air de demon, Gigue, and Ciciliene.

123 MONTÉCLAIR, Michel Pignolet de (1667-1737)

Principes de musique. Divisez en quatre parties. La premiere partie contient tout ce qui appartient à l'intonation; la IIe partie tout ce qui regarde la mesure et le mouvement. La IIIe partie la manière de joindre les paroles aux nottes et de bien former les agréments du chant. La IVe partie est l'abrégé d'un nouveau système de musique, par lequel l'auteur fait voir qu'en changeant peu de choses dans la manière de notter la musique, on en rendroit l'étude et la pratique plus aisées.
*Paris: [veuve Boivin], 1736; 133p.
    Facs. reprint, Genève: Minkoff, 1972.
    English transl. of Part 3, "Sur les agréments du chant," in *Cantates françoises,* ed. by James Anthony and D. Akmajian. Madison, WI: A-R Editions, 1975.

Part 2, pp. 36-43, contains a section on dance music, which Montéclair believes the most suitable of any music for forming one's taste and conveying the sense of various tempos and characters. Single staff musical examples of *airs de danse,* without verbal definition, include an Entrée de ballet, Rigaudon, Gavotte, Bourrée, Marche, Gaillarde, Pastourelle de Jephtë, Pavane, Air vilageois, Tambourin de Jephtë, Courente à la manière françoise, Passacaille, Chacone, Sarabande legère, Passepied, Canarie, Air infernal, Vents, Loure, Gigue, Air—trompettes et haubois,

Cors de chasse [Gigue], Canarie, and Napolitaine. Verbal indications in the score note instrumentation: the Marches en rondeau alternate a solo musette with a full ensemble including trumpets and musettes; the Pastourelle de Jephtë alternates solo musette with an ensemble of strings, oboes, and musettes. Other indications concern the rhythmic and metric notation appropriate to a particular dance melody. The lessons concluding Part 2 include a Gavotte a l'italienne, Allemande, and Courente à l'italienne.

Part 3 on embellishment is said to be one of the most important sources of information about early 18th-c. French vocal ornamentation. It describes and illustrates the Coulé, Port de voix, Chûte, Accent, Tremblement (appuyé, subit, feint, doublé), Pincé, Flaté, Balancement, Tour de gosier, Passage, Diminution, Roulade, Trait, Son filé, Son enflé et diminué, Son glissé, and Sanglot. Comments on each are articulate, practical, and somewhat more technical than those in the average tutor. Examples with realization often provide an appropriate musical context for the ornament, setting the melody to words or representing a mood for which the ornament is suitable. A previous section in Part 3 deals with the setting of words to music.

124 MOREL DE LESCER

Science de la musique vocale, où l'auteur applanit par principes toutes les difficultés de la musique et réunit le beau chant, et le bon goût puisés dans tous les auteurs françois et italiens tant anciens que modernes. Avec lésquels, et le secours d'un bon maître, on peut apprendre facilement, et en très peu de tems cette science si utile à l'éducation de la jeunesse de l'un et de l'autre sexe.

*Charleville: auteur; Paris: aux adresses ordinaires; Liège: B. Andrez graveur; Rheims: De Laitre; Bruxelles: Vonden Berghen, [ca. 1760]; 36p.

Very brief treatment of the rudiments of singing precedes a series of vocal exercises richly interspersed with remarks and performing indications concerning tempo or character, breathing, and phrasing. There is no table of ornaments, but two realizations of trills on p. 7 show the Cadence sans être préparée, or trill with no initial upper auxiliary. An introduction to meters by means of examples of airs (p. 11) relates the use of *notes inégales* to tempo (e.g. in common time, eighth notes are equal if the *mouvement* is *marqué,* but unequal if *lentement)*. An example of meter contrast (p. 14) presents the same 8-measure melody successively in 2/4, 3/4, 3/2, 6/4, 3/8, 6/8, 9/8, and 12/8 meter, indicating for each the tempo and note values to be sung unequally. The 9/8 and 12/8 versions are labeled Gigues. Another lesson in meter (p. 27) offers a continuous air that changes meter and tempo or character every few measures: C *mouvement marqué;* 3 *gratieux: mouvement le sarabande;* 2 *très gay: mouvement de rigaudon;* 6/4 *mouvement de loure;* 3/8 *mouvement de passepied;* 3 *[sarabande];* 6/8 *mouvement de gigue et de sicilienne;* 9/8 *autre mouvement de gigue;* 2/4 *mouvement de tambourin;* 3/2 *lentement: mouvement d'air grave;* 12/8 *autre gigue.* The author recommends learning notes and their ornaments phrase by phrase before singing the words. Examples of *roulés,* or melismas on one syllable (taken from Rameau and Campra), show breath marks during the melisma.

125 MUFFAT, Georg (1653-1704)

Suavioris harmoniae instrumentalis hyporchematicae florilegium secundum, sexaginta duabus excultis modulationibus recentiori stylo choraico sensim magis florescente concinnatis . . . a quatuor vel quinque fidibus, una cum basso continuo.
Passau: Georg Adam Höller, 1698.
*Edited by Heinrich Rietsch as *Florilegium secundum für Streichinstrumente* in *Denkmäler der Tonkunst in Österreich,* v. 4 or Jahrgang II/2 (Vienna: Artaria, 1895; reprinted Vienna: Universal).
*English transl. of the Foreword in Oliver Strunk, *Source readings in music history* (New York: W. W. Norton, 1950), pp. 445-48.
*English transl. of the Preface in Kenneth Cooper and Julius Zsako, "Georg Muffat's observations on the Lully style of performance," *The musical quarterly,* v. 53 (1967), pp. 220-45.

The preface to this collection of ballet suites in the French manner contains invaluable detail concerning performance practice in string orchestras of Lully's time. Presumably the famous 24 Violons du Roi served as Muffat's model as he attempted to demonstrate to his German public the sophisticated charm of French dance music. This music, he advised, was intended not only to please the ear but to convey unmistakeably the movements of the particular dance so that one was inspired to dance in spite of one's self.

186

His preface in 4 languages (Latin, German, French, Italian) treats 5 topics deemed essential to effective performance of French dance music: intonation, bowing, tempo, pitch and instrumentation, and ornamentation. Some 28 musical examples illustrate Muffat's rules for French bowing, many of which refer to specific dance types. The section on tempo illustrates for each meter the proper application of required *notes inégales*. Muffat compares French and German pitch and describes the tenor and bass instruments appropriate to the French string ensemble. With regard to ornaments (or articulation), he defines and illustrates the Pincement, Tremblement (simple, relechissant, roulant), Accentuation (sur-accent, sursaut, accent, relâchement, dispersion), Port de voix, Préoccupation, Coulement (simple, figuré), Exclamation, Involution, Petillement, Diminution, Tirade, and Détachement. (The Cooper and Zsako translation provides a chart comparing names of ornaments in the 4 languages.)

126 MUSSARD

Nouveaux principes pour apprendre à jouer de la flûtte traversière avec des idées précises et raisonnées des principes de musique suivis d'une collection d'airs en duo pour cet instrument. Dédiés à monsieur de la Bussiere . . . Choisies et arrangés par Mr. Mussard, m^e de flûtte.
*Paris: auteur, [1779]; 72p.

This flute instruction manual is notable mainly for its inclusion among the lessons (for 2 flutes) of 5 quick Allemandes, 3 in 2/4, 2 in 3/8 meter. There are also a Gavotte, 11 Menuets, a Marche des janissaires, and a Polonoise & trios. A detailed trill-fingering chart appears in the otherwise elementary instructional text.

127 NIEDT, Friedrich Erhardt (1674-1708)

Handleitung zur Variation, wie man den General-Bass und darüber gesetzte Zahlen variiren, artige Inventiones machen und aus einen schlechten General-Bass Praeludia, Ciaconen, Allemanden, Couranten, Sarabanden, Menueten, Giquen und dergleichen leichtlich verfertigen könne samt andern nötigen Instructionen.
Hamburg: Benjamin Schiller, 1706; 83f.
English transl. of the foreword in Oliver Strunk, *Source readings*

in music history (New York: W. W. Norton, 1950), pp. 454-70.
Musicalische Handleitung zur Variation des General-Basses, samt einer Anweisung wie man aus einem schlechten General-Bass allerley Sachen als Praeludia, Ciaconen, Allemanden, etc. erfinden könne. Die zweyte Auflage verbessert vermehret mit verschiedenen Grundrichtigen Anmerckungen und einem Anhang von mehr als 60. Orgel-Werken versehen durch J. Mattheson. Hamburg: Benjamin Schillers Wittwe und Joh. Christoph Kissner, 1721; 204p.

Facs. reprint, Buren: Frits Knuf, 1976.

This is the second part of Niedt's 3-part manual of thoroughbass and composition, the first part of which appeared as *Musikalische Handleitung* (Hamburg 1700 and 1710). Mattheson's additions in his 1721 edition of Part 2 consist primarily of footnotes with commentary on Niedt's text, plus information on the register dispositions of over 60 northern European organs.

The work is a guide to improvising over a thoroughbass. The first 5 chapters show how to change simple bass progressions into elaborate passagework. Numerous musical examples offer a variety of melodic-rhythmic formulae, systematically covering all intervals from the unison through the octave. Ch. 6-9 show how to vary chords in the right hand with figuration of various kinds; full-length examples appear in ch. 8-9.

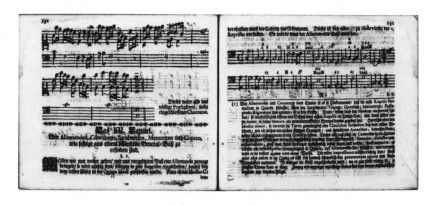

II-127 Friedrich Erhardt NIEDT, *Musicalische Handleitung zur Variation des General-Basses* (Hamburg: Benjamin Schillers Wittwe und Joh. Chr. Kissner, 1721), pp. 130-131. How to create allemandes and other dance tunes by varying a generic thoroughbass line. [Paris, Bibliothèque nationale, 8°B.3228 (R.38.720 Jan. '79)]

Ch. 10 contains a glossary of terms identifying types of composition suitable for such variation: Allemanda, Ballo, Bourée, Boutade, Branle, Caprice, Ciacona, Courante, Double, Fantaisie, Gagliarda/Galliarde, Gavotta/Gavotte, Gigue (Loure), Intrata, Lamento, Madrigali, Menuet, Ouverture, Passagaglio, Passe-pied, Praeambulum, Praeludium, Quodlibet, Rigaudon, Rondeau, Sarabanda, Serenata, Sinfonia, Sonata, Toccata, Trio. The definitions mention etymology, meter, appropriate number of measures, presence of an upbeat, and character of the piece. (Other entries describe tempi and instruments.)

Of greatest interest here are chapters 11-12, in which Niedt demonstrates how to turn a thoroughbass (plain bass with right-hand chord realization) into a variety of specific character pieces, using the variation technique presented in previous chapters. From a single common-time figured bass, presented at the beginning of ch. 11, he creates a Praeludium, Ciacona, Allemanda (2), Courante (2, each with a double), Sarabande (2), Menuet (3), Gigue (2). All appear in fully realized examples. (While Niedt makes no specific distinction between French and Italian versions of the dances, many French characteristics appear in the music.)

128 PRAETORIUS, Michael (1571-1621)

Syntagma musicum ex veterum et recentiorum ecclesiasticorum autorum lectione, polyhistorum consignatione, variarum linguarum notatione, hodierni seculi usurpatione, ipsius denique musicae artis observatione: in cantorum, organistarum, organopoeorum, caeterorumque musicam scientiam amantium & tractantium gratiam collectum; et secundum generalem indicem toti operi praefixum, in quatuor tomos distributum, a Michaele Praetorio.

[V. 2] *Tomus secundus. De organographia. Darinnen aller musicalischen alten und newen, sowol aussländischen, barbarischen, bäwrischen und unbekandten, als einheimischen, kunstreichen, lieblichen und bekandten Instrumenten Nomenclatur, Intonation und Eigenschafft, sampt deroselben justen Abriss und eigentlicher Abconterfeyung: Dann auch der alten und newen Orgeln gewisse Beschreibung, Manual- unnd Pedalclavier, Blassbälge, Disposition und mancherley Art Stimmen, auch wie die Regahl und Clavicymbel, rein und leicht zu stimmen: und wass in Überlieferung einer Orgeln in acht zu nehmen sampt angehengtem ausführlichem Register befindlichen: nicht allein Organisten, In-*

strumentisten, Orgel- und Instrumentmachern, sampt allen den Musis zugethanen gantz nützlich und nötig, sondern auch philosophis, philologis und historicis sehr lustig und anmütig zu lesen. Benebenst einem aussführlichem Register.
Wolfenbüttel: Elias Holwein, 1618; 236p.
Wolfenbüttel: Elias Holwein, 1619; 236p.

Diplomatic facs. reprint ed. by Robert Eitner in *Publikationen älterer praktischer und theoretischer Musikwerk*, v. 13. Berlin: Gesellschaft für Musikforschung, 1884.

Facs. reprint ed. by Wilibald Gurlitt. Kassel: Bärenreiter, 1929.

*Facs. reprint ed. by Wilibald Gurlitt. Kassel: Bärenreiter, 1960 (v. 1), 1958 (v. 2). (Documenta musicologica, I, v. 21 and 14)

English transl. of v. 1 and 2 by Harold Blumenfeld. New Haven: Yale University (The Chinese Printing Office), 1949; vi, a-x, 80 leaves.

[V. 3] *Tomus tertius. Darinnen 1. Die Bedeutung, wie auch Abtheil- unnd Beschreibung fast aller Nahmen, der Italiänischen, Frantzösischen, Englischen und jetziger Zeit in Teutschland gebräuchlichen Gesänge: alss, Concerten, Moteten, Madrigalien, Canzonen, etc. 2. Was im singen, bey den Noten und Tactu, Modis und Transpositione, Partibus seu Vocibus und unterschiedenen Choris, auch bey den Unisonis unnd Octavis zu observiren: 3. Wie die Italiänische und andere Termini Musici, als: Ripieno; Ritornello, forte, pian: presto, lento: capella; palchetto, und viel andere mehr, zu verstehen und zu gebrauchen: Die Instrumenta musicalia zu unterscheiden, abzutheilen, und füglich zu nennen: Der General-Bass zu gebrauchen: Ein Concert mit Instrument- und Menschen Stimmen auff unterschiedliche Choros gar leichtlich anzuordnen: Und junge Knaben in Schulen an die jetzige Italiänische Art und Manier im singen zu gewehnen seyn. Sampt angehengtem ausfürlichem Register.*
Wolfenbüttel: Elias Holwein, 1618; 242+18p.
Wolfenbüttel: Elias Holwein, 1619; 260p.

*Facs. reprint ed. by Wilibald Gurlitt. Kassel: Bärenreiter, 1958 (Documenta musicologica, I, v. 15).

Ed. by Eduard Bernoulli. Leipzig: C. F. Kahnt Nachfolger, 1916; xxxvi+257p.

English transl. by Hans Lampl. DMA thesis, Los Angeles: University of Southern California, 1957; xv+458 leaves.

Theatrum instrumentorum seu sciagraphia Michaelis Praetorii C. Darinnen eigentliche Abriss und Abconterfeyung fast aller derer musicalischen Instrumenten, so j[e]tziger Zeit in Welschland, Engeland, Teutschland und andern Ortern üblich und verhanden seyn: Wie dann auch etlicher der Alten und Indianischen Instrumenten, recht und just nach dem Massstabe abgerissen und abgetheilet.
Wolfenbüttel: 1620; 42pl.+4p.

*Facs. reprint ed. by Wilibald Gurlitt. Kassel: Bärenreiter, 1958 (Documenta musicologica, I, v. 14).

Because v. 2 and 3 of Praetorius' famous encyclopedic study provide us with some of our most detailed information on 17th-c. instruments, instrumentation, and other aspects of performance practice, they are included here despite their largely German-Italian orientation. (Praetorius did compose French dances, published in 1612 as *Terpsichore.*) V. 2 treats nomenclature and classification of musical instruments, then describes the physical characteristics of the various instruments, their shape, compass, quality of tone, etc. Wind, string, and keyboard instruments are covered, including Tromboni, Trom[p]etten, Flötten, Querpfeiffen, Zincken, Pommern/Bombart/Schalmeyen, Fagotten, Sordunen, Doppioni, Racketten, Krumbhörner, Corna-Muse, Bastanelli, Schryari, Sackpfeiffen; Viola de Gamba, Viol Bastarda, Viol de Bracio, Lyra, Laute, Theorba, Quinterna, Pandurina, Pandorra, Penorcon, Orpheoreon, Cithara, Harpa, Scheitholt, Trummscheit, Monochordum, Clavichordium, Spinett, Clavicymbell, Clavicytherium, Claviorganum, Arpicordum, Geigenwerk, Regahl, etc. (The largest part of the volume—the last 3 of 5 sections—is then devoted to historical and contemporary organs.) The *Theatrum instrumentorum,* a set of engravings of instruments published separately, serves as a pictorial supplement to the volume on instruments.

V. 3, in 3 parts, treats genres of composition; theory, notation, and performance practice; and musical terms, figured bass, and instrumentation. Part 1 describes among other types of pieces the Intrada (as prelude to the dance, p. 24, recte 22), the Paduana, Passamezo, and Galliarda (pp. 25-26, recte 23-24), and Bransle, Courant, Volte, Alemande, and Mascharada (pp. 25-26), noting the type of step and motion as well as the repetition pattern in the music. Part 3 describes possibilities for combining instruments into ensembles, following principles of cumulative orchestration (reinforcing fundamental and ornamental parts with a variety of instruments). Praetorius shows how to select reinforcing instruments (according to clefs indicating range) and how to achieve the greatest mixture of sonorities. (The preference for mixed sonorities rather than doubling by instruments of the same type signals his non-French orientation.)

129 PRELLEUR, Peter (fl. 1728-ca. 1755)

The modern musick-master or, the universal musician containing, I. An introduction to singing, after so easy a method, that persons of the meanest capacities may (in a short time) learn to sing (in tune) any song that is set to musick. II. Directions for playing on the flute; with a scale for transposing any piece of musick to the properest keys for that instrument. III. The newest method for learners on the German flute, as improv'd by the greatest masters of the age. IV. Instructions upon the hautboy, in a more familiar method than any extant. V. The art of playing on the violin; with a new scale shewing how to stop every flat or sharp note, exactly in tune, and where the shifts of the hand should be made. VI. The harpsichord illustrated & improv'd, wherein is shewn the Italian manner of fingering, with sets of lessons for beginners, & those who are already proficient on that instrument and the organ; with rules for attaining to play a thorough-bass in which is included a large collection of airs, and lessons, adapted to the several instruments, extracted from the works of Mr. Handel, Bononcini, Albinoni, and other eminent masters. With a brief history of musick, wherein is related the several changes, additions, and improvements, from its origin to this present time. To which is added, a musical dictionary, explaining such Greek, Latin, Italian, and French words as generally occur in musick. Curiously adorn'd with cuts representing the manner of performing on every instrument. Finely engrav'd on above 320 plates.

*London: Printing Office in Bow Church Yard, 1730; 48+48+48+48+48+48+20+4p.

London: Printing Office in Bow Church Yard, 1731.

   *Facs. reprint, Kassel: Bärenreiter, 1965. Notes by A. Hyatt King.

London: Printing Office, 1738.

London: Printing Office and J. Simpson, [ca. 1740].

This is an unusual compendium of instruction for the amateur in singing and playing the recorder, German (transverse) flute, oboe, violin, and harpsichord. The section on German flute is largely abridged from Hotteterre's *Principes* (q.v.). The violin section is based on *Nolens volens* (London: Thomas Cross, 1695). The instructions for tuning harpsichords comes from Gottfried Keller's *A compleat method for attaining to play a thorough bass* (London: J. Cullen, John Young, 1707; see also Corrette, *Maître de clavecin*). Each section is illustrated with a woodcut showing the instrument in performance. The text covers rudiments of technique, augmented by charts demonstrating fingering, available trills, etc. More than half of each section is devoted to music. Minuets, Marches, and Rigadoons (in 6/8 meter) appear in addition to English songs and airs from Italian operas. The harpsichord section contains a Prelude for fingering, Minuets by Lully, a Gavotte, a Jig, a Courant, and a French suite by Mattheson. The section on rules for playing thoroughbass contains several fully realized examples of figured bass accompaniments.

130 QUANTZ, Johann Joachim (1697-1773)

Versuch einer Anweisung die Flöte traversiere zu spielen; mit verschiedenen, zur Beförderung des guten Geschmackes in der praktischen Musik dienlichen Anmerkungen begleitet, und mit Exempeln erläutert. Nebst XXIV. Kupfertafeln.
Berlin: Johann Friedrich Voss, 1752; 334p.+xxivpl.
2nd ed., Breslau: Johann Friedrich Korn der ältere, 1780; 334p.
3rd ed., Breslau: Johann Friedrich Korn der ältere, 1789; 334p.

    Facs. reprint, Kassel: Bärenreiter, 1953 (Documenta musicologica, 2).

    French transl. as *Essai d'une méthode pour apprendre à jouer de la flûte traversière* . . . Berlin: Chrétien Fréderic Voss, 1752; 336p.

    Facs. reprint, Paris: Zurfluh, 1975.

    Dutch transl. by Jacob Wilhelm Lustig as *Grondig onderwys van den aardt en de regte behandeling der dwarsfluit* . . . Amsterdam: A. Olofsen, 1754; 240p.+xxipl.

    *English transl. by Edward R. Reilly as *On playing the flute*. London: Faber and Faber, 1966.

    English transl. of ch. 13-15 as *Easy and fundamental instructions* . . . London: Welcker, [1770]; 32p.

London: Longman and Broderip, [ca. 1790]; 32p.

English transl. of excerpts from ch. 18 in Oliver Strunk, *Source readings in music history* (New York: W. W. Norton, 1950), pp. 577-98.

Japanese transl. by Tsuneko Arakawa as *Flute soho.* Tokyo: Zen On Gakufu, 1976; 340p.

Japanese transl. by Shoji Imoto and Toshinori Ishilala as *Flute soho shiron.* Tokyo: Sinfonia, 1976; 169p.

Ostensibly an instruction manual for playing the flute, Quantz's essay is in fact one of the most comprehensive 18th-c. treatises on contemporary musical performance. Technical instruction for the flute covers construction, embouchure, fingering, notation, tonguing, articulation, and embellishment, from simple ornaments to the improvisation of variations and cadenzas. The last two chapters are virtually separate treatises in themselves. Ch. 17 covers the makeup, size, and seating of the orchestra, describing the respective roles of each instrument as well as the leader in the ensemble. Ch. 18 on musical criticism describes a variety of genres and styles, both functional and national.

While the orientation is primarily toward a mixed German style, sections describing French practices occur throughout. In ch. 17, section 7, par. 56-58, Quantz tries to apply his method of determining tempos (using human pulse beats as a guide) to French dance music. In so doing he briefly discusses the demands made by dancers upon the accompanying ensemble and comments on the tempo and character of the Entrée, Loure, Courante, Sarabande, Chaconne, Passecaille, Musette, Furie, Bourrée, Rigaudon, Gavotte, Rondeau, Gigue, Canarie, Menuet, Passepied, Tambourin, and March. Quantz also remarks upon articulation and rhythmic detail appropriate to the performance of French dance music.

Other sections of the work mention French ornaments (ch. 8, par. 6, 14, 15), *notes inégales* (ch. 11, par. 12), the French manner of ornamenting an Adagio (ch. 14, par. 2), French bowing (ch. 17, section 2, par. 26), French keyboard playing, singing, and opera, especially the suitability of French music to the dance (ch. 18, par. 65-67), the dearth of French musical performances outside of France, where ballets might be seen out of context in Italian operas (ch. 18, par. 73), and the general differences between French and Italian music, as perceived by an experienced German musician (ch. 18, par. 76).

131 RAGUENET, François (ca. 1660-1722)

Paralèle des Italiens et des François, en ce qui regarde la musique et les opéra.

*Paris: Jean Moreau, 1702; 124p.

Facs. reprint, Genève: Minkoff, 1976.

Amsterdam: Estienne Roger, [1708]; 40+8p.

Amsterdam: Pierre Mortier, [ca. 1710].

*English transl. by J. E. Galliard as *A comparison between the French and Italian musick and opera's. Translated from the French; with some remarks. To which is added a critical discourse upon opera's in England, and a means proposed for their improvement.* London: John Morphew, William Lewis, 1709; 86p.

Facs. reprint, London: Gregg International, 1968. Notes by C. Cudworth.

*Ed. by Oliver Strunk in "A comparison between the French and Italian music," *Musical quarterly,* v. 32 (1946), pp. 411-36 (with the original translator's notes) and in *Source readings in music history* (New York: W. W. Norton, 1950), pp. 473-88 (without the original translator's notes).

German transl. in J. Mattheson, *Critica Musica,* v. I/2, Hamburg, 1722. Facs. reprint, 1964.

German transl. in F. W. Marpurg, *Kritische Briefe über die Tonkunst,* v. I, Berlin, 1760. Facs. reprint, 1967.

Raguenet's pro-Italian comparison of French and Italian music highlights general aspects of performance practice in lyric theater. The Italians, unlike the French, have no conductor and no *notes inégales,* sing louder, and make better use of dynamics for expressive purposes. Their violins have heavier strings than those in France, which with longer bows produce greater volume of sound; in comparison, French violins sound muted all the time. Italian arch-lutes and bass viols are bigger than French theorbos, giving more solid support and lower range. The French have the advantage in opera with regard to the use of dance and divertissement (as well as choruses, bass voices, and costuming) to produce variety and an air of grandeur and magnificence. French violinists excel over Italian in the finesse and delicacy of their playing; Italian playing is too much *détaché.* The oboe and flute playing in France is much superior: touching or amorously sighing in the tender and plaintive airs, or in the *airs de mouvement* both mellow and penetrating with an advantage in sonority over the strings.

132 RAMEAU, Jean Philippe (1683-1764)

Code de musique pratique, ou méthodes pour apprendre la musique, même à des aveugles, pour former la voix et l'oreille, pour la position de la main avec une méchanique des doigts sur le clavecin et l'orgue, pour l'accompagnement sur tous les instrumens qui en sont susceptibles, et pour le prélude: avec de nouvelles réflexions sur le principe sonore.
Paris: Imprimerie Royale, 1760; xx+237+33p.

Facs. reprint, New York: Broude Bros., 1965 (MMMLF, 5).

*Facs. reprint, Rome: American Institute of Musicology, 1969 (Complete theoretical writings, v. 4, ed. by Erwin R. Jacobi).

A work intended for the practical musician, primarily the teacher, Rameau's elementary treatise on keyboard playing and accompaniment reflects a lifetime of practical experience on the part of one of the greatest composers of French theatrical dance music. Theories of chord inversion and fundamental bass (or progression of chord roots) are here worked into an orderly, practical method covering rudiments and keyboard harmony. Noteworthy sections treat fingering and finger independence (pp. 6, 11), the French acciaccatura (p. 73), figuring a bass (p. 74), accompanying without bass figures (p. 171), improvising preludes (p. 178), and harmony as a means to expression (p. 165). The sophisticated program of lessons in keyboard harmony emphasizes the expressive role of consonance and dissonance and of fundamental (root) bass progression. The work represents an elaboration of principles established in Rameau's *Traité de l'harmonie,* to which the author frequently refers.

133 RAMEAU, Jean Philippe (1683-1764)

Dissertation sur les différentes métodes d'accompagnement pour le clavecin, ou pour l'orgue; avec le plan d'une nouvelle métode, établie sur une méchanique des doigts, que fournit la succession fondamentale de l'harmonie: et à l'aide de laquelle on peut devenir sçavant compositeur, et habile accompagnateur, même sans sçavoir lire la musique.
Paris: Boivin, Le Clair, 1732; 64p.

*Facs. reprint, Rome: American Institute of Musicology, 1969 (Complete Theoretical Writings, v. 5, ed. Erwin R. Jacobi).
Paris: Bailleux, [ca. 1766]; 64p.
English transl. by Deborah Hayes. Ann Arbor, MI: UM Monograph Service, 1974.

This essay on practical keyboard accompaniment develops ideas on the subject expressed by Rameau in his earlier *Traité de l'harmonie*. Rameau emphasizes fingering of chords, voice-leading in chord progression, and appropriate mingling of consonant and dissonant chords in creating an effective accompaniment. He provides a chart of bass figures somewhat more detailed than the one in the *Traité* and discusses the inefficiency of customary bass figuring and rules for accompaniment. Rameau aims to simplify continuo accompaniment by means of the *basse fondamentale* concept. He relates bass figures to keyboard fingering that produces standard chord progressions. (See Deborah Hayes, "Rameau's Nouvelle méthode," in *Journal of the American musicological society,* v. 27 (1974), pp. 61-74.)

134 RAMEAU, Jean Philippe (1683-1764)

Traité de l'harmonie réduite à ses principes naturels; divisé en quatre livres. Livre I. Du rapport des raisons et proportions harmoniques. Livre II. De la nature et de la propriété des accords; et de tout ce qui peut servir à rendre une musique parfaite. Livre III. Principes de composition. Livre IV. Principes d'accompagnement.

Paris: Jean Baptiste Christophe Ballard, 1722; xxiv+432+18p.

Facs. reprint, New York: Broude Bros., 1965 (MMMLF, 3).

*Facs. reprint, Rome: American Institute of Musicology, 1967 (Complete Theoretical Writings, v. 1, ed. Erwin R. Jacobi).

*English transl. by Philip Gossett as *Treatise on harmony.* New York: Dover, 1971.

English transl. of Book 3 as *A treatise of music, containing the principles of composition.* London: John Walsh, 1752.

London: J. French, 1775-1776.

London: J. French, [1777?].

London: J. Murray, and Dublin: Luke White, 1779. (On the history of English editions, see J. C. Kassler, *The Science of Music in Britain.)*

English transl. by Griffith Jones of Book 4 as *A treatise on harmony, in which the principles of accompaniment are fully explained and illustrated by a variety of examples.* London: Longman & Broderip, [ca. 1795]; 46p.

English transl. of excerpts from the preface and Book 2 in Oliver Strunk, *Source readings in music history,* pp. 564-74.

English transl. of excerpts in Matthew Shirlaw, *The theory of harmony* (1917; 2nd ed., De Kalb, IL: Coar, 1955), pp. 63-133.

The writings of the most influential musical theorist of the period provide not only insight into the structure of his own compositions, but practical application of his ideas to both composition and accompaniment. Book 2, ch. 26, "On the number of measures each air should contain, and on their characteristic movements," comments on the musical structure of dances. Rameau recommends regular phrase structure, especially of 4-measure units or multiples of 4. A table of 16 musical incipits briefly illustrates characteristic rhythms and meters for the Allemande, Courante, Sarabande, Menuet, Passepied, Canarie, Gigue françoise, Gigue italienne, Loure, Gavotte, Rigaudon, and Bourée. Book 3 on composition, in addition to chords, intervals, cadencing, harmonic progression, and modulation, treats the setting of a melody to a bass, setting words to a melody, and construction of a continuo bass to a given melody (especially ch. 38-41).

Possibly no other accompaniment manual of the period applies so directly to both harpsichord and dance idioms as Book 4 of this treatise. Detailed, articulate commentary on fingering, hand position, arpeggiation of chords, reading figured bass, and other purely practical matters dovetails with illustrated description of available chords and progressions. The book's greatest significance must be its association with Rameau's own music. It describes the harmonic vocabulary and keyboard practice of a composer whose own ballet music was celebrated throughout Europe for its felicitousness and originality. At very least, it serves as a guide to the accompaniment of Rameau's own considerable repertory of chamber music based upon the dance.

135 RAPARLIER (18th c.)

Principes de musique, les agréments du chant et un essai sur la prononciation, l'articulation et la prosodie de la langue françoise.
Lille: P. S. Lalau, 1772; 44p.
*Facs. reprint, Genève: Minkoff, 1972.

This instruction manual for vocal ornamentation and diction borrows directly from Montéclair's *Principes de musique* (q.v.), suggesting continuity in French vocal practice throughout the succeeding generation. Clear, precise definitions and careful illustration of ornaments empha-

size the expressive context to which each embellishment is best suited
(pp. 19-28). Each ornament is perceived as an enhancement of the expressive character of the melody or of the meaning of the text. The
author provides details of vocal production and timing, carefully distinguishing between ornaments of similar type, e.g. the 3 degrees of ornamental vibrato (Martellement, Flatté, Balancement). Ornaments discussed include the Coulé, Port de voix (feint, achevé), Accent, Chûte,
Cadence (appuyée/parfaite, subite/jetée, molle, feinte, double), Pincé,
Martellement, Flatté, Balancement, Tour de gosier, Passage, Roulade,
Trait, Sons filés, and Sanglot/Elans. The essay on pronunciation in singing (pp. 29-43) emphasizes the importance of diction as an expressive
component of the music, to be modified to suit the emotion of the specific song.

136 REICHARDT, Johann Friedrich (1752-1814)

Musikalisches Kunstmagazin. Berlin: author, 1782 (v. 1), 1791
(v. 2).
   *Facs. reprint, Hildesheim: Georg Olms, 1969.

This unusual musical periodical addresses itself to the musical connois-
seur in an effort to elevate public taste. It mixes printed music with
commentary, criticism, and literature summary. A wide range of composers (German, Italian, and French), authors, and topics come under
review; ideals of the Enlightenment and early Romanticism prevail. Portions bearing upon French music include (v. 1, p. 80) a review of La
Borde's *Essai* (q.v.), with a table of contents for it; (p. 95) a description
of the character and style of the Polonoise as a Polish national dance
type, with an example scored for violin and keyboard by Grabowiecki;
(p. 141) 3 pieces from Rameau's *Castor et Pollux*—Air gracieux (minuet?), Marche, Gavottes—and an appreciation of Rameau, reproducing
in French La Borde's article on Rameau and Rameau's 1752 letter to the
Mercure de France on d'Alembert's *Élémens* (q.v.); (p. 147) 2 pieces
by Couperin—Sarabande "Les sentimens," "La fleurie ou la tendre
Nanette"—and an appreciation of Couperin, reproducing Couperin's table of ornaments from the *Pièces de clavecin;* (v. 2, p. 74) an Air tendre
from Rameau's *Castor et Pollux* with commentary on p. 96; (p. 100) a
Cavatina from a cantata by Clérambault with commentary on p. 123.

137 ROESER, Valentin (ca. 1735-1782?)

Essai d'instruction à l'usage de ceux qui composent pour la clarinette et le cor. Avec des remarques sur l'harmonie et des exemples à deux clarinettes, deux cors et deux bassons.
Paris: Le Menu, chez Mercier, [1764]; 24p.
*Facs. reprint, Genève: Minkoff, 1972.

The earliest composer's guide to the use of clarinets and natural horns offers scoring suggestions for an ensemble of two clarinets and two horns. Abstract examples show typical writing for the instrument in the proper key for the tonality of the piece. While this appears to be directed toward the Italian symphonic or chamber idioms of the Mannheim school (reference is made to Stamitz), there is one example of a Menuet (p. 22) for two clarinets and two horns, demonstrating the scoring possibility of timbral color contrast upon phrase repetition. (The author lived and performed in Paris from ca.1762 on and was influential in bringing the work of German theorists to the French public by means of his translations.)

138 ROUSSEAU, Jean (1644-?ca. 1700)

Méthode claire, certaine et facile, pour apprendre à chanter la musique, sur les tons transposez comme sur les naturels. A battre la mesure à toutes sortes de mouvemens ordinaires et extraordinaires. A faire les ports de voix, et les cadences sur la musique avec regularité; et à connoître où il faut faire les tremblemens dans les livres où ils ne sont point marquez. Le tout expliqué et mis en ordre par Jean Rousseau.
*Paris: auteur, 1683; 64p.
Paris: auteur, Christophe Ballard, 1691; 38p. *4e édition.*
Amsterdam: P. & J. Blaeu, 1691; 58p. *Le tout mis en ordre par A. Le Chevalier, suivant la copie de J. Rousseau.*
*Amsterdam: E. Roger, [1700]; 87p. *Quatrième édition, revue, augmentée et mise dans un meilleur état.*
Amsterdam: P. Mortier, [ca. 1710]; 87p. *Cinquième édition.*
Facs. reprint, Genève: Minkoff, 1976.

Excellent treatment of French vocal ornamentation emphasizes the context of the ornament, with respect both to poetic and musical metrics and to melodic or rhythmic contour. Only the Port de voix and Cadence or

Tremblement are discussed. Rousseau distinguishes in each case between ornaments that anticipate the beat and those that fall on the beat. Articulate description and explicit musical examples illustrate trills with appoggiaturas falling before the beat (reducing the value of the previous note). Trills without appoggiaturas (which Rousseau later confesses are not true Cadences, but rather Tours de gorges or Tremblements en l'air) occur on ascending short notes in disjunct passages and are found especially in various *airs gays,* such as the Minuet, i.e. minuets in 3/4, 3/8, and similar meters. Among other observations, he describes melodic situations in which it is appropriate to trill only the second half of a long note, after sounding half of its full value. A section on rules for knowing where to trill when no indications appear in the score establishes the melodic, rhythmic, and metric contexts considered to be suitable for adding trills. These rules cover a wider variety of situations than is described in many later instruction manuals.

139 ROUSSEAU, Jean (1644-?ca. 1700)

Traité de la viole, qui contient une dissertation curieuse sur son origine. Une démonstration générale de son manche en quatre figures, avec leurs explications. L'explication de ses jeux différents, et particulièrement des pièces par accords, et de l'accompagnement à fond. Des règles certaines, pour connoître tous les agrémens qui se peuvent pratiquer sur cet instrument dans toutes sortes de pièces de musique. La véritable manière de gouverner l'archet, et des moyens faciles pour transposer sur toutes sortes de tons.

Paris: Christophe Ballard, 1687; 151p.

*Facs. reprint, Amsterdam: Antiqua, 1965.

Facs. reprint, Genève: Minkoff, 1975; 167p.

English transl. in *The consort,* v. 33f. (1977f.).

Dedicated to Rousseau's teacher Sainte Colombe, the viol treatise begins with a brief history of viol playing, naming the greatest French players. Part 1 concerns the holding of instrument and bow, tuning, and the fingerboard. Part 2 describes 5 types of playing customary for the viol: melodic solo, chordal solo, playing a bass to accompany your own singing, providing a bass line in a vocal-instrumental ensemble, and improvising on a given subject. Part 3 describes and illustrates ornaments, including those used customarily by the voice and viol (Cadence ou Tremblement, Port de voix, Aspiration, Plainte, Cheute, Double cadence) and those not idiomatic to the instrument, which must be specifically indicated (Martellement, Battement, Langeur). Rousseau discusses placement of ornaments with reference to the melodic and rhythmic context of the ornamented note; he notes to which of the 5 types of playing each ornament is best suited. Part 4 on bowing states rules for bowing in terms of the metric position of notes in a measure. For each meter, Rousseau indicates which note values are to be played equally and which unequally.

140 ROUSSEAU, Jean Jacques (1712-1778)
Dictionnaire de musique.
Paris: veuve Duchesne, 1768; xii+547p.
  Facs. reprint, Hildesheim: Georg Olms; New York: Johnson, 1969.
Amsterdam: Marc Michel Rey, 1768; xvi+504+372p. (2 v.)
Amsterdam: Marc Michel Rey, 1769; xiv+504+372p. In *Oeuvres de J.-J. Rousseau,* v. 10-11.
Amsterdam: Marc Michel Rey, 1772; 504+372p.
Paris: veuve Duchesne, 1775; 508+372p.
Neuchâtel: Samuel Fauche, 1775; 520+372p. In *Collection complète des oeuvres de J.-J. Rousseau. Nouvelle édition soigneusement revue et corrigée,* v. 11.
London: 1766 [recte 1776]; ix+538p. In *Oeuvres complètes de J.-J. Rousseau,* v. 9.
Genève: 1781; 524+367p.
Genève: 1781; 405+440+304p.
Genève: 1781; xiv+772p.
Genève: 1781; 524+364p. In *Collection complète des oeuvres de J.-J. Rousseau, Citoyen de Genève,* v. 17-18.
Genève: 1782; xiv+772p. In *Collection complète . . . ,* v. 9.
Genève: 1782; 524+400p. In *Collection complète . . . ,* v. 17-18.
Aux Deux-Ponts: Sanson & Comp., 1782; 332+224p. In *Oeuvres complètes de J.-J. Rousseau,* v. 17-18.
Paris: Imprimerie de la Société littéraire-typographique, 1785; 601+424p. In *Collection complète . . . ,* v. 17-18.
Genève, Paris: Volland, 1790; ix+538p. In *Collection complète . . . ,* v. 9-10.

Aux Deux-Ponts: Sanson & Comp., 1792; 290+299p. In *Collection complète . . .* , v. 17-18.

[s.l.]: 1792-93; 460+459+397p. In *Oeuvres complètes . . .* , v. 21-22.

Basel: J. J. Thurneisen, 1793. In *Oeuvres complètes . . .* , v. 17-18.

Paris: Bélin, 1793; 375+402+300p. In *Collection complète . . .* , v. 20-22.

Aux Deux-Ponts: Sanson & Comp., 1798; 290+299p.

Paris: Defer de Maisonneuve, J. E. G. Dufour, 1793-99. In *Oeuvres de J.-J. Rousseau,* v. 10-11.

Paris, Amsterdam: J. E. Gabriel du Four, Didot Le Jeune, 1799; 494+357p. In *Oeuvres de J.-J. Rousseau,* v. 10-11.

*Paris: Lefevre, 1819; 496+352p. In *Oeuvres . . .*

Paris: Crapelet, 1820; 496+352p. In *Oeuvres, nouvelle édition . . .*

Facs. reprint, Genève: Slatkine, 1972.

Amsterdam: M. M. Rey, 1822-24. In *Oeuvres . . .* , v. 17-18.

Paris: P. Dupont, 1824. In *Oeuvres complètes . . .* , v. 12-13.

Paris: Dalibou, 1824-25. In *Oeuvres complètes . . .* , v. 13-14.

Paris: 1839-44. In *Oeuvres . . .* , v. 13-14.

Paris: Société des pubs. illus., 1846. In *Oeuvres complètes . . .* , v. 6-7.

Paris: Galimard, 1959- . In *Oeuvres complètes . . .*

English transl. by William Waring as *A dictionary of music.* London: J. French, [1771]; 468p. 2nd ed. as *A complete dictionary of music. Consisting of a copious explanation of all words necessary to a true knowledge and understanding of music.* London: for J. Murray, Fielding and Water, [ca. 1779]; 468p.

Facs. reprint, New York: AMS Press, 1975.

London: J. Murray; Dublin, Luke White, [1779]; 468p.

Based partly upon Rousseau's articles written for Diderot's and d'Alembert's *Encyclopédie* (q.v.), the dictionary was influential and popular. Though highly opinionated at times, with an undisguised pro-Italian bias previously expressed by Rousseau in his *guerre des bouffons* writings, the technically detailed and clearly written articles have been the source of musical dictionary definitions ever since. The entire work was incorporated into the later *Encyclopédie méthodique* volumes on music by Framery, Ginguené, and Momigny (q.v.); selected articles were translated into German in Johann Adam Hiller's *Wöchentliche Nachrichten und Anmerkungen die Musik betreffend* (q.v.; see the issue of 2 January 1769, pp. 208-10, for the article "Ballet"). Other musical dictionaries indebted to Rousseau include those by Grassineau, Hoyle, and Meude-Monpas. (See the dissertation by Thomas W. Hunt, *The Dictionnaire de musique of Jean-Jacques Rousseau,* North Texas State University, 1967, UM 68-2776.)

Articles on dance types and related pieces include Allemande (distinguishing the danced from the suite versions), Bourrée, Boutade, Branle, Canarie, Chaconne, Contredanse, Courante, Entrée, Fanfare, Forlane, Gaillarde, Gavotte, Gigue, Loure, Marche, Menuet, Musette, Passacaille, Passepied, Pavane, Rigaudon, Rondeau, Sarabande, Sicilienne, Tambourin, and Volte. Ornaments and ornamentation are discussed in articles on Accent, Cadence pleine, Cadence brisée, Coulé, Martellement, Flatté, Port de voix, Port de voix jetté; Agréments du chant, Battement, Broderies (Doubles), Chevrotter, Feinte, Filer, Fusée, Goût du chant, Lourer, Notes de goût, Passage, Pincé, Piqué, Pointer, Proprement, Roulade, Tirade, Transition, Tremblement, and Variations. Other performance practice information may be had from articles such as Accompagnement, Baton de mesure, Battre la mesure, Cadence, Chronomètre, Copiste, Couper, Couplet, Décaméride, Détacher, Doigter, Double, Double-Triple, Expression (Gai, Grave, Légèrement, Lentement, Tendrement, Vite), Goût, Mesure, Mouvement, Opéra, Orchestre, Parties, Phrase, Reprise, Tempérament, Viole, and Violon. With respect to harmony, opposing theories of Rameau, Serre, and Tartini are discussed in articles on Basse fondamental, Harmonie, and Système. Aspects of aesthetics and composition are treated under Dessein, Motif, Nature, Sujet, and Unité de mélodie. There is no coverage of musical instruments, since Rousseau had already written about these in Diderot's *Encyclopédie.* Rousseau's opinions on expressive dance were negative; he saw no point in two languages—song and gesture—vying with one another for attention. There is no entry for dance or chorégraphie. The sarcastic definition of Ballet ("une bizarre sort d'opéra, où la danse n'est guère mieux placée que dans les autres, et n'y fait pas un meilleur effet") became famous.

141 SAINT-LAMBERT, Michel de (fl. ca. 1700)

Nouveau traité de l'accompagnement du clavecin, de l'orgue, et des autres instruments.
*Paris: Christophe Ballard, 1707; 64p.
  Facs. reprint, Genève: Minkoff, 1972.
Amsterdam: Estienne Roger, [ca. 1710]; 134p.

Oriented towards the harsichordist, the 9 chapters of this highly readable manual of thoroughbass and accompaniment treat basic topics such as defining accompaniment, intervals, modes and transposition, motion of the hands, choice of chords, rules for harmonizing an unfigured bass, liberties permitted in accompanying, and taste. Ch. 9 on taste in accompaniment offers remarks on adjusting texture, attack, and rhythm to suit the soloist and type of music. Saint-Lambert distinguishes between treatment of recitative and that of *airs de mouvement,* as well as between harpsichord and organ styles. Ornaments appropriate to the bass or to the accompaniment are indicated, principally the Tremblement.

142 SAINT-LAMBERT, Michel de (fl. ca. 1700)

Les principes du clavecin, contenant une explication exacte de tout ce qui concerne la tablature et le clavier. Avec des remarques nécessaires pour l'intelligence de plusieurs difficultées de la musique. Le tout divisé par chapitres selon l'ordre des matières.
*Paris: Christophe Ballard, 1702; 68p.
  Facs. reprint, Genève: Minkoff, 1972.
  English transl. as *Principles of the Harpsichord* by Rebecca Harris-Warrick. Cambridge: Cambridge University Press, 1984.
Amsterdam: Estienne Roger, [ca. 1710]; 142p.

The 28 chapters of this keyboard manual offer an above average amount of detail concerning keyboard technique, including fingering, ornaments, and articulation. Ch. 8 on metric signatures attempts to describe relative tempos implied by various metric signs in terms of beat equivalence, beginning with a quarter note in common or triple time equal to the step of a man walking 5 quarters of a league per hour. Here Saint-Lambert remarks that minuets for dancing are played at a faster tempo than keyboard minuets; the dances are beaten in one, as if in 3/8 meter. Comments on *notes inégales* point to the Allemande as an exception to the rule: on account of its slowness and common time, inequality falls on 16th notes, if any. He emphasizes that the degree of inequality (the length of the long and short note) is a matter of taste dependent on the type of piece and *mouvement*. Variable texture is considered to be idiomatic to harpsichord music (ch. 9). Ch. 19 on fingering treats intervals, chords, and scales. The extensive discussion of ornaments in ch. 20-28 covers the Tremblement, Double cadence, Pincé, Port de voix, Coulé, Harpegé, Détaché, and Aspiration. An attempt to clarify speed and rhythmic placement of trills is accompanied by examples of various trills and signs used by d'Anglebert and Nivers, with emphasis on the variety of realizations for each type. A complete Menuet and Gavotte appear on pp. 67-68 with ornament signs and fingering. Harris-Warrick's translation provides in appendices the pieces and the ornament tables cited by Saint-Lambert from music by composers Nicolas Lebègue, Jean Henry d'Anglebert, Jean Baptiste Lully, and Guillaume Gabriel Nivers, as well as a compendium of Saint-Lambert's own ornament examples.

143 SIMPSON, Christopher (ca. 1605-1669)

A compendium of practical musick in five parts: teaching, by a new, and easie method, 1. The rudiments of song. 2. The principles of composition. 3. The use of discords. 4. The form of figurate descant. 5. The contrivance of canon.
*London: William Godbid for Henry Brome, 1667; 176p.
*3rd ed., London: Mary Clark for Henry Brome, 1678; 192p. *Together with lessons for viols, etc.*
4th ed., London: W. Pearson for J. Cullen, 1706; 144p. *With additions: much more correct than any former, the examples being put in the most useful cliffs.*
5th ed., London: W. Pearson for John Young, 1714; 144p. *With additions . . .*
6th ed., London: W. Pearson for John Young, 1714. London: W. Pearson for John Young, 1722; 144p.
7th ed., London: T. Astley, 1727; 144p.
8th ed., London: W. Pearson for Arthur Bettesworth and Charles Hitch, 1732; 144p.
9th ed., London: Longman, Lukey and Co., [1775]; 90p. *With material additions, corrected from many gross errors in the former editions, the examples being put in the most useful cliffs.*
Ed. by P. J. Lord, Oxford: Blackwell, 1970.

Part 4, ch. 14 of this composition manual deals with types of instrumental music. Simpson clearly favors those suited to contrapuntal contrivance and so favors the Fancy, Pavan, Galiard, and Almane in order of dignity and excellence. For these he indicates the number of strains, appropriate cadential structure, and structural relation between strains. He regards other dance types (Corants, Sarabands, Jiggs, Country-Dances, etc.) as too common and lacking in potential for musical art to discuss in a treatise on composition. His comments suggest not only which dances were current in the 1660s, but also a snobbish attitude toward dance music among members of the musical establishment. Allied to this may be the British chauvinism evident in his advice to seek examples not necessarily among the works of foreign composers, since none equal the English in matters of importance. (The overall organization and certain details of this treatise are strikingly similar to those in La Voye-Mignot's *Traité de musique,* q.v.)

144 [STADLER, Maximilian (1748-1833)]

Table pour composer des menuets et des trios, à l'infini; avec deux dez à jouer: pour le forte-piano ou clavecin.
*Paris: Wenck, [1780]; 6p.
Paris: Porro, [ca. 1800]; 10p.

Players of this dice game produce 16-measure minuets in D and trios in G major in keyboard score. The method of play is similar to that in Kirnberger's *Der allezeit fertige Polonoisen- und Menuettenkomponist* (q.v.), using two dice (only one for the trios) and numerical tables coordinated with a table of musical measures. The table of numbers is the same as those used in two later dice game publications, the waltz game attributed to Mozart *(Anleitung, so viel Walzer . . . ,* q.v.) and the *Gioco filharmonico, o sia maniera facile per comporre un infinito numero di minuetti e trio anche senza sapere il contrapunto* (Naples: [Marescalchi], 1793), attributed to Joseph Haydn. See Stephen A. Hedges, "Dice music in the 18th century," *Music and letters,* 59 (1978), p. 182; Leonard Ratner, "*Ars combinatoria:* chance and choice in 18th-century music," *Studies in 18th-century music . . . ,* p. 344.

145 TANS'UR, William (1700-1783)

The elements of musick display'd: or, its grammar or groundwork made easy: rudimental, practical, philosophical, historical,

207

and technical. In five books. Containing, I. An universal intro-duction to all the rudiments of musick; shewing the gamut-scale, in its antient, and present, state: and of characters, keys, and of transposition, etc. II. Of time, in all its various moods: with di-rections to performance: and some remarks on the several orna-ments of musick; both vocal and instrumental. III. The structure of musical instruments: with the scale of musick applicable to each; and directions thereunto. Viz. the pitch-pipe, and its use: the organ, or harpsichord: the bassoon and hautboy: the bass-viol, violin, and guittar: the German, and common flutes: the trumpet, and French-horn: the fife, and the clarinet: the drums, and the tabor-and-pipe: and of bells, peals and musical clocks, etc. With sacred lessons; songs in parts; and tunes for instru-ments. IV. The theory of sound, philosophically considered; shew-ing the reasons of concords, and discords: with the principles of composition, in all its branches. V. A new musical-dictionary: explaining, in one view, the technical terms used in music, etc. The whole is faithfully collected from the greatest masters both antient and modern; and methodically laid down for improvement of present, and future ages.

*London: sold by the author and his son; printed for Stanley Crowder, 1772; xiii+232p.

Two earlier versions of this highly conservative treatise were entitled *A new musical grammar: or, the harmonical spectator . . .* (London: the author and Jacob Robinson, 1746; 156p.; 2nd ed. 1753) and *A new musical grammar, and dictionary: or, a general introduction to the whole art of musick . . .* (London: Robert Brown for James Hodges; the author and his son, 1756; xii+176p.). While the orientation is English and Italian, rather than French, the book is noteworthy here for its fa-mous chapter on the pendulum as a musical time-keeping device. A section entitled "The doctrine of pendulums applied to music" (p. 41 in the 1746 version; p. 47, 1756; p. 57, 1772) prescribes a 30-inch pendu-lum to mark a crotchet, etc. The chapter on meters refers to this pendu-lum in suggesting absolute proportional relationships between the tem-pos implied by metric signatures (p. 33, 1756; p. 44, 1772; excerpted in Rosamond Harding, *Origins of musical time and expression*, pp. 17-18).

While the dictionary definitions are too brief to be of great value (though note "Minuet—a quick dance"), an increase in the number of dance terms listed is of possible significance for the history of individual dances. The 1746 version of the work lists Chacone, Ciacona, Minuet, Passepied, Pavin, Rigadoon, Rondeau, Sarabrand (sic), and Sicilian. The 1756 version has Alamande, Galliarda, Gavotta, Giga, Moresk or Morris dancers, Passepied, Pastoral, Pavin, Rigadoon, Rondeau, Sarabrand, and Villanella. The 1772 version includes Alamand, Bourrée, Currant, Dance, Forlana, Galliarda, Gavotta, Giga, Minuet, Musette, Passepied, Passacaglio, Rigadoon, Rondeau, Sarabande (twice), and Saltarella.

146 TARADE, Théodore Jean (1731-1788)

Traité du violon ou règles de cet instrument à l'usage de ceux qui veulent en jouer avec la parfaite connoissance du ton dans lequel on est.

Paris: Melle. Girard, [ca. 1774]; 66p.

*Facs. reprint, Genève: Minkoff, 1972.

Tarade was cited by J. B. Cartier in his *L'art du violon* (Paris: Decombe, 1798) as an authority on bowing, and excerpts from his earlier treatise, *Nouveaux principes de musique et de violon* (Paris: 1774, now lost), appear there. In his *Traité,* pp. 9-16, he provides bowing rules for *notes inégales,* appoggiaturas, *cadences,* and *martellements.* Properly bowed *notes inégales* are considered to be essential to the character of the piece. The section on meters indicates briefly the character implied by each meter and the value of notes to be played unequally. He considers only 2 and 3 to be simple meters; all others are treated as compound meters derived from either 2 or 3. Concerning articulation, he says that staccato dots or slurred staccato marks indicate *notes égales* if the notes normally would be played unequally. Concerning ornaments, he remarks that all French trills are prepared with an appoggiatura, although the preparation is no longer used in modern non-French music.

147 TROMLITZ, Johann Georg (1725-1805)

Ausführlicher und gründlicher Unterricht die Flöte zu spielen.
Leipzig: Adam Friedrich Böhme, 1791; xxiv+376+[10]p.

*Facs. reprint, Amsterdam: Frits Knuf, 1973.

Modeled on the first part of Quantz's flute treatise (q.v.), Tromlitz's instruction manual provides some of our most detailed and extensive

209

information about flute technique in the second half of the 18th c. Chapters on ornamentation, cadenzas, and articulation reflect an international (or German) classic style that draws without acknowledgement upon French and Italian traditions. Treatment of articulation ("Flötensprache") is probably the clearest and most extensive for the period. The treatise is written for the same 2-keyed flute favored by Quantz 40 years earlier; Tromlitz's sequel to the present instruction manual, *Ueber die Flöten mit mehrern Klappen* (Leipzig: Adam Friedrich Böhme, 1800; facs. reprint, Amsterdam: Frits Knuf, 1973), deals with flutes with up to 8 keys.

While there are no specific references to dance music, ch. 5 on meter and tempo notes which meters are frequently used (or not used) in the *style galant,* and many of the musical examples illustrating meter and tempo are dances in character, though not labeled as such (e.g., Minuet, Gigue, Passepied, etc.). A Minuetto on p. 97 illustrates the successful use of the key of C# minor on the 8-keyed flute.

The 15 chapters cover the following subjects: (1) construction, (2) holding the instrument, (3) fingering, (4) notation, (5) meter and tempo, (6) tone and intonation, (7) harmony, keys, (8) articulation, (9) doubletonguing, (10) ornaments (Bebung, Vorschlag/Vorhalt, Nachschlag, Anschlag/doppel Vorschlag, Schleifer, Doppelschlag, Pralltriller & Schneller, Mordent, Battement, Forte & Piano, and Durchziehen), (11) trills, (12) fermatas and cadenzas, (13) breathing, (14) improvising ornamentation, (15) summary. See Thomas E. Warner, "Tromlitz's flute treatise: a neglected source of eighteenth-century performance practice," in *A musical offering: essays in honor of Martin Bernstein,* ed. by Edward H. Clinkscale and Claire Brook (New York: Pendragon Press, 1977), pp. 261-73.

148 TROUFLAUT

Lettre sur les clavecins en peau de buffle inventés par M. Pascal.
*Insert in the *Journal de musique,* Paris: 1773, No. 5; 12p.
Facs. reprint, Genève: Minkoff, 1972.

This panegyric on Pascal Taskin's new leather quilled harpsichord dates the first of such instruments by Taskin to 1768. The leather (peau-de-buffle) is said to last at least five years, and the knee lever permits dynamic flexibility in sound, making the instrument a formidable competitor of the newly emerging pianoforte.

149 TÜRK, Daniel Gottlob (1750-1813)

Klavierschule, oder Anweisung zum Klavierspielen für Lehrer und Lernende, mit kritischen Anmerkungen.
Leipzig, Halle: Auf Kosten des Verfassers; in Kommission bey Schwickert in Leipzig, und bey Hemmerde und Schwetschke in Halle, 1789; 408p.
   *Facs. reprint, Kassel: Bärenreiter, 1962.
Wien: Chr. Gottl. Täubel, 1798; xl+374p. Unauthorized ed. as *Neue Klavier-Schule, oder: Anweisung zum Klavierspielen . . .*
Leipzig: author (Schwickert); Halle: author (Hemmerde und Schwetschke), 1802. *Neue vermehrte und verbesserte Ausgabe. . . .*
Abridged English transl. by C. G. Naumberger as *Treatise on the art of teaching . . .* London: for the proprietor, [ca. 1804].
English transl. by Raymond H. Haggh as *School of clavier playing.* Lincoln: University of Nebraska Press, 1983.

In the appendix of this detailed instruction manual for playing keyboard instruments, ch. 4 describes various dance pieces encountered by the keyboard player: Allemande, Angloise, Ballette, Bourrée, Canarien, Chaconne, Courante, Entrée, Folie d'Espagne, Forlane, Furie, Gaillarde, Gavotte, Gique, Loure, Marsch, Menuett, Musette, Passacaille, Passepied, Pastorale, Polonoise, Rigaudon, Sarabande, Siciliano, Tambourin, and Vaudeville. The descriptions focus upon meter, tempo, character, and expression, with some remarks on the proper performance of certain rhythmic details. Notable is the distinction between the danced and non-danced Allemande. Türk's excellent treatment of ornamentation, fingering, and expressive technique may apply best to the cosmopolitan style of the classic period, but among the examples appended to the book *(Zwölf Handstücke zum Gebrauche beym Unterrichten)* appear a Minuetto, Polonoise, and Marcia. The pieces are completely fingered, with some ornaments, articulation marks, and footnote references to the treatise.

150 VAGUÉ

L'art d'apprendre la musique exposé d'une manière nouvelle et intelligible par une suite de leçons qui se servent successivement de préparation par M\ . V***
*Paris: veuve Ribou et Pierre Ribou; Boivin et le Clair, 1733; 5+2+82p.
*2nd ed. Paris: Mme. Boivin, 1750; 82p.

On pp. 80-82, brief definitions of the various characters of music, showing correspondence between individual meters and dance characters, describe rhythmic details, phrase lengths, repetition schemes, meter, and mood for dance types. These include the Allemande, Bourrée, Bransle, Canarie, Caprice (Fantasie), Chaconne, Courante, Gaillarde, Gavotte, Gigue, Menuet, Passecaille, Passepied, Pavane, Rigodon, Rondeau, Sarabande. The author supports the view of "one of the great and most profound authors" that such pieces are best composed in sections numbering 4, 8, 12, or 16 measures, with caesuras at regular intervals.

151 VILLENEUVE, Alexandre de (1677-after 1756)

Nouvelle méthode très courte et très facile avec un nombre de leçons assez suffisant pour aprendre la musique et les agréments du chant.
Paris: auteur, 1733; [2]+6+39+[1]p.
*Paris: auteur (Bayard, Le Clerc, Castagneri, L'Aigle), 1756; 40p.

This singing manual contains only brief instruction in the rudiments and consists largely of lessons illustrating various keys, meters, characters, etc. In the pieces on pp. 4-15, brief verbal indications tell which note value should be played *inégale*. Those on pp. 24ff. illustrate different sorts of dance rhythms, e.g. Mouvement de courante à la manière françoise, Mouvement de menuet, Passepied, Gigue, Canarie, Loure (grave & animé), Rigaudon, Bourée, Rondeau (gavotte), Sarabande grave, Chaconne gay et leger, Passacaille lent et tendre. The table of ornaments on p. 38 offers one-sentence definitions of Accent, Port de voix, Martellement, Cadence (coupé, double), Pincé, Tremblement, Balancement, Coulement, Hélan, Double cadence battüe, and Double cadence apuyée.

152 VION, Charles Antoine

La musique pratique et théorique, réduite à ses principes naturels, ou nouvelle méthode pour aprendre facilement et en peu de tems l'art de la musique; divisée en deux parties; la première traitant de la musique pratique, la seconde traite de la musique théorique.
Paris: Jean Baptiste Christophe Ballard, 1742; 71p.

*Paris: Jean Baptiste Christophe Ballard, 1744; 71p. *Nouvelle
édition, augmentée d'un nouveau chapitre ou manière de con-
noistre les modes et les tons, ainsi que leurs mutations, secours
très nécessaire pour chanter toute sort de musique à livre ouvert
et sans hésiter; par Monsieur Vion, prêtre, Ordinaire de la musique de l'Eglise de Paris.*

Ch. 4 of this elementary voice tutor has unmeasured exercises in phrasing, with breath marks. Ch. 6 on metric signs illustrates each meter with
several short examples drawn from music of the "most able"
composers—Hotteterre, Lully, L'Affillard, Couperin, Destouches, and
others. Both the remarks and the examples indicate the meter with which
each dance type is associated. The range of meters exemplified is more
extensive than in most such manuals, including C, 2, ₵, 3, 3/2, 3/8,
6/4, 9/8, 12/8, 6/8, 2/4, 4/8, 9/16, 6/16, 3/16, and 12/16.

153 VOGLER, Georg Joseph (1749-1814)

Betrachtungen der Mannheimer Tonschule. 3 v.
Mannheim: 1778-81; 406p., 370p., [241+96+76]p.
*Facs. reprint, Hildesheim: Georg Olms, 1974.

In the last paginated segment of v. 3, Vogler discusses the state of music
in France (pp. 59-76). Taking a highly chauvinistic point of view, he
dismisses French opera before Gluck and praises the theatricality of
modern French opera (presumably Gluck's). In a detailed description of
the French opera orchestra, he notes the presence of 30 violins, 6 violas,
12 violoncellos, 4 contrabasses, 6 bassoons, and all sorts of woodwind
instruments except the serpent. Vogler emphasizes the good effect made
by the quantity of violoncellos, which make the bass line very clear. He
describes the conductor, beating time with a staff while conducting with
gestures employing his whole body, making for more precision in playing than could be achieved with written instructions alone.

154 WALTHER, Johann Gottfried (1684-1748)

*Musicalisches Lexicon; oder, musicalische Bibliothec, darinnen
nicht allein die Musici, welche so wol in alten als neuern Zeiten,
ingleichen bey verschiedenen Nationen, durch Theorie und
Praxin sich hervor gethan, und was von jedem bekannt worden,
oder er in Schrifften hinterlassen, mit allem Fleisse und nach den*

*vornehmsten Umständen angeführtet, sondern auch die in grie-
chischer, lateinischer, italiänischer und frantzösischer Sprache
gebräuchliche musicalische Kunst- oder sonst dahin gehörige
Wörter, nach alphabetischer Ordnung vorgetragen und erkläret,
und zugleich die meisten vorkommende Signaturen erläutert werden.*
Leipzig: Wolffgang Deer, 1732; 659p.
*Facs. reprint, Kassel: Bärenreiter, 1953.

The first comprehensive music dictionary in German draws some of its
material from writings of Brossard and Mattheson, augmented with references to many other musical writings of the 17th c. (and earlier).
Walther includes biographical names in addition to musical terms, with
many French musicians and authors represented. Among the terms appear the names of instruments, French tempo markings, and ornaments
(Agrément, Chûte, Coulé, Couper, Détaché, Lourer, Port de voix, etc.).
For the names of dances, information concerns etymology, phrase structure, number and length of reprises, characteristic rhythm and upbeat,
meter, expression or tempo, and the appropriate keys for cadences. Bibliographic references to Brossard, Mattheson, and Taubert appear within
several of the dance music items. Dances entered include the Allemanda, Bourrée, Canarie, Chaconne, Courante, Entrée de ballet,
Forlana, Gagliarda, Gavotte, Gigue, Loure, Menuet, Passacaglio, Passepied, Pavane, Rigaudon, Sicilienne, and Volte.

A possible forerunner of the dictionary may be the glossary in
Walther's manuscript treatise, *Praecepta der musicalischen Composition* (Weimar 1708; now in Weimar, Landesbibliothek, HS Q 341c; ed.
by Peter Benary, published Leipzig: Breitkopf & Härtel, 1955). Dances
identified there include the Allemanda, Ballo, Borea, Courante, Ciaccona & Chaccone, Entrée, Galliarde, Gavotte, Gigue, Menuet, Paduana
& Pavana, Passagaglia, Passamezzo, Passe Pied, Rigodon, Rondeau,
Saltarella, and Sarabande.

214

PART III

RELATED WRITINGS
ON
THE PERFORMING ARTS

FOREWORD

The writings described in this section provide cultural and aesthetic background for French court dance and dance music of the period. In addition, many works on tangentially related topics incidentally offer specialized information about dance and dance music. Annotations either summarize relevant passages or serve as a general guide to the contents. Items represent a selection of literature on the following topics related to the performing arts (for additional titles, see the index):

A. THE FINE ARTS: DICTIONARIES AND ENCYCLOPE-DIAS Anon. *Encyclopédie méthodique,* Babault, Blankenburg, Bonafons, Corneille, Diderot & d'Alembert, Lacombe *Dictionnaire,* La Valliere *Bibliothèque,* Sulzer

B. AESTHETICS AND AESTHETIC CRITICISM André, Batteux, Beattie, Bielfeld, Chabanon, Chastellux, Crousaz, Decroix, Dubos, Goudar, Gregory, Hogarth, Lacombe *Spectacle,* Lebrun, Le Cerf, Le Pileur, Marpurg, Ménéstrier *Des représentations,* Ménéstrier *Traité*

C. THEATRICAL GENRES (DRAMA, OPERA, PANTO-MIME, BALLET, etc.) Algarotti, Anon. *Comparison,* Aubignac, Bricaire *Lettres,* Chevrier *Observations,* Diderot *Entretiens,* du Roullet, Engel, Krause, La Jonchère, Le Sage, Lambert, Marpurg, Nougaret *De l'art,* Pure, Quatremère, Rémond, Riccoboni

D. MUSICAL POLEMIC issuing from the "Querelle des Bouffons" and the Gluck-Piccini conflict: Castel, Grimm, Rochemont

E. PANEGYRICS, ODES, VERSE ESSAYS Dorat, Titon de Tillet

F. SERMONS AND MORAL ESSAYS ON DANCING Anon. *Cas de conscience,* Gauthier, Languet

G. SATIRE Chevrier *Almanach,* Ralph (Primcock)
H. HISTORIES OF DANCE IN ANTIQUITY Boindin, Boulenger, Burette, Calliachi, Guys, L'Aulnaye, Vossius, Weaver *History*
I. PERFORMANCE INSTITUTIONS
    1. *Academies of Music and Dance:* Anon. *Discours,* Du Coudray, Dumanoir, Parfaict
    2. *Theaters:* Anon. *États,* Boindin, Desboulmiers *Histoire . . . Opéra comique,* Des Essarts, Dury de Noinville, Parfaict, Victor
    • 3. *Performing arts societies, organizations, guilds:* Besche
J. THEATRICAL LIFE
    1. *Theater almanacs, lists of works, collections of texts:* Anon. *Recueil,* Clément & La Porte, Desboulmiers *Histoire anecdotique,* Desboulmiers *Histoire du théâtre,* Gherardi, La Vallière *Ballets,* La Vallière *Bibliothèque,* Le Brun, Léris, Le Sage, Maupoint, Ménéstrier *Recueil,* Molière, Origny, Oulton, Parfaict *Dictionnaire,* Parfaict *Histoire . . . italien,* Parfaict *Histoire . . . français,* Parfaict *Memoires,* Quinault
    2. *Reviews:* Anon. (Potter) *Theatrical*
    3. *Biography and autobiography:* Casanova, Cibber, Constantini, Davies, D'Aquin, Bonafons, Gildon, Gerber, Monnet, Lambert, Le Prévost, Perrault, Titon de Tillet, La Borde
    4. *Diaries, letters, memoires, anecdotes:* Bachaumont, Beauchamps, Gantez, Marolles, Monnet, Mouffle, Clément & La Porte
K. THE SOCIAL CONTEXT OF DANCE
    1. *Dance and manners, therapy, health:* Anon. *Entretiens,* Anon. *A mechanical,* Brown, Essex *Young ladies,* Marquet, Mereau, Nivelon, Rost, Trichter, Weaver *Anatomical*
    2. *Law and the arts:* Carel, Carsillier

ANNOTATED LIST OF WRITINGS

1 ALGAROTTI, Francesco (1712-1764)
Saggio sopra l'opera in musica.
[s.l.]: 1755; 90p.
Livorno: Marco Coltellini, 1763; 157p.
  Facs. reprint, Bologna: FARAP, 1975.
English transl. as *An essay on the opera.*
*London: L. Davis, C. Reymers, 1767; 182p.
  Facs. reprint, London: Press Printers, 1917.
Glasgow: R. Urie, 1768; 124p., 182p.
German transl. by R. E. Raspe as *Versuch über die Architectur, Mahlerey und musicalische Opera.* Kassel: Johann Friedrich Hemmerde, 1769; 300p.
French transl. by F. J. de Chastellux as *Essai sur l'opéra.* Pisa, Paris: Ruault, 1773; viii+190p.
Ed. by G. F. Malipiero in *I profeti di Babilonia.* Milano: 1924.
Excerpts from the 1768 English transl. (ch. 1-2) ed. by Oliver Strunk in *Source readings in music history* (New York: W. W. Norton, 1950), pp. 657-72.

Best known and most influential of the many critics of Italian opera at mid-century, Algarotti upheld a neo-classic ideal of noble simplicity and unified action. In this essay he calls for reform of Italian opera, advocating severity in the drama and the integration of choruses, ballets, and spectacle into the dramatic action (all standard features of lyric tragedy in France). He treats in turn the poetry and subject matter, to which all else is subordinate (ch. 1), the music of recitative, aria, and overture, which all too often violate the spirit of the drama (ch. 2), singing and the abuses of singers more interested in artistic display than in dramatic credibility (ch. 3), dances (ch. 4), and the theater (ch. 5), with a concluding summary. Algarotti is especially critical of dances unrelated to the plot, which he terms "irrational caprioling" (p. 67), always foreign and often repugnant. He insists dance be dramatically relevant, the quintessential abridgment of an action. Two original librettos appended to the essay, *Enea in Troia* and *Iphigénie en Aulide*, demonstrate his ideas for reform. The 1768 English transl. has a short glossary (pp. 187-92). Translator's notes in the 1773 French transl. indicate an expansion of the chapter on dance with a long quotation from Noverre's *Lettres* (q.v.).

2 ANDRÉ, Yves Marie (1675-1764)

Essai sur le beau, où l'on examine en quoi consiste précisément le beau dans le physique, dans le moral, dans les ouvrages d'esprit, et dans la musique.

*Paris: Hippolyte-Louis Guérin, Jacques Guérin: 1741; 302p.

Amsterdam: J. H. Schneider, 1759; 346p. With commentary by Formey.

Amsterdam: J. H. Schneider, 1760; cxxviii+199p.

Paris: L. Etienne Ganeau, 1763; 250+367p.

Amsterdam: J. H. Schneider, 1767.

Paris: L. E. Ganeau, 1770.

German transl. as *Versuch von dem Schönen*. Königsberg: 1753; 142p.

German transl. as *Versuch über das Schöne*. Altenburg: Richter, 1757; 184p.

The author seeks to expose basic principles underlying our perception of beauty. He distinguishes three kinds of beauty: "essential" beauty, which is entirely spiritual and completely independent of the physical world; "natural" beauty, which is both spiritual and corporeal, independent of opinion or taste, but necessarily dependent on the laws of nature (i.e. God); and "arbitrary" or "artificial" beauty, which is spiritual and observes certain rules established by wise men according to reason and experience as guidelines for artistic creativity. Ch. 1 applies these principles to the visible world, ch. 2 the moral, ch. 3 the spiritual, and ch. 4 the musical.

3 [ANONYMOUS]

Cas de conscience sur les danses, décidé par messieurs les docteurs en théologie de la faculté de Paris, où l'on fait voir ce qu'on doit penser des danses en général de celles où les personnes de différent sexe se trouvent ensemble, sur-tout quand elles se sont les jours de dimanche et de fête. Quelles sont les obligations des

*pères et des mères, des seigneurs de paroisse, et de leurs offi-
ciers, par raport aux danses. Des danses qui se sont aux nôces;
des joueurs de violon; de plusieurs abus dont les danses sont la
source, et des différens prétextes que l'on a porté pour autoriser
les danses.*
*Paris: Philippe Nicolas Lottin, 1721; 33p.

Since dancing had become so much in use in the parishes of the country,
a curé, noticing the bad effects following from its practice, sought guid-
ance from *messieurs les docteurs de la Sorbone* in a series of questions.
Among these was the question of whether it was sinful for parents who
did not believe dancing went against Christian piety to send their children to a dancing master. Should they insist that the dancing masters
come to their own houses, so that their children might exercise without
danger under their parents' watchful eyes? The good fathers assured the
curé that parents could take their children to the houses of reputable
dancing masters, always keeping in mind that parents ought to have
confidence in those whom they allow their children to imitate. Advice is
also offered to players of the violin for dancing. This is one of numerous
tracts on attitudes of the Church toward dancing. The general feeling
was that dancing itself was innocent (after all, David danced before the
Lord); its circumstances, however, presented countless perils that led to
the sin of indulgence, the opposite of Christian mortification of the
flesh. It is interesting that this French tract is in many ways quite moder-
ate, in contrast to the vitriolic Puritan tracts of the time.

4 [ANONYMOUS]

*A comparison between the two stages, with an examen of the Gen-
erous Conqueror; and some critical remarks on The Funeral, or
Grief Alamode, The False Friend, Tamerlane and others. In dia-
logue.*
London: 1702; [vi]+200p.
   Facs. reprint, New York and London: Garland, 1973. Preface
by Arthur Freeman.
Ed. with introduction by Staring Bailey Wells, in *Princeton stud-
ies in English*, v. 26. Princeton, London: 1942.
*New York: B. Blom, 1971; xxi+206p.

Theatrical criticism takes the form of a conversation between two gentlemen, Ramble and Sullen, and a critic, Chagrin. Quoting excerpts,

they attack plays and performers at the two London theaters, Lincoln's Inn Fields and Drury Lane. Their critical aesthetic requires the classical unities of action, time, and place. The interest to the dance historian lies in their first-hand account of (1) public reaction to Harlequins and Scaramouches from France pulling the greatest houses that were ever known (p. 47), on the return of the Duke of Monmouth, who brought from France the dancing master St. André (pp. 48-49); (2) the popularity of the French dancer Jean Balon (p. 49); and (3) the problem of introducing dance as part of stage drama (pp. 48-53). The last was seen as decadence, "the blemish of the stage." The book is often wrongly attributed to Charles Gilden, but see S. B. Wells, "An eighteenth century attribution," *Journal of English and Germanic philology,* v. 38 (1939), pp. 239-46.

5 [ANONYMOUS]

Discours académique à l'occasion de l'établissement de l'Académie Royale de Danse en la ville de Paris. Avec un discours académique, pour prouver que la danse dans sa plus noble partie n'a pas besoin des instruments de musique, et qu'elle est en tout absolument indépendante du violon.
Paris: P. Le Petit, 1663; 11p.
*Ed. in part by Charles Pauli, in *Élémens de la danse.* Leipzig: Ulr. Chret. Saalbach, 1756; p. 78.

In order to further the correct teaching of dance, Louis XIV founded the Académie Royale de Danse. The introduction to the letters of patent establishing the school contained this discourse on the importance of dance in training the body, for courtiers in general and for those bearing arms in particular. It argues that dance must be considered an art separate from music, with which it had been combined in the Académie Royale de Musique. (See Dumanoir's *Mariage de la musique avec la dance* for a cogent attack on this position.) For a discussion of the accuracy of dates associated with the existence of the dance academy, see Régine Kunzle, "In search of L'Académie Royale de Danse," *York dance review,* v. 7 (Spring 1978), pp. 3-13. *The French academies of the sixteenth century* by Frances A. Yates (London: The Warburg Institute, University of London, 1947; reprint Kraus, 1968) gives background on the formation of the French academies in general, and on the specific place the academies of music and dance held among them (see especially ch. 12, "Seventeenth-century French academies").

6 [ANONYMOUS]

*Encyclopédie méthodique. Arts et métiers mécaniques. . . .
Tome quatrième.*
*Paris: Panckoucke; Liège: Plomteux, 1788; 812p.

A large portion of the volume is devoted to musical instruments and
their manufacture. The description of instruments by families and individually (pp. 1-148) is extensive in its coverage, though technical detail
is offered for only a few, such as the harpsichord family, violin, harp,
and organ. Included are: Clavecin, Epinette, Manicorde, Clavicorde,
Claquebois, Vielle; Rebec, Violon, Violon d'amour, Alto, Basse de
violon, Basse des Italiens, Basse-double, Violoncelle, Viole, Basse de
viole, Dessus de viole, Lyra de braccio, Baryton, Viole d'amour;
Monocorde, Trompette marine, etc.; Lyre, Harpe, Guittar, etc., Lute,
etc.; Orgue, Orgue à cylindre; Flûte à bec, Flûte traversière; Hautbois,
etc.; Basson; Clarinette; Musette, etc.; Cor, Trompette, Trombone,
Cornet, Serpent; and a long list of percussion instruments. Pages 148-50
provide a table of contents to 21 plates (in v. 3 of the same set) that
illustrate the instruments described. A glossary of terms concerning instruments and their manufacture follows on pp. 150-86.

7 [ANONYMOUS]

Entretiens galans ou conversations sur. . . . Tome II.
*Paris: Jean Ribou, 1681.

The sixth "gallant encounter" (pp. 53-106) takes the form of light conversation about music among two young couples. They observe that
music is much in fashion at court, that ladies and gentlemen are eager to
demonstrate their skill in composing dance tunes and choreographies.
The artistic success of a courante composed by a young duchess leads
them to conclude that with talent and application a dilletante can please
more readily with musical than with literary accomplishment, indeed
that music is currently the fashionable means of pleasing.

**8 [ANONYMOUS] (Sometimes attributed to P. Simon or to
Vente)**

*Etat actuel de la musique du roi et des trois spectacles de
Paris. . . .*
*Paris: Vente, 1759-1778.

223

This almanac appeared annually 1759-1778, offering detailed information about institutions sponsored by royal patronage: Musique (de la Chambre) du Roi, Opéra, Comédie Française, Comédie Italienne, and the royal academies of music and dance. Each year it presented a theatrical calendar (showing how the theater seasons were determined by Church festivals), an introductory essay on the entertainments, and specific information on each institution. For each institution there appears a brief history; a list of personnel indicating the organizational hierarchy of administrators, musicians, singers, dancers, orchestral players, costumers, stage workers, etc., including pensioners both living and recently deceased; and an alphabetized repertory list of all operas, ballets, and other musical stage works performed that year, naming composers and poets. From the lists of performing personnel for the King's chamber music, concerts, and stage entertainments, one can form an idea of the maximum size for musical ensemble accompaniment. The place of dance in the annual entertainment schedule can be seen in the lists of dancers at the Opéra (from *maître des ballets* Mons. Lany to the female supernumeraries; 1760, pp. 35-36 in the second set of numbered pages); of teachers at the Académie de Danse (the list begins with Dupré, p. 42); of dancers at the Comédie Française *(directeur* Bellecourt, principal *danseuses* Allard and Guimard, et al., pp. 86-89) and Comédie Italienne (from *danseurs* to *figurantes,* p. 118). The volume devoted to 1774 also lists public balls, from the time of their origin to 1774 (pp. 68-90), and titles of books offering theatrical information.

9 [ANONYMOUS]

A mechanical essay on singing, musick, and dancing; containing their uses and abuses and demonstrating the alterations they produce in a human body.
*London: J. Pemberton, 1727; [iii]+46p.

This physiology book shows how the body is affected by music and dance: "Dancing is especially good for diseases of consumptions, athmas, hectick fevers, diseases of joynts, agues, suppression of menstrual flux or any other blood related disease" (p. 38).

10 [ANONYMOUS]

Recueil général des opéras représentez par l'Académie royale de musique, depuis son établissement. 16 v.

224

*Paris: C. Ballard, 1703-1746; (v. 1) 444p., (v. 2) 491p., (v. 3) 394p., (v. 4) 486p., (v. 5) 468p., (v. 6) 468p., (v. 7) 468p., (v. 8) 436p., (v. 9) 437p., (v. 10) 609p., (v. 11) 480p., (v. 12) 503p., (v. 13) 524p., (v. 14) 461p., (v. 15) 493p., (v. 16) 539p.
   Facs. reprint, Genève: Slatkine, 1971.
   Facs. reprint, Genève: Minkoff, 1971.

This is said to be the most extensive and accurate edition of opera texts for works performed in Paris, 1669-1745. It contains complete texts for 129 operas set by such composers as Lully, Mouret, and Rameau. The preface in v. 1 begins with a brief history of the invention of opera, in France, from its introduction from Italy early in the 17th c. to the formation of the Académie in 1669, the first "opera" *Pomone* in 1671, the leadership of Lully, the splendor of Pécourt, etc. In the body of the work, the editors (J. N. de Francini, H. de Gaureault, sieur de Dumont, Guyenet, and L. A. E. de Thuret) identify the composers of music and the authors of the poetry, but give only brief mention in the preface to the dancers: les sieurs Dun, Hardouin, Thevenard, Ballon, and Mesd. de Subligny and Maupin. Pécourt is credited with *Ballet de Thétis* and *Ballet de Pélée* (with d'Etang) and other works. The editors intended to compile 56 operas but finally arrived at 126, arranged chronologically. Accuracy is ensured, they claim, because the compilation is being made at the same press that originally published the individual works. Seven volumes were published in 1703; v. 8-10 appeared in the next few years at intervals. Volume 11 was then skipped while the next three appeared in 1734; it was then published, after revision and correction, in 1738. The last two came out in 1739 and 1745. The collection is included here on account of its unusual amount of detail, given in the *avertissements* introducing each work cited, concerning circumstances of production, origin of plots, intent of the author, and ideas on staging. For each opera, there is an illustrative plate, a list of characters (with a few performers named), the poetic text, and a description of staging and machinery.

11 [ANONYMOUS]
The theatrical review: for the year 1757, and beginning of 1758 containing critical remarks on the principal performers of both the theatres [Drury Lane and Covent Garden], *together with observations on the dramatic pieces, new or revived, that have been performed at either house within that period. To which is added, a*

scale of the comparative merit of the above performers.
*London: J. Coote, 1758; v+88p.
Theatrical review, or annals of the drama. V. 1 (Jan.-June, 1763). London: Wilson, Fell, S. Williams, 1763.
[John POTTER (ca.1734-after 1813)] *The theatrical review: or new companion to the playhouse: containing a critical and historical account of every tragedy, comedy, opera, farce, etc. exhibited at the theatres during the last season, with remarks on the actors who performed the principal characters. The whole interspersed with occasional reflections on dramatic poetry in general; the characters of the best dramatic authors; and observation on the conduct of the managers, calculated for the entertainment and instruction of every lover of theatrical amusement. By a society of gentlemen, independent of managerial influence.* 2 v.
London: S. Crowder, 1772; v. 1 Sept.-Dec. 1771; v. 2 Jan.-June 1772.
The theatrical review. [London: 1783.]

These collected reviews of theatrical performances, though uneven in coverage, often describe the work under scrutiny. Some kind of dancing formed a part of many entertainments here reviewed. The reviews constitute a source of information about the two London theaters that supported dance in the third quarter of the 18th c.: Drury Lane and Covent Garden. In the 1758 publication, for example, long critical essays on the productions at the two theaters in 1757 (p. 47) describe not only the action of the plays, but the acting of Mr. Garrick and Mrs. Cibber as well. On p. 45 there is a "Scale of Judgment," from 1 to 18, to measure performances of such actors. Qualities judged included Genius, Judgment, Expression, Acting, and Voice.

12 AUBIGNAC, François Hédelin d' (1604-1676)

La pratique du théâtre, oeuvre très nécessaire à tous ceux qui veulent s'appliquer à la composition des poèmes dramatiques.
*Paris: Antoine de Sommaville, 1657 [sometimes dated 1669]; 514p.
2nd ed., Amsterdam: Jean Frédéric Bernard, 1715; 3 v.
  Facs. reprint, Genève: Slatkine, 1971.
  *Facs. reprint, München: Wilhelm Fink, 1971; lix+357+156+200p.

Ed. by Pierre Martin, with the author's unpublished annotations. Paris: Edouard Champion; Alger: J. Carbonel, 1927; 2+xxx+439p. (See p. 1, note 1, for information on the 1715 edition.)
English transl. as *The whole art of the stage.* [London?]: W. Cadman, 1684.
Facs. reprint, New York: Benjamin Blom, 1968.

Aubignac applies contemporary dramatic theory, especially the notion of "vray-semblance," to drama in which dance plays an intrinsic part. Based upon his personal observations, the book reveals that, even before Molière and Quinault made their contributions to drama, the ballet intermède formed a separate but related embellishment to stage drama. Concerned primarily with spoken as opposed to musical drama, Aubignac nevertheless includes dance with music, poetry, decor, and costume in his discussions of contemporary theatrical works. For information about the second edition (Amsterdam 1715), see the 1927 edition by P. Martin, p. 1, note 1. For discussion of Aubignac by a 20th-c. scholar, see Marie Françoise Christout, *Le ballet de cour de Louis XIV* (Paris: A. & J. Picard, 1967), ch. 5, "Théories et théoriciens: Michel de Pure, Claude-François Ménéstrier (S. J.), d'Aubignac."

13 BABAULT (b. ca. 1780) [A. F. F. MENEGAULT and others]
Annales dramatiques, ou dictionnaire général des théâtres, contenant 1° l'analyze de tous les ouvrages dramatiques: tragédie, comédie, drame, opéra, opéra-comique, vaudeville, etc., représentés sur les théâtres de Paris, depuis Jodelle jusqu'à ce jour; la date de leur représentation, le nom de leurs auteurs, avec des anecdotes théâtrales; 2° les règles et observations des grands maîtres sur l'art dramatique, extraites des oeuvres d'Aristote, Horace, Boileau, d'Aubignac, Corneille, Racine, Molière, Regnard, Destouches, Voltaire, et des meilleurs Aristarques dramatiques; 3° les notices sur les auteurs, compositeurs, acteurs, actrices, danseurs, danseuses; avec des anecdotes intéressantes sur tous les personnages dramatiques, anciens et modernes, morts et vivans, qui ont brillé dans la carrière du théâtre. Par une société de gens de lettres.
Paris: Henée, 1808-12.

*Facs. reprint, Genève: Slatkine, 1967; (v. 1, A-BEA)
xxxix+498p., (v. 2, BEA-COR) iii+496p., (v. 3, COR-E)
476p., (v. 4, F-HOM) 480p., (v. 5, HOM-L) 414p., (v. 6, M)
446p., (v. 7, NOP) 2+536p., (v. 8, Q-S) 428p., (v. 9, T- Z)
2+428p.
2nd ed., 1819.

Though published in the 19th c., this extensive reference work has a
quantity of information concerning theatrical productions in late 18th-c.
Paris. It summarizes works in a variety of genres, describes the theaters,
and provides accounts of celebrated practitioners. Dance information
appears only intermittently among the summaries of tragedies and comedies, which include pieces classified as *ballet, ballet ancréontique, acte
de ballet, ballet pantomime,* and *ballet d'action.* Also treated are the
terms Ballet (v. 1, pp. 457-61), Danse (v. 3, pp. 75-80), Élémens (v. 3,
pp. 357-58), Entrée (v. 3, pp. 398-99), Fêtes (v. 4, pp. 95-97),
Fragmens (v. 4, pp. 162-63), Gavotte (v. 4, p. 216), Intermèdes (v. 5,
pp. 111-12), Machines (v. 6, pp. 4-8), Mascarade (v. 6, p. 145),
Masque (v. 6, pp. 148-59), Mimes (v. 6, pp. 295-97), Opéra (v. 7, pp.
114-33), Pantomime (v. 7, pp. 214-30), Passions (v. 7, pp. 248-50),
and Vaudeville (v. 9, pp. 279-83), and the dancers Beauchamps (v. 1,
pp. 491-92), Blondy (v. 2, p. 65), Camargo (v. 2, pp. 169-71), Didelot
(v. 3, p. 207), Dupré (v. 3, pp. 281-82), Gardel (v. 4, p. 205), Noverre
(v. 7, pp. 64-68; given complete credit for adding expression to dance),
Pécourt (v. 7, p. 266), Sallé (v. 8, pp. 238-39), and the Vestris family
(v. 9, pp. 309-10).

14 BACHAUMONT, Louis Petit de (1690-1771) [and others]
*Mémoires secrets pour servir à l'histoire de la République des
Lettres en France depuis MDCCLXII jusqu'à nos jours, ou journal d'un observateur, contenent les analyses des pièces de théâtre
qui ont paru durant cet intervalle; les relations des assemblées
littéraires; les notices des livres nouveaux, clandestins, prohibés;
les pièces fugitives, rares ou manuscrites, en prose ou en vers; les
vaudevilles sur la cour; les anecdotes et bons mots; les éloges des
savants, des artistes, des hommes de lettres morts, etc.* [1762-
1787] 36 v.
Paris: 1777-1789.
Hollande.

*London: J. Adamson, 1780-1789 (v. 1-14 published 1780; v. 15-16, 1781; v. 17-18, 1782; v. 19-22, 1783; v. 23-24, 1784; v. 25-30, 1786; v. 31-33, 1788; v. 34-36, 1789); (v. 1, covering the years 1762-63) 324p., (v. 2, 1764-66) 304p., (v. 3, 1766-68) 324p., (v. 4, 1768-69) 328p., (v. 5, 1769-71) 328p., (v. 6, 1771-73) 320p., (v. 7, 1773-75) 328p., (v. 8, 1775) 300p., (v. 9, 1776) 302p., (v. 10, 1777) 330p., (v. 11, 1777-78) 238p., (v. 12, 1778) 216p., (v. 13, 1767-79, using subject headings) 328p., (v. 14, 1778-79) 346p., (v. 15, 1780) 311p., (v. 16, 1780 plus supplement on 1762-66) 121+272p., (v. 17, 1781) 384p., (v. 18, 1781 plus supplement to 1765-68) 248+384p., (v. 19, 1781 plus supplement to 1768-71) 336+381p., (v. 20, 1782) 368p., (v. 21, 1782 plus 1771-72) 232+89+90+143p., (v. 22, 1783) 383p., (v. 23, 1783) 354p., (v. 24, 1783 plus 1772-73) 120+360p., (v. 25, 1784) 346p., (v. 26, 1784) 352p., (v. 27, 1784 plus 1773-74) 127+360p., (v. 28, 1785) 332p., (v. 29, 1785 plus 1774-75) 309+358p., (v. 30, 1785 plus 1775) 213p., (v. 31, 1786 plus 1775) 310+360p., (v. 32, 1786 plus 1775) 340+360p., (v. 33, 1786 plus 1775) 321+360p., (v. 34, 1787) 428p., (v. 35, 1787) 508p., (v. 36, 1787) 406p.

Table alphabétique des auteurs et personnages cité dans les mémoires secrets pour servir à l'histoire de la république des lettres en France.
Bruxelles: A. Mertens et fils, 1866.

Facs. reprint, England: Gregg International, 1970; 36 v. after the London 1780-89 ed. plus the 1866 *Table.*

Mémoires secrets de Bachaumont (1762-1771), publiés avec une préface et des notes, et accompagnés de documents inédits par Ad. Van Bever. Tome I avec trente-quatre illustrations d'après les dessins de Carmontelle et les gravures du temps (1762-1767). Tome II avec trente-et-une illustrations d'après les dessins de Carmontelle et les gravures du temps (1768-1771).
*Paris: Louis Michaud, 1912; 2 v.

This collection of journalistic writings by Bachaumont and others of his circle contains literary anecdotes revealing contemporary mores and opinion concerning the theater. They serve to indicate public opinion on specific performances and choreographies, the effectiveness of dances within operas, personal reputations, and the success or failure of new pieces. The 1866 *Table alphabétique* has entries for female dancers Allard, Aurelli, Aurore, Bacceli, Basse, Bassy, Beze, Camargo, Cecile, Crepeux, Despreaux (i.e. Guimard), Dorival, Duperey, the Gardels, Gervaise, Gondolie, Grandi, Heidoux, Heinel, Jude, Lafond, Lany, Laure, Lyonnois, Mire, Paganini, Peslin, Rose, Theodore, Torle, Vernier, Vestris, Zacharie, and Zanuzzi; harlequins Bigotini and Coraly; and dancers Bacquoi-Guédon, Dauberval, the Gardels, Hus (dancer and composer of ballet), Lany, Laval, Nivelon, Noverre (composer), Petit, Pic, Pitro (composer), Veronese, Vestrallard, and the Vestris family. There are also descriptions of *figurantes* and *directeurs de spectacles*. The 1912 ed. provides biographical notes for persons referred to, and appendices in v. 2 have information about Bachaumont and his closest associate, Mme. Doublet.

15 BATTEUX, Charles (1713-1780)

Les beaux-arts réduits à un même principe.
*Paris: Durand, 1746; xiii+291p.
*Paris: Durand, 1747; xiii+308p.
   Facs. reprint, New York: Johnson, 1970.
Leyden: Elie Luzac fils, 1753; 266p.
Göttingen, Leiden: Elie Luzac fils, 1755; 266p. As *Principes de littérature.*
Göttingen, Leiden: Elias Luzac; Paris: Dessaint et Saillant, 1764; 366p. As *Principes de littérature.*
Paris: Saillant et Nyon, 1773; 384p.
   Facs. reprint, Genève: Slatkine, 1969.
Paris: Saillant et Nyon, Vve. Dessaint, 1774; 384p. "Cinquième ed."
Paris: Dessaint et Saillant, 1775; 312p.
   Facs. reprint, Genève: Slatkine, 1967.
Paris: Saillant et Nyon, Vve. Dessaint, 1777; 312p.
Lyon: Amable Leroy, 1800; 312p.
Paris: Nyon, 1810. As *Élémens de littérature.*
German transl. by Philipp Ernst Bertram as *Die schöne Künste aus einem Grunde hergeleitet.* Gotha: Joh. Paul Mevius, 1751; 226p.
German transl. by Joh. Adolf Schlegel as *Einschränkung der schönen Künste auf einen einzigen Grundsatz.* Leipzig: Weidmann, 1751; 408p.

2nd ed., Leipzig: Weidmann, 1759; 615p.

3rd ed., Leipzig: Weidmanns Erben und Reich, 1770; 424+586p.

Facs. reprint of selections from v. 2 and 3, New York: Georg Olms, 1976.

German transl. by Carl Wilhelm Ramler as *Einleitung in die schönen Wissenschaften.* Leipzig: Weidmann, 1756-58; 4 v.

2nd ed., Leipzig: M. G. Weidmanns Erben und Reich, 1762-63; 4 v.

3rd ed., Leipzig: M. G. Weidmanns Erben und Reich, 1769; 4 v.

Wien: Joh. Thomas Edler von Trattner, 1770-71; 4 v.

Wien: Trattner, 1773.

4th ed., Leipzig: M. G. Weidmanns Erben und Reich, 1774; 4 v.

5th ed., Leipzig: 1802.

German transl. of excerpts by Johann Christoph Gottsched as *Auszug aus des . . . schönen Künsten.* Leipzig: Bernhard Christoph Breitkopf, 1754; 218p.

German transl. of excerpts in F. W. Marpurg's *Historisch-kritische Beiträge zur Aufnahme der Musik,* v. 5, 1. Stuck (Berlin: G. A. Lange, 1760), pp. 20-44.

English transl. by Miller as *A course of the belles lettres: or the principles of literature.* London: B. Low & Co., 1761.

Russian transl. by Anna Petrovna Bunina, Moscow: 1808; v+179p.

In this widely influential essay in rationalistic aesthetics, Batteux finds a common motivation in all artistic endeavor: the imitation of nature. Poetry, architecture, painting, music, and dance seek to express universal truth, each in its own way. Music and dance, rather than instructing by means of reason, engage and persuade. Sound and gesture become the means for describing sentiments, or "passions," for arousing in the observer specific emotions or states of mind. Each piece must convey a single state, and all aspects of composition and performance must contribute to that aim, down to the last *agrément* or tilt of the head.

16 BEATTIE, James (1735-1803)

Essays. [On the nature and immutability of truth, in opposition to sophistry and scepticism.] On poetry and music, as they affect the mind. [On laughter, and ludicrous composition. On the utility of classical learning.]

Edinburgh: W. Creech, 1776; xiv+[3]+757p.

Facs. reprint, New York: Garland, 1971.

*London: E. & C. Dilly; Edinburgh: W. Creech, 1778; vi+[3]+555p.

Dublin: C. Jenkins, 1778. *New edition. . . .*

3rd ed., London: E. & C. Dilly; Edinburgh: W. Creech, 1779.

6th ed., Edinburgh: Denham & Dic, 1805; 341p.

Philadelphia: Hopkins [et al.], 1809.

Edinburgh: W. Creech; London: Longman & Co., 1813.

French transl. as *Essai sur la poésie et sur la musique, considérées dans les affections de l'âme.* Paris: F. Benoist, 1798; xxiv+342p.

Paris: Henri Tardieu; Milano: Giegler & Mainardi, 1798; 342p.

German transl. as *Neue philosophische Versuche.* Leipzig: in der Weygandschen Buchhandlung, 1779; 552p.

Written in 1762, Beattie's essay on poetry and music prefigures Chabanon in questioning the aesthetic precept (widely accepted in the 18th c.) that all art imitate nature. The section on music (ch. 6) deals in a straightforward manner with the limitations placed upon music when it is forced to be merely an art of imitation. While imitation may be one aspect of the art, it does not represent the whole of music's value to humanity. After giving several illustrations, he concludes: "If then the highest excellence may be attained in instrumental music, without imitation; and if, even in vocal music, imitation have only a secondary merit; it must follow that the imitation of nature is not essential to this art; though sometimes, when judiciously employed, it may be ornamental" (p. 140). If this be true, he asks, then what does give pleasure in music? His answer deals with (1) the nature of the notes themselves, (2) the relationship between notes, (3) the relationship between words and music, (4) variety and simplicity of structure, and (5) associations aroused. Beattie closes the section on music with a discussion of "sympathy" (what today might be called empathy).

17 BEAUCHAMPS, Pierre François Godard de (1689-1761)
Recherches sur les théâtres de France, depuis l'année onze cens soixante et un, jusqu'à présent. 3 v.
*Paris: Prault père, 1735; v. 1, 22+508p.; v. 2, 544p.; v. 3, 523p.
Facs. reprint, Genève: Slatkine, 1968.

Rather than a continuous history, this is a collection of information of interest to the author, published for those who love theater. Volume 1 dips into Jean de Nostradamus for lives of the poets of Provence (probably from *Les vies des plus célèbre et anciens poètes provençaux*, Lyon 1575); discourses on the origin of spectacles in France; summarizes in list form the establishment of theaters and performing groups in Paris; offers miscellaneous information and quotations about "entremets, mistères, moralités, farces & sotties avant Jodelle;" and closes with a list of their authors, with miscellaneous information about authors and their works (pp. 1-356). The rest of v. 1 and all of v. 2 cover the French theater, divided into "four ages." For the dance historian, most useful is v. 3 entitled *Tournois, Carousels, Pas d'armes, Comédies, Mascarades, Mommeries, et Ballets, depuis 1548 jusqu'en 1735*, especially the list of ballets (etc.) on pp. 1-202. The information, however, is uneven, as is that in the following sections on the Théâtre de l'Opéra, the Italian theater, the Opéra Comique, and a final section on the lives of some French actors. Three final tables list authors, chronologically and alphabetically, and the works discussed, alphabetically.

18 BESCHE l'ainé
Abrégé historique de la ménestrandie. Dans lequel on rapporte les différents Arrêts du Conseil et Lettres-Patentes rendus en faveur de l'art musical, contre la communauté de Saint-Julien des Ménétriers.
*Versailles: 1774; 36p.

This lively summary history documents the strife between independent musicians and the guild of dancing masters and players of instruments, known as the Confrérie de Saint Julien des ménétriers (descended from the guild established ca.1330 for jongleurs and menestrels). Besche traces the guild's efforts to control all instrumentalists through a series of legal battles with the Organistes du Roi that from the 1690s to the 1770s repeatedly brought about royal restriction of the guild's jurisdiction. See Robert Isherwood, *Music in the Service of the King*, pp. 154ff.

19 BIELFELD, Jacob Friedrich von (1717-1770)

L'érudition complète . . . Les premiers traits de l'érudition universelle ou analyse abrégée de toutes les sciences, des beaux-arts et des belles-lettres par M. le baron de Bielfeld. Tome second.

Leiden: Sam. et Jean Luchtmans, 1767; 350p.

L'érudition universelle, ou analyse abrégée de toutes les sciences, des beaux-arts et des belles lettres. Par M. le Baron de Bielfeld. Tome troisième, qui traite des parties de l'érudition qui prennent leur source dans le génie.

*Berlin: 1768; 448p.

English transl. by W. Hooper as *The elements of universal erudition, containing an analytical abridgment of the sciences, polite arts and belle lettres.*

*London: G. Scott for J. Robson & B. Law, 1770; v. 2, 433p.; v. 3, 444p.

Dublin: H. Saunders, 1771.

For Bielfeld, the aim of science is utility or instruction, while the aim of polite or liberal arts is pleasure. The arts discussed in v. 2 of the 1770 English translation include eloquence (pp. 53-75), rhetoric (pp. 131-52), poetry (pp. 190-296), music (pp. 297-347), painting (pp. 348-77), engraving (pp. 378-84), sculpture and plastic art (pp. 385-98), architecture (pp. 399-418), and declamation (pp. 419-33). Dancing is treated as part of exercise (v. 3, pp. 359-76; pp. 380-93 in the French ed. of 1768). In offering criteria for judging works of genius, Bielfeld emphasizes the need for the unexpected and for good taste. The best must imitate nature, have perspicuity, and elevate sentiment; the most sublime will combine a vision of great perspicuity with the strictest adherence to truth.

The third volume (intended as a guide to youth for the wise employment of time at the academy and university) defines belles lettres as the instructive and pleasing sciences that occupy memory and judgment. The 38 chapters deal exhaustively with several subjects, from blazonry to geography. "Digression on exercises," the chapter in which dance is treated, echoes the sound-mind-in-a-sound-body idea of Greek antiquity. Those who devote themselves to study should also become expert in praiseworthy exercises: dancing, riding, fencing, leaping, wrestling, swimming, shooting, games of address, art of drawing, raising of fortifications, forming and polishing optic lenses. The section on dance (ch. 14) provides a succinct account of the state of dance in the

1760s and its role in educating the young to deport themselves in society with grace, ease, and dignity. The author defines dance in its modern practice as "the art of expressing the sentiments of the mind or the passions, by measured steps or bounds that are made in cadence, by regulated motions of the body, and by graceful gestures; all performed to the sound of musical instruments or of the voice, and which forms at once an exercise agreeable to the performer and pleasing to the spectator." It is not a "jumble of freaks and gambols" as the vulgar think; the dance of people of education always expresses some idea (p. 363 in the 1770 transl.).

The author emphasizes the importance of expressive pantomime in stage dance and describes various genres of theatrical and social dancing. To assist in characterization and in the depiction of specific subjects or sentiments, the ballet master relies upon music of specific mood or character, to which the steps correspond: Sarabande, Courante, Loure, etc. for the grave and serious; Menuet, Passepied, Chaconne, Gavotte, Rigaudon, Gigue, Musette, Bourrée, etc. for the gay, playful, lively, or comic. Among social dances, only the Minuet and Contredanses continue to be current. According to the author, the once majestic air of the parading Pavane now appears comic. In like manner dismissed are the Vainquers, Passepiés, Sarabands, and Courants of Louis XIV. A reference to "choreography" counsels its study.

A general discussion of music as one of the fine arts (ch. 8, pp. 233-74 in the 1768 French ed.) contrasts Italian and French tempo markings by noting that the French combine the concepts of musical expression and dance character, using the names of dances as guides to expression, e.g. Loure, Sarabande, Menuet, Gavotte, Gigue, Bourrée, Rigaudon, Musette, Courante, Chaconne, Passepied, etc. When discussing different types of music, Bielfeld lauds the excellence of French dance music (p. 256 in the 1768 ed.), in which the melodies agree so very well with both the character of each dance and the nature of the steps—a feature essential to the success of dance music. He criticizes French opera performances for the distracting practice of audibly beating time with a baton and for the poor musicianship of some female singers who sacrifice artistic qualities for the sake of vocal showmanship.

20 BLANKENBURG, Christian Friedrich von (1744-1796)

Litterarische Zusätze zu Johann George Sulzers allgemeiner Theorie der schönen Künste, in einzelnen, nach alphabetischer Ordnung der Kunstwörter aufeinander folgenden Artikeln abgehandelt. 3 v.
*Leipzig: Weidmann, 1796-98; (v. 1, A-G) 651p., (v. 2, H-R) 578p., (v. 3, S-Z) 518p.
Facs. reprint, Frankfurt: Athenäum, 1972.

Conceived as a supplement to Sulzer's encyclopedia of fine arts (q.v.), Blankenburg's additions to the original articles include bibliographies, etymologies, and historical sketches; there are also a few new articles. (The supplement first appeared in Sulzer's enlarged ed. of 1786-87, and was then augmented for the Leipzig ed. of 1792-94, of which this title is a separate but similar publication.) The article Ballet includes a historical sketch of the growth of modern ballet from the early 17th c. to the end of the 18th c., listing poets and composers who made notable contributions to the genre; a paragraph on Noverre and ballet as an art separate from spectacle; and a bibliography on ballet. The article Choreographie (sic) consists of a bibliography, not comprehensive. The article Tanzkunst presents a classified bibliography covering (1) the art of dancing in general, including publications from 1557-1797; (2) writings for and against the dance on moral grounds, 1752-1795; (3) history of the dance, 1712-1759; (4) origin of the dance; (5) dance of individual peoples. No entries appear for individual dance types. Entries on other relevant topics include Comödie, Musik, Oper, Operetten, Pantomime, Rhythmus, Schön. The articles, however, convey little new information beyond that found in Sulzer's original.

21 BOINDIN, Nicholas (1676-1751)

Discours sur la forme et la construction du théâtre des anciens, où l'on examine la situation, les proportions, et les usages de toutes les parties.
[s.l.] 1710.
Reprinted in v. 1 of *Histoire de l'Académie royale des inscriptions et belle lettres, depuis son établissement jusqu'à présent. Avec les mémoires de littérature tirez des régistres de cette Académie, depuis son renouvellement jusqu'en M.DCCX.*
Paris: Imprimerie Royale, 1717, 1736, 1761, 1786. (Pages 136-53.)

This is a study of ancient Greek and Roman theaters in which dance was presented. Two clear illustrations contrast Greek and Roman theater architecture. The book is included here primarily because it serves as a companion study to Burette's *Treize mémoires sur la gymnastique des anciens* (q.v.), which refers to it.

22 BOINDIN, Nicholas (1676-1751)

Lettres historiques sur tous les spectacles de Paris.
*Paris: Pierre Prault, 1719; iv+92+134p.+50p.+59p.

This pot-pourri of history, documentary, almanac, and criticism devotes its two main sections to the Comédie Françoise and the Opéra. (The Comédie Italienne was treated in Boindin's earlier publication *Lettres historiques à Mr. D*** sur la nouvelle Comédie Italienne. Dans lesquelles il est parlé de son établissement, du caractère des acteurs qui la composent, des pièces qu'ils ont représentées jusqu'à present, & des avantures qui y sont arrivées,* Paris: Pierre Prault, 1717.) The first part gives a history of the Comédie Françoise from its origins to 1718; a list of actors employed as of January 1718 and an overview of financial matters, organization of the institution, and personnel (the orchestra consists of 6 instruments: 3 violins, 1 oboe, and 2 bassoons); and a summary of rules and regulations governing job requirements, perquisites, conduct of rehearsals, choice of productions, royalties, etc. (pp. 1-18). It continues with a review of each production since January 1718, with brief comment upon public reception, citing details supporting the successes of individual works, acts, or actors, sometimes with more elaborate personal description of players' skills (pp. 18-26). There follows a transcription of the actors' statement upon closure of the theater in April 1718 (p. 26) and M. de Fontenay's statement upon opening of the theater (p. 30), followed by an account of the controversy and a brief biography of each of the actors (tenure, roles, career). On page 50 begins a plot summary of the play *Artaxere* of May 1718, with a critique of the play on p. 66. This is followed by a month-by-month summary of new actors and plays through the end of 1718.

Part 2 on the Opéra begins with a summary history from 1645, interrupted by the libretto of the prologue to *L'Hercule amoureux*, described as the first opera printed in France, and a plot summary for the rest of the work, indicating the subject matter of the ballets. On pages 35-71 appears the poetic *livrée* for 18 *entrées de ballets* from *L'Hercule amoureux*, indicating to which members of the royal family and court were assigned various allegorical roles. The history of the Opéra continues with an account of Lulli's life and career. Pages 93-111 briefly treat operas performed 1672-1718, mentioning significant roles, notable singers, and high points in the history of the production. *Le triomphe de l'amour* of 1681 is cited as the first work in which female dancers were introduced, among them Mlle. de la Fontaine. Pages 112-18 list names of then current singers (p. 113), dancers (p. 114), and orchestral musicians (pp. 115-18) classified by instrument and function *(petit choeur, grand choeur)*. Names of other figures in the directorship and administration appear on pp. 119-20, including ballet and chorus masters, designers of sets and machines, etc. A brief description of the building (p. 120), a list of principal composers and poets in the employ of the Opéra (p. 121), and a list of publishers of libretti and music follow. The last section (pp. 122-34) reviews the productions of 1718, with remarks on audience reception and occasional general evaluation of the dances. The critique of *Ballet des âges* is especially long; other titles include *Isis, Bellerophon, Tancrède, Rolland, Amadis de Gaule, Le jugement de Paris, Acis & Galathée, Le ballet des âges, Semiramis,* and revivals of *Les caractères de la dance* (Rébel), *La cantate d'Enone* (Destouches), and *Les caractères de la guerre* (Andrieux).

(A third part, "Troisième lettre sur tous les spectacles de Paris," comments on attempts to accommodate modern French taste; a fourth continues efforts begun in the 1717 *Lettres historiques sur la nouvelle Comédie Italienne* by reviewing productions from November 1717 to October 1718.)

23 BONAFONS, Louis Abel de, abbé de Fontenai (1737-1806)

Dictionnaire des artistes, ou notice historique et raisonnée des architectes, peintres, graveurs, sculpteurs, musiciens, acteurs et danseurs, imprimeurs, horlogers et méchaniciens. 2 v.
*Paris: Vincent, 1776; (v. 1, A-K) xiv+772p., (v. 2, L-Z) 795p. Facs. reprint, Genève: Minkoff, 1972.

Wishing to show the progress of the human spirit, Bonafons gathers information on the origin and development of each art listed in the title and on artists both ancient and modern. Based on *La danse ancienne et moderne* by L. Cahusac (q.v.) and *Anecdotes dramatiques* by J. La Porte (q.v.), the work is a derivative but nonetheless useful source. See Acrobates, Archimime, Baltazarini, Batyle, Blondy, Camargo, Danse, Dumoulin brothers, Dupré (taken from Noverre's *Lettres,* q.v.), Empuse, Fontaine, Hylas, Laval, Memphis, Mimes, Pantomime, Pécourt,

Pélissier, Prévost, Pylade, Rameau (musician), Riccoboni family, Schoenbates. The definition in the article Danse synthesizes all views: "La danse est un mouvement du corps en cadence, à pas mesurés, au son de la voix et des instruments; ou, selon les philosophes qui l'ont le mieux connue, l'art des gestes, c'est à dire l'art de les faire avec grace et mesure, relativement aux affections qu'ils doivent exprimer. La nature a fourni les positions; l'expérience a donné les règles" (v. 1, pp. 462-63). Extensive articles on Lully and Rameau compare the two composers. Other musicians cited include d'Aquin, Blavet, Boesset, Campra, Chambonières, Charpentier, Clairembault, Colasse, Couperin, Desmarets, Destouches, de la Guerre, LaLande, Lalouette, Lambert, Marais, Marchand, Mondonville, Montéclair, Philbert, Philidor, Rébel, and Senallié.

24 BOULENGER DE RIVERY, Claude François Félix

Recherches historiques et critiques sur quelques anciens spectacles et particulièrement sur les mimes et sur les pantomimes, avec des notes.
*Paris: Jacques Merigot, 1751; 176p.

This study brings together much information on a question of primary interest to 18th-c. theoreticians, whether in England, Germany, or France: what kind of dance was honored by the ancient Greeks and Romans? Once known, it could serve as a model for emulation by contemporary dancers. In Part 1, Boulenger de Rivery delves into the Greek and Latin origins of mime. In Part 2, he then describes ancient pantomimes both artistically (dances, costumes, masks, movements) and socially (favoritism, wealth, honors, rivalry, popularity). For the author, the contemporary choreographer now creating a similar, meaningful kind of dance is Jean-Baptiste de Hesse, for whom Boulenger de Rivery has high praise.

25 BRICAIRE DE LA DIXMERIE, Nicolas (1731-1791)

Les deux âges du goût et du génie français sous Louis XIV et sous Louis XV ou parallèle des efforts du génie et du goût dans les sciences, dans les arts et dans les lettres, sous les deux règnes.
*La Haye, Paris: Lacombe, 1769; 532p.
  Facs. reprint, Genève: Minkoff, 1970.
  Facs. reprint, Genève: Slatkine, 1971.
Amsterdam: B. Vlam, 1770; 387p.

The author takes a long view, comparing cultural life under Louis XIV and Louis XV, first in a broad survey, then in an examination of individual disciplines. According to his general thesis, the age of Louis XV enjoyed the fruits of labor undertaken in the previous era. In his summary evaluation of the progress of dance (pp. 170-71), he finds merit in the state of the art under Louis XIV, despite advances made thereafter. A section on music treats opera; those on instrumental music and singing focus on virtuosi. A section devoted to comic opera credits Le Sage (q.v.) with the creation of the genre. The section on ballet ("La Danse," pp. 520-26) begins by asking whether it is indeed an art. Many would answer yes, says this author, and would even consider it equal to the other arts. Dance is similar to painting in that it speaks to the eye; in addition it has the advantage of coordination with music, and thus speaks to the ear as well.

A very brief historical survey of dance quickly arrives at Louis XIV, who is said to have quit dancing when reminded by the dramatist Racine of the dancing Nero's unenviable demise. After Louis stopped dancing, the art became like the statue of Pygmalion—inanimate. In two pages the author offers succinct evaluation of many 18th-c. dancers, from the celebrated Dupré to the young Gardel. He expresses concern that dance too often reaches the far limits of taste: "Ce sont des bornes qu'elle doit respecter" (p. 526).

26 BRICAIRE DE LA DIXMERIE, Nicolas (1731-1791)

Lettres sur l'état présent de nos spectacles, avec des vues nouvelles sur chacun d'eux, particulièrement sur la Comédie Française et l'Opéra.
*Amsterdam, Paris: Duchesne, 1765; 83p.

Bricaire's letters provide an overview of stage and spectacle in his day. They offer a positive assessment of the states of the Comédie Française (ch. 1, pp. 3-40) and the Opéra (ch. 3, pp. 48-73), and recommend merging the Comédie Italienne and the Opéra Comique (ch. 2, pp. 41-47). Their references to dance suggest the subordinate position and limited extent of the dance in these spectacles. See especially pp. 65-68; the ballets are "très bien adaptés au sujet, et très engénieusement variés et composés. Quant à l'execution, elle est parfaite" (p. 65).

27 BROWNE, Richard

Medicina musica; or a mechanical essay on the effects of singing, musick, and dancing, on human bodies. Revis'd and corrected. To which is annex'd a new essay on the nature and cure of the spleen and vapours.
*London: John Cooke, J. & J. Knapton, 1729; 125p.

An 18th-c. physiotherapist, Browne shows that singing, music, and dancing can cure certain diseases, especially among the fair sex, whose tender and delicate constitutions make them susceptible. On the contribution of dancing to good health specifically (pp. 51-69), he finds dancing superior to riding in the cure of the spleen and vapours, "melancholick affection," in agues and in suppression of the "catamania." Dancing is superior also because the accompanying music fills the mind with gay enlivening ideas and makes the spirit flow with vigor and activity (p. 55). For agues, Browne recommends that the practice of dancing begin two hours before a paroxysm is expected, "which may prevent it, or at least the cold fit will soon be over" (p. 56). Remember how the person bitten by the tarantula is cured by the motion and heat of the blood, which cause the body to throw off the poison of the bite. But any person can overdo, so one must be sure to get enough sleep. Also, dancing must not become boring; one must take frequent intervals of refreshment. Thus after exercising sensibly, "the spirits will briskly actuate and invigorate the body, the blood will flow on in a full uninterrupted course, and in short the whole animal machine will be render'd more fit for the execution of its various functions" (p. 69).

28 BURETTE, Pierre Jean (1665-1747)

Treize mémoires sur la gymnastique des anciens: premier mémoire pour servir à l'histoire de la danse des anciens; second mémoire pour servir à l'histoire de la danse des anciens; mémoire pour servir à l'histoire de la sphéristique ou de la paume des anciens. [s.l.] 1710.
*Reprinted in v. 1 of *Histoire de l'Académie royale des inscriptions et belles lettres, depuis son établissement jusqu'à présent, avec les mémoires de littérature tirez des régistres de cette Académie, depuis son renouvellement jusqu'en M. DCCX.*
Paris: Imprimerie royale, 1717, 1736, 1748, 1761, 1786; pp. 93-116, 117-35, 153-77.

Italian transl. as *Prima, e seconda memoria per servire alla isto-ria del ballo degli antichi.* Venezia: Antonio Groppo, 1746; 44+42p.
3rd ed., Venetia: Antonio Groppo, 1759.

These 3 studies on dance in the ancient world provided background and a rationale for 18th-c. writers trying to find an academic basis for dance aesthetics. The first defends the excellence of dance and traces its vener-able origins among all ancient peoples. The second divides dance into functional types, choosing to concentrate upon religious, military, theat-rical (tragedy, comedy, satire, and pantomime), and ceremonial dance (for marriages, festivals, and similar occasions of rejoicing). The third essay describes technical gymnastic training among the ancients, with a section devoted to those exercises using balls.

29 CALLIACHI, Niccolo (1643?-1707)

De ludis scenicis, mimorum et pantomimorum syntagme posthu-mum, quod e tenebris erutum recensuit, ac praefatione auctum Petro Garzonio, senatori amplissimo. Dicavit Marcus Antonius Madero, Venetae D. M. Bibliotheca, curator.
*Patavii: Tipis Seminarii, apud Joannem Manfré, 1713; iv+ xxii+98p.
Reprinted with *De pantomimus et mimis dissertatio* by Octavio Ferrari (Wolfenbüttel: Gottfried Freytag, 1714; 63p.) in Tome 2 of A. H. de Sallengre, *Novus thesaurus antiquitatum romanorum.* Venetiis: 1718, 1735.

Written by a professor at the University of Padua, this posthumously published book focuses on the origins of Greek mime theater in Dionys-ian rites and the development of mime into the complex theater of Ro-man pantomime. Both Calliachi's and Ferrari's tracts provided back-ground for the formation of an 18th-c. philosophy of expressive dance based on the models of ancient dances. Calliachi's chapters are: 1 (pp. 1-4) *De scenae etymologie;* 2 (pp. 4-12) *Scena vetus, ejusdemque partes singulae curatius describuntur;* 3 (pp. 13-22) *An poetae et actores ve-teres in eadem fabula;* 4 (pp. 22-28) *Inquiritur prima scenicorum lu-dorum origo;* 5 (pp. 28-34) *Ostenditur, qua ratione scenici ludi in Dionysiacis sacris primum fuerint exorti;* 6 (pp. 34-40) *Quid fit mimus, et quaenam mimorum origo et antiquitas;* 7 (pp. 41-43) *Referuntur va-riae mimorum species apud Graecos;* 8 (pp. 44-48) *De mimus*

242

latinorum; 9 (pp. 49-52) *De pantomimus, eorumdemque prima origine;* 10 (pp. 53-60) *Sententia salmasii expenditur;* 11 (pp. 61-67) *Prima pantomimorum origo diligentius exponitur;* 12 (pp. 67-75) *Exponitur pantomimicae saltationis artificium;* 13 (pp. 75-82) *Exponitur pantomimicus apparatus scena, vestitus, instrumenta musica;* 14 (pp. 82-89) *Perquiritur, quid esset . . . in pantomimicis ludis;* 15 (pp. 89-95) *Examinatur, quas fabulas pantomimi desalturent;* 16 (pp. 96-98) *Exponuntur pantomimorum certamina.*

30 CAREL

Réponse du Sieur Carel, maître de danse, privilégié du roy, à la lettre de M. Deshayes, maître des ballets de la Comédie Fran-çoise, inserée dans le Mercure d'août 1764, p. 177.
*Paris: Mercure de France, October 1764; pp. 197-204.

Arguments are here presented in the continuing debate concerning ownership of a dance. (The question of property rights for works of art remained troublesome throughout the 18th c. and into the 20th.)

31 [CARSILLIER et GUIET]

Mémoire pour le Sieur Blanchard, architecte juré- expert. Contre la Demoiselle Deschamps, actrice de l'Académie royale de musique et contre le Sieur Burze Deschamps, ci-devant acteur à l'Opéra Comique.
*Paris: Cellot, 1760.

In this brief, a lawyer makes a case against the artists named who did not keep a contract. In such legal documents reside nuggets of information for the dance historian about the artist's place in society.

32 CASANOVA DE SEINGALT, Giacomo Girolamo (1725-1798)

Mémoires . . .
Written in French in the 18th c., first published in Germany in 1822. For publication history, see the 1922 French ed. with *avertissement* by Raoul Vèze and introduction by Octave Uzanne (Paris: Éditions de la Sirène, 1922; 12 v.). Many modern editions exist. For discussion of the references to music and dance, see Paul Nettl, *The other Casanova* (New York 1950).

First published in German transl. by Wilhelm von Schutz as *Aus den Memoiren des Venetianers Jacob Casanova de Seingalt oder sein Leben, wie er es zu Dur in Böhmen niederschrieb.* Leipzig: Brockhaus, 1822.
First French edition as *Mémoires de J. Casanova de Seingalt, écrits par lui-même.* Leipzig, Paris: 1826.
English transl. by Arthur Machen as *The memoirs of Jacques Casanova de Seingalt, 1725-1798.* Introduction by Havelock Ellis. Edinburgh: R. & R. Clark, 1940; 8 v.
English transl. by Arthur Machen as *The Life and Memories.* . . . Ed. by G. Gribble. New York: Da Capo Press, 1984.
*Ed. by Robert Abirached and Elio Forzi with a preface by Gerard Bauer. Paris: Gallimard, 1958-60; (v. 1, 1725-56) lv+1262p., (v. 2, 1756-63) xv+1253p., (v. 3, 1763-74) 1325p. New edition as *Histoire de ma vie.* Wiesbaden: F. A. Brockhaus, 1960-62; 6 v.

Casanova's memoires contain many passing references to dancers. He traveled freely in Italy, Germany, England, Switzerland, France, Russia, Poland, Bohemia, and the Netherlands, with sojourns in Venice, Lyons, Paris, Dresden, Prague, Vienna, Berlin, St. Petersburg, London, and Warsaw, and his tastes led to encounters with women at all levels of society. Dancers mentioned are primarily Italian, performing both in Italy and abroad, but enough French dancers surface in these volumes to warrant mention here. The description (v. 1, p. 649) of Louis Dupré performing at age 53 is especially famous, since little information about this dancer has emerged elsewhere. In context, the passage is part of a description of the opéra-ballet *Les fêtes venitiennes,* and Casanova's comments on the costumes and staging document the pseudo-Italian style then favored in Paris. The famous Camargo is also discussed—does she or does she not wear *caleçons?* Casanova's observations are also interesting for their unflattering view of life at the courts where ballet flourished. He is especially disparaging of the Duc de Wurtemberg and his court at Stuttgart (v. 2, ch. 14), which supported the choreographer J. G. Noverre for several years of importance to his development. There is also background on the court of Frederick the Great in Berlin and the life of La Barbarini (v. 3, ch. 17). Ange and Sarah Goudar pass in and out of his life (v. 3), the former introduced as the one "qui me parla de jeu et de filles" (v. 3, p. 184)—the 18th-c. stereotype of theatrical women, many of whom were dancer-courtesans. Finally, the memoires paint a lively picture of the Italian theater as it flourished in cities frequented by this Italian adventurer.

33 CASTEL, Louis Bertrand (1688-1757)

Lettres d'un académicien de Bordeaux sur le fonds de la musique, à l'occasion de la lettre de M. R[ousseau] contre la musique françoise . . . Tome premier.
London, Paris: Claude Fosse, 1754; 74p.
   *Facs. reprint, Genève: Minkoff, 1973 *(La querelle des bouffons,* v. 2, no. 49).

In the last of his 8 letters comparing French and Italian music (p. 72; p. 1438 of the Minkoff anthology), Castel describes those features of French music contributing to what he perceives to be its unpleasant air of monotony. He finds French music too flowing, unified, and conjunct owing to mannerisms of harmony, rhythm, and melody that emphasize connection and transition. The result is an effect of timidity, discretion, and regularity in strong contrast to the boldness of Italian music, in which unadorned leaps abound. His criticism attacks chiefly continual ornamentation that smooths out the melodic line to the point of blandness.

34 CHABANON, Michel Paul Guy de (1729-1792)

Observations sur la musique, et principalement sur la metaphysique de l'art.
Paris: Pissot père et fils, 1779; xx+215p.
   Facs. reprint, Genève: Minkoff, 1969.
   *Facs. reprint, Genève: Slatkine, 1969.
German transl. by Johann Adam Hiller as *Über die Musik und deren Wirkungen, mit einigem Anmerkungen.* Leipzig: Friedrich Gotthold Jacobäer & Sohn, 1781; xxviii+228p.
   Facs. reprint, Leipzig: Zentralantiquariat der DDR, 1974.

De la musique considérée en elle-même et dans ses rapports avec la parole, les langues, la poésie et le théâtre.
*Paris: Pissot, 1785; 460p.
   Facs. reprint, Genève: Minkoff, 1969.
   *Facs. reprint, Genève: Slatkine, 1969.

The second version, *De la musique considérée,* is a revised and enlarged treatment of the original *Observations.* Its three parts consist of the original first, considering music in itself and its relationship to other arts (pp. 25-194), the new second, on the musical properties of language (pp. 195-396), and the new third, on qualities of languages in general (pp. 398-459). The 1785 edition serves for the present description.

Chabanon did not accept the Aristotelian view that all art is an imitation of nature and that music necessarily imitates words—a view that dominated 18th-c. aesthetic thought. With this treatise he upholds the integrity of music as a self-contained language, capable of independence as an artistic medium, though often relating to poetry and dance by choice of the composer. His writings construct the first carefully reasoned musical aesthetic furthering the notion of music in and of itself, anticipating by a century the writings of Eduard Hanslick. Chabanon similarly insists that dance as imitation is pantomime, a genre best suited to actors in the theater, not essential to dance itself.

Several portions bear upon dance and dance music. In arguing that the character of a nation's music is not a reliable guide to the character of the nation itself, he views the popular stereotypes derived from characteristic dances of various nations (ch. 8, p. 93): the grave and majestic Spanish dances such as the Folie d'Espagne, the proud Polonoise in contrast to the mournful and phlegmatic gravity of Spain, the graceful gaity, sweetness, and dignity of French dances such as the Minuet and Courante, etc.

In ch. 12 on the dance (pp. 117-28), he recognizes that dance can imitate functional activity, but denies that such imitation is the essence of the art; rather, dance is the art of forming with grace and measure all the movements required by the music; it is rhythm made perceptible to the eye, with all of its divisions and subdivisions, while the pantomime often associated with dance is merely an inessential addition, best left to actors. He acknowledges one man (J. G. Noverre?) whose ballet pantomimes succeeded in making his reputation throughout Europe, but nonetheless, Chabanon insists, good dancers appear to be writing the music to which they dance; when in addition they express extra-musical meaning, they merely add another talent—pantomime—to what is indeed properly theirs—dancing (p. 124). In arguing that music itself can engender physical movement, he points to the competent conductor, whose gestures express the desired articulation and expression in great detail (p. 129; this suggests sophistication of conducting technique, although Chabanon does not indicate whether his conductor is French or perhaps one of the German symphonists admired earlier in the book).

Later in ch. 12, Chabanon emphasizes the unity of a dance and its music (p. 128): both say the same thing, one to the eye, the other to the ear, but each communicating only a vague sensation rather than a specific message. The association of this sensation with analogous situations and words requires intellectual exertion; it is only this intellectual effort to use music symbolically that makes the music in any way "imitative."

Granting that such association of music with situation is an important aspect of theater, Chabanon attempts in ch. 16 (pp. 145-57) to distinguish the various characters of music, their natural usage, and their appropriate imitative use. He divides musical character or expression into 4 types *(tendre; gracieuse; gaie; forte et bruyante)* and examines the use of each type. His purpose is to (a) establish a "universal language" of song types and (b) show how this "musical language" serves as a referent for the musical art of imitation as it is adapted to the illusions of the theater. For each character type, he describes the range of sentiment or emotion associated with it, suggests appropriate human situations that give rise to the particular sentiment, and mentions specific musical traits that distinguish it from other types, including relative tempo, articulation, rhythmic style, etc. The discussion thus provides a useful supplement to dictionary definitions of terms indicating musical character or tempo.

35 CHASTELLUX, François Jean de (1734-1788)
Essai sur l'union de la poésie et de la musique.
*Den Haag, Paris: Merlin, 1765; 94p.
  Facs. reprint, Genève: Slatkine, 1971.

Chastellux's essay deals primarily with the relationship of text and music in opera, emphasizing the need to give both poetry and music equal consideration if a unified musico-poetic structure is to be achieved. His remarks on the structure of dance music arise incidentally during a comparison of Italian and French styles. The author favors Italian music over French, but finds that the same ideals of simplicity, thematic unity, and formal proportion based on strict periodicity that he admires in Italian instrumental music are also evident in Lully's *airs de danse*. He defines unity (p. 17) in terms of the single idea or motive that pervades a piece, providing the skeleton fleshed out and ornamented by means of musical variation and nuance, as Lully's dance melodies demonstrate. However, while French dance music may be phrased symmetrically, he believes it is not therefore necessarily "periodic," since it often fails to unify phrases into rounded periods, the way Italian music does. Both Lully and Rameau serve as negative examples in this regard, while Geminiani's minuet receives praise. Finally, he insists that for a song to be periodic, both the poetry and music must show the same symmetry and sense of proportion.

36 CHEVRIER, François Antoine de (1721-1762)

Almanach des gens d'esprit, par un homme qui n'est pas sot. Calendrier pour l'année 1762 et le rest de la vie: publié par l'auteur du Colporteur.
*Londres: M. Jean Nourse, 1762; 119p.

Written in a satiric tone, this almanac admittedly mimics other such "productions immortelles qui sont la fortune de ceux qui les impriment et l'ennui de ceux qui les lisent" (p. 5). There are sections on French theater in Paris (pp. 21-35), the Théâtre Italien (pp. 35-41), and a monthly almanac (pp. 85-109). The "portraits" of the nations of Europe (pp. 41-85) also give information on theater. Bound with this tract is the author's *Le Colporteur, histoire morale et critique* (London: Jean Nourse [1761?]), a similarly ribald description of 18th-c. life.

37 CHEVRIER, François Antoine de (1721-1762)

Observations sur le théâtre dans lesquelles on examine avec impartialité l'état actuel des spectacles de Paris.
Paris: Debure le jeune, 1755; 86p.
    *Facs. reprint, Genève: Slatkine, 1971.

The author writes as a citizen who has studied literature, who loves the arts and who, although not an artist himself, believes he can serve the public by his disinterested zeal. He considers each type of Parisian theater in order: Théâtre François (pp. 16-41), Théâtre Italien (pp. 42-57), Opéra (pp. 64-79), and Opéra Comique (pp. 80-85). A section on *Théâtres particuliers* (pp. 58-63) refers to such special performances as those at Sceaux. No theater is covered very thoroughly; dance appears only under the Opéra, where, after attacking the opera ("Les accessoires . . . sont trop négligés, des habits peu convenables, des machines trop lourdes, et des décorations mal entendues en gâtent souvent la pompe"), he treats the ballet with similar disdain (p. 77). He judges the female dancers good but the men lacking in excellence, though many aspire. If one has seen Camargo and Dupré, can one hope that someone will imitate them? In the final chapter on the Opéra Comique, he recommends the ballets of Noverre.

38 CIBBER, Colley (1671-1757)

An apology for the life of Mr. Colley Cibber, comedian, and late

patentee of the Theatre-Royal. With an historical view of the stage during his own time.
London: John Watts, 1740; 8+346p.
  Facs. reprint, Ann Arbor, MI: University of Michigan Press, 1968.
Dublin: G. Faulkner, 1740; 6+346p.
2nd ed., London: John Watts, 1740; 488p.
An apology . . . view of the stage to the present year. Supposed to have been written by himself, in the style and manner of the poet laureat. London: 1741.
3rd ed., *To which is now added a short account of the rise and progress of the English stage; also a dialogue on old plays and old players.* London: R. Dodsley, 1750; 12+555p.
4th ed., London: Watts, 1740; 2 v.
4th ed., Dublin: G. Faulkner, 1740.
London: J. Watts, 1750; 346p.
New ed. with notes and commentary by Edmund Bellchambers, London: W. Simpkin & R. Marshall, 1822; xxiii+514+viip.
London: Hunt & Clarke, 1826; 5+ii+340p.
London: Whittaker, Treacher & Arnot, 1829; 6+340p.
London: Whittaker, Treacher & Arnot, 1830; 10+ii+340p.
New ed. with notes and supplement by Robert W. Lowe, with portraits by R. B. Parkes and 18 etchings by Adolphe LaLauze, London: J. C. Nimmo, 1889; (v. 1) lxxi+337p., (v. 2) vi+416p.
  *Facs. reprint, New York: AMS Press, 1966.
London: J. M. Dent & Sons, [1914]; xv+302p.
New York: E. P. Dutton & Co., [1914]; xv+302p.
Wattham St. Lawrence: Golden Cockerel Press, 1925; 2 v.
London: J. M. Dent & Sons, [193?].
New York: E. P. Dutton, [193?]; xv+302p.

Cibber's famous *Life* provides background on the English stage in the first third of the 18th c., a time in which French dancers were imported at intervals and the two theaters (Lincoln's Inn Fields and Drury Lane) associated with dancers John Weaver and John Rich were thriving. The 1889 ed. contains notes correcting errors of fact. Additional documents fill in the history before and after Cibber's stage career, including James Wright's *Historia histrionica* and the Patent granted to Sir William Davenant, an account of chief incidents in theatrical history prior to

Cibber's death, and Anthony Aston's "Brief Supplement to Colley Cibber." Appendices list Cibber's dramatic productions and provide a bibliography of works by and about him.

39 CLÉMENT, Jean Marie Bernard (1714-1812) and Joseph de LAPORTE (1713-1779)

Anecdotes dramatiques contenant 1°. Toutes les pièces de théâtre, tragédies, comédies, pastorales, drames, opéra, opéra-comiques, parades, proverbes, qui ont été joués à Paris ou en province, sur des théâtres publics, ou dans des sociétés particulières, depuis l'origine des spectacles en France, jusqu'à l'année 1775, rangés par ordre alphabétique. 2°. Tous les ouvrages dramatiques qui n'ont été représentés sur aucun théâtre, mais qui sont imprimés, ou conservés en manuscrits dans quelques bibliothèques. 3°. Un receuil de tout ce qu'on a pu rassembler d'anecdotes imprimées, manuscrites, verbales, connues ou peu connues; d'évènemens singuliers, sérieux ou comiques; de traits curieux, d'épigrammes, de plaisanteries, de naïvetés et de bons-mots, auxquels ont donné lieu les représentations de la plupart des pièces de théâtre, soit dans leurs nouveauté, soit à leurs reprises. 4°. Les noms de tous les auteurs, poètes ou musiciens, qui ont travaillé pour tous nos théâtres, de tous les acteurs ou actrices célèbres qui ont joué à tous nos spectacles, avec un jugement de leurs ouvrages et de leurs talens, un abrégé de leur vie, et des anecdotes sur leurs personnes. 5°. Un tableau, accompagné d'anecdotes, des théâtres de toutes les nations. 3 v.
*Paris: veuve Duchesne, 1775; 590+580+576p.

Facs. reprint, Genève: Slatkine, 1971.

This guide to theater gossip provides (1) an alphabetical list of stage works performed in Paris to the year 1775; dances appear here as *opéra-ballet, fêtes, comédie-ballet, ballet-pantomime, parodies, divertissement, ballet-héroique, intermèdes,* and *spectacles,* as well as *ballet;* (2) an additional list of works not staged in Paris but available in written form (primarily ancient and foreign works); (3) anecdotes and gossip concerning incidents at performances, the King's reaction, identity of characters satirized in the action, etc.; (4) a listing of all actors, musicians, and other participants, with biographical information (birthplace, account of career, evaluation of character and of strengths as an artist), quotations from contemporaries, personal and professional anecdotes, and a brief, non-comprehensive list of works or roles; (5) an overview of theater in other cities. Part 4 appears in v. 3; the biographical article on Lully occupies 5 pages. Dancers are listed among the personnel for the Académie Royale de Musique and the Comédiens Ordinaires du Roy for 1775. Entries can be found for dancers Allard, Beauchamp, Beaujoyeulx, Benserade, Blondy, Camargo, DeHesse, Deshayes, Dupré, Lany (Jean and Mlle), Lyonnais, Marcel, Pécourt, Prévot, Puvigné, Sallé, and Subligny, as well as for historians Cahusac and de Pure.

40 CONSTANTINI, Angelo (ca. 1655-1730)

La vie de Scaramouche.
Paris: Claude Barbin, 1695; 134+[6]p.
2nd ed., Paris, Lyon: Thomas Amaulry, 1695.
Brussels: 1699, 1708.
Troyes: 1729.
Reprinted in *Trésor des Arlequinades,* 1856.
Paris: Bonnaissies, 1876.
Torino: G. Einaudi, 1973.
English transl. by A. R. London: Robert Gifford, 1696.
Italian transl. as *Nascita, vita, e morte del famoso Scaramuzza comico napolitano.* Venice: 1726.
*English transl. by Cyril W. Beaumont as *The birth, life and death of Scaramouch.* London: C. W. Beaumont, 1924; xlii+[20]+86p.

These are the memoirs of one who made a career of playing the *commedia dell'arte* character called Mezzetin (Mezzetino), based on the old comic figure known as the Captain—braggart, boaster, and liar. Before and after 1700, dancers appeared at both the court opera and the lowly fairground theaters, especially at the Opéra Comique; thus a life such as this becomes a source of background information on dance. (For other titles related to *commedia dell'arte,* see Lambranzi and Le Sage.)

41 CORNEILLE, Thomas (1625-1709)

Le dictionnaire des arts et des sciences. 2 v.
*Paris: chez la veuve de Jean Baptiste Coignard, 1694.
   Facs. reprint, Genève: Slatkine, 1968; 2 v., 1276p.
Paris: Rollin père, 1732.

A companion to the French Academy's *Dictionnaire de l'Académie Françoise* (Paris 1694), this dictionary of technical terms is heavily indebted to earlier French language dictionaries, especially Furetière's. (Compared to Furetière, Corneille provides more detailed description of the music for a given dance type; however, Furetière offers fuller treatment of the Menuet, Pavane, and Sarabande.) Definitions of dance and musical terms are for the most part brief, but they occasionally contain useful technical detail. Relevant entries include Allemande (music), Bourrée (musical structure), Baguette (drumsticks), Canaries (dance and music), Chaconne (musical structure), Coupé (step), Courante (musical structure and dance steps), Danse (haut/bas), Danseur (*danseurs de corde* only), Gavote (musical structure, dance steps), Gigue (music), Loure (instrument), Menuet ("Air à danser dont le mouvement est fort viste"), Musette (instrument), Passecaille (music, dance), Passepied (dance), Pavane (dance), Sarabande (dance, music).

42 CROUSAZ, Jean Pierre de

Traité du beau. Où l'on montre en quoi consiste ce que l'on nomme ainsi, par des exemples tirez de la plupart des arts et des sciences.

Amsterdam: François L'Honoré, 1715; 302p.

*Facs. reprint, Genève: Slatkine, 1970.

*New ed., Amsterdam: L'Honoré & Châtelain, 1724; 524+398p.

German transl. of excerpts in Johann Nikolaus Forkel, *Musikalisch-kritische Bibliothek*. Gotha: C. W. Ettinger, 1778-79; v. 1-2 ("Abhandlung vom Schönen").

In his treatise on beauty, Crousaz seeks universal principles of beauty that apply to the multiplicity of experience in life and art (architecture, manners, the human body; the sciences, virtue, eloquence, music). Ch. 3 on the characteristics of beauty emphasizes the importance of diversity, but diversity tempered by uniformity, regularity, and order (i.e. consistency in the quality of connection) with a proper regard for proportion (i.e. consistency in relationship between the various details comprising the whole). Crousaz observes a certain degree of relativism in man's perception of beauty and even admits to the pleasing effect, in certain contexts, of diversity not subordinated to an overall unity, although he explains these divergences as the product of insufficient education in the true principles of beauty or as lack of taste.

Ch. 11 on beauty in music (pp. 171-203) does not appear in the other-wise expanded version of 1724. In applying the basic principles to music in general, it deals primarily with acoustic phenomena, sound produc-tion, and modes. Among other demonstrations of interaction between unity and diversity, Crousaz compares the cadences appropriate to the ends of sections in dance airs *en rondeau* or in fast tempo (Gigue, Ga-votte) with those in binary form dance tunes (pp. 292-93). The need for considering the effects of tempo upon sound and expression of the text is illustrated by the case of a Menuet with many notes to a measure, which if set to a text would sound ridiculous, owing to the overly rapid decla-mation of the text enforced by the presumed dance tempo (p. 294). Crousaz stresses in music, as in rhetoric, the importance of an organic unity in which each passage seems to develop naturally and without contrivance from the preceding (p. 297).

43 D'AQUIN DE CHÂTEAU-LYON, Pierre Louis (1720-1797)

Lettres sur les hommes célèbres, dans les sciences, la littérature et les beaux-arts, sous le règne de Louis XV. Première partie.
*Amsterdam, Paris: Duchesne, 1752; 191p.
Siècle littéraire de Louis XV ou lettres sur les hommes célèbres.
Première partie. Amsterdam: Duchesne, 1753; 220p.
Amsterdam: Duchesne, 1754.
Facs. reprint, New York: AMS Press, 1978.

The son of the famous organist Louis Claude D'Aquin defends the prog-ress of the arts after the demise of the Sun King in a series of letters on famous practitioners known to him. The original 1752 volume continues in the re-titled 1753 publication; the 1754 edition supplements both. The first volume deals almost exclusively with music and musicians. Letter 2 on the opera lauds the accomplishments of more recent composers at the expense of Lully. It describes the success and character of operas by Rameau, Desmarets, Montéclair, Campra, Destouches, Mouret, Rebel and Francoeur, Blamont, Boismortier, and Royer (emphasizing the po-etry). Letter 3 is a panegyric on Rameau's music and career, praising his achievement in unifying Italian brilliance with the inexpressible charm of French music. D'Aquin describes the effect of especially dramatic scenes from *Hippolyte, Thesée,* and *Les Indes galantes,* praising the Chaconne in *Les sauvages* for its variety, harmony, and nobility and marvelling at the descriptive power of Rameau's music. Letters 5 and 6 discuss French virtuosi on keyboard (organ, harpsichord) and string (vi-olin, viol, etc.) instruments, their reputations, playing, etc. Letter 6 treats famous singers and dancers. D'Aquin is an apologist for the prominent role of ballet in opera. Dupré merits an enthusiastic eye-witness account of his talent. Other dancers mentioned include Marcelle, Lani, Lavalle, Javillier; La Fontaine, Subligny, Sallé, Guyot, Camargo, Puvigné, and Lyonnois. Beauchamps and Pécourt are mentioned as well.

44 DAVIES, Thomas (1712?-1785)

Memoirs of the life of David Garrick, esq. 2 v.
London: 1780.
2nd ed., London: 1780.
   Facs. reprint, Hildesheim: G. Olms, 1972.
Dublin: J. Williams, 1780.
*3rd ed. as *Memoirs of the life of David Garrick, esq. interspersed with characters and anecdotes of his theatrical contemporaries. The whole forming a history of the stage, which includes a period of thirty-six years.* 2 v. London: author, 1781; xvii+352p., xiv+429p.
4th ed., London: 1784.
New ed., London: Longman, Hurst, Rees & Orme, 1808.
   Facs. reprint with notes by Stephen Jones, New York: Benjamin Blom, 1969.
German transl. as *Leben von David Garrik* [sic]. Leipzig: 1782.

David Garrick's fame as an actor was international in the 18th c. He stood at the intersection of dance and dramatic acting. He figured in the lives of such dancers as John Weaver, John Rich, Marie Sallé, and especially J. G. Noverre, whose London production with Garrick of his *Fêtes chinoises* initiated a riot (see v. 1, pp. 186-92). Garrick's influence on the development of the *ballet d'action* is immeasurable; hence a contemporary account of his life is here included.

45 DECROIX, Jacques Joseph Marie (?-1827)

L'amie des arts ou justification de plusieurs grands hommes.
*Amsterdam, Paris: Les marchands de nouveautés, 1776; xi+233p.

The section on opera and Rameau (pp. 94-189) defends Rameau against the criticism of Rousseau and others, pointing to Italianate elements inherent in French style. Decroix reports on a new pamphlet concerning the ballet héroique *Titus à l'empire,* in which ballet master Gardel attests to Rameau's role in bringing dance to its present perfection: with his vivid expression and the great variety of airs in his ballets, Rameau has truly created the dance. Decroix describes what he believes were Rameau's ideals for opera (as opposed to ballet). He stresses the novelty and variety of airs in the divertissements, their relevance to the dramatic action, and the appropriate use of local color. Above all is Rameau's ability in monologues, choruses, and ballets to use in a manner appropriate to the circumstances the most sublime harmony and seductive melody.

46 DESBOULMIERS, Jean Auguste Jullien (1731-1771), known as JULLIEN DES BOULMIERS
Histoire anecdotique et raisonée du Théâtre Italien, depuis son rétablissement en France, jusqu'à l'année 1769. Contenant les analyses des principales pièces, et un catalogue de toutes celles tant italiennes que françaises, données sur ce théâtre, avec les anecdotes les plus curieuses et les notices les plus intéressantes de la vie et des talens des auteurs et acteurs. 7 v.
*Paris: Lacombe, 1769; v. 1 (to 1721) 512p., v. 2 (1721-26) 528p., v. 3 (1726-32) 538p., v. 4 (1733- 40), 556p., v. 5 (1741-51) 531p., v. 6 (1751-63) 546p., v. 7 (1763-68) 510p.
   *Facs. reprint, Genève: Slatkine, 1968.
Paris: Des Ventes Deladoué, 1770.

This account of performances of the Théâtre Italien begins with a sketch of the early history of Italian comedians in France, then describes in chronological order each of the works performed there, starting with undated works prior to 1762 and proceeding through 1768. The years 1716 through 1768 are treated in most detail. For each work, the author gives performance dates, plot summary with excerpts from the dialogue, and information about the more famous actors, dancers, composers, and poets or authors represented. The works include ballets and plays with added songs (ariettes and vaudevilles). Here may be found descriptions of *ballets pantomimes (Les filets de Vulcain,* v. 4, pp. 336-40, or *La vallée de Montmorenci,* v. 5, pp. 34-40) and *ballets héroiques (Le Sultan généreux,* v. 6, p. 370). Ballets within larger works receive passing notice *(Le colier de perle,* "comédie en trois actes . . . mêlée de ballets et de musique," v. 1, p. 101, in which "la pièce finit par un grand balet pantomime figuré," v. 1, p. 112). Performers described include J. F. De Hesse, who made his debut at Fontainebleau to "beaucoup d'applaudis-semens, qu'il a longtemps merités . . . pour la composition des balets" (v. 4, p. 112).

Following this *Histoire,* a *Catalogue raisonné* (v. 7, pp. 219ff.) lists in alphabetical order all the theatrical works, then all authors and actors (and presumably singers) not previously discussed, with a summary paragraph on the life and career of each. Next appears a list (p. 461) of works performed in the old Théâtre Italien (1682-1695), compiled by Gherardi (q.v.). There follows (p. 467) a list of works for which texts were extant at the Théâtre Italien itself, including French and Italian works and opéras-comiques, grouped by language and genre (number of acts). A final list for this section presents the titles of plays mixed with ariettes and vaudevilles, in alphabetical order, with names of their authors and composers (pp. 475-81). The remainder of v. 7 is devoted to lists of personnel: ballet masters (p. 485), dancers (p. 486), orchestral musicians (p. 487), set designers and costumers (p. 489), and administrators. The orchestra, under Lejeune, consisted of 10 violins, 2 flutes and oboes, 2 hunting horns, 3 violoncellos, 2 bassoons, 2 violas, 2 contrebasses, and percussion; personnel lists indicate 5 first and 5 second violins. The final section of the work describes organization and operation of the theater and the regulations governing it.

47 DESBOULMIERS, Jean Auguste Jullien (1731-1771), known as JULLIEN DES BOULMIERS

Histoire du théâtre de l'Opéra Comique. 2 v.
Paris: Lacombe, 1769; 497p., 558p.
*Paris: Des Ventes Deladoué, 1770; 8+497p., 558p.
Facs. reprint, New York: AMS Press, 1978.

In his preface, the author states his intention of avoiding dry lists of dates concerning who danced where, when, and with whom. He intends rather to offer information about popular works performed at the Opéra Comique in an agreeable manner. The information is therefore uneven and often incomplete. Volume 1 covers the period 1712-1747; v. 2, 1752-61, each with alphabetical lists of works. Entries include the setting, sometimes a date, sometimes a summary description, excerpts of dialogue, an evaluation or a report of the work's reception. Sometimes author and composer are mentioned, but in no place are performers listed. At the end of v. 2 (p. 133f.), miscellaneous items have been assembled in alphabetical order, rather than in chronological order as in the body of the work. Examples of ballets treated more extensively are *Les fêtes chinoises* (v. 2, pp. 323-24) and *La fontaine de jouvence* (v. 2, p. 334-35).

48 DES ESSARTS, Nicolas Toussaint Lemoine (1744-1810)
Les trois théâtres de Paris, ou abrégé historique de l'établissement de la Comédie Françoise, de la Comédie Italienne et de l'Opéra; avec un précis des loix, arrêts, règlemens et usages qui concernent chacun de ces spectacles.
*Paris: Lacombe, 1777; 300p.

A lawyer summarizes the history of legal regulations governing the 3 major theatrical institutions of Paris. Three chapters deal respectively with the Comédie Française (pp. 8-188), the Comédie Italienne (pp. 189-212), and the Opéra (pp. 213-300). For the Opéra, regulations issued in 1713 and revised in 1714 describe the duties and privileges of the musicians, singers, and dancers. Articles 26-29 of the 1714 revision specify separation of the functions of *batteur de mesure* (conductor) and *maître de musique* for the stage singers, formerly a single post, the duties of which are now recognized as impossible of fulfillment by a single person. Information concerning the musicians' hours, payment, rehearsal schedule, and dress code also appears here. Article 29 on the duties of the *maître de ballet* indicates that he teach dance not only to the dancers, but to the singers as well. Other regulations govern the conduct of public balls at the Académie Royale de Musique for 1715 (pp. 257-60). Article 2 of the 1713 regulations provides for the establishment of the royal schools of music and dance.

49 DIDEROT, Denis (1713-1784) and Jean le Rond D'ALEMBERT (1717-1783)
Encyclopédie, ou Dictionnaire raisonné des sciences, des art et des métiers, par une societé de gens de lettres. Mis en ordre et publié par M. Diderot, de l'Académie Royale des Sciences et des Belles-Lettres de Prusse; et quant à la partie mathématique, par M. D'Alembert, de l'Académie Royale des Sciences de Paris, de celle de Prusse, et de la Societé Royale de Londres . . . 35 v.
*Paris: Briasson, David, Le Breton, Durand, 1751-1780 (v. 1-7, 1751-57; v. 8-17, 1765; Plates, 11 v., 1762-72; Supplement, 5

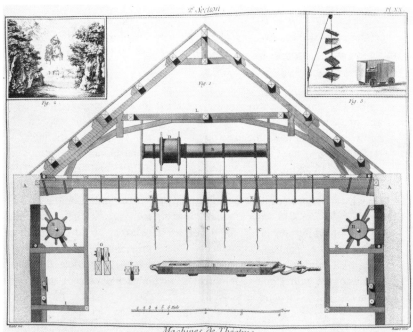

258

v., 1776-77; Index, 2 v., 1780). (For publication history, see Richard N. Schwab, et al., "Inventory of Diderot's Encyclopédie," *Studies on Voltaire and the eighteenth century,* v. 80, 83, 85, 91-93.)

Facs. reprint, Stuttgart-Bad: Friedrich Frommann, Gunther Holzboog, 1967 (35 v., 1751-1780 ed.).

Facs. reprint, Milano: Franco Maria Ricci.

Facs. reprint of the illustrations as *Diderot encyclopedia: the complete illustrations, 1762-77.* New York: Abrams, 1978; 5v.

Facs. reprint of selected illustrations as *Theatre architecture and stage machines: engravings from the Encyclopédie of Diderot and D'Alembert, 1762-72.* New York: Benjamin Blom, 1969; 22p., 89pl.

The most famous and comprehensive encyclopedia of the 18th c. contains hundreds of articles concerning music, dance, and instrument making, many illustrated by elaborate engraved plates. Louis de Cahusac contributed dance articles to the first 7 v.; after his death in 1759, few articles appeared on dance of the lyric theater. There are nevertheless some 120 entries signed with his mark (B), among them Ballet, Bourrée, Branle, Chaconne, Changement, Contredanse, Coupé, Courante, Danse, Danseur, Double, Egalité, Entrée, Expression, and Fête. The extensive article Chorégraphie, on dance notation, was written by Louis Jacques Goussier, a professor of mathematics. Two plates (Plates, v. 7) accompany this article. The first condenses the chorégraphie signs into boxes 1 to 76; the second contains the first 10 musical and chorégraphie measures of a *Pas de deux lutteurs* (danced in the opera *Les fêtes grecques et romaines),* with additional signs depicting body movement. Plates, v. 10 *(Machines de théâtre merveilleux)* contains 49 plates showing the machines used at the Paris opera. The diagrams of working parts have insets showing the disposition of dancers on the finished machines.

Jean Jacques Rousseau provided many of the music articles; these became the basis of his dictionary of music (1768), which in turn was the source of Rousseau's additional articles in the supplement to the Encyclopédie. Dance types described by Rousseau include Allemande, Courante, Gaillarde, Gavotte, Menuet, Passacaille, Passepied, Rigaudon, Tambourin, and (in the supplement) Bourrée and Bransle. The articles on Chaconne and Gigue were written by D'Alembert. Diderot contributed articles on the Canarie, Loure, Menuet, Musette, Rigaudon, Sarabande, Sicilienne, Tambourin, and Tordion, as well as those on dance steps (Balancé, Pas de gaillarde, Glissé, Pas, Saut, Sisson, etc.) and musical instruments. Other contributors on music and dance include Castillon fils (Comergo, Pavan, Alla francese, Alla polacca, etc.), Sul-

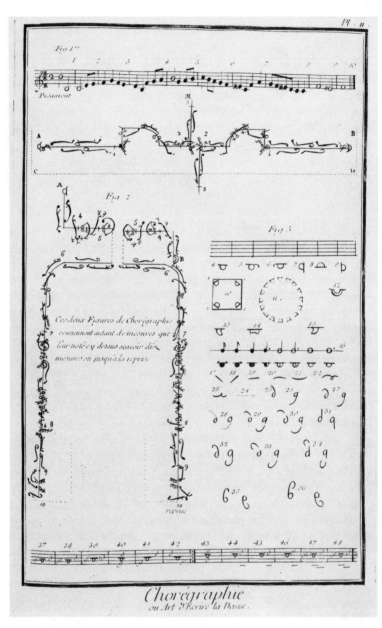

III-49 Denis DIDEROT and Jean le Rond D'ALEMBERT, *Encyclopédie* (Paris: Briasson, David, Le Breton, Durand, 1751-80), Plates v. 7, Plates I and II. Dance notation symbols for the article "Chorégraphie." [Repro-

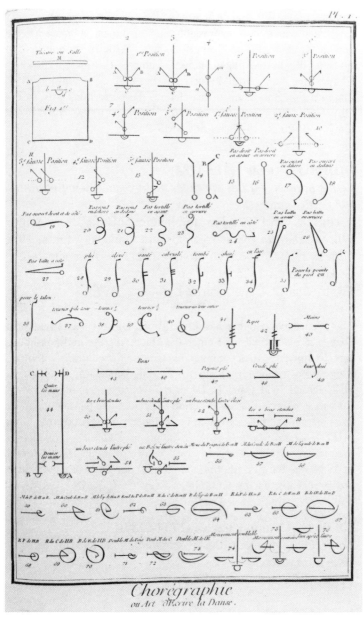

Chorégraphie
ou Art d'écrire la Danse.

261

zer (Ballet), Marmontel (Opéra), and de Jaucourt (Pavane, Tempo de gavotte, tempo di menuetto). Among the many relevant entries are terms associated with tempo, expression, embellishment, musical articulation, and instrumental ensemble performance. Articles serving as explanations to illustrative plates include Lutherie (instrument making) and Chasse (the hunt, with French hunting calls), in addition to Chorégraphie. For authorship of articles on the performing arts, see A. R. Oliver, *The encyclopedists as critics of music* (New York: Columbia University Press, 1947; reprint AMS Press).

50 DIDEROT, Denis (1713-1784)

Le fils naturel, ou Les épreuves de la vertu [including *Entretiens sur Le fils naturel*].
4 editions in 1757. For publication history, see Arthur M. Wilson, *Diderot* (New York: Oxford University Press, 1972).
*Ed. by J. Assézat and M. Tourneux in *Oeuvres complètes*. Paris: Garnier frères, 1875; v. 7, pp. 1-168.
Ed. by Jean P. Caput. Paris: Larousse, [1970].

The French philosopher and critic Denis Diderot was an advocate for change in many areas of French life, including the tradition-bound theater. In this essay to accompany his play *Le fils naturel,* Diderot offered suggestions for the lyric theater, including ballet. Influenced by the English actor David Garrick, Diderot advocated meaningful movements for ballet, going so far as to define ballet as "une pantomime mesurée" (p. 158), an example of which he included (pp. 158-66). M. H. Winter in *Pre-romantic ballet,* p. 152, mentions Diderot's influence on the practice of staging scenes after well-known paintings. *La fille mal gardé* of 1789 was the first important example. See *Diderot's writings on the theatre* (1936), ed. by F.C. Green (New York: AMS Press, 1978).

51 [DORAT, Claude Charles (1734-1780)]

La déclamation théâtrale, poëme didactique en trois chants, précédé d'un discours.
*Paris: Sébastien Jorry, 1766; 128p.

La danse, chant quatrième du poeme de la déclamation, précédé de notions historiques sur la danse et suivie d'une réponse à une lettre écrite de province.
*Paris: Sébastien Jorry, 1767; 198p.

Both titles in a new ed., as *En quatre chants, précédé d'un discours et de notions historiques sur la danse*. Paris: Sébastien Jorry, 1767; 176p. Paris: Delalain, 1771; 238p.
*Reprinted in v. 3 of *Chef-d'oeuvres de Dorat*. Paris: Belin, [179?]; pp. 1-30 *(Discours)*, 31-52 *(Notions)*, 53-136 *(La déclamation . . . en quatre chants)*.

Each section of the 1766 *discours*—on tragedy, comedy, and the opera— is preceded by a charming illustration. The poem *La danse* praises dance. It should be "natural et libre" (p. 161), and "l'âme doit commander: que les pieds obéissent;" one should study under a "maître qui pense" (p. 165). In *Notions*, Dorat states that he regards dance as "déclamation muette;" its movements, when expressive, become as intelligible as the spirit and the mind, even as the articulation of the word. He especially praises the expressive dancing of Marie Sallé (pp. 175-76). Other dancers he honors are Préville, Dauberval, Dupré (who moves among mortals like a god), Camargo, Lani, Allard, Noverre ("quel feu!"), Dumesnil, Clairon, Dubois, Montmesnil, Dufresne, and Démars. In v. 1 of the *Chef-d'oeuvres*, there is a short account (pp. 7-18) of the life of this prolific poet, who challenged Voltaire *(Le poëte universel)*, but had to be content to be known as "le poëte des femmes." His poetic hommage to expressive dancing provides lively—if highly opinionated—portraits of some of the most important French ballet dancers of the century.

52 DU BOS, Jean Baptiste (1670-1742)

Réflexions critiques sur la poésie et sur la peinture. 2 v.
Paris: Jean Mariette, 1719; 692p., 529p.
Utrecht: Etienne Neaulme, 1732; 3 v.
Paris: P. J. Mariette, 1733; 3 v.
Paris: P. J. Mariette, 1740, 1746, 1755.
Dresden: 1760.
Paris: Pissot, 1770.
  Facs. reprint, Genève: Slatkine, 1967; 308p.
Dutch transl. by Philip Zweerts as *Oordeelkundige aanmerkingen over de pöezy,* 3 v. Amsterdam: J. Loveringh, 1740.
  Amsterdam: Hermann de Wit, 1760.
  Leiden: C. van Hoogeven junior, 1774.
*English transl. by Thomas Nugent as *Critical reflections on poetry, painting, and music; with an inquiry into the rise and prog-*

ress of the theatrical entertainments of the ancients.
London: John Nourse, 1748; 3 v., 356p., 420p., 292p.
   Facs. reprint, New York: AMS Press, 1978.
German transl. as *Kritische Betrachtungen über die Poesie und
Mahlerey.* København: in der Mummischen Buchhandlung,
1760; 3 v.

Du Bos's famous treatise on aesthetics was one of the earliest to affirm
the idea that art imitates nature. The essay on the theatrical arts of the
ancients briefly digresses to the then present (Part 3, ch. 10) to compare
changes in Roman declamation during the time of Augustus with those
in music and dance under Louis XIV. In two chapters of Part 3 (pp. 199-
320 of the 1748 English transl.), the author discusses theatrical dance,
drawing upon his knowledge of antiquity and his extensive observation
of contemporary dancing, including that at the Comédie Italienne. In Du
Bos's view, music and dance in the last 120 years (prior to 1719) had
become gradually more expressive, faster, more varied, and more distinctly characterized. Music increased in speed and sophistication of execution; ballet airs became faster and less uniformly sedate. Before Lully's innovations were accepted, the older airs were executed with lutes,
theorbos, and viols mixed with some violins, and the steps and figures of
the ballets were slow and simple. Dancers observed all possible decency
in execution; movements scarcely differed from those of common
dances. Lully introduced quick airs that required dancers to move with
greater celerity and action, sometimes choreographing them himself; Du
Bos cites examples from *Cadmus* and *Galatea.* Lully individualized the
dances in support of dramatic characterization. Later, dancers learned to
do this themselves and even suggested ideas for airs of new character to
enhance the ballet, reversing the earlier situation in which the music
dictated the character of the dance. Sixty years ago the Fauns, Shep-
herds, Peasants, Cyclops, and Tritons danced alike, but now their
dances had different character, each with its proper steps, attitudes, and
figures upon the stage. Both women and men entered into these characterizations. The public approved of the new trend (despite those who
decried the vulgar excesses of certain artists) and have now become so
accustomed to it that they would find the taste of sixty years ago quite
insipid.

53 DU COUDRAY, Alexandre Jacques

Lettre d'un parisien à son ami, en province, sur le nouveau spectacle des élèves de l'Opéra, ouverts le 7 janvier.
*Paris: les marchands de nouveautés, 1779; 16p.

An enthusiastic and totally partial review of a performance opening the new theater for pupils of the theatrical dance school (7 January 1779) briefly describes the action, sets, and ballets ending each of 4 acts. The work, *Jerusalem delivrée, ou Renaud et Armide,* a *tragédie-pantomime* by Leboeuf, is described as a pantomime spectacle with machines, quite unique in conception. The 4 ballets depict (1) an allegory in the *genre pittoresque,* personifying demons and passions; (2) pleasures, games, and passions; (3) the demons evoked by Armide's fury (upon learning that Renaud must return to the Christian camp), armed with fiery torches in a *pittoresque* ballet; (4) nymphs and dryads, with fauns and satyrs near the soldiers' camp, at the beginning of the act.

54 DUMANOIR, Guillaume (1615-1679)

Le mariage de la musique avec la dance, contenant la réponce au livre des treize prétendus académistes, touchant ces deux arts.
*Paris: Guillaume de Luyne, 1664; [x]+120p.
   Facs. reprint, Bologna: Arnaldo Forni, 1969; 130p.
Ed. by J. Gallay. Paris: Librairie des Bibliophiles, 1870; xxvii+91p., appendices pp. 93-129.

Dumanoir vehemently criticizes the newly established Académie de Danse (formed by dissenting dancers wishing independence from the performers' guild—the Confrérie St. Julien—of which Dumanoir was the leader), arguing that dance is necessarily dependent upon music and must not be separated from it. In examining the articles of patent that established the academy, he takes a negative view of the dancers involved in the project, reasoning against their attempts to separate dance from music. You say, he charges, that you can dance well and satisfy spectators without the least participation of instruments and music. But can you prove this? You who cannot move in dance without touching an instrument or singing a song or beating a rhythm? And are dances not made to music, never without it? And performed to it? Just remember that music can get along without dance, but dance never does without music.

55 DUREY DE NOINVILLE, Jacques Bernard (1683-1768)
Histoire du théâtre de l'Opéra en France depuis l'établissement de l'Académie Royale de Musique jusqu'à présent. En deux parties. 2 v.
*Paris: Joseph Barbou, 1753; 264p., 221p.
2nd ed. as *Histoire du théâtre de l'Académie Royale de Musique en France, depuis son établissement jusqu'à présent. Seconde édition, corrigée et augmentée des pièces qui ont été représentées sur le théâtre de l'Opéra par les musiciens italiens, depuis le premier août 1752 jusqu'à leur départ en 1754 avec un extrait de ces pièces et des écrits qui ont paru à ce sujet.* By Louis Travenol and J. B. Durey de Noinville. Paris: Duchesne, 1757; 320p., 221+11p.
*Facs. reprint, Genève: Minkoff, 1972.

This well organized reference book provides information on a variety of topics concerning the origins and development of the Paris Opéra. It devotes sections to the origins of opera in France, with a chronological summary, 1645-1674 (v. 1, pp. 1-30); the life of J. B. Lully, with remarks on his work and personal life (v. 1, pp. 31-76); names of directors of the Opéra, 1669 to the present, and the regulations concerning their function (v. 1, pp. 77-104); statutes, regulations, and privileges pertaining to the Opéra since the establishment of the Académie Royale de Musique (1669-1714; v. 1, pp. 105-43), with a segment on the performing personnel—their numbers, pay status, auditions, vacations, duties, and seasons (v. 1, pp. 119ff.); regulations concerning the permission accorded the Académie to give public balls in the Salle de l'Opéra (v. 1, pp. 148-72); the Concert Spirituel au Château des Tuilleries, with names of orchestral musicians and singers (v. 1, 173-76); lives of poets (v. 1, 177-272) and musicians (v. 2, pp. 1-53) employed at the Académie Royale de Musique, with catalogues of their operas, including Cambert, Lully, Colasse, Louis and Jean Lully, Theobalde, de Gatty, Marais, Desmarets, Charpentiers, Mlle de la Guerre, Gervais, La Coste, Campra, Destouches, La Barre, Bouvard, Rebel père, Bertin, Batistin, Salomon, Bourgeois, Matho, Mouret, Montéclair, La Lande, Colin de Blamont, Aubert, Rebel fils, Francoeur, Villeneuve, Guinault, Royer, Brassac, Rameau, Du Plessis, Boismortier, Niel, La Dlle Duval, Grenet, Mion, Mondonville, La Garde, D'Auvergne; lives of deceased singers and dancers (Fontaine, Prevost) of the Opéra (v. 2, pp. 54-71); cast lists of productions from 1660 to 1756 including musicians and dancers who appeared on stage (v. 2, pp. 72-137), also a classified list of performers at the Académie Royale de Musique, including dancers and musicians for each year through 1756 (v. 2, pp. 138-54); a chronological catalogue of operas performed in Paris, 1660-1752 (v. 2, pp. 145-69); and an alphabetical catalogue of operas performed in Paris, 1645-1752 (v. 2, pp. 170-201). The second edition adds a section on the Italian comic operas presented at the Opéra 1752-54 by the so-called Bouffons, with plot summaries and commentary (v. 1, pp. 273-320); a list of books on music and dance relevant to the history of the Opéra (11p. appendix), and a list of pamphlets published during the years of the lively quarrel known as the Guerre des Bouffons, between partisans of French and Italian opera.

56 DU ROULLET, Marie François Louis Gand Leblanc (1716-1786)
Lettre sur les drames-opéra.
*Amsterdam, Paris: Esprit, 1776; 55p.

Upholding Greek authors and Quinault as model dramatists, du Roullet criticizes opera, specifically the *opéra-tragédie.* His cogent remarks deal with all aspects of the genre: subject, exposition, action, situations, climax and ending, characters, sets, style, meter, music, unity of time and place, the *merveilleux,* spectacle, fêtes and divertissements (with and without dance), pantomime, and costume.

57 ENGEL, Johann Jakob (1741-1802)
Ideen zu einer Mimik. 2 v.
Berlin: August Mylius, 1785 (v. 1, 381p.), 1786 (v. 2, 314p.).
　　Facs. reprint, Darmstadt: Wissenschaftliche Buchgesellschaft, 1968.
　　Facs. reprint, Hildesheim: Georg Olms, 1969.
In *Sämtliche Schriften* (12v.), Berlin, 1801-6; v. 7-8.
　　Facs. reprint, New York: Johnson Reprint, 1986.
Berlin: Mylius, 1804. Plates added by Johann Wilhelm Meil.
Berlin: 1812.
Ed. by Theodor Mundt, Berlin: Mylius, 1845; vii+212p., vi+194p.
*French transl. by H. Jensen as *Idées sur le geste et l'action théâtral.* 2 v., 34pl. Paris: Barrois l'âiné; Strasbourg, Den Haag, 1788-89; [570p.]. Paris: Jensen, [1789]. Paris: H. J. Jensen & Co., [1794]; 324+295p.

English adaptation by Henry Siddons as *Practical illustrations of rhetorical gesture and action, adapted to the English drama . . . embellished with numerous engravings expressive of the various passions, and representing the modern costume of the London theatres.* *London: Printed for Richard Phillips, 1807; iv+387+23p.
*Revised ed., London: Sherwood, Neely and Jones, 1822; viii+393+[15]p.
Italian transl. by L. Riccoboni as *Lettere intorno alla mimica.* Milano: G. Pirotta, 1818-1819; xxviii+251p.+40pl., 239p.+pl.41-60.
Milano: Presso Botellie Fanfani, 1820.
Italian transl. by Rasor, 1820.

In 44 letters with 34 illustrative plates (a format similar to that of Noverre's *Lettres)*, Engel argues the virtue of acknowledging precise rules as a basis for criticism of the art of gesture. For the 18th-c. idea that exterior modification of the body mirrors the interior condition of the spirit, he finds support in quotations from both ancient and contemporary writers—Lessing, Cahusac, Lucien, Du Bos, Sulzer, Horace, Descartes, Le Brun, Garrick, Diderot. He gives specific direction on how to act in general, and how to express emotions in particular, how to differentiate among the kinds of desire, how the body is affected by different emotions such as hatred and its permutations, how the spirit is like an instrument with strings, the vibrations of which continue long after being plucked, quieting only imperceptibly. Letters 29 and 30 ("Mr. Noverre's idea of a pantomime . . ." and "Farther disquisition on the subject of pantomime") refer specifically to Noverre's practices in making ballet pantomimes, quoting extensively from his letters. Engel's work, however, applies his theory of pantomime to all the performing arts— musical, declamatory, poetic, dramatic—as well as to painting, and his descriptions are a good source of information about 18th-c. theatrical expression. For a recent discussion of this work, see Jarmila Veltrusky, "Engel's ideas for a theory of acting," *The drama review,* v. 24 no. 4 (December 1980), pp. 71-80.

58 [ESSEX, John]

The young ladies conduct; or rules for education, under several heads; instructions upon dress, both before and after marriage. And advice to young wives.
*London: John Brotherton, 1722; xl+134+[2]p.

This courtesy book gives a complete picture of the expectations of behavior for young women in the 18th c.: "Sometimes to read, to write, to meditate or reflect on what you read, and to contemplate; sometimes to walk, or dance, or sing, to play upon a musical instrument, or use any modest and decent exercise; and to refrain from no fitting honourable work or labour, whereby to imploy yourselves" (p. 56). Thus she spent her time—but also in a certain manner, that is, with a certain air, that of "complaisance," or good breeding. This book by dancing master Essex is evidence of the importance of that person in the education of the young. All aspects of behavior are considered, especially chastity, but also temperance, industry, humility, sincerity, vanity, sensibility, how to dress, how to choose a husband, how to act as a wife, how to speak to an inferior or approach a superior, how to enter and leave a room. An understanding of the style with which a young 18th-c. woman moved may be acquired from etiquette books such as this.

59 FURETIÈRE, Antoine (1619-1688)

Dictionnaire universel, contenant généralement tous les mots françois, tant vieux que modernes, et les termes des sciences et des arts.
La Haye, Rotterdam: Arnout & Reignier Leers, 1690; 3 v.
   Facs. reprint, Genève: Slatkine, 1970; 3 v.
Revised by Henri Basnage de Beauval, La Haye & Rotterdam: Arnout & Reignier Leers, 1701; 4 v.
*Le Haye: Pierre Husson, Thomas Johnson, Jean Swart, Jean van Duren, Charles le Vier, La veuve van Dole, 1727; 4 v.
Paris: Vve Delaulne, 1732; 5 v.
[Other editions to 1771 (Paris, 8 v.).]

Essais d'un dictionnaire universel.
Amsterdam: 1684.
Amsterdam: 1685.
Amsterdam: H. Desbordes, 1687.
   Facs. reprint, Genève: Slatkine, 1968; [xii]+317p.

Furetière's work has been called the most extensive French language dictionary of the 17th c. The earlier *Essais,* a brief version of the subsequent dictionary, has musical terms, but entries relating to dance music are more numerous in the later work. The definitions are not necessarily comprehensive, referring either to the dance, dance music, steps, or

instrument of the same name, but seldom to all of these. The entry
Chachone (1690 ed.) may be the earliest dictionary description of the
term as a musical one; the entry on the minuet step (e.g. 1694 ed.) may
be the earliest French description of the minuet as a dance. Other dance
terms found in the 1727 ed. include: Allemande, Bal, Ballet, Bourrée
(on dance steps), Canaries, Chaconne, Coupé, Courante (steps and music), Danse, Danseur, Entrée, Forlane, Gaillard (both 16th and 18th-c.
types of music), Galant, Gavote, Gigue, Loure (instrument), Menuet
(music, dance step), Musette (instrument), Passepieds, Passecaille, Pavane, Rondeau, Sarabande, Sicilienne. (See Albert Cohen, "Early
French Dictionaries as Musical Sources," *A musical offering: essays in
honor of Martin Bernstein,* ed. by H. Clinkscale and C. Brook [New
York: Pendragon Press, 1977], pp. 97-112.)

60 GANTEZ, Annibal (ca. 1600-ca. 1668)

L'entretien des musiciens.
Auxerre: Jacques Bouquet, 1643.
Ed. with commentary by Ernest Thoinan (pseudonym for A. E.
Roquet). *Paris: A. Claudin, 1878; xxxii+269p.
  Facs. reprint, Genève: Minkoff, 1971.

This epistolary essay on the musical and artistic life of 17th-c. France,
in the form of 57 letters to a friend by a worldly cleric, musician, and
teacher, is useful for Gantez's personal evaluations of musicians in Paris
during the reigns of Louis XIII and XIV, among them A. Boesset,
Bournonville, Du Caurroy, Lambert, Mersenne, and Veillot.

61 [GAUTHIER, François Louis (1696-1780)]

*Traité contre les danses et les mauvaises chanson, dans lequel le
danger et le mal qui y sont renfermés sont demontrés par les
témoignages multipliés des Saintes Ecritures, des SS. Pères, des
Conciles, de plusieurs évêques du siècle passé et du nôtre, d'un
nombre de théologiens moraux et de casuistes, de jurisconsultes,
de plusieurs ministres protestans, et enfin des païens même.*
*Paris: Antoine Boudet, 1769; lii+286+120p.
2nd ed., Paris: Boudet, 1775; lx+426p.
Paris: Frouelle, 1785; 347p.
Italian transl. as *Trattato contro i balli e le cattive canzone.*
Venezia: Simone Occhi, 1787; 344p.

If all the tracts against dance published during this period were here included, the number of entries would swell considerably; this one appears here as an example. Part 1, the "discours préliminaire," consists of Biblical quotations followed by a long section reflecting on the quotations. Part 2, "Traité contre les danses," meets all the objections to this evidence against dancing. Part 3, "Traité contre les mauvaises chansons," attacks obscene songs, love songs, drinking songs, etc. Within these diatribes are embedded description of dance and song practice that may be used, with caution, as primary source material by dance historians.

62 GERBER, Ernst Ludwig (1746-1819)

Historisch-biographisches Lexicon der Tonkünstler, welches Nachrichten von dem Leben und Werken musikalischer Schriftsteller, berühmter Componisten, Sänger, Meister auf Instrumenten, Dilettanten, Orgel- und Instrumentenmacher enthält; zusammengetragen von Ernst Ludwig Gerber . . . [2 v.] [Anhang, welcher Nachrichten von Bildnissen, Büsten und Statüen berühmter Tonlehrer und Tonkünstler . . . und ein Instrumenten-Register enthält.]

*Leipzig: Johann Gottlob Immanuel Breitkopf, 1790-92; xiv p., 992+860 col., xvi+86p.

   *Facs. reprint, Graz: Akademische Druck- und Verlagsanstalt, 1977.

The first major self-contained dictionary of musical biography expands the biographical content of Walther's *Musikalisches Lexikon*. This 2-volume edition served as the basis for the first important French biographical dictionary, A. Choron's and F. Fayolle's *Dictionnaire historique des musiciens* (Paris: Valade, 1810-11; Paris: Chimot, 1817; facs. reprint, Hildesheim: G. Olms, 1970) and the first extensive biographical dictionary of musicians in English, *A dictionary of musicians* (London: Sainsbury, 1824 and 1827; facs. reprint, New York: Da Capo, 1966). A later 4-volume ed., the *Neues historisch-biographisches Lexikon der Tonkünstler* (Leipzig: A. Kühnel, 1812-13), revises rather than replaces the original.

   Information on the lives and works of French performers, composers, and authors is drawn from the writings of Laborde and others. Major composers are provided with a list of works, others with an overview. Dates and other pertinent biographical information are often lacking for

secondary figures. Coverage of French musicians is said to be less complete than that of Germans and other Europeans. (The Graz facs. reprint,
edited by Othmar Wessely, includes a supplementary volume of additions and corrections made by Gerber's contemporaries, as well as the
author's own manuscript revisions.) An appendix provides a list of portraits and statues of persons cited in the dictionary, as well as a list of
instrument makers.

63 GHERARDI, Evaristo (d. 1700), ed.
*Le théâtre italien, ou le recuëil de toutes les scènes françoises,
qui ont esté joüées sur le théâtre italien de l'hôtel de Bourgogne.*
Paris: Guillaume de Luyne, 1694; 545p.
Genève: J. Dentand, 1695-96; 2 v.
Mons: A. Barbier, 1696; 2 v.
Amsterdam: Adrian Braakman, 1695-98; 3 v.
Paris: Héritiers de Mabre-Cramoisy, 1695-98; 3 v.
Paris: Jean Bapt. Cusson, Pierre Witte, 1700; 6 v. . . . *Enrichi
d'estampes en taille-douce à la tête de chaque comédie, à la fin
de laquelle tous les airs qu'on y a chantez se trouvent, gravez,
notez, avec leur basse-continuë chiffrée.*
Amsterdam: A. Braakman, 1701.
London: Jacob Jonson, 1714.
Paris: P. Witte, 1717.
*5th ed., Amsterdam: Michel Charles Le Cene, 1721; (v. 1)
xx+472+16p., (v. 2) 541p., (v. 3) 561+8p., (v. 4) 524+36p.,
(v. 5) 460+24p., (v. 6) 512+40p.
Paris: P. Witte, 1738.
Paris: Briasson, 1741.
   Facs. reprint, Genève: Slatkine, 1969.

The world of Harlequin and Italian comedy was a world of movement.
Many dancers, including Marie Sallé, emerged from this stratum of the
theater. Information on the Italian theater therefore belongs here. In his
preface Gherardi explains that none of the comedies printed in this collection is complete, since the Italian actors learned nothing by heart. In
order to play a comedy, it sufficed that they merely be informed of its
subject a moment before entering the theater. The rest was theater: the
interplay of words and actions among the players. The comedies here
recorded thus derive from the reminiscences of several persons, printed
because the much admired performances in France (1682-1697) were

discontinued. Some of the comedies are assigned specific authors, named in the frontispiece to the play. Each comedy is illustrated with an engraving of the scene and the character, thus providing information on setting and costume. The printed plays themselves consist variously of dialogues and monologues (a mixture of French and Italian), interlaced with long paragraphs on the complications of the plot, the "business" of the scene, and, infrequently, corrections and additions. At the end of each volume (1700 ed. on) appears music for a few of the songs.

64 GILDON, Charles (1665-1724)

The life of Mr. Thomas Betterton, the late eminent tragedian wherein the action and utterance of the stage, bar, and pulpit are distinctly consider'd, with the judgment of the late ingenious Monsieur de St. Evremond, upon the Italian and French music and operas; in a letter to the Duke of Buckingham. To which is added the Amorous widow, or the Wanton wife, a comedy. Written by Mr. Betterton, now first printed from the original copy.
*London: Robert Goslin, 1710; xiv, 176p.
   *Facs. reprint, London: Frank Cass & Co., 1970.
   Facs. reprint, Clifton, NJ: Kelley, 1970; Fairfield, NJ: Augustus M. Kelley, s.d.

This biography contains a practicing actor's rules for imitating the passions in order to reflect nature. The eminent tragedian Thomas Betterton had just died, and in an account of the great actor's life, Gildon records for posterity the master's rules for acting: "Action is motion . . . life is motion," the passions must be suitable to the character and the subject, the actor must transform himself into the person he represents, etc. These ideas are echoed in 18th-c. writings, such as the *History of the English stage* (London 1741) and Noverre's *Lettres* (q.v.), and works such as Weaver's *Loves of Mars and Venus* (q.v.), advocating that dance similarly imitate the passions.

65 GOUDAR, Sara (? - ?) or Ange (1720-1791)

Oeuvres mêlées de Madame Sara Goudar, Angloise, divisées en deux tomes. Tome premier: lettres sur les divertissements du carnaval de Naples et de Florence. Tome second: remarques sur la musique italienne et sur la danse à Milord Pembroke.

273

*Amsterdam: 1777; v+xii+203p., 198p.

Italian transl. of a portion (v. 2, pp. 1-88) as *Osservazioni sopra la musica ed il ballo, ossia estratto di due lettere di Mr. G. a Milord P., tradotte dal francese par F. T.* Milano: Gaetano Motta, [1773]; 110p.

This collection gathers together writings of Sara (or Ange) Goudar, possibly an 18th-c. couple who traveled throughout Europe writing perceptive, opinionated letters about contemporary life and art. It contains all but three of the letters most relevant to the arts. Of the three, two are available at the Walter Hines Page Library, Ashland, Virginia: (1) *Lettre d'un François à Londres à un de ses amis à Paris: ou relation de ce qui s'est passée sur le théâtre anglois, à l'occasion du Sieur Noverre.* *[1755]; 7p. This contains a valuable eye-witness account of the anti-French demonstrations at the Drury Lane Theater, November 1755, aroused by performance of Noverre's *Fêtes chinoises.* (2) *Lettre critique sur les acteurs et actrices des trois spectacles de Paris, à Monsieur Garich acteur et directeur du théâtre de Drurylane à Londres. Où l'on trouve les portraits de tous les acteurs et actrices, qui se distinguent aujourd'hui sur la scène françoise.* *La Haye: 1760; 19p. Only Gaetan Vestris rates a positive assessment in this scathing attack on actors and dancers in Paris by these observers who believe that "le tendre et le gracieux sont les sublime de la danse" (p. 17). (3) *Observations sur les trois derniers ballets pantomimes qui ont paru aux Italiens et aux François: sçavoir, Télémaque. Le sultan généreux. La mort d'Orphée.* 1759; 46p.

In the 1777 collection of letters, a preface (pp. v-xii) sketches in a few words the writers' point of view. They maintain that it is not politics that teaches about humanity; to know a nation, they look to the mores and customs that are its touchstone. The first volume offers specific descriptions of spectacles and balls given at festivals in Naples and Florence, 1774-1776. The authors can not stand a ballet that includes someone dying while dancing. For them, rules are violated when ballet pantomime depicts great battles: "La guerre et la danse ne sont pas faites pour être ensemble" (v. 1, p. 30), especially before women. All of the successful *ballets d'action* by Noverre were anathema to the Goudars. Putting gods on the stage in dances degrades those supreme beings, they insisted. (The ancients could do so with impunity, since they had so many gods that some could easily be used for this purpose without degrading the entire divine community.) The letters in v. 2 unmercifully attack music and dance, especially on the Italian stage. Those two arts have degenerated proportionately as the other arts have been perfected, the authors complain. The letters are full of sarcasm and satire, especially about the impresarii, who are like merchants who go to America to buy monkeys and parrots, the first to sell for their beauty, the second for their speech. They continue their attack on Noverre: until his ballets appeared, dance was done on feet; with his, dance is done with heads. Of Noverre's book *(Lettres,* q.v.), the Goudars admit that it is full of spirit: "Il n'y manque que du bon sens" (v. 2, p. 28). As to his grand ballets, however, they find them often unintelligible and almost always too long. As the authors rant on—especially on the stupidity of resurrecting ancient pantomime—they provide useful description of current practice. Concerning authorship of the letters (Sara or Ange), see Frances L. Mars, "Ange Goudar, cet inconnu," *Casanova gleanings,* v. 14 (1966), pp. 1-65. See also [Ange Goudar's] *Le brigandage de la musique italienne* (1777; reprinted New York: AMS Press, 1978).

66 GREGORY, John (1724-1773)

A comparative view of the state and faculties of man with those of the animal world.
*London: J. Dodsley, 1765; 203p.
2nd ed., London: J. Dodsley, 1766.
3rd ed., London: J. Dodsley, 1766.
4th ed., London: J. Dodsley, 1767.
4th ed., Dublin: W. Sleater, et al., 1768.
5th ed., London: J. Dodsley, 1772.
6th ed., London: J. Dodsley, 1774.
7th ed., London: J. Dodsley, 1777.
8th ed., Dublin: W. Sleater, et al., 1778.
New ed., London: J. Dodsley, 1785.
London: A. Strahan and T. Cadell, 1788.
Edinburgh: W. Creech, 1788.
New ed., London: T. Cadell, Jr. and W. Davis, 1798.
French transl. by J. B. Robinet as *Parallèle de la condition et des facultés de l'homme avec la condition et les facultés des autres animaux.* (After the 4th English ed.)
Paris: Lacombe; Bouillon: Société typographique, 1769; 272p.

Gregory's philosophical essay communicates the aesthetic belief that in late 18th-c. France served as the rationale for the developing *ballet d'action.* He explains that in contemporary civilized society, the fine arts are incapable of cultivation in a manner useful to life. Only in a simpler, freer, more natural society does the exertion of fancy and passion permit an atmosphere favorable to the arts. The author looks back to classical antiquity for the time when "philosophy not only gave to the world the most accomplished generals and statesmen but presided with the greatest lustre and dignity over Rhetoric, Poetry, Music, and all the elegant arts that polish and adorn Mankind" (p. 162). Specific observations on dance occur in a section on the union of music, dance, and poetry (pp. 122-87 in the 1769 French ed.).

67 GRIMM, Friedrich Melchior, Baron von (1723-1807)

Lettre de M. Grimm sur Omphale, tragédie lyrique, reprise par l'Académie royale de musique le 14 janvier 1752.
Paris: 1752; 52p. (Originally in *Mercure de France,* January 1752.)

> *Facs. reprint, Genève: Minkoff, 1973 (*La querelle des bouffons: texte des pamphlets,* v. 1, pp. 1-54; introduction by Denise Launay).

Grimm's letter attacks *Omphale,* comparing it unfavorably with *Pygmalion,* J. P. Rameau's opera-ballet of 1748. Interest for the dance historian lies in the description of a scene in which the statue, danced by Mlle. Puvignée, comes to life (pp. 39-48). Launay's comments introducing the Minkoff reprint, as well as the other pamphlets in the collection (two in answer to Grimm on *Omphale,* pp. 55-117) documenting a lively argument on the merits of French versus Italian music, describe the historical context of Grimm's remarks.

68 HOGARTH, William (1697-1764)

The analysis of beauty. Written with a view of fixing the fluctuating ideas of taste.
London: J. Reeves, 1753; 153p.
  Facs. reprint, New York: Garland, 1973.
London: W. Strahan for Mrs. Hogarth, 1772.
London: [1791]. With rules for drawing caricatures, and an essay on comic painting by F. Grose.
London: R. Scholey, 1810.
London: S. Bagster, [1810].
Philadelphia: G. Paine & Son, 1900. As v. 6 in *The Works of*

276

William Hogarth.
Chicago: Reilly and Lee, [1908].
Pittsfield, MA: Silver Lotus Shop, 1909.
Ed. with commentary by Joseph Burke, with rejected passages from the manuscript drafts and autobiographical notes. *Oxford: Clarendon Press, 1955.
Ed. with commentary by R. Woodfield. Great Britain: Scolar Press, 1971.
German transl. by C. Mylius as *Zergliederung der Schönheit, die schwankenden Begriffe von dem Geschmack festzusetzen.* London: A. Linde, 1754. Berlin: C. F. Voss, 1754.
   Facs. reprint, Hildesheim: Georg Olms, 1974.
Italian transl. as *Analisi della bellezza.* Livorno: 1761.
French transl. with biography by Hendrik Jansen as *Analyse de la beauté, destinée à fixer les idées vagues qu'on a du goût.* Paris: author; Levrault, Schoell et compagnie, 1805. 2 v.
French transl. with commentary by Olivier Brunet. Paris: A. G. Nizet, 1963.

In this treatise on beauty, the famous English painter denies symmetry as fundamental to beauty in the visual arts and instead affirms a pleasing variety, embodied in the serpentine line. In ch. 15 devoted to the face, ch. 16 to attitude, and ch. 17 to action, closing with a section "On dancing" (pp. 146-53 in the original edition), Hogarth offers analytical criteria for the perception of beauty in physical motion. According to his theory, graceful curvilinear motion is more beautiful than straight or circular motion. He therefore differentiates elegant from grotesque (comic) styles of dancing according to the characteristic degree of serpentine movement. The minuet and the contredanse come under scrutiny for their pleasing character of motion. If the minuet is thought to be the pinnacle of refinement in dance, it is because the minuet provides the maximum variety of serpentine motion: in the wavelike rise and fall of the body, in the S-curves of the floor patterns, in the presentation of hands, etc. Further comment on the character of comic dances for the stage ("elegant wantonness," such that serious dancing is even "a contradiction in terms") and final remarks on stage action provide insight into practices of the theater. Remarks on the aristocratic self-assurance necessary to the proper performance of courtly dance communicate not only the ethos of the ballroom, but the essential expressive purpose of this kind of dancing.

69 KRAUSE, Christian Gottfried (1719-1770)

Von der musikalischen Poësie.
Berlin: Johann Friedrich Voss, 1752; 484p.
Berlin: Johann Friedrich Voss, 1753; 484p.
*Facs. reprint, Leipzig: Zentralantiquariat der DDR, 1973.
Facs. reprint, Kassel: Bärenreiter, 1973.

One of the earliest treatises devoted to the setting of words to music, this contains in its final chapters a discussion of opera in Germany. The contribution of dance to stage entertainment comes under consideration in ch. 11 (the final chapter). Dance is discussed as an element of opera (where it must have variety, meaning, and invention, pp. 442-44) and as an independent stage genre (ballet is defined as a short play providing joy and amusement, pp. 464-66). The former reference includes a detailed description of the ballet *Pygmalion*.

70 LACOMBE, Jacques (1724-1811)

Dictionnaire portatif des beaux-arts, ou abrégé de ce qui concerne l'architecture, la sculpture, la peinture, la gravure, la poésie et la musique; avec la définition de ces arts, l'explication des termes et des choses qui leur appartiennent: ensemble les noms, la date de la naissance et de la mort, les circonstances les plus remarquables de la vie, et le genre particulier de talent des personnes qui se sont distinguées dans ces différens arts parmi les anciens et les modernes; en France et dans les pays étrangers.
Paris: veuve Estienne et fils, Jean-Th. Hérissant, 1752; xiii+707p.
*Paris: Jean-Th. Hérissant, les frères Estienne, 1753; 752p.
Paris: Jean-Th. Hérissant, les frères Estienne, 1755; 758p.
Paris: Jean-Th. Hérissant, 1759; 636p.
Paris: Jean-Th. Hérissant, 1766; vi+754+20p.
Italian transl. as *Dizionario portatile delle belle arti.*
Venezia: Remondini, 1758. Venezia: nella stampiera de Bassano a spese Remondini, 1768. Bassano a spese Remondini de Venezia, 1781; 390p.

This general dictionary of the fine arts has entries on a variety of musical subjects, such as dance types, instruments, genres, national styles, and names of composers and musicians. The articles tend to be brief, superficial, and opinionated, the coverage uneven. There are articles on Musique and Ballet ("On entend aussi par ce mot, une suite d'airs de plusieur mouvements, dont les danses figurent quelque sujet," p. 49), but not Danse. The description of the Menuet mentions meter, phrase length, geographic origin, number of measures in each reprise, length of the upbeat, etc., but most of the other dances receive briefer treatment. Included are Allemande, Chaconne, Courante, Gaillard, Gavotte, Gigue, Loure, Menuet, Musette, Passecaille, Passemezze, Passepied, Pavanne, Rigaudon, Sarabande, Tambourin, and Volte. Biographical coverage is erratic; columns are devoted to Lully and Elizabeth Jacquet de la Guerre, but no entry appears for Rameau, Campra, or Delalande.

71 LACOMBE, Jacques (1724-1811)

Le spectacle des beaux arts; ou considérations touchant leur nature, leurs objets, leurs effets et leurs règles principales; avec des observations sur la manière de les envisager; sur les dispositions nécessaires pour les cultiver; et sur les moyens propres pour les étendre et les perfectionner.
*Paris: Hardy, 1758; xxii+374+8p.
[Paris: Vincent et Lobin Le Jeune], 1761; xix+374p.
   Facs. reprint, Genève: Slatkine, 1970.

Part 1 considers the nature of the fine arts and the advantages secured, as well as the difficulties encountered, in cultivating them. Part 2 treats poetry in particular, Part 3 music. Lacombe's aesthetics follow the prevailing theory of imitation. Music supposedly imitates not only natural sounds, sights, and events, but human passions and actions as well. Such imitation, he believed, is the primary purpose of theatrical music. Only dance music can be considered to be absolute music ("mélodie pure"), although if the dancing articulates specific sentiments, the music ought to become imitative as well (Part 3, ch. 5, "De la mélodie"). Part 2 considers poetry in all its aspects, including opera-ballet, especially when composed of several short poems united by a general title. These he finds agreeable, since the subject allows contrast and gives a free hand to the musicians. *L'Europe galante* serves as an example of this type, but any subject based on fable, history, or allegory will do. Men, he observes, are attracted by tableaux that expose their own traits, emotions, passions—i.e. their nature: "C'est la peinture de nos moeurs qui nous touche; plus la copie sera vive et ressemblante, plus elle procurera de satisfaction" (p. 165). Part 3 upholds opera as the highest form of musical expression, because all the arts enter into its composition: "le jeu de la scène, l'action du poëme et de la musique, les danses et les machines avec les loix de la vraisemblance, de l'unité, l'intérêt . . ." (p. 334).

72 LA JONCHÈRE, Vénard de
Théâtre lyrique. 2 v.
*Paris: Barbou, veuve Duchesne, Jombert, 1772; 343+362p.

This collection of opera texts on heroic subjects is preceded by a testy essay on opera (v. 1, pp. 1-178) reflecting pro-French opinion of the Guerre des Bouffons era. The author deplores the effects of Italian influence upon French musical taste and argues at length for the support and betterment of traditional French opera. (He calls for government support of the fine arts in order to encourage poets and composers in this direction.) He deplores the opera-ballet as a genre, citing integrity of plot as the first criterion for judging lyric entertainment. He defends French music against pro-Italian criticism, including the typically French use of divertissements, choruses, and the *merveilleux.* In a section on the abuse of instruments (p. 88), he castigates composers and musicians for the modern tendency of instruments to dominate the voice, instead of supporting it. In discussing individual genres of instrumental music, he lauds the French *airs de danse* as France's most original and persuasive contribution to stage music. He attributes their pleasing effect and international success to their variety, to their distinctiveness of character that does not, however, preclude imitation of nature or the passions. La Jonchère justifies the French habit of loudly beating the measure on the grounds that no other type of opera uses such complicated theatrical forces. The section on dance (pp. 135-52) answers objections to the dance and distinguishes two types of dances: imitative or pantomimic ones and those that express the passions. Additional topics include uses of dance, characters of the dance, expression, cause of uniformity among dances and means of varying them, additional arguments in favor of the dance, and the impossibility of creating a spectacle from dance alone.

73 LAMBERT, Claude François
Histoire littéraire du regne de Louis XIV. Dédiée au Roy.
*Paris: Prault fils, Buillyn, Quillau, 1751; 3 v.

Prefacing a section devoted to poets and musicians under Louis XIV is an essay (inserted between pp. 280 and 281 of v. 2) on the progress of poetry and of music under Louis XIV. Concerning music (pp. v-xii), Lambert considers Lully's instrumental music to be his weakest contribution, though he admits that modern ignorance of performance techniques and limitations in Lully's time might color the modern view. He observes that Lully's instrumental pieces were considered extraordinary in their day, and the courantes and sarabandes danced at Louis XIV's wedding were held in highest regard. Campra's *L'Europe galant* receives high praise as the model for all subsequent ballets; most admirable are Campra's *airs de violon* (dances?), with a novelty and variety quite unlike those of Lully. Destouches' pastorale *Issé*, hailed as a success, is criticized for its monotony and mannered character, its instrumental numbers *(symphonies)* for feebleness and general inferiority to those of Campra. Marais receives praise, largely for his vocal music. The subsequent *Éloge* praising poets and musicians contains short accounts of the lives and reputations of prominent musicians under Louis XIV (pp. 281-502), including Colasse, Delalande, Michel Lambert, and Lully (with quotations from *Le Parnasse françois,* q.v.).

74 L'AULNAYE, François Henri Stanislas de (1739-1830)

De la saltation théâtrale, ou recherches sur l'origine, les progrès, et les effets de la pantomime chez les anciens, avec neuf planches coloriées.
*Paris: Barrois l'aîné, 1790; 100p.

The essence of the dance must be gesture arising from imitation. Without this, dance is inexpressive and without interest. To prove this thesis, L'Aulnaye summons all the references available to the scholar on the dance *(saltation)* practices of the ancients—Quintilian, Lucian, Aristotle, Homer, Xenophon, Herodotus, Scaliger—as well as stories from China and the Americas. He draws upon verbal quotations, etymology, inscriptions, epitaphs, and decrees, illustrated with 9 beautiful plates. The largest section is devoted to dance among the Romans (pp. 40-100), in which he discusses miming, games, declamation, comedy, and the pantomimes themselves (dress, masks, instruments, *pièces*, games). Unique is a detailed description of a pantomimic scene, *Le jugement de Paris* (pp. 90-94).

75 [LA VALLIÈRE, Louis César de la Baume le Blanc, duc de (1708-1780)]
Ballets, opéra, et autres ouvrages lyriques, par ordre chrono-logique depuis leur origine; avec une table alphabétique des ouvrages et des auteurs.
*Paris: Cl. J. Baptiste Bauche, 1760; 298p.
Facs. reprint, London: H. Baron, 1967.

This was intended to be a comprehensive catalogue of works for the French lyric stage. It begins with a chronological list of poets who wrote for the genre (pp. 1-26) and one of musicians (pp. 27-39), from 1552 onward. Most of the book then devotes itself to a list (pp. 40-254) of ballets, mascarades, entrées, etc. in two time periods: 1548-1673 and 1673-1759. Works from the latter years inevitably have more informa-tion noted concerning composers, librettists, number of acts or entrées, characters, performance locations, number of performances, and subse-quent changes. An alphabetical table (pp. 255-78) lists authors and works.

76 LA VALLIÈRE, Louis César de la Baume le Blanc, duc de (1708-1780)
Bibliothèque du théâtre françois, depuis son origine; contenant un extrait de tous les ouvrages composés pour ce théâtre, depuis les mystères jusqu'aux pièces de Pierre Corneille; une liste chronologique de celles composées depuis cette dernière époque jusqu'à présent; avec deux tables alphabétiques, l'une des auteurs et l'autre des pièces. 3 v.
Dresden: Michel Groell, 1768; (v. 1) xx+576p., (v. 2) 584p., (v. 3) 504p.
*Facs. reprint, Genève: Slatkine, 1969.

Following a brief introduction to the origins and development of French drama from the Middle Ages to the present, La Vallière lists alphabeti-cally and describes extant plays for the French stage. The descriptions variously offer details about performers, plot summaries with quota-tions, or criticism. The author disputes facts with the compilers of simi-lar catalogues, especially the brothers Parfaict *(Dictionnaire des thé-âtres,* q.v.). Each play is identified by type—pastorale, tragedy, farce, etc. Of interest to the dance historian is the gradual appearance of references to dance. In v. 3, p. 82, Geneviève de Brabant is cited for a 5-act work with a ballet closing each act; p. 89 identifies Molière's *Malade imaginaire* as a 3-act play mixed with dances and music. As the list proceeds, more and more comedies appear to contain music and dance. Volume 1 lists plays before 1552 through 1627; v. 2, 1628-1636; v. 3, 1637-1765. Page 226 of v. 3 begins the list of plays presented in translation from Greek, Latin, Italian (or presented in Italian), Spanish, English, German, with additional plays "des poètes du pays du Nord et même des nations hors de l'Europe." A special descriptive section is devoted to *pièces satyriques* (pp. 263-319). Appended are two alphabetical tables of authors and of titles of plays.

77 LE BRUN, Antoine Louis (1680-1743)

Théâtre lyrique; avec une préface, où l'on traite du poëme de l'opéra. Et la réponse à une épître satyrique contre ce spectacle.
*Paris: Pierre Ribou, 1712; 318+[3]p.

Le Brun prefaces this collection of his opera librettos with a discussion of the elements of a good opera, emphasizing the relation of the dances to the work as a whole. (The librettos themselves provide no description of the dances, other than the infrequent "on fait plusieurs dances," e.g. p. 198.) He argues for a balanced mixture of songs and dances. Opera is a spectacle made for the eyes (owing to the machines and dances) as well as for the ears. Opera's chief virtue consists in its combination of media; it is not only dance, not only music, not only a theme: it is all of these things. When rightly conceived, the dances extend the subject and do not interrupt the flow of the opera, as a detractor claimed. Le Brun has hereby recorded his plays, because he wrote them in his youth and now sees them purloined. Furthermore, his words were often ruined on the stage by poor productions. The collection contains poetry for the plays *Zoroastre* (pp. 36-80), *Arion* (pp. 81- 122), *Mélusine* (pp. 123-54), *Sémélé* (pp. 155-98), *Hippocrate* (pp. 199-236), *Frédéric* (pp. 237-62), and *Europe* (pp. 263-318).

78 LEBRUN, Charles (1619-1690)

A method to learn to design the passions, proposed in a conference on their general and particular expression. Written in French, and illustrated with a great many figures excellently designed, by Mr. Le Brun, chief painter to the French King, chan-

cellor and director of the royal academy of painting and sculpture. Translated into English, and all the designs engraved on copper, by John Williams, esq.
London: author, 1734.

*Facs. reprint, Los Angeles, CA: William Andrews Clark Memorial Library, 1980 (publication numbers 200-201). Introduction by Alan T. McKenzie.

Based on Lebrun's lectures of 1667 (or 1668) at the Académie Royale de Peinture et de Sculpture, this series of annotated drawings depicting facial expressions appeared in numerous French editions from 1696 on, with English translations appearing by 1701 and an Italian translation in 1751. Lebrun classifies the passions according to a scheme heavily indebted to those of Poussin and Descartes. Drawings and text specify how the individual passion may be expressed in facial gestures or postures. Lebrun's scheme of expressing specific emotions by means of corresponding facial gestures probably influenced French acting in the second half of the 17th century. In the 18th century his scheme—or others derived from it—was urged upon actors by authorities such as Betterton, Hill, and Cibber and apparently supported by Hogarth (e.g. in his depiction of Garrick as Richard III; see McKenzie's introduction to the 1980 reprint).

This 1734 edition represents a literal translation of the French original, with exact copies of the drawings. Passions depicted include: Admiration, Esteem, Veneration, Veneration (issuing from faith), Extasy (sic), Contempt, Horrour, Fright, Pure love, Desire, Hope, Fear, Jealousy, Hatred, Sadness, Bodily pain, Joy, Laughter, Weeping, Anger, Extream despair, Rage. (The selection and ordering of drawings differ among the various editions.) Commentary for each describes physical responses to the specific emotion, e.g. motion or condition of the eyes, brows, forehead, mouth, etc. Lebrun pays special attention to eyebrows, which he believes of all facial features best express the passions.

79 LE CERF DE LA VIÉVILLE, SEIGNEUR DE FRESNEUSE, Jean Laurent (1674-1707)

Comparaison de la musique italienne et de la musique françoise. Où, en examinant en détail les avantages des spectacles, et le mérite des compositeurs des deux nations, on montre quelles sont les vrayes beautéz de la musique.
Bruxelles: François Foppens, 1704; 183p. (Part 1 only.)

Bruxelles: François Foppens, 1705; Part 1 (2nd ed.), x+183p.;
Part 2, 352p.; 1706, Part 3, 212+53p.
*Facs. reprint, Genève: Minkoff, 1972.
Reprinted as v. 2-4 in the 1721 and subsequent editions of J.
Bonnet, *Histoire de la musique et de ses effets* (q.v.).
Facs. reprint, Graz 1966.
German transl. by J. Mattheson in *Critica musica,* v. 1. Hamburg: author, 1722.
Facs. reprint, Buren (Netherlands): Frits Knuf, 1964.
German transl. by F. W. Marpurg in *Kritische Briefe über die Tonkunst,* v. 1. Berlin: F. W. Biernstiel, 1759.
Facs. reprint, Hildesheim: Georg Olms, 1974.
English transl. of excerpts from the 6th dialogue in Oliver Strunk,
Source readings in music history (New York: Norton, 1950),
pp. 489-507.

This collection of dialogues, letters, and essays replies to the criticism of French music in Raguenet's *Parallèle* (q.v.). In defending the musical world of Lully against pro-Italian critics, Le Cerf describes the musical aesthetic of late 17th-c. France that sought simplicity, reasonableness, and naturalness in art, as opposed to sensuality. He reports briefly on Lully's composition for dance (Part 2, pp. 228-29) and on Lully's life. Brief treatment of choreographer Pierre Beauchamps appears in Part 1, p. 11.

80 LE PRÉVOST D'EXMES, François (1729-1793)

Lully, musicien.
*Paris: [ca. 1780]; 48p.

This biography and appreciation, rich in citations from contemporary history, aesthetics, chronicle, anecdote, journalism, etc., was compiled chiefly by Le Prévost d'Exmes from various articles by Sénecé, de Fresneuse, and Titon du Tillet (q.v.). It recounts the reception of each opera, quoting newspaper critics, etc.

81 LÉRIS, Antoine de (1723-1795)

Dictionnaire portatif des théâtres, contenant l'origine des différens théâtres de Paris; le nom de toutes les pièces qui y ont été représentées depuis leur établissement, et des pièces jouées en province, ou qui ont simplement paru par la voie de l'impression depuis plus de trois siècles; avec des anecdotes et des remarques sur la plupart: le nom et les particularités intéressantes de la vie des auteurs, musiciens et acteurs; avec le catalogue de leurs ouvrages, et l'exposé de leurs talens: une chronologie des auteurs, et des musiciens, les opéras et des pièces qui ont paru depuis vingt-cinq ans.

Paris: C. A. Jombert, 1754; xl+557p.

*2nd ed., Paris: C. A. Jombert, 1763; xxxiv+738p.

Paris: Bauche, 1763.

Facs. reprint, Genève: Slatkine, 1970.

Less complete than other theater catalogues, this serves as a concise theater-goer's guide to works and personalities associated with the Parisian stage. The preface in the second ed. provides a brief account of the origins of the various Parisian theaters; an evaluation of various *spectacles de Paris* presented June 1, 1763 at the Académie Royale de Musique; and lists of singers, dancers, teaching personnel, and pensioners at the Comédie Française and the Comédie Italienne. Part 1 begins with a list of stage works (pp. 1-461), indicating title, type, author, and place and date of performance. Two chronological charts (pp. 494-95) list authors, then composers, indicating how many works each contributed during the years 1300-1763. Part 2 offers anecdotes and commentary concerning authors, musicians, and actors, organized alphabetically by name (pp. 495-701). Two chronological tables list operas presented at the Académie Royale de Musique, 1645-1763 (pp. 702-8), and plays presented or published 1729-1763 (pp. 708-23). A supplement occupies pp. 723-30.

82 LE SAGE, Alain René (1668-1747) and D'ORNEVAL (d. 1766)

Le théâtre de la foire ou l'opéra comique. Contenant les meilleures pièces qui ont été représentées aux foires de S. Germain et de S. Laurent. Enrichies d'estampes en taille douce, avec une table de tous les vaudevilles et autres airs gravez-notez à la fin de chaque volume. Recueillies, revûës, et corrigées. 6 v.

*Paris: Etienne Ganeau, 1721-31; v. 1 (1721) 388+64p., v. 2 (1721) 448+64p., v. 3 (1721) 434+88p., v. 4 (1724) 502+40p., v. 5 (1724) 432+56p., v. 6 (1731) 493+65p.

*Paris: Pierre Gandouin [et al.], 1721-1737; 10 v.: v. 1 (1737), v. 2 (1737), v. 3 (Etienne Ganeau, 1721), v. 4 (Etienne Ganeau, 1724), v. 5 (Etienne Ganeau, 1724), v. 6 (Pierre Gandouin, 1731), v. 7 (1731), v. 8 (1731), v. 9 (1737), v. 10 (veuve Gandouin, 1734).

Paris: Pierre Gandouin [et al.], 1724-1737; 10 v.: v. 1 (1737) 427+68p., v. 2 (1737) 448+64p., v. 3 (1737) 454+88p., v. 4 (Etienne Ganeau, 1724) 502+40p., v. 5 (Etienne Ganeau, 1724) 431+59p., v. 6 (veuve Pissot, 1728) 493+68p., v. 7 (Pierre Gandouin, 1731) 436+88p., v. 8 (1731) 367+60p., v. 9 (1737) 568+69p., v. 9 part 2 [=v. 10] (1737) 534+52p.

*Facs. reprint, Genève: Slatkine, 1968; v. 1 (i.e. v. 1-5 newly paginated) 652p., v. 2 (i.e. v. 6-10 newly paginated) 702p.

Amsterdam: Châtelain [et al.], 1722-38.

Amsterdam: L'Honoré et Châtelain, 1723-37; 9 v. in 10.

Amsterdam: 1764; 10 v.

Amsterdam: 1783.

Paris: 1783.

This collection of texts (librettos) to comic operas presented at the fairs of St. Germaine and St. Laurent illustrates the history of the genre from 1713 to 1728. These supposedly represent the best plays of the *opéra comique,* excluding those derived from Italian plays and those whose success depended solely on brilliant ballets or good actors. The repertory divides into 3 groups representing chronological changes within the genre: plays performed with signboards (when fair actors were forbidden to present spoken plays), works consisting of *vaudevilles* sung by the actors, and works that mingle songs with prose dialogue. Each complete text appears with an indication of the original date and place of performance and the original actors, but without commentary. An appendix to each volume gives the tunes to all vaudevilles included in the texts (the tunes are referred to in the text by serial number). These airs were selected or composed by Jean Claude Gillier, the composer of the fair theater. Stage directions indicate where dances occur, but dances are merely named rather than described. An illustrative plate accompanying each text shows clearly the scene design and characters in costume. These works provide insight into popular theater, serving as background to the innovations of those celebrated dancers (such as Marie Sallé) and musicians whose careers began with the comic operas and ballets of the fair theaters. An 1887 study by V. Barberet entitled *Le Sage et le théâtre de la foire* (Genève: Slatkine, 1970) gathers together the *pièces foraines* omitted by Le Sage in *Le théâtre de la foire* and lists all of his works chronologically, both those written by Le Sage alone and those written with collaborators. Barberet also provides an analysis of Le Sage's theater, including a chapter on the *divertissements* (pp. 202-207).

The works included in either of the 10-volume Gandouin editions are as follows (volume, title, date of first performance, author, page number):

V. 1—*Arlequin roy de Sérendib*, 1713, Le Sage, 16-63; *Arlequin Thétis*, 1713, Le Sage, 64-83; *Arlequin invisible*, 1713, Le Sage, 84-104; *Le foire de Guibray*, 1714, Le Sage, 105-31; *Arlequin Mahomet*, 1714, Le Sage, 132-69; *Le tombeau de Nostradamus*, 1714, Le Sage, 170-99; *Arlequin, sultane favorite*, 1715, LeT . . . , 200-85; *La ceinture de Vénus*, 1715, Le Sage, 286-349; *Parodie de l'opéra Télémaque*, 1715, Le Sage, 350-84; *Le temple du destin*, 1715, Le Sage, 385-427; 185 airs.

V. 2-*Arlequin defenseur d'Homère*, 1715, Louis Fuzelier, 1-43; *Arlequin Colombine*, 1715, Le Sage, 44-79; *Les eaux de Merlin*, 1715, Le Sage, 80-131; *Arlequin traitant*, 1716, D'Orneval, 132-225; *Les arrests de l'amour*, 1716, D'Orneval, 226-58; *Le temple de l'ennuy*, 1716, Le Sage et Fuzelier, 259-75; *Le tableau du mariage*, 1716, Le Sage et Fuzelier, 276-315; *L'écôle des amans*, 1716, Le Sage et Fuzelier, 316-52; *Arlequin Hulla*, 1716, Le Sage et D'Orneval, 353-97; *Le Pharaon*, 1717, Fuzelier, 398-448; 188 airs.

V. 3—*Les animaux raisonnables*, 1718, Fuzelier et M. A. Alexandre Le Grand, 1-35; *La querelle des théâtres*, 1718, Le Sage et Fuzelier, 36-59; *Le jugement de Paris*, 1718, D'Orneval, 60-93; *La princesse de Carizme*, 1718, Le Sage, 94-199; (remaining works in v. 3 all composed by Le Sage and D'Orneval) *Le monde renversé*, 1718, 200-67; *Les amours de Nanterre*, 1718, 268-329; *L'isle des Amazones*, 1718, 330-76; *Les funérailles de la foire*, 1718, 377-410; *Le rappel de la foire à la vie*, not performed, 411-54; 237 airs.

V. 4—(all composed by Le Sage and D'Orneval) *La statue merveilleuse*, 1719, 1-94; *Le diable d'argent*, 1720, 95-123; *Arlequin roi des ogres*, 1720, 124-73; *Le queue de vérité*, 1720, 174-211; *Prologue*, 212-31, to *Arlequin Endymion*, 1721, 232-304, and *La forêt de Dodone*, 1721, 305-51; *La fausse-foire*, 352-74, *Prologue* to *La boîte de Pandore*, 1721, 375-428, and *La tête-noire*, 1721, 429-502; 133 airs.

V. 5—(all composed by Le Sage and D'Orneval) *Le régiment de la calotte*, 1721, 1-46; *L'ombre du cocher poëte*, 47-69, *Prologue* to *Le*

rémouleur d'amour, 1722, 70-106, and *Pierrot Romulus,* 1722, 107-40;
Le jeune-vieillard, 1722, 141-268; *Prologue,* 269-80, to *La force de
l'amour,* 1722, 281-364, and *La foire des fées,* 1722, 365-431; 154 airs.

V. 6—(all composed by Le Sage and D'Orneval) *L'enchanteur Mirli-
ton,* 1725, 1-28; *Le temple de mémoire,* 1725, 29-69; *Les enragés,*
1725, 70-122; *Les pèlerins de la Mecque,* 1726, 123-230; *Les comédiens corsaires,* 231-56, *Prologue* to *L'obstacle favorable,* 1726, 257-
312, and *Les amours déguisés,* 1726, 313-72; *Achmet et Almanzine,*
1728, 373-493; 162 airs.

V. 7—(all composed by Le Sage and D'Orneval) *La Pénélope moderne,* 1728, 1-84; *Les amours de Protée,* 1728, 85-120; *La princesse
de la Chine,* 1729, 121-212; *Les spectacles malades,* 1729, 213-40; *Le
corsaire de salé,* 1729, 241-94; *L'impromptu du Pont-Neuf* (by M.
P . . .), 1729, 295-322; *Les couplets en procès,* 1730, 323-49; *La reine
du Barostan,* 1730, 350-401; *L'Opéra-Comique assiégé,* 1730, 402-36;
204 airs.

V. 8— *La grand'mère amoureuse,* 1726, Fuzelier et D'Orneval, 1-65;
(remainder composed by Le Sage, Fuzelier, and D'Orneval) *L'industrie,*
66-89, *Prologue* to *Zémine et Almanzor,* 1730, 90-134, and *Les routes
du monde,* 1730, 135-83; *Le mariage du caprice et de la folie* (by
M . . .), 1724, 1730, 184-238; *L'indifférence,* 239-66, *Prologue* to
L'amour marin, 1730, 267-317, and *L'espérance,* 1730, 318-67; 140
airs.

V. 9—(all composed by Le Sage and D'Orneval) *Roger de Sicile,*
1731, 1-115; *Les désespérés,* 116-52, *Prologue* to *Sophie et Sigismond,*
1732, 153-219, and *La sauvagesse,* 1732, 220-74; *La première représentation* (by Le Sage), 275-97, *Prologue* to *Les mariages de Canada*
(by Le Sage), 1734, 298-362; *Le mari préféré* (by Le Sage), 1736, 363-
421; *Les trois commères,* 1723, 422-563; 157 airs.

V. 10—(all composed by Le Sage and D'Orneval) *Le réveil de
l'Opéra-Comique,* 1732, 1-15; *La lanterne véridique,* 1732, 16-72; *La
parterre merveilleux,* 73-84, *Prologue* to *Le rival de lui-même,* 1732,
85-122; *La mère jalouse,* 1732, 123-67; *L'allure,* 1732, 168-215; *L'isle
du mariage,* 1733, 222-79; *Le retour de l'Opéra-Comique,* 1734, 286-
321; *Le père rival,* 1734, 322-83; *Les audiences de Thalie,* 1734, 384-
427; *Les petites maisons,* 1732, 433-88; *L'amour désoeuvré,* 1734, 489-
534; 66 airs.

83 MAROLLES, Michel de (1600-1681)

Les mémoires de M. de M., abbé de Villeloin. Divisée en trois parties, contenant ce qu'il a vû de plus remarkable en sa vie, depuis l'année 1600. Ses entretiens avec quelques-uns des plus sçavants hommes de son temps. Et les généalogies de quelques familles alliées dans la sienne, avec une briève description de la très-illustre maison de Mantouë et de Nevers.
Paris: Antoine de Sommaville, 1656-57.
*2nd ed., Amsterdam: 1755; (v. 1) xiii+396p., (v. 2) 416p., (v. 3) 392p. (Genealogies omitted.)

These memoires give a personal view of the court life in which ballet developed under the reign of Louis XIII, then matured during the reign of Louis XIV. Marolles' firsthand account includes descriptions of famous ballets such as *Les fées de forêts de S. Germain* (1625; v. 1, pp. 114-16; v. 3, p. 220), *Danse de Sompy* (1625; v. 1, pp. 120-21), *Les noces imaginaires de la douairière de Bilbahaut* (1626; v. 1, pp. 132-35), *Le ballet de la prospérité des armes de la France* (1640; v. 1, pp. 237-39), and *Ballet en triomphe de la beauté* (1640; v. 1, pp. 239-40). He provides information on the order for making *révérences,* the order of seating by rank, the formalities of promenades, the festivities for court marriages, baptisms, dinners, and visits. In addition, v. 3 contains an extensive essay on ballet ("Neuvième discours du ballet," pp. 110-56). Here he comments on the importance of novelty and the *merveilleux* for rendering a ballet pleasing and proper: "Que si le ballet n'est point du tout sérieux, il faut néanmoins que la manière et l'invention nouvelle le rendent agréable et honnête, y mêlant des choses extraordinaires qui tiennent du merveilleux" (pp. 119-20). The essay also provides summaries of several ballets: *Ballet du tems* (pp. 127-39), *Ballet des armoires* (pp. 139-45), *Ballet des emblèmes et des hiéroglyphiques* (pp. 146-50), *Ballet des muses* (pp. 150-56).

84 MARPURG, Friedrich Wilhelm (1718-1795)

Historisch-kritische Beyträge zur Aufnahme der Musik. 5 v.
*Berlin: (v. 1) Joh. Jacob Schützens Wittwe, 1754[-1755]; xx+562p.; (v. 2-5) Gottlieb August Lange, 1756-1778; 576p., 560p., 564p., 534p.
Facs. reprint, Hildesheim: Georg Olms, 1970.

In discussing opera (v. 2, pp. 90-91), Marpurg takes the (French) point of view that to please, the ballets in opera productions—though they need not be as fully integrated into the plot as the chorus in a tragedy— ought to have some connection with the subject or action of the opera. (He implies that the dances ending each act of an opera on the German stage do not typically attain this goal.) Later (v. 2, pp. 181-84), he augments his argument by paraphrasing the thoughts of Rémond de St. Mard on the same subject (after *Oeuvres*, v. 5, p. 141). Another section (pp. 232-60) presents a chronological index of operas staged in Paris from 1645 to 1754. This list is periodically interrupted by biographical notices for some composers, including Marais, Desmarets, Charpentier, de la Guerre, Mouret, Montéclair, de la Lande, and others.

85 MARQUET, François Nicolas (ca. 1687-1759)
Nouvelle méthode facile et curieuse, pour apprendre par les notes de musique à connoître le pouls de l'homme et les différens changemens qui lui arrivent, depuis sa naissance jusqu'à sa mort, tirée des observations faites par M. F. N. Marquet.
Nancy: veuve N. Baltazard, 1747; 34p.
*2nd ed., Amsterdam, Paris: P. Fr. Didot, 1769; v+216p.

For the purpose of communicating exact tempo, a physician advocates applying to music the medical distinction between patterns of human pulse beats. Six plates illustrate 24 pulse patterns, differing in either the intensity or frequency of the pulsations, or both. Marquet equates the natural regular pulse beat to the downbeat of a minuet measure and to the one-second swing of a well regulated pendulum, resulting in a calculated 60 minuet measures per minute! The 14 critical essays that augment the second edition attest to a certain amount of controversy over Marquet's thesis that pulse patterns, and therefore musical patterns, express specific physical-emotional states.

86 MAUPOINT
Bibliothèque des théâtres, contenant le catalogue alphabétique des pièces dramatiques, opéra, parodies, et opéra comiques; et le tems de leurs représentations. Avec des anecdotes sur la plûpart des pièces contenuës en ce recüeil, et sur la vie des auteurs, musiciens et acteurs.
*Paris: Laurent François Prault, 1733; 369p.
*Paris: Pierre Prault, 1733; 369p.

This reference book on stage productions in Paris begins with an alphabetical list by title of plays, ballets, operas, etc., presented during the years ca.1450-1732. Entries state the genre, author or poet, composer, place and date of first performance, names of participants (actors, singers, dancers), and success of the production. Multiple settings of the same title or libretto are treated individually. An appendix (pp. 321-329) provides additions and corrections. Subsequent appendices include a chronological list of operas by year of first performance (1671-1732; pp. 330-32); a chronological list of composers of the operas and ballets cited in the main listing (with year and number of works cited; p. 333); an alphabetical list of *opéras comiques* performed at the Théâtres de la foire de St. Germain et de St. Laurent (pp. 334-42); a chronological list of dramatic authors, 1450-1730 (pp. 343-56); and a general index of authors, musicians, and actors, with reference to the works under which they are mentioned (pp. 357ff.). Composers of operas and ballets listed on p. 333 (with date of first mentioned performance and number of works cited) include: Aubert (1725, 1), Batistin (1709, 3), Bertin (1706, 4), Bourgeois (1713, 2), Bouvard (1702, 1), Cambert (1659, 3), Campra (1697, 16), Charpentier (1694, 1), Colasse (1688, 9), Colin de Blamont (1723, 2), De la Barre (1700, 2), De la Coste (1697, 7), De la Lande (1666, 3), Desmarest (1693, 7), Destouches (1697, 9), Gervais (1697, 3), Lully (1660, 17), Louis and Jean de Lully (1688, 2), Marais (1693, 4), Mathau and Alarius (1718, 1), Mouret (1714, 6), Quinaut (1729, 1), Rebel père (1703, 1), Rebel and Francoeur fils (1726, 2), Royer (1730, 1), Salomon (1713, 2), Theobalde (1691, 2).

87 MÉNÉSTRIER, Claude François (1631-1705)
Recueil des devises et des poésies.
*[Lyon? Paris?]: [1663-1689].

This is a collection of descriptions of edifices and decorations produced under Ménéstrier's direction for royal wedding processions, festivals, and ceremonies. Published separately 1663-1689, they were collected by the author, interleaved and bound with holograph notes, manuscript letters, poems, etc., most written in French, some in Latin, Greek, or Italian. The separate publications are: (1) *L'Amour, autheur et conservateur du monde; dessein des peintures du plafond de l'alcove de leurs Altesses Royales* (s.l., 1663?; 4p.), (2) *Description de l'arc de la porte du chasteau. Les noeuds de l'amour de la France et de la Savoye* (s.l., 1663; 4p.), (3) *Description de l'arc dressé par les soins du Souverain Senat de Savoye, pour l'entrée de leurs Altesses Royales à Chambery* (Lyon: Pierre Guillimin, 1663, 32p.), (4) *Dessein de la course à cheval, faite à l'occasion des nopces de Madame Françoise d'Orleans-Valois avec S. A. Royale Charles Emanuel II, Duc de Savoye, Roy de Chypre, etc.* (Chambry: Par les FF. Du-Four, 1663; 16p.), (5) *Dessein de la machine du feu d'artifice pour les nopces de leurs Altesses Royales* (s.l., 1663?; 17p.), (6) *Les honneurs funèbres rendus à la mémoire de très-haut, très-puissant, très-illustre et très-magnanime prince Monseigneur Louis de Bourbon, Prince de Condé, et premier prince du sang de France* (Paris: Estienne Michallet, 1687; 40p.), (7) *Les noeuds de l'a-mour; dessein des appareils dressez à Chambery à l'entrée de leurs Altesses Royales à l'occasion de leurs nopces* (Chambry: Par les FF. Du-Four, 1663; 51p.), (8) *Description de l'arc dressé par les soins des magistrats de la Souveraine Chambre des comptes de Savoye, en la place du chasteau* (s.l., 1663?; 31p.), (9) *La statuë de Louis le Grand, placée dans le temple de l'honneur. Dessein du feu d'artifice dressé devant l'Hôtel de Ville de Paris, pour la statuë du Roy, qui y doit estre posée* (Paris: Nicolas et Charles Caillou, 1689, 29p.). See also Ménéstrier's *L'art des emblèmes* (1662) and *La philosophie des images* (1682), both reprinted in facsimile (New York: Garland, 1979) with introductory notes by Stephen Orgel.

88 MÉNÉSTRIER, Claude François (1631-1705)

Des représentations en musique anciennes et modernes.
Paris: René Guignard, 1681; 333p.
  *Facs. reprint, Genève: Minkoff, 1972.
Paris: Robert Pépié, 1684; 333p.
Paris: Robert Pépié, 1685; 333p.

This study deals with historical, theoretical, and practical aspects of courtly entertainment, entering into philosophical speculation. An opening section describes practices of the ancients (pp. 1-133). Ménéstrier then expresses the aesthetic ideal prevalent throughout the next century—that art should imitate nature, mirroring the actions of the spirit in a natural manner (p. 134). Detailed descriptions of selected theatrical events include the entertainments at Tortone for the wedding of the Duc de Milan (pp. 157-60), at Paris for the wedding of the Duc de Joyeuse, and others in Bavaria, Florence, Austria, Savoy, Germany, and England. In France, the activities of Jean Antoine de Baïf, the influence of Cardinal Mazarin, the establishment of the academy of music, etc., interweave with numerous descriptions of perfect "actions" of the theater, which, at their best, correspond to St. Augustine's perfect harmonies, in the author's opinion.

89 MÉNÉSTRIER, Claude François (1631-1705)

Traité des tournois, joustes, carrousels et autres spectacles publics.

*Lyon: Jacques Muguet, 1669; 6+400p.

Facs. reprint, New York: AMS Press, 1978; 400p.

Facs. reprint in series *The philosophy of images,* ed. with introductory notes by Stephen Orgel, New York and London: Garland, 1979; [ii]+400+[ii]p.

Meticulous descriptions and beautiful illustrations here provide a record of court entertainment in Ménéstrier's remote and recent past. An ecclesiastic in charge of Jesuit courtesies, the able scholar traveled from court to court preparing *ballets ambulataires* and *ballets à entrées* for various festivals and public celebrations. Seeking models for his work, he gathered and printed this treasury of sources both ancient and modern. Clearly organized chapters tell how to select machines, *récits,* subjects, decoration, and *devises,* as well as how to stage quadrilles, carrousels, *divertissemens militaires,* mascarades, and *naumachies.* Included is information on the rich entertainments at the court of Savoy and on the noblemen—the Marquis Ludovico d'Aglié San Martino and Count Filippo d'Aglié San Martino—who were active in producing the splendid displays there.

90 MEREAU

Réflexions sur le maintien et sur le moyen d'en corriger les défauts.
*Gotha: Mevius & Dieterich, 1760; [xxv]+193+[3]p.

Containing quotations from John Locke among others, this education manual tells how to train children in bodily movement. Although there is no reference to dance per se, the principles of body mechanics, including the correction of faults, reveal the prevailing emphasis on movement in education.

91 MOLIÈRE, Jean Baptiste Poquelin (1622-1673)

Les oeuvres . . .

Paris: 1666. (For publication history, see Robert Jouanny, ed., *Oeuvres complètes de Molière,* Paris: Éditions Garnier Frères, 1962; 2 v.)

DES
COMPARSES.

A Comparſe eſt aux Carrouſels,ce qu'eſt l'Entrée aux Ballets , & la Scene aux Comedies, & Trage-dies. C'eſt à dire qu'elle eſt l'En-trée des Quadrilles dans la Carrie-re , dont elles font tout le tour pour ſe faire voir aux Spectateurs, & s'al-ler rendre aux Pavillons,& aux Po-ſtes qu'on leur a deſtinez. Elle ſert auſſi a meſurer la Li-ce pour la Courſe, & l'vſage en eſt ſi ancien que Virgile decrivant les Ieux qu'Enée fit pour ſon Pere, a remarqué expreſſément les Comparſes,quand il dit :

Poſtquam omnem læti conceſſum , oculoſque ſuorum
Luſtravere in Equis.

Apres

III-89 Claude François MÉNÉSTRIER, *Traité des tournois, joustes, carrousels et autres spectacles publics* (Lyon: Jacques Muguet, 1669), p. 203. Illustration of a horse ballet. [New York Public Library at Lincoln Center, Astor, Lenox, and Tilden Foundations, Dance Collection, [*MGRZ-Res.]]

Nouvelle édition, revuë, corrigée et augmentée, enrichie de figures en taille-douce. 4 v. Amsterdam: Pierre Brunel, 1713; 37+448p., 504p., 538p., 487p.

Although it is difficult to reconstruct dances within Molière's plays, owing to the lack of descriptive information, the important role of dance in many of his stage works must be acknowledged. His *comédies-ballets,* initially in collaboration with choreographer-dancer Pierre Beauchamps and decorator-designer Jacques Torelli, then with composer Jean Baptiste Lully, combined ballet scenes with stage comedy, allowing dance to penetrate the action of the play. The 1713 edition of Molière's works contains the author's statements of intention for each play. Indications for dancing consist of minimal stage directions. (Details of the dance *intermèdes* in some of Molière's comédie-ballets may be found in the collected edition of Lully's music, *Oeuvres-complètes,* begun in Paris in 1930 and never completed.) For a modern treatment of Molière's role, see Marie-Françoise Christout, *Le ballet de cour de Louis XIV, 1643-1672* (Paris: Picard, 1967).

92 MONNET, Jean (1703-ca. 1785)

Supplément au roman comique, ou mémoires pour servir à la vie de Jean Monnet, ci-devant directeur de l'Opéra-Comique à Paris, de l'Opéra de Lyon, et d'une Comédie Françoise à Londres, écrits par lui-même. 2 v.
London: 1772; 200+288p.
*London: 1773; 135+192p.
Ed. with commentary by Henri d'Almeras as *Mémoires de Jean Monnet, directeur du théâtre de la foire.* Paris: Louis-Michaud, [1909]; 278p.
English transl. by Richard Mayne as *Memoirs,* with commentary by George W. Ball. Garden City, NJ: Doubleday, 1978; 544p.

Jean Monnet was an impresario active in the theatrical productions of the fairground theaters, one of which, the Opéra-Comique, gave the great choreographer J. G. Noverre his start. The relationship between aristocratic dance institutions and these theaters with their own ballets is a fascinating part of 18th-c. dance history. These memoirs are therefore important for their account of the activities in these theaters of such French dancers as Marie Sallé, Marie Camargo, Gaetan Vestris, Jean Barthélemy Lany, Louis Dupré, and others. They also document professional mobility, showing interaction among the theater communities of different cities, especially London (where Monnet worked with the mime John Rich), Paris, and Lyon.

93 MOUFFLE D'ANGERVILLE (d. ca. 1794)

Vie privée de Louis XV, ou principaux événements, particularités et anecdotes de son règne. 4 v.
London: J. P. Lyton, 1781.
London: 1781. *Nouvelle édition, augmentée sur les manuscrits de l'auteur.*
London: 1785.
London: J. P. Lyton, 1788.
Ed. by Albert Meyrac, Paris: Colmann-Lévy, 1921; 431p.
English transl. by J. O. Justamond as *The private life of Lewis XV.*
London: C. Dilly, 1781. Dublin: Whitestone, 1781.
Paris: B. Mathé, 1976. Ed. by Arnoux Laffrey as *Siècle de Louis XV.*
*English transl. by J. S. Mingard, annotated and amplified by quotations from original and unpublished documents by Albert Meyrac, as *The private life of Louis XV.* New York: Boni & Liveright, 1924; ix+364p. London: John Lane, 1924; ix+364p.

With a view of life in the court of Louis XV (reigned 1715-1774), these memoirs provide background on the persons who supported the cost and determined the ambience of entertainment in which dance flourished.

94 NIVELON, F[rancis?] (fl. 1720-1740?)

The rudiments of genteel behavior.
*[s.l.]: 1737; [27p.+12pl.]

This brief but precise etiquette book contains large illustrations of 6 female and 6 male figures similar to, but more expressive than, those in Pierre Rameau's *Maître à danser* (q.v.). The accompanying verbal description also derives from Rameau, but it is limited to the curtsey and bow, giving of hands, proper standing and walking, receiving, offering, and passing. Only one brief paragraph concentrates on the minuet. The exceptional detail in the plates makes this a valuable reference on carriage and ettiquette.

95 NOUGARET, Pierre Jean Baptiste (1742-1823)

De l'art du théâtre en général, où il est parlé des spectacles de l'Europe, de ce qui concerne la comédie ancienne et nouvelle, la tragédie, la pastorale-dramatique, la parodie, l'opéra sérieux [v. 2: l'opéra bouffon] et particulièrement la comédie-mêlée-d'ariettes [v. 1: avec des observations sur les différens genres de musique] [v. 2: avec l'histoire philosophique de la musique, et des observations sur ses différens genres reçus au théâtre].
*Paris: Cailleau, (v. 1) 1768, 1769; xxiv+382p.; (v. 2) 1769; viii+370p. (1769 ed. of v. 1 entitled *De l'art du théâtre; où il est . . .)*

Facs. reprint, Genève: Slatkine, 1971.

Nougaret takes the entire gamut of theatrical spectacle as his subject. He examines critically each genre from the highest order of tragedy to the lowest *opéra bouffon,* applying to all the same critical principles, such as unity of time and place. In Book 1, after an opening section cogently defending the theater as a place of virtue and instruction (v. 1, pp. 1-20), Nougaret quickly sketches the history of spectacle from antiquity (pp. 21-39) to the rise of the Opéra Comique and the coming of the Italians (pp. 40-66). Book 2 examines and advocates the new theater (pp. 1-72, 108-14). A section on *opéra bouffon* compares it to ancient comedy (pp. 73-107). Book 3 gives advice to poets on the difficulties of composition (pp. 115-60); Book 4 (pp. 161-363) provides extensive detail concerning the subject, its exposition, climax and denouement; unities of time, place, and person; the number of actors, use of scenes; verisimilitude, style; the place of dialogue, decorations, etc. Book 5 (v. 2, pp. 1-124) is a survey of theatrical genres; Book 6 concentrates upon musical theater (pp. 125-344). A chapter on music discusses how music affects animals, how it is useful in love, how women must not be exposed to it too long or too much. Identifying Quinault's and Lully's *Le triomphe de l'amour* (1681) as the first *opéra-sérieux,* Nougaret reflects upon the theater of grand opera, on the operas of Italy, on ballets and their place in opera (they are often badly placed and occur too frequently), closing with more advice to the poet (the music must reinforce the poetry, and the poem must suit the music). In essence, this overview of 18th-c. theater reveals the minor role dance played within it.

96 ORIGNY, Antoine Jean Baptiste Abraham d' (1734-1798)

Annales du théâtre italien, depuis son origine jusqu'à ce jour. 3 v.

*Paris: veuve Duchesne, 1788; 333p., 315p., 308p.
  Facs. reprint, Genève: Slatkine, 1970.
Paris: veuve Duchesne, 1793.

Purporting to have compiled the definitive history of Italian theater in France, Origny offers observations on the art of Italian comedy and catalogues Italian productions in France from 1597 (the arrival date of the first Italian actors in France) to 1786. He systematically lists dates of openings, closings, and revivals and comments on the authors and actors. He discusses the vicissitudes of fortune suffered by the Comédie Italienne and the laws that governed that theater. Volume 1 provides a glance at early Roman origins, beginning with the first comedy known to the author—*La calandra*, 1524—and moving swiftly through the early years of Italian comedy in France, 1577-1761. Volume 2 continues more expansively through 1781, while v. 3 proceeds through 1786 in a more detailed manner. There are occasional specific references to choreographers, dancers, and dances. Tables at the end of each volume chronologically list the subjects discussed.

97 OULTON, Walley Chamberlain (1770?-1820)

The history of the theatres of London: containing an annual register of all the new and revived tragedies, comedies, operas, farces, pantomimes etc. that have been performed at the Theatres-Royal, in London, from the year 1771 to 1795. With occasional notes and anecdotes. 2 v.
*London: Martin and Bain, 1796; 196p., 271p.

Information on pantomimes, ballet pantomimes, ballets, interludes, and ballet spectacles appears here among notes on theatrical productions. A continuation of Benjamin Victor's *History of the theatres of London and Dublin* (q.v.), which in 3 v. covered the years 1730 to 1770, this register records how plays were received, which speeches were made and occasions commemorated (especially deaths); who performed, gave benefits, quarreled; how expensive a spectacle was. Such works show dance as part of the total spectrum of theatrical offerings.

98 PARFAICT, Claude (1705-1777) and François (1698-1753) [finished and edited by Godin d'ABGUERBE]

Le dictionnaire des théâtres de Paris, contenant toutes les pièces qui ont été représentées jusqu'à présent sur les différens théâtres françois, et sur celui de l'Académie royale de musique; les extraits de celles qui ont été jouées par les comédiens italiens, depuis leur rétablissement en 1716 ainsi que des opéras comiques et principaux spectacles des foires Saint Germain et Saint Laurent. Des faits, anecdotes sur les auteurs qui ont travaillé pour ces théâtres, et sur les principaux acteurs, actrices, danseurs, danseuses, compositeurs de ballets, dessinateurs, peintres de ces spectacles etc. 7 v.

Paris: 1745-49.

*Paris: Lambert, 1756; v. 1 (A-BY) xvi+508p; v. 2 (CA- GA) 667p.; v. 3 (GA-OB) 519p.; v. 4 (OB-SA) 566p.; v. 5 (SA-TY) 592p.; v. 6 (VA-ZU) 338p.; v. 7 (corrections and addenda) pp. 339-757.

Paris: Rozet, 1767; 7 v.

Facs. reprint, Genève: Slatkine, 1967; 2 v.

In this ambitious catalogue the brothers Parfaict list alphabetically all stage works (including plays, operas, and ballets) performed in Paris from 1552 to the mid-18th c. Each work is identified by title, genre, and date and location of performance (with a physical description of the theater). They provide a summary of each work, the words to the airs when possible, and examples of dialogue. Most important, they give cast lists, which include ballet dancers, even taking note of cast changes for subsequent performances. Lively descriptions of individual performers emphasize personal features, habits, and character, in addition to birthplace, teachers, establishments with which associated, difficulties and triumphs. For large works, individual acts may be described; occasionally a description covers an entire program that may have combined several pieces. Volume 7 is especially useful for dance references; here are described several ballet scenarios by Jean Baptiste François DeHess (also known as DesHaies, Dezaies, or Deshayes).

99 PARFAICT, François (1698-1753) and Claude (1705-1777)

Histoire de l'ancien théâtre italien, depuis son origine en France, jusqu'à sa suppression en l'année 1697, suivie des extraits ou

canevas des meilleures pièces italiennes qui n'ont jamais été imprimées.
Paris: M. Lambert, 1753; 455p.
*Paris: Rozet, 1767; xiv+455p.
Facs. reprint, New York: AMS Press, 1978; xiv+455p.

As Marion Hannah Winter has so well documented *(Pre-romantic ballet,* London: Pitman, 1974), the influence of the Italian theater on French dance was vital and consistent throughout this period. Hence we include this early history of the Italian theater in France, written by the foremost chroniclers of theater history in France, the indefatigable Parfaict brothers. It begins with an account of the first visits and the final sojourn of the Italian troupe in France. There follows a combined description of characters (Scaramouche, Pantalon, etc.) and performers (Tiberio Fiorilli and others). On page 130 begin the summaries of over 40 plays presented between 1667 and 1674. Based partly on an Italian manuscript of Dominique Biancolelli, the book tries to present these summaries in a form that suggests exactly what occurred in a theater where the main concern was to be amusing.

100 PARFAICT, François (1698-1753) and Claude (1705-1777)
Histoire générale du théâtre françois depuis son origine jusqu'à présent avec la vie des plus célèbres poètes dramatiques, un catalogue exact de leur pièces, et des notes historiques et critiques.
Paris: A. Morin [et al.], 1734-1749; 15 v.
Facs. reprint, Genève: Slatkine, 1967; 3 v.
Amsterdam: 1735-1749; 15 v.
Paris: P. G. Le Mercier, 1745-1749.
*Paris: Mercier et Saillant, 1745-1749 *(Histoire du théâtre français . . .);* v. 1 (1745) xxiv+486p., v. 2 (1745) xvii+568p., v. 3 (1745) xv+582p., v. 4 (1745) xii+549p., v. 5 (1745) xii+489p., v. 6 (1746) xvi+428p., v. 7 (1746) vi+452p., v. 8 (1746) xvi+427p., v. 9 (1746) xx+421p., v. 10 (1747) viii+454p., v. 11 (1747) x+502p., v. 12 (1747) xi+562p., v. 13 (1748) xvi+454p., v. 14 (1748) vii+572p., v. 15 (1749) vii+494p.
Facs. reprint, New York: B. Franklin, 1968; 3 v.

The historical writings of François Parfaict and his brother virtually established written theater history in France and remained among the most significant 18th-c. publications on French theater. Their work on annotated catalogues of plays grew into this comprehensive literary history long considered to be an essential source for French theater history. It treats all genres of French theater, from its origins in the time of Charlemagne into the 18th c., with greatest detail presented for the periods after 1380. The first 3 v. try to bring order to the miscellany of *mystères, moralités, soties,* and *farces* that comprised the beginnings of the French theater. Separate sections deal with the founding of various theatrical entities (theaters, troupes, genres). By the middle of v. 3, the listing of plays and poets becomes regular enough to progress by years, here 1552-1602; v. 4 covers the period 1601-1632. With v. 5 (1633-1638), reporting becomes orderly enough to permit appended indexes of titles, authors, and poets, and sometimes actors. The authors proceed similarly in v. 6 (1639-1645), 7 (1646-1653), 8 (1654-1660), 9 (1661-1665, with a chronological list on pp. 1-40), 10 (1666-1669), 11 (1670-1676), 12 (1677-1685), 13 (1686-1695), 14 (1696-1708), and 15 (1709-1721). They include descriptions and summaries of the plays, quotations from scenes and prefaces, extracts from newspaper reviews, and information concerning events that affected performances: biographies of poets and performers (sometimes with work lists), royal and official decrees, etc.

101 PARFAICT, François (1698-1753) and Claude (1705-1777)

Mémoires pour servir à l'histoire des spectacles de la foire, par un acteur forain. 2 v.

*Paris: Briasson, 1743; lxxxiii+240p., 321p.

Facs. reprint, New York: AMS Press, 1978.

The work deals with performances at the two famous fairs, one at St. Germain from the 12th c. on and one at St. Laurent, then 4 centuries old. Volume 1 covers the period 1697-1721, v. 2 through page 162 the period 1722-1742. For each item, the brothers Parfaict give the title of the work performed, scenario with *intermèdes* containing divertissements or dances, the name of the fair at which it was performed, the troupe and performers involved (including "sauteurs et danseurs de corde et pantomime"), and dates of opening and closing. Their survey provides an excellent panorama of the varied entertainment available at the fair theaters. There follows an alphabetical list (v. 2, p. 163) of the *opéras comiques* and other works (name, acts, place, date, sometimes performers); next a chronological list of the names of entrepreneurs of the principal spectacles (v. 2, p. 284); and finally an alphabetical list of the authors and their plays (v. 2, p. 295). The brothers present this information with pride, since three dancers now at the Opéra— Demoiselle de Lisle, Mlle Mènes, and Mlle Sallé—owe their origins to these entertainments.

102 PERRAULT, Charles (1628-1703)

Les hommes illustres qui ont paru en France pendant le XVIIième siècle, avec leurs portraits au naturel. 2 v.
*Paris: 1696-1700.
Facs. reprint, Genève: Slatkine, 1970.
*English transl. by J. Ozell as *Characters historical and panegyrical of the greatest men that have appear'd in France during the last century.* London: Bernard Lintott, 1704-1705; [26]+221p., [6]+224p.

The English translation omits the beautifully engraved portraits of the famous men of French culture here eulogized. Only two musicians are included: Lully (English transl., v. 1, pp. 192-95) and Mersenne (v. 2, pp. 47-50). Among his musical innovations, Lully is said to have made the inner parts of scores as interesting as the treble; introduced new, previously unknown characters or *mouvements* into instrumental music; used drums and tympani in concert music, usually for warlike and triumphal effects; and perpetuated a deft use of dissonance. He also improved the level of musicianship among professionals; sight-singing and thorough-bass became common skills in France only after his arrival.

103 PURE, Michel de (1634-1680)

Idée des spectacles anciens et nouveaux. Des anciens cirques, amphithéâtres, théâtres, naumachies, triomphes. Des nouveaux comédies, bals, mascarades, carosels, courses de bagues et de testes, joustes, exercices et reveuës militaires, feux d'artifices, entrées des rois, et des reynes.
[s.l.: 1658]
Paris: Michel Brunet, 1668; 318p.
*Facs. reprint, Genève: Minkoff, 1972.

This guide to court ballet entertainment during the reigns of Louis XIII and Louis XIV devotes lesser space to other forms of courtly diversion,

Generallement parlant, il n'y a que le Violon qui soit capable du mouvement François, de répondre à la prestesse de nostre Genie, & de continuer avec égalité & avec justesse, toute la suite & la durée d'un grand Balet. Les délassemés qui se font successivement deviennent imperceptibles: & de trois Violons, qui joüent, l'un qui se reposera, le peut faire sans retrancher beaucoup de l'harmonie, ou du moins sans faire prejudice à l'air que l'on dancera. Les desacords sont aussi-tost rajustez, & la modique longueur du Dessus, faisant moins de violence aux chordes, les tient plus long-temps accordées, & moins sujetes à se relâcher.

Ie conclus donc absolument pour eux : Ie desire toutefois qu'ils soient bien choisis, bien concertez, & bien sages. Car quand la main est sans guide, ou quand le caprice la conduit, tout aussi-tost l'habileté se débauche & s'efface : & mille cous d'archet égarez & extravagans, font des agréements forcez, & jettent ceux qui dancent ou dans des

contre-temps impreveus, ou bien tout à fait hors de cadence. Le Poëte ou celuy qui a la direction du Balet, doit prendre un soin exact de faire joüer note pour note l'Air du Balet, sans y permetre ny redouble ny batterie qu'alors qu'on ne dance point. Car aussi-tost que l'Entrée est commencée, la gloire du Violon n'est plus qu'à joüer juste de mesure & de mouvement, sans vouloir affecter ny passage ny diminution, parce que vous ne sçauriez prendre ou derober si adroitement un temps pour faire vostre baterie, que vous n'interrompiez en quelque façon le train de celuy qui dance : & que ce moment suspendu ne face une notable méconte mesme parmy les gens de la meilleure oreille. Il y en a toutefois d'incorrigibles, & qui éblouïs de la vitesse de leurs doigts, ne regardent plus aux pieds du Danceu, ny au pas de Balet. C'est un des principaux soins de l'Entrepreneur ou du Poëte, & sur lequel il ne doit rien relâcher ny en faveur d'une bonne main, ny sous le pretexte de son habileté.

III-103 Michel de PURE, *Idée des spectacles anciens et nouveaux* (Paris: Michel Brunet, 1668), pp. 276-77. Discussion of instruments to accompany dancing, especially the violin. [New York Public Library at Lincoln Center, Astor, Lenox, and Tilden Foundations, Dance Collection, [*MGRK-Res.]]

SECTION XIII.·

Des Danceus.

ON ne fçauroit parler des Dan-
ceus de Balet, qu'on ne touche quelque chofe de la Dance en
general : & l'on ne peut decider ce
qui peut faire un bon Danceur,
qu'on n'ait quelque teinture de ce
qui compofe la belle Dance. Ie n'en-
tends pas toutefois par ce dernier
mot de belle Dance, ce rampant
mol & pareffeux, que les corps foi-
bles & abbatus ont introduit dans
les Bals. Ie ne veux pas forcer ny
la mode ny le temps; ny mefme m'é-
tendre fur les belles manieres de la
Dance publique & domeftique, où
les deux fexes ont droit d'agir & de
paroiftre. Ie n'en diray qu'un feul
mot en paffant, Que la Dance qu'on
nomme la belle, qui confifte en fim-
ples demarches, à bien obferver le
pas,& à garder des temps reguliers
& juftes, eft toûjours plus maje-

ftueufe, & fent mieux fa perfonne
de qualité, & ce qui vaut encore
beaucoup mieux, la modeftie & la
vertu. Qu'il n'eft rien qui foit de
meilleure grace pour une belle Dame, & qu'elle doit infailliblement
reüffir dans les Courantes & dans les
Sarabandes. Le Branle veut plus de
gayeté, & femble eftre plus propre
pour les hômes qae pour les femmes.
Car s'il eft un peu gourmandé par
le premier, qui eft grave & ferieux,
il eft auffi-toft emporté par le fecond
où l'on ne fait que fauter, & par le
troifiéme, où l'on court toûjours ; &
la Gavote débauche bien-toft toute
la gravité qui peut fe trouver dans
les uns ou dans les autres, & enga-
gê l'un & l'autre Sexe à des agita-
tions & à des fecouffes tout autre-
ment vigoureufes. Pour ce qui eft
de toutes les nouvelles inventions,
ces Bourées, ces Menuets,ce ne font
quedes redites deguifées des joüets
des Maîtres à dancer, & d'honne-
ftes & fpirituelles philouteries pour
atraper les dupes qui ont dequoy les
payer.

III-103 Michel de PURE, *Idée des spectacles anciens et nouveaux*
(Paris: Michel Brunet, 1668), pp. 278-79. Discussion of dancers for ballet
de cour. [New York Public Library at Lincoln Center, Astor, Lenox, and
Tilden Foundations, Dance Collection, [*MGRK-Res.]]

including comedy (pp. 162-77), balls (pp. 177-83), and fireworks, tilting matches, and parades (pp. 183-208). A historical comparison between ancient (Book 1, p. 1-160) and modern (Book 2)—e.g. French court—entertainment emphasizes similarity of forms and of political justification in the two eras. Book 2 on modern forms contains the following chapters: I. *Des spectacles nouveaux;* II. *De la comédie;* III. *Du bal;* IV. *Des feux de joye;* V. *Des joustes;* VI. *Des courses de bague & de testes;* VII. *Des carozels;* VIII. *De la mascarade;* IX. *Des exercices ou revuëes;* X. *Des entrées faites aux rois & reines;* XI. *Du balet:* i. *Du nom & de l'essence du balet;* ii. *Du sujet;* iii. *Du titre;* iv. *Du corps;* v. *Des parties;* vi. *Des entrées;* vii. *Des incidents;* viii. *Du pas de balet;* ix. *Des figures;* x. *Des airs de balet;* xi. *Des récits;* xii. *Des instruments;* xiii. *Des danceux;* xiv. *Des habits;* xv. *Des masques;* xvi. *Des vers;* xvii. *Des machines;* xviii. *De la boutade;* xix. *Du lieu fixe & du mobile.*

In the lengthy chapter on ballet, de Pure insists upon unity of conception (pp. 215-23). The subject must be pleasing but seemly, the title relevant (pp. 223-27). No part should take precedence over another, each maintaining its independence, even though spontaneously and inevitably linked together. Sections devoted to dance steps (pp. 243-51, 278-85) urge attention to the quality of the performers, if corruption of the steps by inexpert amateurs is to be avoided. All aspects of the ballet come under scrutiny: the figures (pp. 251-58), music and text (pp. 258-77, 296-300), costumes, masks, and machines (pp. 285-96, 301-18).

In the section on dance music (pp. 258-65), de Pure makes the poet responsible for the quality of movement in the dance airs. He emphasizes the appropriateness of the tune for expressing the mood of the action or representation; this entails an appropriate key and mode and a melody suited to the steps required by the subject matter. The composer must walk a fine line between interpreting the dramatic action and serving musical beauty; when dealing with bizarre subjects, the musician should react conservatively rather than suggest poor musicianship in an effort to portray the bizarre. Rhythmic movement must be more deliberate in danced than in sung airs, the ornaments shorter and less elaborate for the sake of supporting the dancer's actions. The two sections of the binary dance air need not be equal in length, at the composer's discretion.

The section on instruments (pp. 271-77) comments on the suitability of various instruments for accompanying dancing. The theorbo and lute are described as suited only for accompanying singing, or for playing Allemandes and Sarabandes, etc., in which the majesty of the melody is greater than the energy of the dance; the superfluity of notes in this style tends to confuse the dancers, while the languishing harmony tends to subvert the action. The musette has associations of innocence and the pastoral appropriate to dancing, but has too coarse and thin a sound for the sophisticated style of the theater. The oboe, as played in France, merits praise for its expressiveness and wonderfully accurate execution of ornaments, but tends to be tiring to play and unreliable. Organ and clavier are not portable enough for divertissements. The harp is no longer used for dancing. The guitar is disparaged. Finally, the violin is lauded as the most appropriate accompaniment to dancing, especially in multi-voiced string ensembles. However, musicians must avoid fancy virtuoso playing and excessive ornamentation that confuses the dancers with too many fast notes and additional accents; an unornamented style is preferred, coordinated to the steps of the ballet.

104 QUATREMÈRE DE QUINCY, Antoine Chrysostôme (1755-1849)

Dissertation sur les opéras bouffons italiens.
*Paris: 1789; 38p.
In *Archives littéraires de l'Europe,* v. 16 (1807), pp. 1-39.
German transl. by F. August Weber in *Correspondence musicale de Spire* (1792), pp. 122, 149, 167, 197, 203, 209.

This appreciation of Italian comic opera stresses the divergent tastes of France and Italy. On the last two pages, the author discusses dancing as an example of the different way each regards the relation between dance or gesture and dramatic action: the Italians use dance as a type of panto-mime only, to further or elaborate upon the action, while the French are content to highlight the dance and temporarily abandon action. This is because the Italians are not good dancers, aside from pantomime, while the French are virtuosos who know how to please with their art alone. The Italians act more than they dance; the French dance more than they act, with the dances independent of the dramatic interest. "On danse à Paris pour danser, comme en Italie l'on chante pour chanter."

105 QUINAULT, Phillippe (1635-1688)

Le théâtre de Quinault, contenant ses tragédies, comédies et op-éra.
In *Oeuvres de M. Quinault.* Paris: G. de Luyne, 1659.
Amsterdam: A. Wolfgang, 1663; 2 v.
Amsterdam: A. Schelte, 1665, 1677.

Amsterdam: Pierre de Coup, 1715; 2 v.

2nd ed., with biography and commentary, Paris: P. Ribou, 1715; 5 v.

Paris: Compagnie des librairies, 1739; 5 v.

*Paris: Les libraires associés, 1778; 465p., 502p., 512p., 413p., 450p.

Facs. reprint, Genève: Slatkine, 1970.

Paris: Petite bibliothèque des théâtres, 1783; 1 v., as *Chef-d'oeuvres de . . .*

Paris: P. Didot l'ainé, F. Didot, 1811; 2 v., as *Oeuvres choisies.*

Paris: 1824; 2 v., with biography by G. A. Crapelet, as *Oeuvres choisies.*

Paris: Laplace, Sanchez, 1882; with biography by V. Fournel and illustrations by H. Allouard, as *Théâtre choisi.*

The 1715 Paris edition of Quinault's works has a particularly good essay (pp. 3-62) on the collaboration between Quinault, poet of the *ballet de cour* from 1672 until his death, and composer J. B. Lully. Frequent reprints throughout more than a century witness the attraction these librettos had for composers long after the *ballet de cour* had developed into French operatic genres. The texts here included provide lists of characters, but no names of performers or performing instructions.

106 RALPH, James [pseud. A. PRIMCOCK] (?1705-1762)

The touchstone: or historical, critical, philosophical & theological essays on the reigning diversions of the town. Design'd for the improvement of all authors, spectators, and actors of operas, plays and mascarades. In which everything antique, or modern, relating to music, poetry, dancing, pantomimes, chorusses, cat-calls, audiences, judges, criticks, balls, ridottos, assemblies, new oratory, circus, bear-garden, gladiators, prize-fighters, Italian strolers, montebank stages, cock-pits, puppet-shews, fairs and publick auctions is occasionally handled. By a person of some taste and some quality, with a preface, giving an account of the author and the work.

*London: Booksellers, 1728; xxvii+237p.

*Facs. reprint, New York: Garland Press, 1973; 7+ xxviii+237p.

2nd ed., London: for J. Crokatt, 1729.

Reissued as *The taste of the town: or, a guide to all publick diversions. Viz. I. Of musick, operas and plays. Their origines, progress, and improvement, and the stage-entertainment fully vindicated from the exceptions of Old Pryn, the Reverend Mr. Collier, Mr. Bedford and Mr. Law. II. Of poetry, sacred and profane. A project for introducing scripture-stories upon our stage, and acting them on Sundays and Holy-days after divine service, as is customary in most polite parts of Europe. III. Of dancing, religious and dramatical. Reflections on this exercise, public and private, with the learned Bishop Potter's sentiment thereon. IV. Of the mimes, pantomimes and choruses of the antients; and of the imitation of them in our modern entertainments after plays. V. Of audiences, at our theatrical representations, their due behaviour, and of cat-calls and other indecent practices, concluding with remarks on our pretenders to criticism. VI. Of masquerades; ecclesiastical, political, civil and military: their antiquary, use and abuse. Also of ridottos, assemblies and Henley's oratory. VII. Of the athletic sports of the antients. Their circus compared with our bear-garden, and their gladiators with our prize-fighters. Of cock-fighting, puppet shows, montebanks and auctions.*
*London: Booksellers of London and Westminster, 1731; xxviii+237p.

In a wholly irreverant manner, "Primcock" devotes his third essay in this book to dancing (pp. 86-114). He offers historical background found in other legitimate histories, all the way back to Bacchus (who introduced grapes into Greece, "for which I thank him"). He then turns to pantomimes (they were so corrupt they corrupted Rome), meaning-dances, voice accompanied with emphatic motions, ancient sacred and profane dance, non-valid and conflicting claims for dance, dances that uplift, dance description, dance and pedagogical method, and dancing as a universal language. The work is not only an antidote to the overly serious treatment of dance by other writers; the author's keen eye for detail often clarifies obscurities met in serious descriptions by other writers.

107 RÉMOND DE SAINT-MARD, Toussaint de (ca. 1682-1757)
Réflexions sur l'opéra.
*Den Haag: Jean Neaulme, 1741; x+104p.
  Facs. reprint, Genève: Slatkine, 1970.
  Facs. reprint, Genève: Minkoff, 1972.
As v. 2 in *Les oeuvres melées de Mr. Rémond de Saint-Mard.*
Den Haag: J. Neaulme, 1742.
As v. 5 in *Oeuvres.* Amsterdam: P. Mortier, 1749-50.
Amsterdam: Changuion; Paris: P. de Lormel, 1777; 58p.
German transl. in J. W. Hertel, *Sammlung musikalischer Schriften, grosstentheils aus den Werken der Italiäner und Franzosen übersetzt und mit Anmerkungen versehen.* Leipzig: Johann Gottlob Immanuel Breitkopf, 1757-58; 254p.

Rémond's criticism is founded upon the idea of art imitating natural passions. If opera is to be compelling, true, and agreeable, then poetry, music, and dance must combine in the service of the passions. Too much emphasis on technique at the expense of expressiveness spoils the opera. Dance is especially deplorable when it gives pleasure only to the eye, rather than appealing to all the sensibilities. Dancers who move mechanically bore the audience and retard the progress of the opera. The spectators come to see the passions vividly depicted, and they deserve to be moved. Dance should thus be an integral part of a unified spectacle; dance not intended to be expressive has no place in opera. During the course of this general critique of lyric tragedy and ballet, in which he criticizes the deteriorating quality of instrumental music, the author ponders the inexplicable mechanical connection between beautiful melodies and the affections of our hearts, affirming the power of characteristic pieces (such as those of Lully and Campra) to stir the affections. In so doing, he describes vividly the specific passions aroused by the Gavotte, Gigue, Passacaille, Chaconne, Courante, and Sarabande.

108 RICCOBONI, François (1707-1772)
L'art du théâtre. Lettre de M. Riccoboni fils a M*** au sujet du théâtre.
*Paris: C. F. Simon, Giffart fils, 1750; 104+32p.
  Facs. reprint, Genève: Slatkine, 1971; 104+33p.

The scion of a dynasty of Italian actors, friend and long time associate of Marie Sallé, Riccoboni was an author, actor, choreographer, and gifted dancer in the Italian tradition. His career was associated principally with the Théâtre Italien in Paris, with only occasional forays abroad. With Sallé, he contributed to the development of action ballet in the 1720s, synthesizing Lambranzi elements with the *danse d'école* and Anglo-Italian pantomime techniques. Since both dancers were firmly trained in these techniques, they lead the development of new forms during the 1730s and 1740s. Specifically, they carried the comic episodes depicted by Lambranzi (q.v.) into the developed *ballet d'action* with their individual versions of *Pygmalion,* presented within 5 months of each other, Sallé's in London, Riccoboni's in Paris. Drawing upon his many years of experience as a choreographer and dancer, as well as actor, Riccoboni used dance terminology to describe how the body should be expressive. The book was widely used by ballet pantomimists in their training for expressive dancing. *Le geste, L'expression, La force, La fureur, L'entousiasme, La noblesse, La majesté, Le jeu muet, Le jeu de théâtre* are a few of the sub-headings in this little manual. (For another guide to attaining bodily expressiveness in portraying the passions, see C. Gildon's *Life of Mr. Thomas Betterton.*) For an account of the relationship between Marie Sallé and François Riccoboni and the latter's influence on the choreographers De Hess and Hilverding, see Marion Hannah Winter, *Pre-romantic ballet* (London: Pitman, 1974), pp. 83-99 and infra.

109 ROCHEMONT, de

Réflexions d'un patriote sur l'opéra françois, et sur l'opéra italien, qui présentent le parallèle du goût des deux nations dans les beaux-arts.
*Lausanne: 1754; xii+137p.
> Facs. reprint, Genève: Minkoff, 1973 *(La querelle des bouffons,* v. 3, pp. 2025-2173).

In this comparison of French and Italian opera, a brief section on dance (pp. 66-68) compares the foreign (e.g. Italian) dancer, whose circus-like elevation makes him half dancer and half acrobat, to the French ballet celebrity Louis Dupré, whose subtle ease is peerless. The author then distinguishes between the noble style in dance, which expresses the elevated sentiments of a grand spirit, and the comic or grotesque styles, which express naive joy and related sentiments of the ordinary mortal.

110 ROST, Johann Leonhard [pseud. MELETAON] (1688-1727)

Von der Nutzbarkeit des Tantzens. Wie viel selbiges zu einer galanten und wohlanständigen Conduite bey einem jungen Menschen und Frauenzimmer beytrage; auch wie man dadurch sowol die Kinder als erwachsene Leute von beederley Geschlechte, zur Höflichkeit, Artigkeit und Freymüthigkeit anweisen solle, verfasset von Meletaon.

Frankfurt, Leipzig: Joh. Albrecht, 1713; 244p.

Frankfurt, Leipzig: Joh. Albrecht, 1713; 270p.

F. Derra de Moroda, in "Dancing for Health in the 18th Century," *The dancing times* (January 1931), pp. 453-54, describes this book as a defense of dance against those who do not understand the noble art. It stresses proper performance, lists dances (Courante, Menuets, Passepieds), and lays out a recommended course of study. Detailed rules for ballroom etiquette and healthful living make this source a confirmation of the extensive spread of French court dance into Germany.

111 SULZER, Johann Georg (1720-1779)

Allgemeine Theorie der schönen Künste, in einzeln, nach alphabetischer Ordnung der Kunstwörter auf einander folgenden Artikeln abgehandelt. 2 v.

Leipzig: M. G. Weidmanns Erben und Reich; Berlin: George Ludwig Winter, 1771 (v. 1), 1774 (v. 2).

Leipzig: M. G. Weidmanns Erben und Reich, 1773-1775; 764p., 948p.

Biel: Heilmann, 1777; xvi+764p., 948p.

2nd ed., Leipzig: M. G. Weidmanns Erben und Reich, 1778-1779; 4 v., xx+390p., 391p., 480p., 470p.

Leipzig: M. G. Weidmanns Erben und Reich, 1786-1787; 4 v., xx+506p., 589p., 638p., 678p. *Neue vermehrte Auflage.*

Leipzig: Weidmann, 1792-1794; 4 v., xxiv+755p., 707p., 760p., 814p. *Neue vermehrte zweyte Auflage.*

*Facs. reprint, Hildesheim: Georg Olms, 1967 (v. 2, E-J, 707p.; v. 3, K-Q, [vi]+760p.; v. 4, R-Z, 814p.; "Register," ii+198p.), 1970 (v. 1, A-D, xix+xxiv+755p.).

Karlsruhe: Christian Gottlieb Schmieder, 1796-1797; 4 v., xxiv+819p., 763p., 829p., 896p. *Neue vermehrte dritte Auflage.*

*Frankfurt und Leipzig: 1798; 4 v., xxiv+819p., 763p., 829p., 896p. *Neue vermehrte dritte Auflage.*

This encyclopaedia of the fine arts promulgates ideas current a generation earlier, deriving from authors of the French and German Enlightenment such as Du Bos, Batteux, Schlegel, and Baumgarten. The articles on musical topics as far as "Modulation" (but including "System") were written jointly by Sulzer and J. P. Kirnberger; those from "Preludiren" up to the letter S were written by Kirnberger and his pupil J. A. P. Schulz; the remainder were written by Schulz alone.

Articles appear for the following dance types (page references are to the Olms facsimile reprint): Allemande (v. 1, pp. 112-23), Bourrée (p. 429), Ciaconne/Chaconne (p. 475), Courante (p. 589), Englische Tänze/Contretänze/Angloise (v. 2, p. 66), Folie d'Espagne (p. 249), Forlane (p. 250), Gavotte (p. 309), Gigue, Harlekin (pp. 469-70), Loure (v. 3, pp. 292-93), Marsch, Menuet (pp. 388-89), Musette (p. 421), Passacaille (p. 650), Passepied (p. 655), Pastoral (p. 660), Polonoise (p. 716), Rigaudon (v. 4, p. 106), Rondeau, and Sarabande (p. 128). There is also a general article Tanzstück (v. 4, pp. 511-14) emphasizing the role of dance music in expressing national character. These articles report on the character, rhythmic and metric structure, and historical origin of the dance tunes, as well as the character and function of the dances. "Allemande" distinguishes between instrumental, social dance, and folk dance types. "Loure" describes the character of the dancing, criticizing gestures customarily seen in staged loures. "Menuet" provides the most information on musical structure, also discussing the character and social currency of the minuet as a dance.

Articles devoted to the art of dancing include Ballet (v. 1, pp. 289-96, on Noverre, imitation, aesthetic questions, history), Choreographie (pp. 472-73, notation), Gesellschaftstänze (v. 2, pp. 402-3), Tanz (v. 4, pp. 503-7), Tanzkunst (pp. 507-11), Figur, Figuranten (dancers), Pantomime (v. 3, pp. 647-49), Schritt (steps, v. 4, pp. 345-46). In addition, the work deals with topics bearing upon aesthetic ideals (Charakter, Edel, Empfindung, Erfindung, Erhaben, Genie, Heroisch, Kenner, Klarheit, Kunst, Leidenschaften, Liebe, Nachahmung, Natur/natürlich, Reitz, Schön/Schönheit, Style, Vollkommenheit, etc.), upon artistic structure (Bindung, Einheit, Einschnitt, Ende, Entwicklung, Form, Ganz, Mannigfaltigkeit, Ordnung, Regelmässig, Symmetrie, Veränderungen/Variationen, Verbindung, Verzierung, etc.), and upon the stage (Opera, Kleidung, Operetten/comische Opern, Comödie, Stellung, etc.). A lengthy bibliography accompanies the article on Tanzkunst. In the facsimile reprint of the 1792-94 edition, an introduc-

313

tion and bibliography by Giorgio Tonelli appears in v. 1; additions and
corrections appear in v. 4, pp. 792-814. (For a bibliographic supplement
to Sulzer's encyclopaedia, see Blankenburg's *Litterarische Zusätze.*)

112 TITON DU TILLET, Évrard (1677-1762)
*Description du Parnasse françois, exécuté en bronze, suivie
d'une liste alphabétique des poëtes et des musiciens rassemblés
sur ce monument.*
Paris: Jean Baptiste Coignard fils (veuve Ribou; P. Prault; veuve
Pissot), 1727; xxviii+366p.
*Paris: Jean Baptiste Coignard fils, 1732; 660p. Entitled *Le
Parnasse françois, dedié au roi.*
*Suite du Parnasse françois, jusqu'en 1743. Et de quelques au-
tres pièces qui ont rapport à ce monument. Remarques sur la
poësie et la musique, et sur l'excellence de ces deux beaux arts.
Avec des observations particulières sur la poësie et la musique
françoise et sur nos spectacles.* [Paris: Coignard fils, 1743];
832+xciiip.
> Facs. reprint of *Le Parnasse . . .* [1732] and *Suite du
> Parnasse . . .* , Genève: Slatkine, 1971. From a copy with an-
> notations by the author.

*Second supplément du Parnasse françois, ou suite de l'ordre
chronologique des poètes et des musiciens que la mort a enlevés
depuis le commencement de l'année 1743 jusqu'en cette année
1755.* [Paris: Jean Baptiste Coignard fils, 1755]; 86p.
Description du Parnasse françois . . . 3e supplément. Paris:
1760; 48+122p.
> Facs. reprint of *Second supplément* and *3e supplément,*
> Genève: Minkoff, 1984.

The author, a disciple of Boileau and devoté of French arts and letters,
describes an allegorical bronze monument (never executed) to the glory
of Louis XIV and the great poets and musicians of France. Under
Apollo (Louis XIV) and the three graces stand the nine muses, among
them Lully. Among portraits of the 25 next most important poets and
musicians are those of Delalande, Marais, De la Guerre, Campra, and
Destouches. The roughly 160 names on scrolls include those of about 40
composers of the 17th and 18th c. The ensuing work is a catalogue of
writers and musicians so honored, providing for each a brief biography

and appreciation, some with personal anecdotes or a list of works. In addition there is brief acknowledgement (in a special section, pp. 789-816) of famous actors and actresses from the Comédie and the Opéra, including dancers. Very briefly described (a sentence or two) are dancers Françoise Prévost, La Fontaine, Marie Thèrèse Subligny, Marie Camargo, and Marie Sallé (pp. 800-16). Merely mentioned are Louis Pécourt, Jean Ballon, and Louis DuPré. A hypothetical "Orchestre du Parnasse" is described, listing musicians (p. 674). The biographical entries are numbered; those for musicians include Lully (139, pp. 393-401), Molière (102, pp. 308-20: concerns Lully), Cambert (135), Du Mont (136), Lambert (137), Chambonnière, the Couperins, Boivin, Le Bègue and other keyboard composers (140), the Gaultiers (141), Quinault (142, pp. 406-11; with information on Lully), Bensérade, M. A. Charpentier (177), F. Charpentier (178), Ménéstrier (232, pp. 601-3), Boesset (233), Delalande (237), Theobalde (240), Marais (242), Lalouette (243), De la Guerre (249), Brossard (255, pp. 652-53), and Marchand (259). The first supplement adds Moreau (260), F. Couperin (261), Senallié (266), Bernier (267), Montéclair (272), Mouret (274), Dandrieu (276), Rousseau (280, pp. 732-52), Desmarets (282). The second supplement adds Gervais (297), Campra (298), Destouches (313), Clairambault (314), Bourgeois (316), La Barre, Rebel, Bertin, La Coste (331). For a detailed study of this monumental work, see Judith Colton, *The Parnasse françois* (New Haven: Yale University Press, 1979).

113 TRICHTER, Valentin

Curiöses Reit-Jagd-Fecht-Tantz-oder Ritter-Exercitien-Lexicon, worinne der galanten ritterlichen Uibungen Vortreflichkeit, Nutzen und Nothwendigkeit, nebst allen in denselben vorkommenden Kunst-Wörtern hinlänglich erkläret, insonderheit aber der Pferde Arten, Eigenschaften, Gestalt, Mängel und Gebrechen, nebst deren wohlbewährten Heil-Mitteln, deren Fortpflanzung, Erziegung, und künstliche Abrichtung, auch alles, was zur Reuterey gehöret; ferner die hohe und niedere Jagd-Wissenschaft, der völlige Jagd-Zeug, die Eigenschaften kleiner und grosser Hunde, wie auch verschiedener Thiere und Vögel; ingleichen das Forst-Wesen; sodann das wahre Fundament der Fecht-Kunst mit dem Floret sowol als Degen; das Voltigiren auf dem Pferde; ingleichen die niedrigen Cammer- und hohen theatralischen Täntze, und die mit der Tantz-Kunst unzertrennlich verbundene musikalische Wissenschaft; das Ball- und Ballonen-Schlagen; die alten sowol als noch gebräuchlichen Ritterlichen Ernst- und Lust-spiele; welchen noch beygefüget ist die Wappen-Kunst, als eine dem Adel eigenthümliche und unentbehrliche Wissenschaft, alles in alphabetischer Ordnung und dergestalt eingerichtet, dass junge Herren von Adel angewiesen werden, wie sie durch eine gefällig-machende Aufführung sich in Stand setzen können, dereinst vollkommene Hof-Leute, gute Soldaten und geschickte Hauswirthe abzugeben, verfasset von Valentino Trichtern, Königl. Gross-Britannischem Stallmeister der G. A. Universität Göttingen.

*Leipzig: Johann Friedrich Gleditsch, 1742; 2366 cols.

This dictionary of chivalric exercise—directed to those members of the middle class privileged to serve the nobility in military or civil capacity—offers detailed treatment of terms and topics pertaining to a variety of noble sports and active pastimes, including riding, hunting, fencing, dancing, music, games, and heraldry. Articles on the dance types comment on character and affect, musical form, rhythmic characteristics, dance steps, and comparison with other dances, including the Allemande (distinguishing the dance from the musical composition), Angloise, Bourrée, Canarien, Chaconne, Courante, Entrée, Forlana, Gaillarde/Gagliarda, Gavotte, Gigue, Loure, Marsch, Passecaille, Passepied, Polonoise, Rigaudon, Rondeau, Menuet, Sarabande. Entries appear for various ornaments (Accent, Coulé, Lourer, Mordant, Tremolo, etc.) and musical instruments (Basse-Taille, Basse Continuë, Basse, Basson, Castagnettes [with reference to Taubert], Cembalo, Chalumeau, Chitarra, Claquebois, Clarino, Clarinette, Cornemuse, Cromorne, Fagot, Flauto traverso, Flute, Geigen, Harfe, Laute, Musette, Orgel, Posaune, Serpent, Tambour, Theorbo, Trompette), plus miscellaneous musical topics (Cammer-Ton, Capellmeister, Componist, Deutlichkeit einer Melodie, Fanfare, Musick, Opera, Serenade). Dance related entries include Bal, Ballet, Cadence, de Caprice tantzen, Chorégraphie, Danse, Figuren, Porte les bras, Prosaisches Tantzen, Tantzen, Tantz-Kunst (etiquette), Tanzmeister, and various steps (Balanciren, Caprioles, Chassé, Contretems, Coupé, Demi-coupé, Fleuret, Pas, etc.). Of additional interest are articles on sport and entertainment in various places (Copenhagen, Cassel, Cremona, Dessau, Dresden, Frankreich, Fulda, Gross-Britanien, Hanau, Leipzig, Lobkowitz [family], Mantua, Modena, München, Münster, Oesterreich, Preussen, Salzburg) and on rhetorical figures (e.g. Evolutio, Exclamatio).

114 VICTOR, Benjamin (d. 1778)

The history of the theatres of London and Dublin, from the year 1730 to the present time. To which is added, an annual register of all the plays, etc. performed at the Theatres-Royal in London, from the year 1721, with occasional notes and anecdotes. 2 v.
*London: T. Davies, R. Griffiths, T. Becket, P. A. De Hondt, G. Woodfall, J. Coote, G. Kearsly, 1761; vii+222p., 218p.
The history of the theatres of London, from the year 1760 to the present time, being a continuation of the annual register of all the new tragedies, comedies, farces, pantomimes, etc. that have been performed within that period, with occasional notes and anecdotes. London: T. Becket, 1771; xi+232p.
Facs. reprint of all 3 v., New York: Benjamin Blom, 1969.

Among histories of English theater, this work falls between Colley Cibber's *Apology for his life* (1740, q.v.) and Walley Oulton's *History of the theatres of London* (1796, q.v.). A behind-the-scenes account of theater in London and Dublin, written by someone who was deeply involved in theatrical life, the work contains anecdotes about audience-actor relationships, actor-gentleman status, licensing and patents, financial precariousness, ticket prices and performance wages, sabotage (the audience effectively cancelled a performance of a French company by drowning out the sound of the orchestra with their own instrument sounds and by rolling peas on the stage to prevent the dancers from appearing). The narrative in v. 2 emphasizes the work of specific actors (pp. 1-90), after which begins the register. The listing reveals a plethora of pantomime offerings in England. Of special interest is the account of the ill-fated attempt to stage Noverre's *The Chinese festival* in London at a time when England and France were at war (pp. 131-36). An appendix consists of letters about theatrical matters.

115 VOSSIUS, Isaac (1618-1689)

De poematum cantu et viribus rythmi.
*Oxford: E. theatro sheldoniano, 1673; 136p.
*German transl. as *Vossius vom singen der Gedichte, und von der Kraft des Rhythmus,* in *Sammlung vermischter Schriften zur Beförderung der schönen Wissenschaften und der freyen Künste.* Berlin: Friedrich Nicolai, 1759; pp. 1-84, 216-314.
German transl. (incomplete) in J. N. Forkel, *Musikalisch-kritische Bibliothek,* v. 3. Gotha: 1779.

317

In "The *ballet d'action* before Noverre," *Dance Index,* v. 6 no. 3 (March 1947), pp. 52-72, Artur Michel writes, "The first to gauge the dance of his day expressly in relation to the dance of antiquity was the great Netherlands philologist, Isaac Vossius (1618-1689). His script . . . did not, it is true, directly affect the dance. But due to the fame of its author, it was known to all later scholars and, directly and indirectly, it reached out far beyond academic circles. A German translation appeared in 1759, at the height of the battle for and against the *ballet d'action.* " Vossius' writings dealt with music in terms of poetic meter and rhythm, which he considered to be the source of expression of feelings in music, as well as in poetry. His ideas influenced J. S. Bach and especially J. Mattheson, who in his *Der vollkommene Kapellmeister* (q.v.) applied principles of poetic meter to the analysis of dance music.

116 WEAVER, John (1673-1760)

The history of the mimes and pantomimes, with an historical account of several performers in dancing, living in the time of the Roman emperors. To which will be added a list of the modern entertainments that have been exhibited on the English stage, either in imitation of the ancient pantomimes, or after the manner of the modern Italians; when and where first performed and by whom composed.

*London: Roberts, 1728; 56p.

   Facs. reprint in Richard Ralph, *The life and works of John Weaver* (New York: Dance Horizons, 1985), pp. 675-732.

In this history, Weaver most clearly states his definition of pantomime as an entertainment of dancing in which all is performed by gestures and the action of the head, fingers, legs, and feet—without the use of words. His own works strove toward this ideal, works with both tragic and comic characterization conveyed in action alone. He appends a list of modern "entertainments," beginning with his own *The tavern bilkers* (1702) and ending with *The rape of Proserpine* (1726).

CHRONOLOGICAL
SHORT-TITLE LIST

1690	FURETIÈRE: Dictionnaire
1694	CORNEILLE: Dictionnaire
1694	GHERARDI: Le théâtre italien
1694	L'AFFILARD: Principes . . . musique
1695	CONSTANTINI: Vie de Scaramouche
1696	LOULIÉ: Éléments . . . de musique
1696	PERRAULT: Les hommes illustres
1697	MASSON: Nouveau traité . . . composition
1698	MUFFAT: Suavioris harmoniae
1699	HELY: The compleat violist
1700	FEUILLET: Chorégraphie
1700	FEUILLET: Le passepied
1700	FREILLON-PONCEIN: Véritable
1701	BROSSARD: Dictionnaire
1702	ANONYMOUS: Comparison
1702	FEUILLET: P^{er} recueil
1702	RAGUENET: Paralèle
1702	SAINT-LAMBERT: Principes
1703	ANONYMOUS: Recueil . . . opéras
1704	FEUILLET: Recueil de dances
1704	LE CERF: Comparaison
1705	MASSON: Divers traitez
1706	FEUILLET: Recueil de contredances
1706	NIEDT: Handleitung zur Variation
1707	HOTTETERRE: Principes de la flûte
1707	PASCH: Beschreibung
1707	SAINT-LAMBERT: Nouveau traité
1709	BEHR: Wohlgegründete
1709	FEUILLET: IX Recueil de danses
1709	MONTÉCLAIR: Nouvelle méthode
1710	BURETTE: Treize mémoires
1710	GILDON: Life of Mr. T. Betterton
1711	BONIN: Die neueste Art . . . Tantzkunst
1711	HEINICHEN: Neu-erfundene . . . Anweisung
1711	PEMBERTON: An essay . . . dancing
ca.1712	GAUDRAU: Novueau recueil de danses
1712	LEBRUN: Théâtre lyrique
1712	WEAVER: An essay . . . dancing
1713	BEHR: L'art de bien danser
1713	CALLIACHI: De ludis scenicis
1713	DUPONT: Principes de musique
1713	MATTHESON: Neu-eröffnete Orchestre

1713	PEMBERTON: The Pastorall
1713	ROST: Von der Nutzbarkeit
1715	BONNET: Histoire de la musique
1715	CROUSAZ: Traité du beau
1716	COUPERIN: L'art de toucher
1716	LAMBRANZI: Neue . . . Tantz-Schule
1717	BOINDIN: Discours sur la forme
1717	TAUBERT: Rechtschaffener Tanzmeister
1717	WEAVER: Loves of Mars & Venus
1718	DUPONT: Principes de violon
1718	WEAVER: Orpheus & Eurydice
1719	BOINDIN: Lettres historiques
1719	DU BOS: Réflexions critiques
1719	HOTTETERRE: L'art de préluder
1720	TOMLINSON: Six dances
1721	ANONYMOUS: Cas de conscience
1721	LE SAGE: Théâtre de la foire
1721	WEAVER: Anatomical . . . lectures
1722	ESSEX: Young ladies conduct
1722	RAMEAU, J.: Traité de l'harmonie
1723	BONNET: Histoire générale
1724	THURMOND: Harlequin Dr. Faustus
1725	RAMEAU, P.: Abbrégé
1725	RAMEAU, P.: Maître à danser
1725	SOL: Méthode . . . de bien dancer
1727	ANONYMOUS: Mechanical essay
1727	BARON: Historisch-theoretisch
1727	LANG: Dissertatio de actione
1727	TITON DU TILLET: Description
1728	DUFORT: Trattato del ballo
1728	RALPH: The touchstone
1728	WEAVER: History of the mimes
1729	BROWN: Medicina musica
1729	JENYNS: Art of dancing
ca.1730	ANONYMOUS: Rules
1730	PRELLEUR: Modern musick-master
1730	THEOBALD: Perseus
1732	KELLNER: Treulicher Unterricht
1732	RAMEAU, J.: Dissertation
1732	WALTHER: Musicalisches Lexicon
1733	GERVAIS: Méthode . . . accompagnement
1733	MAUPOINT: Bibliothèque

1733	VAGUÉ: L'art d'apprendre la musique
1733	VILLENEUVE: Nouvelle méthode
1733	WEAVER: Judgment of Paris
1734	LEBRUN: Method . . . passions
1734	PARFAICT, F.: Histoire général
ca.1735	MONTÉCLAIR: Petite méthode . . . musique
1735	BEAUCHAMPS: Recherches
1735	TOMLINSON: Art of dancing
1736	LA CHAPELLE: Vrais principes
1736	MONTÉCLAIR: Principes de musique
1737	ANONYMOUS: Kurzgefasstes
1737	DAVID: Méthode nouvelle
1737	HOTTETERRE: Méthode . . . musette
1737	NIVELON: Rudiments of . . . behaviour
1738	CORRETTE: L'école d'Orphée
1739	MATTHESON: Vollkommene Capellmeister
ca.1740	CORRETTE: Méthode . . . flûte
1740	CIBBER: An apology
1740	GRASSINEAU: Musical dictionary
1740	LE BLANC: Défense . . . viole
1741	ANDRÉ: Essai sur le beau
1741	CORRETTE: Méthode . . . violoncelle
1741	DUPUIT: Principes . . . vièle
1741	RÉMOND DE ST.-MARD: Réflexions
1742	TRICHTER: Curiöses . . . Lexicon
1742	VION: La musique pratique
1743	PARFAICT, F.: Mémoires
1745	FERRIOL Y BOXERAUS: Reglas
1745	PARFAICT, C.: Dictionnaire
1746	BATTEUX: Les beaux-arts
1746	BOLLIOUD DE MERMET: Corruption
1746	BORIN: L'art de la danse
1747	MARQUET: Nouvelle méthode
ca.1750	CROME: Fiddle new model'd
ca.1750	LEPITRE: L'art de la danse
ca.1750	METOYEN: Démonstration
1750	MARPURG: Critischer Musicus
1750	RICCOBONI: L'art du théâtre
1751	BOULENGER: Recherches
1751	DIDEROT: Encyclopédie
1751	LAMBERT: Histoire littéraire
1751	LANGE: Anfangsgründe zur Tanzkunst

1752	D'ALEMBERT: Élémens de musique
1752	D'AQUIN DE CHÂTEAU-LYON: Lettres
1752	GRIMM: Lettre de M. Grimm
1752	KRAUSE: Von der musikalischen Poesie
1752	LACOMBE: Dictionnaire portatif
1752	LECOINTE: Apologie de la danse
1752	QUANTZ: Versuch . . . Flöte
1753	BACH, C. P. E.: Versuch . . . Clavier, I
1753	CORRETTE: Maître de clavecin
1753	DUREY DE NOINVILLE: Histoire
1753	HOGARTH: Analysis of beauty
1753	PARFAICT, F.: Histoire . . . italien
1754	BÉTHIZY: Exposition de la théorie
1754	BLAINVILLE: L'esprit de l'art
1754	CAHUSAC: La danse ancienne
1754	CASTEL: Lettres d'un académicien
1754	LÉRIS: Dictionnaire portatif
1754	LUSTIG: Muzykaale spraakkonst
1754	MARPURG: Historisch-kritische Beyträge
1754	ROCHEMONT: Réflexions d'un patriote
1755	ALGAROTTI: Saggio sopra l'opera
1755	BÉRARD: L'art du chant
1755	BORDET: Méthode raisonnée
1755	CHEVRIER: Observations
1756	BLANCHET: L'art . . . du chant
1756	PAULI: Élémens de la danse
1757	DENIS, C.: Nouvelle méthode
1757	DIDEROT: Le fils naturel
1757	KIRNBERGER: Der allezeit fertige
1758	ANONYMOUS: Ludus melothedicus
1758	ANONYMOUS: Theatrical review
1758	CORRETTE: Parfait maître à chanter
1758	LACOMBE: Spectacle des beaux-arts
1758	MINGUET E YROL: Arte de danzar
1759	ANONYMOUS: État actuel de la musique
1759	CHOQUEL: La musique rendue sensible
1759	MAHAUT: Nieuwe manier . . . dwarsfluit
ca.1760	MOREL DE LESCER: Science de la musique
1760	CARSILLIER: Mémoire
1760	LA VALLIERE: Ballets, opéras
1760	MEREAU: Réflexions sur le maintien
1760	NOVERRE: Lettres sur la danse

1760	RAMEAU, J.: Code de musique pratique
ca.1761	MERCHI: Guide des écoliers de guitarre
1761	BOUIN: La vielleuse habile
1761	L'ABBÉ LE FILS: Principes du violon
1761	LUSSE: L'art de la flûte
1761	VICTOR: History of the theatres
1762	BACH, C. P. E.: Versuch . . . Clavier, II
1762	CHEVRIER: Almanach des gens d'esprit
1762	GALLINI: Treatise . . . dancing
1762	LANGE: Tôton harmonique
1762	MALPIED: Élémens de chorégraphie
1762	MARPURG: Clavierstücke
1763	BRIJON: Réflexions sur la musique
1763	HOEGI: Tabular system
1763	MEYER: Essai . . . harpe
1763	URIOT: Description des fêtes
1764	CAREL: Réponse . . . à . . . Deshayes
1764	DUVAL: Principes de la musique
1764	ROESER: Essai . . . clarinette
1765	ANGIOLINI: Dissertation
1765	BRICAIRE DE LA DIXMERIE: Lettres
1765	CHASTELLUX: Essai sur l'union
1765	GREGORY: Comparative view
1765	MAGNY: Principes de chorégraphie
1766	DORAT: Déclamation théâtrale
1766	HECK: Art of fingering
1766	HILLER: Wöchentliche Nachrichten
1766	LACASSAGNE: Traité . . . chant
1767	BIELFELD: Érudition complète
1767	BLAINVILLE: Histoire . . . musique
1767	BONÉM: Tratado . . . dança
1767	CHAVANNE: Principes du menuet
1767	MACE: Musick's monument
1768	DENIS, P.: Méthode . . . mandoline
1768	LA VALLIERE: Bibliothèque
1768	LEONE: Méthode . . . mandoline
1768	NOUGARET: De l'art du théâtre
1768	ROUSSEAU, J. J.: Dictionnaire
1769	BRICAIRE DE LA DIXMERIE: 2 âges
1769	DARD: Nouveaux principes
1769	DESBOULMIERS: Histoire anecdotique
1769	DESBOULMIERS: Histoire du théâtre

1769	GAUTHIER: Traité contre les danses
1769	GUILLAUME: Caractères de la danse
1769	LÉCUYER: Principes . . . du chant
ca.1770	FOUCHETTI: Méthode . . . mandoline
ca.1770	MALPIED: Traité . . . danse
1770	BAILLEUX: Méthode . . . vocale
1770	BORDIER: Traité de composition
1770	GALLINI: Critical observations
1770	HOYLE: Dictionarium musica
1771	BURNEY: Present state . . . France
1771	CLÉMENT: Principes de corégraphie
1771	LAUS DE BOISSY: Lettre . . . danse
1771	SULZER: Allgemeine theorie
1772	CUPIS: Méthode . . . violoncelle
1772	FELDTENSTEIN: Erweiterung
1772	FRANCOEUR: Diapason général
1772	LA JONCHÈRE: Théâtre lyrique
1772	MONNET: Supplément
1772	RAPARLIER: Principes de musique
1772	TANS'UR: Elements of musick
ca.1773	ANONYMOUS: Instruction . . . tambours
1773	ANGIOLINI: Lettere . . . a M. Noverre
1773	BURNEY: Present state . . . Germany
1773	TROUFLAUT: Lettre sur les clavecins
ca.1774	TARADE: Traité du violon
1774	BESCHE: Abrégé historique
1774	NOVERRE: Due lettere
1775	CLÉMENT: Anecdotes dramatiques
1775	ENGRAMELLE: La tonotechnie
1776	AZAIS: Méthode de musique
1776	BEATTIE: Essays
1776	BONAFONS: Dictionnaire
1776	BURNEY: General history of music
1776	DECROIX: L'ami des arts
1776	DU ROULLET: Lettre sur les drames
1776	HAWKINS: General history . . . music
1777	BACHAUMONT: Mémoires secrets
1777	DES ESSARTS: Les trois théâtres
1777	GOUDAR: Oeuvres mêlées
1777	MERCHI: Traité des agrémens
1777	MILANDRE: Méthode . . . viole d'amour
1778	BORSA: Saggio filosofico

1778	VOGLER: Betrachtungen
1779	CHABANON: Observations
1779	DU COUDRAY: Lettre
1779	DE PILEUR: Traité sur la musique
1779	LORENZONI: Saggio . . . flauto
1779	MAGRI: Trattato . . . ballo
1779	MUSSARD: Nouveaux . . . flutte
ca.1780	DUBOIS: Principes d'allemandes
ca.1780	LE PRÉVOST: Lully musicien
1780	BRIJON: L'appolon moderne
1780	DAVIES: Memoirs of . . . Garrick
1780	LA BORDE: Essai sur la musique
1780	STADLER: Table pour composer
1781	MOUFFLE: Vie privée de Louis XV
1782	CHRISTMANN: Elementarbuch
1782	MARCOU: Élémens . . . de musique
1783	CORRETTE: La belle vielleuse
1784	BACQUOY-GUÉDON: Méthode . . . danse
1784	GUILLEMIN: Chorégraphie
1784	JONES: Treatise on . . . music
1784	LÉGAT DE FURCY: Seconds solfèges
ca.1785	DESPRÉAUX: Cours d'éducation
1785	CHABANON: De la musique
1785	ENGEL: Ideen zu einer Mimik
1785	LACÉPÈDE: Poétique de la musique
ca.1786	BUSBY: Complete dictionary
1786	ANONYMOUS: Encyclopédie méthodique . . . danse
1786	BORNET: Nouvelle . . . violon
1786	CRAMER: Kurze Uebersicht
1787	COMPAN: Dictionnaire de danse
1787	KOCH: Versuch . . . Composition
1787	MEUDE-MONPAS: Dictionnaire
1788	ANONYMOUS: Encyclopédie méthodique . . . mécaniques
1788	ORIGNY: Annales du théâtre italien
1789	QUATREMÈRE DE QUINCY: Dissertation
1789	TÜRK: Klavierschule
ca.1790	ANONYMOUS: Anleitung so viel walzer
1790	ALBRECHTSBERGER: Gründliche
1790	GERBER: Lexikon
1790	L'AULNAYE: De la saltation
1791	FRAMÉRY: Encyclopédie méthodique. Musique

1791	REICHARDT: Kunstmagazin
1791	TROMLITZ: Ausführlicher . . . flöte
1793	DURIEU: Nouvelle méthode . . . vocale
1793	ROJO DE FLORES: Tratado . . . danza
1795	ALTENBURG: Versuch . . . Trompeter
1796	BLANKENBURG: Litterarische Zusätze
1796	MOREAU DE ST.-MÉRY: Danse
1796	OULTON: History of the theaters
1797	DAUBE: Anleitung zur Erfindung
1797	DREWIS: Freundschaftliche Briefe
ca.1798	HAYN: Anleitung Angloisen
ca.1798	LANGLÉ: Traité de la basse
1798	BAILLEUX: Méthode . . . violon
1799	KOLLMANN: Essay on . . . composition
1800	KATTFUSS: Chorégraphie
1808	BABAULT: Annales dramatiques
1822	CASANOVA: Mémoires

INDEX

GUIDE TO THE INDEX

The index combines names, titles, and subjects drawn from both the bibliographic data and the annotations for each item in Parts I, II, and III of this *Guide*. Subjects representing broad classes of literature such as dictionaries, histories, or periodicals are entered in the index, but see also the classification lists in the Forewords to each of the three parts of the *Guide*.

Many specific subjects appear in the index under broad subject headings. The following summary presents these subject headings in the order in which they appear. The subject **DANCE TYPES** encompasses both musical and choreographic aspects of the dances. Names of authors, ballet masters, composers, dancers, musicians, and so forth, appear together under **NAMES**. Titles of stage works, individual dances, and printed books may be found respectively under **BALLETS, DANCES, OPERAS, PLAYS,** and **PUBLICATIONS**. General information about ballets, operas, plays and other types of social or theatrical diversion is cited under **ENTERTAINMENT**.

All references in the index are to serial numbers of entries in Parts I, II, and III of the *Guide*. Subject headings appear in boldface upper case letters. Personal names of authors of main entries in the *Guide* appear in upper case letters; for these names, the serial number references in boldface indicate items for which the person is the author, rather than a subject mentioned in the notes. Similarly, for titles listed under PUBLICATIONS a boldface serial number reference indicates a main entry for that title. Specific subjects and names of persons treated as subjects appear in lower case letters. All titles of publications, stageworks, and dances are italicized. Uniform spelling of personal names conforms whenever possible to that in *The new Grove dictionary of music and musicians*.

SUMMARY OF SUBJECT HEADINGS

AESTHETICS AND CRITICISM
General
Dance
Music

BALLETS (By title; see also **ENTERTAINMENT, THEATRICAL**)

BIBLIOGRAPHY

BIOGRAPHY, AUTOBIOGRAPHY, MEMOIRS

COLLECTIONS OF NOTATED DANCES

DANCE
Social
Theatrical

DANCE INSTRUCTION AND STUDY

DANCE MUSIC (See also **DANCE TYPES**)

DANCE NOTATION, CHORÉGRAPHIE

DANCE NOTATION MANUALS

DANCE PEDAGOGY

DANCE PERFORMANCE AND TECHNIQUE
Arms (Ports de bras)
Ballet master (Maître de ballet)
Body
Bows, Honors (Révérences)
Cadence—See Relation of music and dance
Composition of ballets
Composition of dances
Dancers
Dancing master (Maître à danser)
Danse bas, danse haut
Danse chantée
Danse comique
Danse de demi-caractère

DICTIONARIES
General
Dance
Music

ENCYCLOPAEDIAS

ENTERTAINMENT, SOCIAL
General
Assembly (Assemblée)
Ball (Bal)
Carrousel
Festival (Fête)
Fireworks (Feu de joie, Feu d'artifice)
Jousts, Tilting matches
Mascarade (Bal masqué)
Naumachie
Parades
Ridotto

ENTERTAINMENT, THEATRICAL
General
Acte de ballet
Ballet
Ballet à entrées
Ballet ancréontique
Ballet comique
Ballet d'action
Ballet de cour
Ballet héroique
Ballet intermède
Ballet pantomime
Ballet sérieux
Comédie
Comédie ballet
Commedia dell'arte (See also Théâtre italien)
Divertissement
Drama—See Play
Élémens
Entr'acte
Entrée
Fragments
Harlequinade
Intermède
Masque

Romance
Rondo
Serenata
Sonata
Symphony
Suite
Toccata
Trio
Vaudeville
Villanella

NAMES

OPERAS (By title; see also **BALLETS; OPÉRAS COMIQUES;** and **ENTERTAINMENT, THEATRICAL**)

OPÉRAS COMIQUES (By title; see also **BALLETS; OPERAS;** and **ENTERTAINMENT, THEATRICAL**)

PERFORMANCE INSTITUTIONS
Académie Royale de Danse
Académie Royale de Musique
Académie Royale de Peinture et de Sculpture
Comédie Française
Comédie Italienne
Concert Spirituel au Château des Tuilleries
Covent Garden
Drury Lane Theater
Lincoln's Inn Fields
Musique du Roi
Opéra
Opéra Bouffon
Opéra Comique
Théâtre de la Foire (St. Germain, St. Laurent)
Théâtre Italien—See **ENTERTAINMENT, THEATRICAL**—Théâtre italien
Vauxhall
Vingt-quatre Violons du Roi

PERIODICALS

PLACE NAMES

PLAYS (By title; see also **ENTERTAINMENT, THEATRICAL**)

POETRY AND POETS

PUBLICATIONS (By title; includes articles, books, essays, multi-volume sets, pamphlets, periodicals)

INDEX

342

DANCE TYPES

345

349

NAMES

351

361

367

OPÉRAS COMIQUES (By title; see also **BALLETS; OPERAS;** and **ENTERTAINMENT, THEATRICAL**)

377

378

383

SATIRE AND PARODY I-39; III-28, 39, 65, 76

SCENIC ELEMENTS III-12

    Costume I-5, 6, 16, 22, 30, 32, 34, 35, 36, 46, 48, 50, 56, 58, 60, 63; II-2, 78, 131; III-8, 12, 24, 32, 37, 46, 56, 57, 58, 63, 74, 82, 103, 111

    Device (Devise) I-45, 46; III-89

    Machines I-5, 6, 45, 46, 58, 68; III-10, 13, 22, 37, 49, 53, 72, 77, 89, 103

    Masks I-34, 46, 50; III-24, 74, 78, 103

    Production I-5, 34, 35, 45, 46, 58; III-10, 22, 88, 89, 92, 10

    Properties I-35, 46, 58; III-82, 87

    Staging and Sets I-5, 6, 34, 35, 46, 58; II-21, 32; III-10, 12, 22, 32, 37, 46, 50, 53, 56, 63, 82, 87, 89, 95

SERMONS AND MORAL ESSAYS I-51, 60; III-20, 61